*The Automobile
and American Life*

The Automobile and American Life

JOHN A. HEITMANN

McFarland & Company, Inc., Publishers

Jefferson, North Carolina, and London

LIBRARY OF CONGRESS CATALOGUING-IN-PUBLICATION DATA

Heitmann, John Alfred.
The automobile and American life / John A. Heitmann.
p.   cm.
Includes bibliographical references and index.

ISBN 978-0-7864-4013-9
softcover : 50# alkaline paper ∞

1. Automobile industry and trade — United States — History.
2. Automobile industry and trade — Social aspects — United States — History.
I. Title.
HD9710.U52H39   2009   338.4'76292220973 — dc22   2009001474

British Library cataloguing data are available

Cover photograph ©2009 Classic Stock

Manufactured in the United States of America

*McFarland & Company, Inc., Publishers
Box 611, Jefferson, North Carolina 28640
www.mcfarlandpub.com*

For Fred Schroth (1931–2007),
who was the first to teach me
about cars, and car culture.

ACKNOWLEDGMENTS

Many people along the way were important to the completion of this study. During the summer of 2008, Peter Cajka, a former student of mine at the University of Dayton and now a graduate student at Marquette University, played a critical role in acquiring materials and in analysis. Peter exhibited considerable grace under pressure, and his efforts in exploring the topics of labor history and World War II were most significant. Niki Johnson, also a former student who is now an editor at the University of Dayton Research Institute, has done so much on this project over the years, beginning with a review of paper presentations and ending with a careful edit and reformatting of the manuscript for the publisher. Many students in my seminars taught me much over the years, including Elaine Berendsen, Caitlin Toner, Collin Delany, Maria Stanzak, and Greg Winters.

Student office assistant Rania Shakkour used her online and computer skills to help greatly in collecting a large number of historical images. My administrative assistant, Carolyn Ludwig, not only made numerous runs to the library, but also kept things going in the Alumni Chair in Humanities office when I had to sequester myself and write. Former colleague and friend Edward Garten not only supplied considerable information on his grandfather's Ford dealership in Hinton, West Virginia, but also team-taught several auto history courses with me. Several of my colleagues in the history department at the University of Dayton were most supportive of my work, including Department Chair Julius Amin and Professor Marybeth Carlson, who encouraged me to follow my passion for automobile history and leave other studies behind. Professor Larry Schweikart, a former rock band drummer, made sure that I was up on a number of songs about cars. College of Arts and Sciences Dean Paul Benson not only provided funds, but also has been a constant source of encouragement. And finally, without folks in the Roesch Library — Robyn Reed, Bob Leach, and Diane Hoops — I never would have gotten the materials I needed to write the story that I did.

Outside of the University of Dayton community, a number of individuals also assisted me. My good friend Bill Leslie at Johns Hopkins University always believed in my ability to do good scholarship, and his *Boss Kettering* was one of the first serious scholarly works on auto history that I read. Further, it was his seminar on the automobile and American life that set me on my present course. At the National Automotive History Collection in Detroit, Mark Patrick and Barbara Thompson obtained the materials I asked for without delay. Jon Bill at the Auburn Cord Duesenberg Museum was a great help in obtaining photographs.

I doubt if I would have written this work if I had not purchased a worn-out 1971 Porsche 911T Targa twelve years ago. Over time, it has become my "solid gold" Irish green Porsche, so to speak. I got plenty of help from my mechanic and friend Cliff Brockman. And while my wife Kaye has never "got it" that when you work on your car you work on yourself, I thank her for putting up with a seemingly quixotic quest to raise "Lazarus" from the dead.

TABLE OF CONTENTS

INTRODUCTION: THE AUTOMOBILE, ITS HISTORY AND INFLUENCE, AND SOME CONTRADICTIONS

I wonder if anybody has yet written a History of the Motor-Car. I am certain thousands must have written books more or less purporting this; I am also certain that most of them consist of advertisements for particular makes and models.— G. K. Chesterton, 1936.[1]

In an introduction to an undergraduate course syllabus, historian of technology Stewart W. Leslie said it well with the assertion that "the automobile is the perfect technological symbol of modern American culture, a tangible expression of our quest to level space, time and class, and a reflection of our restless mobility, social and otherwise." To expand on that comment with the goal of writing a definitive and complete monograph is daunting to say the least. However, in this work that has emerged from my teaching undergraduate students, I plan to expand on Leslie's comment and explore how the automobile transformed business, life on the farm and in the city, the nature and organization of work, the environment, leisure time, sexuality, and the arts. It might seem that my foci are rather obvious, given the overall topic. However, my experience has been that despite the passing of more than 70 years, G. K. Chesterton's above-quoted comments ring true to this day. Many of the books on the history of the automobile that can be found in bookstores remain advertisements of sorts, sometimes focusing on a single marque, sometimes on a decade or an era, but whatever the case uncritical, simplistic, and superficial. Whatever the shortcomings of this study, I promise the reader a different kind of book. While there must be sections that develop historical literacy about the automobile in American life, there are also encounters with new material not to be found in the literature to date. I want the reader to think deeply about the car and American culture, as well as the transformative power of technology upon society and everyday life.[2]

The automobile and its related infrastructure transformed everyday life as well as our basic values. From top to bottom in American society, it created wealth and jobs. It played a crucial role in transforming Americans from producers of a limited number of goods to mass production manufacturers and consumers living in a Machine Age. It influenced, among other things, the nature and structure of the communities we live in, how we define and value community, and the design of our homes and other living spaces. Over the course of the twentieth century, the car whetted our appetite for new things conveying status and personal attractiveness, petroleum-based energy sources, engaging action movies, primal rock-and-roll music, and high-fat fast food.

To characterize this complex transition is quite a challenge, but crucial in developing a general understanding of the very essence of what it means to be human in a technologically-

1

centered Western society. Our loves, hopes, fears, ambitions, and disappointments are all
somehow tied to the automobile.

While sitting at a dinner table several years ago during a Society of the History of Technology annual meeting in Dearborn, Michigan, I became engaged in an interesting conversation with a talented graduate student from Columbia University, soon to become a successful
academic. The topic was writing a book to supplant James Flink's well-regarded *Automobile
Age*, which I had used for several years in undergraduate classes focusing on the history of
car culture in America.[3] The two of us concluded that it would be extremely difficult to take
on this task, and that it would take at least 10 years to accomplish it, if it was possible at
all.

Despite this well-meant warning, I began to collect materials for precisely such a project. Fools rush in where angels fear to tread. After all, my students resisted reading Flink's
book, unless they were prodded by the big stick of a weekly quiz. Despite my encouragement
and enthusiasm for the substance, insights, and synthesis contained in it, students disliked
the extreme detail of this definitive text. Secondly, *Automobile Age* was becoming dated, as
the automobile industry and its technology and organization were being transformed at
light-speed pace, and a vast amount of scholarship on the topic had been generated since
the late 1980s. In this emerging new world of alternative energy sources, rising petroleum
costs, shifting centers and methods of production, and differing generational responses to
the automobile, a vastly different car culture has emerged, quite a contrast to that of 30 years
ago.

Finally, as I became more and more involved in automobile history as opposed to my
former interests in the history of chemical technology, I increasingly wanted to say something
new about the automobile in American life. One can say only so much about Henry Ford,
mass production, Alfred Sloan and organization, design and designers, and the decline of
Detroit's Big Three. The literature on the history of the automobile is replete with well-worn
topics. Thus, the challenge was to get underneath the surface, address new questions, and to
dig deep into American society and culture. And to me, new and fresh perspectives were far
riper for picking on cultural fronts rather than in more well-worn areas of economic, business, or technological history. It was culture —film, literature, music — along with social change
that piqued my students' interests, far more than lectures on businessmen and their strategies
or refinements of engines and powertrains.

That is not to say those areas are no longer worth pursuing. Rather, culture and the social
construction of technology may be a way to readdress these more familiar areas of scholarly
endeavor.[4] What follows, then, is the result of this quixotic quest to learn more about the
world that I have lived in and the cars I have loved, hated, felt indifferent towards, and sometimes driven. I make no claims concerning completeness or closure; it is merely an exploration. In a sense, this work is my "auto-biography," as in the process of researching and
writing I have learned much about myself, the times I have lived in, and my country.

*   *   *

The automobile is an *inanimate thing* that many Americans have fallen in love with, and
continue to love in a new world of microprocessors, laptops, digital cameras, cell phones, and
flat screens. Despite the proliferation of similar looking "econoboxes," a large proportion of
Americans do not see the car as simply an appliance, like a toaster or refrigerator. Elegantly
shaped and finely engineered cars are loved by many and admired by many more. Despite the

constraints of aerodynamics and increased gasoline costs, contemporary cars can still be luscious objects, like the Dutch Darrin-designed Packards of the late 1930s.

Choices on the personal and societal level concerning the automobile have led to sweeping economic, psychological, and social changes, and perhaps there should be more awareness brought to this one *thing*, the car, and its impact on our lives. For many Americans living in the twentieth century and beyond, the automobile has become an idol to be worshipped, conferring power, freedom, and pleasures to its owners. In ignoring the warnings of the prophet Isaiah concerning idols, however, perhaps it has brought judgment on us as well, particularly at the time I am writing this work.

Fundamentally, we may wonder to what degree we are masters of this technology, and to what degree we are its slaves. If we are its slaves, we rarely recognize it. David Gartman, in his interesting yet stretched Marxist analysis of the automobile assembly line, asserted that line-workers were akin to slaves, but it takes little thought before one may challenge that bizarre claim.[5] Indeed, there is little, if anything, in common between a nineteenth century African American working on a Louisiana sugar plantation and the auto worker putting parts on a 2008 Chevrolet Cobalt at the Lordstown, Ohio, GM factory. In general, work and life are often hard, but for a twenty-first century American, the possibilities for living the good life remain endless. For an Antebellum slave, to be someone's property and to be legally restricted in movement and class says it all.

Since its introduction more than a century ago, the car has often been seen as a freedom machine — ask any American teenager with a newly issued license. With it, we can go and come as we please, and whether the monitor is a parent or a government, our whereabouts and behavior are difficult to follow. It is a catalyst for the making of a mobile society in terms of race, class, and geographical location.

Yet, for most Americans, the automobile is also seen as an absolute necessity. For a senior citizen, the loss of driving privileges is staggering. For a working adult, access to the automobile is often critical to get to the job and back home.

This often commonplace, sometimes beautiful vehicle is a manufactured, mass-produced product that has displaced the horse, omnibus, railroad, bicycle, and trolley in the course of history, and has brought with it a remarkable sense of individuality and autonomy. Along with the inherent freedom that the automobile has brought, however, have come constraints, to the degree that we may thoughtfully ask whether the automobile has led human beings into a largely unrecognized dependency in which the machine now rules over us in subtle if not imperceptible ways. While we are not slaves to the car, certainly many of us have made choices involving it that in the long term may not have been in our best interests. Economically, it saddles many Americans with car payments while at the same time greatly depreciating in real value. The family car is a poor investment. Young people often work during high school to pay for their cars at the expense of studies. Furthermore, the automobile demands a highway network requiring extensive capital investment, one that cuts through city neighborhoods, thus dividing urban communities and often aesthetically reducing the city to one largely consisting of concrete and asphalt. Its concentration in cities has resulted in extended commuting times; its misuse by negligent or risk-taking drivers, along with product failures, has led to more than 40,000 highway deaths each year. And yet within hours of a fatal accident the scene is cleaned up to the point where it appears the accident never happened, thus obliterating negative impressions of how the machine can change lives forever. Only rarely do we see roadside memorials that remind us of those loved ones who are now gone due to a fatal accident. Would we as Americans put up with any other technology that took so many more lives per year than any war since 1945?

*   *   *

Indeed, like the tension between freedom and constraints, the automobile has resulted in a number of other puzzling contradictions. Car culture, with two very different Janus-like faces, is associated with inherent dichotomies concerning uniform goods and individuality, and public and private space.

To begin with, the automobile is far more than a means of transportation; it is manufactured in all kinds of sizes, shapes and colors so that people can choose that which is best suited to them and best expresses their status, lifestyle and personality.[6] It is the job of the automotive stylist and the advertising people to induce those personal feelings inside of us, so that we cannot live without the car of our dreams. Cars are also one measure of our identities. They provide hints to the world concerning our values, aspirations, and our present-day economic situation. Who among us has not felt the effects of depersonalization born out of the bureaucracy of the modern age, with its reliance on badges, identification numbers and cards, form letters, blanket e-mails, and all the rest? And yet they are means for us to assert individuality within a hostile, competitive environment that wants to reduce us and make us faceless. Certainly our automobiles are one rather powerful means to make us feel more important than we really are. Yet they are made of interchangeable parts by largely interchangeable workers.

Styling is an important attribute of the automobile in a way that is certainly unique in American life. Thus, the car is an expression of our individuality; it is very much like fashionable clothing that moves. Once an accessory market developed in the wake of the uniformly produced and black Model T, cars could be changed to suit personal taste. Therefore, the common citizen could distinguish himself from others. Beginning in the mid–1920s, this trend was accelerated with the development of flexible mass production, so that the range of colors, engine and transmission options, and accessory choices seemed nearly limitless. For example, in 1965, the Chevrolet division of General Motors offered 46 models, 32 engines, 20 transmissions, 21 colors plus 9 two-tone options and more than 400 accessories.[7] Designer cars and sport utility vehicles bearing the names Bill Blass and Eddie Bauer have taken this desire for individual expression to the next level. But it is more than simply style. A Hyundai Tiburon has a serious style to it. It is Brand as well. And the badge that represents that Brand has enormous significance.

The owner of a Mercedes possesses refined elegance. Similarly, a Lexus driver is a person who has wealth and often a sense of economic stability. Audi owners are well-off and like to think of themselves as a bit different. Can anyone behind the wheel of a Porsche be a loser?[8]

Brands must be protected by their manufacturers at all costs. A C-30 Volvo with a problem of unintended acceleration must be dealt with by the organization immediately and conclusively, for above all Volvos are equated with safety. Some would argue that the Depression-era decision to broaden the Packard market base beyond its elite niche to the middle classes might have temporarily saved the company, but in the long run weakened the Brand.

Psychologists have asserted that the colors of our vehicles tell much about the owners. Supposedly, cars are usually painted in bright colors and primary tones like yellows, light blues and reds during economic boom times. On the other hand, when the economy cools, so do the colors to include gray, brown, and dark blue. On one website the following is said about colors and who you are:

Black: First choice of ambitious drivers who want to project an image of success.
Red: You're outgoing and impulsive with a youthful attitude, but easily bored.
Silver: You have great style and are often successful, but tend to be pompous.
White: The first choice of doctors and drivers who are reliable and methodical.
Gray: Expresses understated good taste and indicates a safe, cautious driver.
Blue: A team player who's sociable and friendly, yet lacks imagination.[9]

To further individualize our cars, in more recent times we have resorted to "identity bracelets," or vanity car tags that allow us to get in a final word about ourselves. These vanity tags may be official state license plates or custom tags that are especially popular in states where only one tag is required on the rear of the automobile. Of course names are important, proper or otherwise, including: "Parrot Head," "High Roller," "Country Boy," and "Pork Chop." So too are religious inscriptions, like "Meet Me in Church on Sunday," "Galatians 2:20," "Happy Christians," "Prayer Changes Things," or the sign of the fish, a fish encircling the name of Darwin, or cross. Then there are business names, patriotic license plates, and names and inscriptions about sweethearts.[10]

We often have a relationship with this mass-produced machine, right or wrong, demented or healthy. As in a more primitive society where one has a relationship with animals where both partners profit from it — say, the North American Indians who once relied on the buffalo for their existence — we live in a largely urban, third wave industrialized post-modern society, where we identify and depend on the car.[11] We repay it with a passion often bordering on obsession. It is that affinity, or love, that results in our naming these machines Lulu, Lazarus (because it was raised from the dead), Betsy, Bessie, Freddy, Nellie, Pumpkin, Little Willy, White Pony, and so on. We talk to these machines as if they have a mind of their own, pleading with them to go another mile in a violent rainstorm, or in extreme hot or cold temperatures. We also pray for them as we would for an afflicted relative, as we drive through a storm or sense a faltering motor as we drive down a lonely stretch of highway.

For my generation, and the two generations before it, the automobile was at the center of our family life. It was so important that many of my photographs that include my mother, father, relatives and me feature an automobile at the center. For a family whose fortunes were ravaged by the rise of Nazism and World War II, the progression of photos reflected our annual increased fortunes, as well as the well-dressed children who were growing up.

If we think about it, this behavior of attachment to a thing is rather silly, but it is one reflection of an attachment to more than an object. One such relationship is mentioned in the thoughtful book *Driving Obsession*. It is the case of multimillionaire oil heiress Sandra West, who stipulated in her will that upon her death she be buried in a lace nightgown in her baby-blue 1964 Ferrari, with the seat comfortably slanted. In 1977, with West dead, her executor, eager to comply with instructions because only then would he inherit $5 million, precisely followed instructions and buried her in a 9-foot deep concrete tomb at the wheel of her beloved car.[12] Communities also bury cars. In 1957, the citizens of Tulsa, Oklahoma, buried a 1957 Plymouth, using it as a 50-year time capsule. Oil, gasoline, and a case of Schlitz beer were put in the trunk, just in case these commodities would not be available in 2007.[13] Unfortunately, 1957 Plymouths were prone to rust even without being buried, and thus when the car was unearthed during the summer of 2007 it was a near blob of iron oxide, although its elegant Virgil Exner–designed fins remained clearly recognizable.

For many Americans the automobile — the apex of twentieth century mass production technology — is also at the heart of an internal contradiction concerning individuality. Out of a drive for sameness and regularity, born on an assembly line so ably but comically depicted in Charlie Chaplin's *Modern Times* or Ben Hamper's *Rivethead*, we achieve the ultimate expression of self and personal freedom. At the extreme of expressions of individuality we have art cars. Harrod Blank, who wrote a book and made a video on the topic, has perhaps done more than anyone to publicize these very funny examples of artistic desire, like that of Volkswagen with a television mounted on top, a car covered with glued-on buttons, or a vehicle possessing scales imitative of a fish.[14]

Indeed, it can be said that cars are an art form, as Le Corbusier commented in 1928 when he claimed that the car was as powerful a symbol of the Machine Age as the Gothic Cathedral was of the Middle Ages. They can be very beautiful — or ugly — things, but whatever the case, we worshiped them at mid-twentieth century and for some, the obsession with them continues to this day.

Enhanced mobility brings with it not only the freedom to be a unique individual and associate with others of one's choosing, but also isolation as well. Thus, we have a second important contradiction. Without doubt, the car has changed the nature of space and time, and with it human settlement patterns, social relations, and the spatial relationship between work and home and cities and industry. In the process of changing space, it has empowered people in many ways, most evidently women and teenagers, by enabling them to leave the confines of home. For many young people, it was a place for forbidden sexual activity. But along with this enhanced mobility came also an increased tendency towards social isolation, for the idea that the automobile is an extension of the home remains a central feature of car culture. Cars are parked in the home garage. It is a place no longer removed from the home proper like a shed, but rather integrally attached to the home and often a central design feature of it. So when we take to the road a part of our home goes with us, and indeed perhaps that is why agoraphobics (those who fear going outside the home) are usually quite content to go out in cars, but are terrified of using public transportation. Inside our cars we feel sheltered in a private place, so much so that people at a stop light pick their noses and put on makeup as if they were not observed. For the harried mother, driving alone is the one time during the day when she can re-establish her equilibrium.

There are undoubtedly many more inherent contradictions associated with the automobile and American life. But by focusing only on contradictions, one misses a full understanding of the role played by the automobile in shaping American life. What follows is the story of how the essence of life in America changed because of the widespread adoption of a complex machine. How those changes took place, in terms of key historical individuals and institutions, as well as how that change was represented in film, song, poetry and literature, is at the heart of what follows. In order to fully characterize this transition, a discussion of the history of automotive technology and its business and economic history, including organizations, markets, and consumer preferences, follows as well. Further, government is also a part of this story, as local, state, and federal authorities made public policy that created our roadways, often at the expense of mass transit, and regulated the auto in terms of safety, energy consumption, and the environment. It is also interesting to note that government is the largest single purchaser of automobiles, and this has been the case since the 1960s. The automobile and the nation-state is a topic that will be only cursorily addressed here, but one that demands further scholarly investigation.

To encapsulate all of these themes in a brief work is a daunting challenge, but one with extreme rewards, for with it comes an enhanced understanding of what it meant to be an American living in the twentieth century, and who we are as a people today in the early twenty-first century. With the future of the American automobile industry in flux, it may well be worth our time to revisit the past once again.

1

Beginnings: From a Mechanical Curiosity to a Plaything for the Well-to-Do

Musicians, like poets, are often keen to comment on subtle changes that take place in everyday life. Frank Banta's ragtime instrumental "Kareless Koon, an Ethiopian Two Step" was released in 1899. Unwittingly, perhaps, it was one of the first cultural representations of the automobile in America.[1] The song's sheet music cover depicts a wealthy and well-attired Black couple riding in a new electric vehicle driven by a White chauffer. Its occupants are shown throwing coins to a group largely comprised of White folks, in what was a total social reversal uncharacteristic of the age of Jim Crow.

It is doubtful, however, that the artist of this cover could have foreseen just how revolutionary the automobile would become, not only in terms of everyday life, but also in facilitating social change. The automobile would become a tremendous source of new wealth, and in the process elevate African Americans and Whites, but usually not to the extent projected on the cover. And while the automobile did not have its origins in America, it would transform her people and her land as no other technology during the twentieth century.

European by Birth, American by Adoption

An apt but worn-out cliché concerning the early history of the automobile is that "the automobile was European by birth, American by adoption." Indeed, the visionary idea of the automobile — in the words of James Flink, "the combination of a light, sprung, wheeled vehicle; a compact, efficient power unit; and hard surfaced roads" — gradually became a reality during the last half of the nineteenth century, primarily in Europe and to a lesser degree in America.[2] The idea was transformed into a complex artifact, one that quickly hardened in fundamental design. For example, the basic configuration of the modern automobile with the radiator and engine in the front, followed by the clutch, transmission and rear axle drive, the *système Panhard*, was devised in France in 1891.[3] A decade later, the 1903 De Dion-Bouton followed this scheme with a honeycomb radiator, sliding design four-speed transmission, and a steel frame, clearly distinct from the horseless carriage. Most importantly, the De Dion used an ingenious rear axle that replaced the cumbersome chain drive with half shafts transmitting power to the drive wheels. And finally, the 1903 "Sixty" Mercedes, despite its chain drive, had a magneto ignition, six-cylinder engine, and a top speed of 60 miles per hour.[4] In fundamental terms, the modern automobile crystallized technologically very quickly, and thus its origins are a most important object for study.

After the idea and pioneering artifact came the commonly-used term *automobile*. Tracing its introduction (a semantic history) tells us much about the early history of the *automobile* in America. As Patricia Lipski skillfully pointed out, the word was French, but key to its adoption in America was its acceptance by New York City's high society.[5] The term "automobile" was first used in America in 1895 and fully adopted in the U.S. by 1899, but other words were proposed and debated during this time — horseless carriage, motocycle, motor vehicle, automation, mocle, autom, polycycle. Members of high society in New York City, including William Rockefeller, George Gould, Edwin Gould, John Jacob Astor, Jacob Ruppert, C. P. Huntington, and Claus Spreckels, owned the first cars. This Gilded Age aristocracy paraded their vehicles at Newport, Rhode Island, in the summer of 1899, and influenced the editorial writers of the new magazines *The Automobile* and *The Automobile Magazine* to endorse *automobile* as a universally accepted term. In sum, while the beginnings of the automobile are often attributed to a group of visionary tinkerers, engineers, inventors, and mechanical geniuses, the upper classes were the consumers of this product, and they cast a lasting imprint on its place in culture in ways perhaps more complex than just the choice of a term.

The key innovations associated with this new transportation technology, its gradual diffusion and acceptance, first public impressions, and initial cultural responses are the most significant areas of research. These topics have received considerable scholarly attention, and indeed the present study must begin here, at the critical moment of creation.[6]

While the origins of a new technological system are undoubtedly important, historians often work backwards in time to fully trace strands of seminal ideas and techniques. That tendency can often prevent scholars from addressing more recent pressing and relevant matters. With the passage of time, perspectives become clearer, records are discovered and catalogued, and historical actors with a penchant to refute one's story die. Yet the recent past often has the most relevance for the living, despite the many methodological and practical obstacles in pursuing it.

Whatever the time frame under investigation, the tension between continuity and change challenges the historian in a unique manner. What distinguishes the historian from the sociologist or philosopher, however, is the scrupulous adherence to chronology and time.

Technological antecedents to the automobile included the work of Nicholas Joseph Cugnot between 1765 and 1770 on a three-wheel steam tractor for pulling cannons; Richard Trevithick and his experiments with a steam locomotive conducted during the years 1801 and 1803; and Philadelphia inventor Oliver Evans and his "Orukter Amphibolos" or "Amphibious Digger." All of these early efforts have been described in detail elsewhere, but are mentioned here to provide a sense of the long sweep of history concerning this form of transportation technology.[7]

Steam carriages appeared on the scene primarily in England beginning in the 1820s, although in 1865 horse-drawn transportation interests suppressed mechanical road vehicles with the passage in Parliament of the so-called Red Flag Act. This legislation limited the speed of "road locomotives" to 2 mph in towns and 4 mph on the open highway. It also required that an attendant walk 60 yards ahead carrying a red flag by day and a red lantern by night. Until its repeal in 1896 at the request of wealthy automobile pioneers, the act militated against the development of the automobile idea in Great Britain, for by 1890 there were light steam vehicles capable of speeds of 15 mph over long distances. David Beasley's *The Suppression of the Automobile: Skullduggery at the Crossroads* discusses this chapter in history, important in terms of British developments, but tangential to mainstream developments in the emergence of the internal combustion engine (ICE) that would prove key to the automobile's acceptance in Europe and America.[8]

Technological Antecedents: The Bicycle

Concurrent to ICE technological advances were developments related to the bicycle that took place in America between 1880 and 1900. The bicycle created a widespread demand for flexible, personal transportation, and it brought freedom to both women and young people. While the nineteenth century railroads exposed Americans to rapid (for the day) land transport, the very fact that tracks limited transverse spatial mobility opened the door to possibilities for more adaptable movement on roadways. Bicycles, despite their shortcomings associated with muscle power, difficult terrain, and weather, put urban dwellers in motion. In particular, their introduction and diffusion raised important questions concerning the quality of roads, manufacturing techniques, social changes, and legislation. Without exaggeration, the bicycle set the stage for the automobile that followed.

The bicycle story began in Europe around 1819 with the introduction of a hobbyhorse design. Its historical evolution is traced in David Herlihy's beautifully illustrated monograph.[9] The first mechanical bicycle is credited to the Scotsman Kirkpatrick Macmillan, who in 1839 constructed a home-built, treadle-driven device so that he could more easily visit his sister who lived some 40 miles away. This invention was for the most part ignored until the 1860s, when in France so-called pedal velocipedes were manufactured by carriage maker Pierre Michaux and his son Ernest. These designs were a cross between the modern bicycle and the wooden hobbyhorse. The velocipede's wheels consisted of wooden spokes and rims held together by a steel band. The front wheel was larger than the rear, and pedals were attached directly to the axle. With ivory handlebar grips, and a seat resembling an animal's spine, this awkward-looking device weighed sixty pounds. It quickly earned itself an appropriate nickname —"the bone-shaker"— as it traversed the rough roads of that era. In 1869 the velocipede made its way to American shores, where a number of American firms improved its design. An American version incorporated hollow instead of solid steel tubes, and a self-acting brake. To stop, the rider pushed against the handlebars, thus compressing the seat spring and causing a brake shoe to engage against the rear wheel. It was seat-of-the-pants driving at its best, more a curiosity and sport than everyday technology.

A brief velocipede craze followed in the late 1860s. At the same time, several social clubs were organized. It was difficult to ride the velocipede on the bumpy roads of the day, and one had to walk it uphill. But after 1871 interest in this less-than-practical device waned, in part because so many of the machines built were poorly designed. A radically new design was needed, and that would come as a result of the efforts of Englishman James Starley, whom, to this day, the British honor as the father of the bicycle industry.

In 1870 Starley introduced his Ariel bicycle. Like its predecessors, the Ariel featured front drive pedals. However, for greater efficiency Starley made the front wheel as large as it could be, limited only by the length of the rider's legs, and thus increased the wheel circumference and relative efficiency. Correspondingly, the rear wheel was reduced in size, making it just large enough to maintain balance. Thus, the era of the bone-shaker had ended and that of the "high wheeler" or "ordinary" began.

English production techniques soon incorporated steel tubes, ball bearings, and solid rubber tires. One riding a high-wheeler could reach 20 mph, but it was dangerous and there was always the possibility of the rider "talking a header," and flying over the handlebars. It was awkward and precarious, but in Britain a wide following soon emerged as clubs of cyclists were formed.

The American ordinary craze was fueled by the efforts of manufacturer Colonel Albert A. Pope, a Civil War veteran from Boston who traveled to England, began importing British models, took the lead in establishing the American League of Wheel Men in 1880 and built his own models under the Columbia trademark. By 1884, Pope's firm made some 5,000 "Columbia" units, and the technological gap between the U.S. and the British narrowed.[10] The inherent problem with the ordinary, however, was that its size was connected with the stature of its rider, and thus standardization was impossible. Therefore, economies of scale in manufacturing could not be truly achieved.

The greatest advantage of British bicycle manufacturers during the 1880s lay in superior metallurgical techniques. Birmingham's W.C. Stiff (an appropriate name given the technology he developed!) perfected a method of weldless tube manufacture that permitted the brazing of light tubing to solid forging. By limiting the use of heavy gauge metal to stress points, a considerably lighter bicycle could be made without any loss of strength. Throughout the 1880s, American manufacturers were forced to use English tubes if they aspired to build first-class products. The British also modified the ordinary's design by introducing gearing in the front of the vehicle, thus allowing the rider to pedal easier. These geared bicycles were called Dwarfs or Kangaroos, but most bicyclists saw them as no safer than the conventional design. If safety was an issue, and it certainly was for many women, they moved to a tricycle. American designers also attempted to reverse the large and small wheels of the ordinary, putting the large wheel in the back and gearing it, thus reducing the possibility of a rider going over the handlebars due to a sudden stop or maneuver.

Americans made valuable technical contributions to bicycle design, particularly during the 1880s and 1890s. Just as the Americans seemed to be taking a lead in bicycle technology, in the mid–1880s John Kemp Starley, nephew of the creator of the Ariel, came up with the concept of the safety bicycle. This design featured a triangular frame, two wheels of about 2 feet in diameter, and a rear wheel driven by a sprocket connected to a chain. While the idea was not totally new, it was the industrial commitment to this design that was so important. Indeed, what emerged was the notion that safety was important, so much so that high wheelers became market curiosities by 1890.

The social impact of the safety bicycle was enormous, particularly after 1888 when the design was coupled with John Boyd Dunlop's pneumatic tires. The cycling population expanded greatly, and women, who had shunned the earlier models, embraced the dropped frame safety bicycle design. The dropped frame was introduced in 1888, and shortly thereafter women bicyclists' skirts were shortened and their ankles exposed. Women began wearing bloomers, leading Elizabeth Cady Stanton to remark, "Many a woman is riding to the suffrage on a bicycle."[11] Further, young men and women could now go for rides without third party supervision. Patriarchal and matriarchal controls were increasingly being challenged by a machine, and as machines would become more complex with the coming of the automobile, so would the resulting social changes.

Sales leaped forward in the 1890s, and an acetylene flame lamp was introduced in 1895 so that cyclists could travel safely at twilight and in the dark. For several years during the trend-driven Gay 90s, bicycling became a full-fledged boom. Bicycle racing became a popular sport, and many colleges established bicycling teams. Further, the bicycle inspired sheet music, trading cards, and board games. Undoubtedly the most famous of all songs inspired by the bicycle was Harry Dacre's "Daisy Bell," composed in 1892 with its chorus:

> Daisy Daisy,
> Give me your answer do!
> I'm half crazy,
> All for the love of you!
> It won't be a stylish marriage,
> I can't afford a carriage,
> But you'll look sweet upon the seat
> Of a bicycle built for two![12]

By 1900, some 300 firms made more than a million bicycles in the United States, making it a world leader. Innovations that followed included the coaster brake, a springed fork in the front, and cushioned tires. The cost of the bicycle halved from $100 to $50 during the 1890s, and thus American industry liberated the bicycle from its status as a plaything for wealthy sportsmen to a far more popular tool for travel. In doing so, the bicycle in a sense paved the way for the automobile, including the innovations of Henry Ford that would follow in the first decade of the twentieth century.

Apart from raising consciousness concerning flexible travel and its impact on road improvements in the United States, no preceding technological innovation — not even the internal combustion engine — was as important to the development of the automobile as the bicycle. The bicycle was the object of scorn by horsemen and teamsters long before the appearance of the horseless carriage. Further, bicyclists gained the legislative right to use public roads in Massachusetts as early as 1879. Key elements of automotive technology that were first employed in the bicycle industry and then subsequently made their way into early automobiles included steel-tube framing, ball bearings, chain drive, and differential gearing. The bicycle industry also developed the techniques of quantity production using specialized machine tools, sheet metal, stamping, and electric resistance welding that would become essential elements in the volume production of motor vehicles.

An innovation of particular note is the pneumatic bicycle tire, invented by Dr. John B. Dunlop in Ireland in 1888.[13] Dunlop was far from working in a vacuum, however, as numerous inventors patented similar designs during the late 1880s and early 1890s. Also, the rubber tire had a long history that Dunlop undoubtedly built upon. Solid rubber tires were first introduced around 1835, and in 1845 Robert William Thompson, a civil engineer from Middlesex, England, patented a pneumatic tire similar to Dunlop's design. An important issue was how to keep the tire on the rim, and it was not until the early part of the twentieth century that a system employing a wire-reinforced bead was widely adopted. Bicycle tires were the basis of automobile tires in France by 1895 and in the United States in 1896 when the B. F. Goodrich Company scaled up a single-tube bicycle tire for one of Alexander Winton's early vehicles.

The greatest contribution of the bicycle, however, was that it provided its owner with the ability to go when and where he wanted to. Sunday trips to out-of-the-way scenic places were now within the reach of the common man and his family. As one commentator of the period poignantly remarked, "Walking is on its last legs."[14] Thus, the bike was the first freedom machine, as it remains to this day for younger children who want to travel beyond the watchful eye of an observing and controlling parent. It demanded, however, muscle power and a willingness to be exposed to the weather. To this day in many European cities the bicycle is an environmentally friendly alternative to the automobile.[15]

Compact Power: The Internal Combustion Engine

Along with the development of the bicycle, the internal combustion engine (ICE) was most critical to developments in early automobile history. Credit for the ICE is normally given to Belgian inventor Étienne Lenoir (1822–1900). Living in France, Lenoir patented a two-stroke engine in 1860 that used illuminating gas (gas derived from heating coal in large retorts) that was ignited by a spark generated by a battery and coil. Lenoir's engine was noisy and inefficient, and it tended to overheat. Used in stationary applications to power pumps and machines, some 250 were sold by 1865. And while the editor of *Scientific American* proclaimed in 1860 that with the coming of the Lenoir engine the Age of Steam was coming to an end, it took more than four decades before the ICE would eclipse the steam engine.[16]

In 1876, Nicholas Otto (1832–1891) developed a four-cycle engine (intake, compression, power, and exhaust), and Lenoir came up with a similar design during 1883 and 1884. Two engineers who had once worked for Otto, Gottlieb Daimler (1834–1900) and Wilhelm Maybach (1846–1929), designed a 1.5 horsepower, 110 pound, 600 rpm "high speed engine" in 1885, and built several experimental vehicles between 1885 and 1889. Maybach, one of the most important engineer-inventors of this early period, designed the modern carburetor for mixing air and gasoline in 1893.[17]

De Dion motor carriage #2, 1901. The French and the Germans were the true pioneers of the automobile in terms of technology and manufacturing (Library of Congress).

In the meantime, Karl Benz (1844–1929) built a tricycle in 1885 to 1886 and exhibited a design at the 1889 Paris Exhibition. By 1893 he had constructed an improved four-wheel car with a three-horsepower engine that sold well and was fairly reliable. More than 100 Benz vehicles were sold by 1898. An early leader, Benz was soon passed technologically, especially by French manufacturers.

James Laux, in his book *First Gear*, discusses in detail the French automobile industry before 1914.[18] The key French inventor-engineer of the late nineteenth century was Émile Constant Levassor, who took Gottlieb Daimler's engine and placed it in the front of the vehicle. Before Levassor's untimely death, he proved the merits of his design — that a vehicle of his design could be practical — in the 1895 Paris-Bordeaux-Paris race. At first, and for only a relatively short time, Paris was the center of the nascent global automobile industry. Perhaps this was due to excellent French roads or social, economic, or political factors that remain to be explicated and are currently discounted. James Flink has argued that the importance of Paris was accidental rather than a crystallization of a complex network of relationships that included German, French, and Belgian inventors and businessmen.[19]

The importance of the early French auto industry is reflected in the following table.[20]

TABLE 1: GROWING POPULARITY OF THE
AUTOMOBILE IN FRANCE, 1899–1908

Year	Vehicles in Use	Year	Vehicles in Use
1899	1,672	1905	21,543
1900	2,897	1906	26,262
1901	5,386	1907	31,286
1902	9,207	1908	37,586
1903	12,984	1909	46,000
1904	17,107		

While a number of entrepreneurs in England, America, and Germany were only beginning to catch up to the French by the end of the nineteenth century, there was a concurrent Darwinian-like competition among three rival technologies in terms of power — the ICE already mentioned, steam, and electricity. In the end the most economically efficient technology would prevail, but that was by no means clear to those living in 1900.

Choices Made: Competition from Steam Engines and Electric Motors

The early designs of the internal combustion engine were primitive to say the least, and thus these power plants were anything but reliable and smooth running. At the turn of the century steam cars dominated the automotive field. An alternative was the electric car, but they were expensive and limited in range and speed. As it turned out, there was a short window of time in which these three technological rivals were engaged in a contest that revolved around which would be the chief power source for this new form of flexible and personal transportation, the automobile. The end result would have enormous consequences for the remainder of the twentieth century, economically and environmentally. As Tom McCarthy has pointed out, during the first decade of the twentieth century, a number of experts warned of the environmental consequences of ICE–powered vehicles, including the issues of oil depletion and toxic exhausts. However, McCarthy contends that the widespread adoption of the automobile by a consuming public allayed concerns at a time when adjustments could have been far more easily made than those that we, in the early twenty-first century, are now making.[21]

Steam had a long history going back to the eighteenth century as the chief power source for factories, railroad locomotives, and electrical generation. For automobiles, steam engines were quieter than internal combustion. With fewer moving parts, steam engines had been manufactured for generations, and with less exacting tolerances. In addition, a steam engine had remarkable torque, especially from a dead stop. Steam pressure could be built up and stored, to be released at full force on demand. An internal combustion engine must turn within a narrow range of revolutions per minute to operate efficiently. Additionally, as anyone who has looked at a schematic of a transmission or differential knows, gears and small parts result in a power transmission system that can only be deemed ingenious to the mechanically uninitiated. Moreover, in the cylinder of a gas engine, the greatest force is exerted at the explosive instant of ignition, with the power dissipating as the piston completes its stroke. But in the cylinder of a steam engine, the steam enters, expands and continues to push for as much as 90 percent of the stroke.

Steam engines had both limitations and advantages.[22] With its extensive piping and metalwork, a steam car was heavier than an ICE car of comparable horsepower. Steam engines ran at lower thermal efficiencies than gas engines, losing much of their heat to the atmosphere. And while the working parts of a steam engine were quite simple and durable, the ancillary equipment — boiler, burner, and all manner of pumps, valves, and gauges — was dauntingly complex, demanding constant attention and maintenance. Most critically, the

A White Steamer is pushed across the finish line in a 1907 hill climb. Steamers were a very popular form of propulsion during the early days of motoring. Though reliable and fast, they were limited in range, expensive and heavy (Library of Congress).

popular steam cars of the early 1900s — Stanley, White, and Locomobile — took 10 to 30 minutes to work up adequate steam pressure from a cold start and then had to stop for water every 30 to 100 miles. By contrast ICE–powered cars started faster and had greater range, an advantage in rural areas where service stations were sparse.

After the turn of the century, steam car technology remained essentially stagnant for years until Abner Doble introduced advanced designs, while ICE–powered cars quickly improved. By the end of the first decade of the twentieth century, steam cars were technologically obsolete and economically unviable. Given these winds of change, White and Locomobile both converted to internal combustion by 1910, leaving only Stanley to fill a market with a curiosity that in recent times has been resurrected in as an interest in "buff" circles by car collector and comedian Jay Leno.

In addition to the ICE– and steam-driven automobiles, there were also electric models at the turn of the century, partly the consequence of work by Thomas Edison and others to improve battery design.[23] Electrics had several distinct advantages. They were especially attractive to those in the taxi business and women who wished to avoid the crank starting, noise, vibration, and pollution of ICE–powered vehicles. Low-end torque characteristics of electric motors ensured quick starts. However, in the early twentieth century any advantages were

Charging the battery of a Detroit electric automobile, 1919. It was the electric cord that ultimately limited the acceptance of the electric car in America during the first two decades of the twentieth century (Library of Congress).

greatly outweighed by the many serious liabilities. Electrics were far more expensive than the gasoline automobile to manufacture and about three times more expensive to operate. Batteries could weigh a ton or more. There was the ever-present wire or cord that had to connect to a discharged electric car. As late as 1910, their range was only 50 to 80 miles on a battery charge, charging facilities were virtually nonexistent outside large cities, the storage batteries of the day deteriorated rapidly, and hill climbing ability was poor due to the excessive weight of the batteries for the horsepower generated.[24] These relative liabilities have persisted to the present, despite recent improvement in storage batteries.

American Pioneers

The transition in national automotive leadership away from Europe and to the United States that took place during the first decade of the twentieth century is complex. One aspect that remains to be explored is the immigration of European automotive engineers to the United States. This matter of technology transfer certainly happened in the case of the Thomas Company located in Buffalo, New York, where a number of French engineers were employed, and may have occurred elsewhere as well.[25] Much of the automotive history literature published in the United States celebrates American innovation but ignores European influence on the early development of the industry, as if the American industry evolved out of virgin soil—a highly unlikely proposition given the nature of the trans–Atlantic connections of that day. Certainly the United States had its native pioneers who constructed prototype vehicles or produced cars in small numbers. It also had automobile manufacturers, who more often than not had previously been bicycle or carriage and wagon manufacturers.

The pioneers included Charles and Frank Duryea, who assembled their first vehicle in 1893.[26] The brothers would later engage in bitter priority disputes that continued to the early 1940s. Elwood Haynes and Edgar and Elmer Apperson built their first car in 1894 in Kokomo, Indiana. In 1895 Hiram Maxim installed a gasoline engine on a tricycle, and a year later Henry Ford demonstrated his Quadricycle.[27] Alexander Winton, a bicycle manufacturer in Cleveland, Ohio, would soon follow with an unoriginal design of his own, but he was also among the first to manufacture vehicles in some quantity, marking him as a leader in the early automobile business, along with the aforementioned bicycle manufacturer Colonel Albert A. Pope of Hartford, Connecticut.

While Pope's influence in the business would last only two years, to 1899, the Winton Motor Carriage Company flourished into the early twentieth century. Winton, like Henry Ford, raced his cars, and in 1903 a Winton became the first car to cross the continental United States.

Other manufacturers of the period included George N. Pierce in Buffalo and Thomas L. Jeffery, who built the Rambler. Most significant was Ransom Eli Olds, whose curved-dash "Merry Oldsmobile," built in Michigan, became an industry leader, with a production volume of 5,000 units in 1904. A dispute unfortunately followed—disputes were all too common among pioneer inventors and manufacturers of the era—and while Olds would later set up another company called REO, his influence on the industry diminished. Former employees of Olds who got their start there and then proved to be influential later in the automobile industry included Jonathan D. Maxwell, Robert C. Hupp, Roy D. Chapin and Howard E. Coffin.

During the first decade of the twentieth century, the number of firms active in the industry is staggering by today's standards. Some of the names of the early car companies were Orient, Monarch, Walker, Gale, Wolverine, Maxwell, Stoddard-Dayton, Wayne, Holsman, Logan, and Lambert. John Rae summarized the state of the infant industry as characterized by easy entry, virtually no government restrictions, literally hundreds of companies, and sources of capital varying from giants like J. P. Morgan to local banks and patrons.[28]

As the superiority of the gasoline automobile was increasingly demonstrated over its steam and electric competitors, the geographic center of automobile manufacturing in the U.S. shifted from New England to the Midwest. The early, overwhelming choice of the internal combustion engine by Midwestern manufacturers was influenced by the region's poor roads, which were nearly impossible for electrics to negotiate, relatively vast spaces when compared to the East, and by the availability of gasoline for fuel in sparsely settled rural areas that lacked electricity. Since village blacksmiths were accustomed to repairing wagons and carriages, they can be considered the first generation of auto mechanics.

The presence of a vibrant carriage trade and other economic and geographic factors contributed to the emergence of Detroit as the hub of automotive manufacturing in America. Most certainly, however, the elusive factor of personality and the presence of the likes of Ransom Olds, Henry Ford, Henry Leland, and Billy Durant proved critical to the rise of Detroit as the "Motor City."

To make a single prototype of a car is one thing, but to make it with uniform quality and in quantity is a very different challenge. Recognition of the importance of high tolerance, uniformly machined parts like crankshafts and engine blocks is usually credited to Henry Leland.[29] Leland learned machine tool techniques from a craft tradition that can be traced back to Eli Whitney at the Mill Rock armory and was later diffused and improved upon by Simeon North at Springfield and Roswell Lee at Harpers Ferry. High volume and economies of scale would be the central achievement of Henry Ford and his key employees at Ford Motor Company after 1908. The spectacular rise in American auto production is reflected in Table 2.

TABLE 2: AMERICAN MOTOR VEHICLE
PRODUCTION, 1899–1910[30]

Year	Number	Value ($)
1899	600	1,290,000
1903	10,576	16,000,000
1904	13,766	24,500,000
1905	20,787	42,000,000
1906	23,000	50,000,000
1907	42,694	105,000,000
1908	49,952	83,000,000
1909	114,891	135,000,000
1910	200,000	225,000,000

Despite the presence in Cleveland, Ohio, of pioneering firms that included Winton, Stearns, Gaeth, Washburn, Marr, Owen Rogers & Hanford, and Pennington, Richard Wager made the argument that Cleveland's decline as the center for the automobile industry was the consequence of conservative bankers. In contrast, Detroit's financial institutions were far more willing to take risks.[31]

Alexander Winton driving his automobile on the racetrack, 1901. Winton was certainly one of the most important of the pioneer automobile manufacturers in America (Library of Congress).

Organization as Power

With the introduction of a small number of experimental vehicles and the realization that they had commercial possibilities, trade organizations were quickly established. In October 1895, the month before the first race of experimental automobiles that was to take place in Chicago, Charles B. King, a Detroit manufacturer, wrote to the editor of the new magazine *The Horseless Age*:

> Realizing the fact we have already a large number of people in the country interested in the coming evolution, the motor vehicle, and in order to pave the way for this vehicle of the future, it is proposed to form a national organization which will have as its object the furtherance of all details connected with the broad subject, and hold stated meetings where papers can be read and discussions follow as to the respective merits of all points in question. Such an organization is needed now, and upon its formation would meet with the hearty co-operation of the newspapers, the friends of good roads and the public at large.
>
> It is therefore proposed that such an organization be now formed and have as its name "The American Motor League."[32]

The first meeting of this proposed group would take place November 1, 1895, in Chicago, with interested parties coming from Cincinnati; Philadelphia; Boston; Springfield, Massachusetts; Kokomo, Indiana; New York City; Canada; and Detroit. A draft constitution was adopted that called for this organization to "educate and agitate," to "direct and correct legislation," and to defend "the rights of ... vehicles when threatened by adverse judicial decisions."[33]

The Association of Licensed Automobile Manufacturers (ALAM) proved to be a more

A 1902 theater poster from Cincinnati, Ohio. In addition to the challenges of the machine and the environment, flat tires were an all-too-frequent matter for the automobilist to deal with (Library of Congress).

significant and studied trade organization. Its basis and actions have been thoroughly examined elsewhere.[34] In short, the ALAM was the result of patent 549,160 granted to Rochester, New York, attorney George B. Selden for a road vehicle that was to use an internal combustion engine using liquid hydrocarbons. It was an egregious error on the part of the Patent Office to grant such a patent, but it led to the formation of a number of car manufacturers who charged a license fee to anyone making an ICE–powered car and then distributed the proceeds to a Selden, a group of electric car manufacturers, and the ICE vehicle makers who had joined the group and adhered to its policies. Many car manufacturers, including Henry Ford, disregarded the ALAM and fought it in court, eventually winning their case, which led to the disbanding of this retrogressive organization. The ALAM story, however, illustrates the place in the automobile story for a study of organizations, including the National Automobile Chamber of Commerce (NACC), the Automobile Manufacturers Association, and the Motor Vehicle Manufacturers Association, which remain to be more fully examined by scholars.

In addition to the trade organizations that emerged during the late 1800s, social organizations were quickly established once a critical number of automobiles fell into the hands of the well-to-do.[35] The most significant of these early automobile clubs was the Automobile Club of America (ACA), established in New York City in 1899. Its mission was clearly stated in its 1903 *Yearbook*:

> The objects of this corporation are the formation of a social organization or club, composed in whole or in part of persons owning self-propelled pleasure vehicles for personal or private use. To furnish a means of recording the experience of members and others using motor vehicles or automobiles. To promote original investigation in the mechanical development of motor carriages, by members and others. To arrange for pleasure runs and to encourage road contests of all kinds among owners of automobiles. To co-operate in securing rational legislation and rules governing and regulating the use of automobiles in city and country. To maintain the rights and privileges of all forms of self-propelled pleasure vehicles whenever and wherever such rights and privileges are menaced. To encourage the construction of good roads and improvement of the public highways. And generally to maintain a social club devoted to the sport of automobilism throughout the country.[36]

In addition to the ACA and the American Automobile Association (AAA), by 1903 there were thirteen automobile clubs in the state of New York, nine in Massachusetts, five in Ohio and four in Pennsylvania, with nineteen in other states and the District of Columbia. The AAA was organized in Chicago in March 1902.[37] As a national federation of eight leading clubs, including the ACA, the AAA's key role was to lobby for improved public highways, protect the legal rights of drivers, and regulate auto racing and endurance trials. In subsequently pursuing those objectives, the automobile became less a plaything for the elite and more a necessity for the rural and urban middle classes.

The Automobile for Better or Worse?

The idea that the horseless carriage would have an enormous impact on American society did not escape the pioneers of that device. In a March 1896 article in the *Horseless Age* it was stated that the auto

> will make the suburbs easier of access, improve the trade of country hotels in many places, and still further depress the business of horse-raising. Much of the land now used for horse-raising

John Jacob Astor, 1864–1912, with his chauffeur standing beside the car. Chauffeurs are a largely neglected figure in the early history of the automobile (Library of Congress).

and growing horse feed will in process of time find other uses more in harmony with the trend of progress.[38]

The immediate social impact of the newly developed automobile during the first decade of the twentieth century was significant. The thoughts of a person first seeing this belching, stinking, noisy device making its way are difficult for a historian to recapture. To be sure, horses often reacted violently to an encounter with an early car. So did many people, especially rural folks who were fearful of change and urban dwellers who were concerned over their rights while walking the street. Rural residents often thought of the automobile as a "devil-wagon," and as Lowell Julliard Carr demonstrated in a pioneering sociological study, their attitudes only changed when the car came to have a commercial presence in their community.[39]

Of course, notions of the automobile's rivalry with the horse surfaced quickly and comparisons between the horse and the car were common. The advantages of a machine over a horse prompted one inventor in 1895 to build his own horseless carriage. Ironically, given the carnage that would later be a consequence of the automobile, *The Horseless Age* reported

> Carlos Booth, M.D. of Youngstown, Ohio had a terrible runaway last June, in which his wife came near losing her life and the horse was killed. Reading of the Paris Race about this time he at once made a design for a motor carriage, which he is now having constructed.[40]

As it turned out, Booth's vehicle would be completed by the summer of 1896. Made by Fredonia Manufacturing of Youngstown, Ohio, it weighed more than 1,000 pounds and earned Dr. Booth the distinction of being the first physician in America to own an automobile.[41]

The cost of a car with upkeep contrasted to maintaining a horse was a key question that early automobile advertising often addressed. For example, an advertisement in the *Ford Times* in September 1913 depicted a scale with a horse and a Model T on the two pans, the weight of the horse far exceeding that of the car. The ad further read, "Old Dobbin, the family coach horse, weighs more than a Ford car. But — He has only one-twentieth the strength of a Ford car — cannot go as fast nor as far — costs more to maintain — and almost as much to acquire." Cars also eliminated the horse manure problem on city streets.

While an exact date cannot be ascertained, sometime during the second decade of the twentieth century the automobile became a primary article of consumption for middle America, and no longer a plaything for the rich summering at Newport, Rhode Island, or the sporting set on Long Island. After initially finding the auto a "devil wagon," rural Americans in particular embraced the car as essential to improving their lives. Booth Tarkington's 1918 *Magnificent Ambersons* captured the social and economic complexities of that transition as well as any contemporary account of the day.[42] The novel is a love story involving the Ambersons, the Morgans, and the Minafers, set in a Midwestern town at a time of profound economic and social change. With the widespread diffusion of the automobile, landed elites, complacent and spoiled, who were living in prosperous mid-sized towns, lost their economic power at the expense of the new auto-centered manufacturing class comprised of investors, entrepreneurs and engineers.

The automobile gradually knitted urban and rural areas more tightly together, although evidence indicates that initially city and country folk really did not want to partake in this kind of social togetherness. During the first decade of the twentieth century city folk began to go for country rides, at times trespassing on farmers' property while picnicking, and eating the farm's fruits and vegetables as well. Some individuals and rural communities took

A 1915 advertisement design study for Pierce Arrow automobiles showing a man talking to three women and a man in a car. Early automobiles were largely for the rich, at least until the coming of Henry Ford's Model T (Library of Congress).

Poster of a woman wearing a driving coat, gloves and a hat secured by a scarf, with a car in the background, 1906. Just as clothing was fashionable, so was the automobile to millions of status-conscious Americans (Library of Congress).

appropriate steps to discourage these upper middle class urbanites from intruding.[43] An extreme reaction was the spanning of roadways with barbed wire, sure to cause injury to the unsuspecting automobilist. And there was also the ever-present speed trap to worry about, along with laws calling for a red flag to precede the car or even requiring calling ahead to the next town warning of the car's appearance on local roads.

This was a time in American history when farmers perceived themselves to be exploited by city-based institutions like banks and corporations, and thus resentment spilled over to those taking Sunday drives, with excessive repair and towing charges, food bills, and gasoline purchases often the result. On the other hand, those living in rural areas soon recognized that there was an economic benefit to having these urbanities take excursions to the country. Thus, travelers were often welcomed because of the money they brought with them.

The automobile slowly but surely diffused into rural America and with it came many improvements in the quality of life. By World War I, the automobile enabled physicians to make their rounds more efficiently and rural areas established hospitals to serve surrounding communities. A decade later the one-room schoolhouse gradually gave way to centralized schools, and thus the automobile improved education. While some church leaders railed against the car because of Sunday drives that would decrease church attendance, in reality the auto enabled once-isolated members to attend worship services. On economic terms, the appearance of the automobile broadened the market of farm goods for farmers, and in general made life easier.

Music Galore

Culturally, the automobile was featured prominently in popular music as early as 1899, when the first promotional song, "The Studebaker March," was released."[44] A number of these early songs about automobiles had no words, but rather were composed in a manner that imitated automobile noises — fast, slow, jerky, and droning. "The Motor Car," released in 1903, and "The Auto Race," published in 1904, were of this variety. As automobiles became a fixture in American life, so were songs about them, for in 1905 some 29 songs appeared, 40 in 1906, and 53 in 1908. Romance was at the heart of this early genre of song (see chapter 5 for more on this topic), but so then was the Ford, in lyrics either about Henry or his car. Indeed, more than 60 songs about Ford were written between 1908 and 1940:

"Love in an Automobile." 1899. By Alfred Dixon.
"My Automobile Girl." 1900. Lyrics and music by R. J. Morris.
"My Auto Lady." 1901. By George S. Atkins.
"Jes Come Aroun' Wid an Automobile." 1902. Lyrics by R. Melville Baker, music by Josephine Sherwood.
"When Isabella Green Went Automobiling." 1902. By Harry Marshall.
"The Girl on the Automobile." 1905. Lyrics by Sam Lewis, music by Joe Nathan.
"In My Merry Oldsmobile." 1905. Lyrics by Vincent Bryan, music by Gus Edwards.
"On an Automobile Honeymoon." 1905. Lyrics by William Jerome, music by Jean Schwartz.
"Take a Little Ride with Me." 1906. Lyrics by Jack Drislane, music by Theodore Morse.
"The Gay Chauffeur." 1907. By F. L. Valentine.

"The Ford." 1908. By Jarry H. Zickel.

"I'd Rather Have a Girlie Than an Automobile." 1908. By William A. Dillon.

"The Motor Girl." 1909. Lyrics by Charles J. Campbell, music by Julian Edwards.

"Motor King." 1910. Lyrics by Jack Drislane, music by Henry Frantzen.

"Keep Away from the Fellow Who Owns an Automobile." 1912. By Irving Berlin.

"He'd Have to Get Under — Get Out and Get Under." 1913. Lyrics by Grant Clarke and Edgar Leslie, Music by Maurice Abrahams.

"The Packard and the Ford." 1915. Lyrics by Harold R. Atteridge, music by Harry Carroll.

"On the Old Back Seat of the Henry Ford." 1916. Lyrics by Will Dillon, music by Lawrence Dillon.

"Don't Take Advantage." 1919. Lyrics by Howard Rodgers, music by James V. Monaco.[45]

The Mechanical Arts and the Coming of the Machine Age

Modern culture as we understand it owes much to the concurrent emergence of the automobile and motion picture. Introduced at roughly the same time, cars and film grew in a synergistic relationship with one another. One would be hard pressed to find a film depicting modern life where the automobile does not carry some significance in the progression of the story. From simply transporting people from one place to another to conveying nostalgia, creating the elaborate chase scenes found in so many modern action films, or enabling characters to converse while in an isolated space, the automobile has an established role in film.

Thus, it is virtually impossible to understate the significance of the automobile in the evolution of film. From being a vehicle for transporting characters from scene to scene to a weapon in the hands of a demented driver, much drama, comedy and tragedy in film have taken place in and around the automobile. Despite this, the topic of automobile and film has rarely been addressed systematically or comprehensively. Film can sell automobiles and automobiles can sell a particular film. The automobile strongly influenced the film industry, from being a major "character" to shaping film techniques involving motion and camera angle.

Several decades ago, film scholar Julian Smith drew on the vast collection at the Library of Congress to survey hundreds of films made before 1920. Smith's work uncovered short documentaries like *Automobile Parade* or the 1902 one reel *A Unique Race Between Elephant, Bicycle, Camel, Horse and Automobile*. Each of these short films featured mechanical novelty associated with the early automobile.[46] The first film to depict the automobile was Thomas Edison's 1900 short, *Automobile Parade*. It featured cars driven by Newport, Rhode Island's motoring elite, along with stray pedestrians, horse-drawn carriages, and bicycles and tricycles.[47]

Cars were first featured in the 1903 narrative film *Runaway Match*. This work employed a theme that was to recur again and again — a rebellious couple elopes in a car to avoid the insensitive opposition of her rich father to their intentions to marry. Because of the car, young lovers, characteristically never thinking of the long term, escaped from a father who was perhaps more wise and practical than given credit for. Thus, traditional courtship patterns were challenged by the possibilities of flexible transportation. Now a middle-class man had the same freedom as one more affluent, and glandular impulses were triumphant.

Racing was critical to early technological developments, enhancing a manufacturer's reputation as well as fueling popular enthusiasm for the automobile among all classes. In October 1904 the Vanderbilt Cup races on Long Island, New York, were filmed for the American Mutoscope and Biograph Company. The scenes in this film are remarkable and include an international cast of cars, what appeared to be a challenging road course, and a variety of camera angles. It set the standard for the hundreds of racing films that would follow.[48]

Early films played off the dangerous side of the automobile. The portrayal of risky accidents evidently enhanced a sense of adventure; however, crashes as depicted in the 1909 Edison film *Happy Accidents* rarely killed anyone in action-adventure films and certainly not comedies. With few exceptions, the villain got what he deserved. Slapstick accidents, a staple of early comedy like Mack Sennett's Keystone Kops series, trivialized crashes — they resulted from clear incompetence rather than automobile design, and driver and passengers were never killed or seriously injured.[49]

One such example was Sennett's *Gussle's Day of Rest*, produced in March 1915 and featuring a Ford Model T. The day at an ocean resort begins with an accident in which Gussle's plain-looking, overweight wife is run over by a Model T driven by a middle-aged man with a beautiful young companion at his side. Perhaps the first message of the film is that a car — even a Ford Model T — can take you far with attractive women. But this blonde has eyes elsewhere, including for Gussle, who ends up trying to escape from his wife and the woman's friend by taking the Ford on what becomes a rollicking chase. A second theme might be that while you can attract girls with a car, you might not be able to keep them. Ultimately, Gussle and his blond companion are buried in a landslide, and the story ends with a grin.[50]

Ralph Beardsley and J.D. Coote in a 1910 Simplex. One can never underestimate the significance of racing in the broader context of technological developments and the diffusion of the automobile (Library of Congress).

Five men trying to pull an automobile out of mud during the New York to Paris automobile race, 1905. Early endurance races demonstrated the supposed reliability of this relatively new transportation technology (Library of Congress).

Crowd at the start of the New York to Paris race, New York, 1905 (Library of Congress).

The Quest for Speed

In real life, however, an out-of-control automobile could easily prove to be deadly, especially when it came to racing. The origins and early history of the automobile in America are closely tied to competitions, including endurance and reliability runs, road racing, hill-climbs, and oval track events. Indeed, the automobile took on new significance in American life when, on November 28, 1895, "The Race of the Century" took place in Chicago.[51] Sponsored by the *Times-Herald* and run during a snow storm, the race ran from Chicago to Evanston and back, a distance of 53 miles. Frank Duryea won with a time of just over 10 hours. While rival newspapers were harshly critical of the event, the race sparked America's fascination with the automobile. Racing resulted in considerable publicity and this fact did not elude many of the early manufacturers, including Alexander Winton, Henry Ford, and Ransom Olds. Match races, high-speed runs, competitions on the glass-smooth beaches at Daytona and Ormond Beach, Florida, and the Vanderbilt Cup races on Long Island that began in 1904 became very popular during the first decade of the twentieth century.[52] The first generation of American race heroes included Willie K. Vanderbilt, Bob Berman, and Barney Oldfield, whose name would become a household word ("Who does that guy think he is, Barney Oldfield?").[53] The Glidden Tour, which took place on public roads between 1905 and 1913, emphasized relia-

Automobile racing on a curved wood track, probably at or near Washington, D.C., ca. 1922 (Library of Congress).

bility over speed, and enabled the leading luxury marque (Pierce-Arrow) to establish an enviable reputation among the well-to-do. Events became transnational as well; the 1908 New York to Paris race featured seven cars from France, Germany, Italy, and the United States, with a Buffalo, New York–made Thomas winning the 17,000-mile event.[54] And while road racing's popularity would decline somewhat by 1910, the construction of large wood plank circular racetracks across the country beginning in 1913 ensured that automobile racing was here to stay as an important spectator sport in America.[55] That same year the mass-produced Ford Model T was introduced. With its low cost and reliability, even an Alabama farmer at the wheel of a modified Model T at the local county fair could at least think he was driving like Barney Oldfield.

THE INSCRUTABLE HENRY FORD
AND THE RISE OF THE MACHINE AGE

I don't know anything about history, and I wouldn't give a nickel for all the history in the world. The only history that is worth while is the history we make day by day. Those fellows over there in Europe knew all about history; they knew all about how wars are started; and yet they went and plunged Europe into the biggest war that ever was. And by the same old mistakes, too. Besides, history is being rewritten every year from a new point of view; so how can anybody claim to know the truth about history?

History is more or less bunk. It is tradition. We want to live in the present, and the only history that is worth a tinker's dam is the history we make today.[1]

The man who possibly did more to alter the history of the twentieth century than any other had little use for history, or so it was commonly thought. As reflected in the artifacts and shops of Greenfield Village, however, he did have a passion for the history of the common person. Like all of us, he was a person of contradictions, with both a public and a private face. But with Henry Ford, the inconsistencies were stark and the appearances clouded. On one hand he was a simple man, tied to rural American folkways; yet he was also a driven and quixotic individual, an anti–Semite who proved to be an inspiration to fascist leaders in Europe. Purportedly a champion of the common man, he drove his son Edsel mercilessly and hired thug Harry Bennett to run his company and keep the union at bay during the 1930s and 1940s. He preached old-fashion morality, yet met furtively with his mistress by taking a small boat moored behind his Fair Lane mansion. While his Model T's and A's created a new place beyond the haystack for lovemaking, Ford personally designed front seat dimensions that supposedly prevented lovers from having sex. John Rae's conclusion about Ford remains true to this day: "His personality ... continues to elude us: was he a simple man erroneously assumed to be complex, or an enormously complex individual with a misleading aura of simplicity?"[2] At the heart of Ford was a drive to control — his son, his employees, the firm he founded, and perhaps even the world that he lived in.

In sum, Ford did much to create a world in which paradoxically he was far from comfortable. Perhaps it was because this world driven by machines and organizations was so complex and inherently so uncontrollable. As historian Robert Wiebe once argued about the 1880 to 1920 era, America was searching for order, impossible perhaps to attain, given the host of forces at work, including those of globalization and industrialization.[3]

Henry Ford was a child of the nineteenth century, but his leadership in developing mass production created a Machine Age in which individuality and worker satisfaction were diminished. Rapid, sometimes capricious change became increasingly common. It was a world in which efficiency rather than close human relationships reigned supreme.

From a Dearborn Farm to the World Stage

So much has been written about Henry Ford that it is difficult to say something new about his life or work. He was born in the midst of the Civil War on July 30, 1863, in Dearborn, Michigan,[4] the son of a well-to-do farmer. By the time young Henry was thirteen, his mother and a number of siblings had died. Left with five surviving brothers and sisters and plenty of farm chores, young Henry was not keen on farm life; however, that would not stop him from later interrupting his career as a machinist or from celebrating rural living after he became famous. There seem to have been questions about young Henry's abilities, for it is said that his father once remarked, "Henry had wheels in his head. John and William [two other sons] are all right, but Henry worries me. He doesn't seem to settle down and I don't know what will become of him."[5]

Henry did find joy in the farm workshop. As he matured, he became increasingly obsessed with machines, including watches, the most complex of all machines of that day. He left the Dearborn family farm at age 16 and found employment in Detroit as a mechanical apprentice. He learned how to repair steam engines, and that experience later convinced him that the steam engine was too heavy for a personal vehicle. He also worked part-time repairing clocks and watches. He next moved to the Flower Brothers machine shop and then to the Detroit Drydock Company, where he continued to learn more about machines and materials. By age 17 he had became a journeyman machinist who possessed the remarkable gift of understanding how machines worked, and how to improve them.

Ford next worked for noted inventor George Westinghouse on thresher and sawmill steam engines. In 1885 Henry repaired an internal combustion engine while in the employ of the Eagle Ironworks in Detroit. It was some time afterwards that he decided to take an internal combustion engine and wed it to a vehicle. What distinguished him from other pioneer tinkerers and engineers of the period was that he wanted to achieve economies of scale and thus make automobiles in large numbers and lower production costs. At first he thought of watches as the product he would focus his energies on, but he soon turned to vehicles powered by the internal combustion engine.

Despite all that has been written on Henry Ford, it remains somewhat a mystery how he developed the idea that the automobile was to be a universal necessity that would be in demand in good times and bad. In part, his thinking was the result of his common sense approach to life shaped by his early life on the farm. While American life was shifting from being predominately rural to urban at the turn of the century, many Americans remained tied to the land and lived in relative isolation without electricity or telephone. In spite of this, Americans were restless and desired mobility, spatial and social, and the automobile would provide both: spatial in terms of a constant desire to move from place to place; and social, as a tool to increase one's economic opportunities.

Certainly, the ideas that resulted in the Model T were well formed by 1906, when Ford wrote the following to readers of *The Automobile*:

> There are more people in this country who can buy automobiles than in any other country on the face of the globe, and in the history of the automobile industry in this country the demand has never yet been filled....
>
> The greatest need today is a light, low-priced car with an up-to-date engine of ample horsepower, and built of the very best material. One that will go anywhere a car of double the horsepower will; that is in every way an automobile and not a toy; ... It must be powerful

enough for American roads and capable of carrying its passengers anywhere that a horse-drawn vehicle will go without the driver being afraid of ruining his car.[6]

Perhaps his understanding of the common person and his ability to read the market for automobiles when few could was derived in part from his understanding of self. Since the colonial era, Americans have been on the move, seeking new opportunities or simply to reinvent themselves. Additionally, American society was not nearly as starkly stratified as in Europe, and thus the automobile, with all of its class implications, played a very different role in an America where rigid class lines hardly existed. Equality led to widespread buying power, and this potential buying power of Americans, in Ford's mind, was enormous. Ford somehow envisioned that as more automobiles were produced, more industrialization would follow, in turn resulting in even more buying power among the middle and working classes. While most of the early pioneers in the automobile industry in America thought of their cars as leisure objects for the well to do, only Ford, Ransom Olds, and Billy Durant thought differently. This triumvirate found ways to meet the demand from a mass consumer market that desired to break the bonds of place.

In 1891 Ford moved on to the Detroit Edison Company, and five years later he had a fateful encounter with Thomas Edison. Ford later saw that meeting as decisive to his future in the automobile business. He later claimed that Edison encouraged him to move forward with his car project as Edison advised, "There is a big future for any light-weight engine that can develop a high horsepower and is self contained. Keep on with your engine. If you can get what you are after, I can see a great future."[7] Ford never forgot that moment with Edison, and later he would develop a unique friendship with America's most useful citizen. Later he would move Edison's Menlo Park laboratory to Dearborn as a part of his historical Greenfield Village, and in that museum is a glass tube that purportedly contains the last breath of Edison, collected at his deathbed on the wishes of Ford.

Ford's first prototype was constructed in 1891. In 1896 a refined model was built, the Quadricycle, and if we are to believe the legend, Ford found it too big for the woodshed door. He then knocked down a wall, and pushed the car on a rainy street. With wife Clara holding an umbrella and a friend on a bicycle warning horsemen along the way, Ford started his engine and took his first ride.

Ford faced many more obstacles and challenges along the way before founding the Ford Motor Company in 1903. Two precursor companies failed, as Ford and his financial backers differed as to the target market and the role of racing in publicizing his cars.

Racing was extremely important to Henry Ford and others during the pioneer days of the automobile industry. As now, racing results in publicity that cannot be acquired any other way. It cultivates a following interested in speed, a powerful and attractive quality associated with any form of transportation. Racing success was reflective of technological sophistication, and racing tested, both then and now, demonstrator technologies that were eventually introduced into everyday vehicles.

At the turn of the twentieth century no production automobile in America had a greater sophistication or reputation than the Winton, a car made in Cleveland, Ohio. In 1903, a Winton driven by Horatio Nelson Jackson would be the first to cross America. In October 1901, Ford challenged Alexander Winton to a match race, and won. A year later, Ford built the famous 999 and set a new speed record.[8] Consequently, he was known all over America and recognized as a key player on the Detroit automobile scene.

It was from racing that Ford recognized the importance of shedding weight at every instance to gain more speed. A powerful engine is only one part of a racer's equation, for the ratio of horsepower to weight is far more critical than total horsepower alone in a racing machine. It was that quest for strength and lightness that led Henry to his discovery of vanadium alloy metal. He did not originate the use of vanadium in the automobile industry, for the French manufacturer Peugeot used it in racing machines prior to Ford's discovery. But he understood the alloy's utility in a production vehicle, and vanadium alloy steel became a critical material used in the Model T. Until metal could be alloyed into a very hard material, it could not be machined with the precision needed for parts interchangeability. The alternative was softer metal pieces that had to be "fitted" with files and jigs, one by one, to each vehicle. As the story goes, Ford was on the beach after a race in Florida where there had been an accident. Ford would later recount that, "There was a big smashup and a French car was wrecked.... After the wreck I picked up a little valve strip stem. It was very light and very strong. I asked what it was. Nobody knew."[9] Ford had the valve stem analyzed and discovered that it was vanadium steel, and that this material gave three times the strength per weight when compared to production steel.

In 1903, Henry Ford made a third attempt to establish an automobile firm with himself at the helm, and the Ford Motor Company as we know it today was founded. It began with $28,000 in capital, and the firm never raised another cent by selling stock until after Henry Ford died in 1947. A number of early models were produced between 1904 and 1908 which sold for a low price and had a reputation for reliability. In 1906 Ford produced the Model N, a $600 car, and the firm sold a record 9,000 cars and had revenues of $5.8 million. In the wake of this success with the Model N during the winter of 1906 and 1907, plans began to evolve for the production of Model T, one of the most important vehicles in the history of the automobile.

Once the T was designed, it was fixed, thus eliminating expensive retooling costs. With the design "frozen," the focus of activities at the Ford Motor Company shifted to production. While the practice of mass production emerged at Ford after 1908, it was both a reflection of distinctively American developments within the nascent auto industry beyond those taking place at the Ford Motor Company.[10]

From the mid–1890s to 1908, skilled machinists dominated automobile production. They commanded the production processes of small-scale firms. Usually British, German, or generational Americans, they moved to the automobile industry from carriage making operations, bicycle manufacturing, or other trades. The highly skilled machinists determined the pace of work, set the standards for the finished product, and hired or fired unskilled workers. "As the aristocrat of the shop," wrote Stephen Meyer "the all-around machinist knew some mechanical drawing and mathematics, how to operate different classes of machine tools, and how to perform fitting, filing, and assembly operations at the bench."[11] The machinist used finely honed skills while leading a team of apprentices and laborers. Meyer concluded that "Their knowledge represented their power in the production process and resulted in the powerful shop traditions of the autonomous craftsmen ... this shop culture controlled and regulated production through various output quotas and restrictions on the amount of effort exerted or output manufactured."[12] As a result, production was slow and car prices were high. Early automobiles were novel, and sold to the elite. James Flink asserted that "so long as and wherever such artisanal production persisted, labor productivity was extremely low."[13]

However, throughout the nineteenth century these and other artisanal skills were challenged by new technologies aimed at supplanting manual labor and raising production volume. Americans had been fascinated with motion and its role in production going back to Oliver Evans' late eighteenth century automated flour mill. The nineteenth century pork disassembly line as perfected in Cincinnati, Ohio, was another example of the American interest in production flow. While Ford claimed the meat processing disassembly line had influenced his thinking, his assistant, Charlie Sorenson, later denied it.

Others in Detroit were also thinking of economies of scale and efficiencies during this time. For example, Billy Durant's Buick, under the helpful guidance of Walter P. Chrysler, was making 5,000 cars a year in 1912. Indeed, many elements of mass production existed long before events would unfold at Ford's Highland Park factory.

Frederick Winslow Taylor and "One Best Way"

To understand the context of the development of the assembly line at Ford's Highland Park facility, one must first discuss the work of Frederick Winslow Taylor. In *Principles of Scientific Management*, Taylor acknowledged the power of the craftsman and railed against their "systematic soldiering," or output restriction.[14] Stephen Meyer has pointed out this aspect of scientific management, as he asserted that "With Frederick W. Taylor, early automobile industry engineers and managers found such skilled workers an obstacle to their plans for a more systematic organization of production."[15] For Taylor and his followers, the task was, either subtly or forcefully, to shift power relations on the shop floor.

Taylor was born in 1856 to a wealthy Philadelphia family. After an abortive semester at Harvard, where young Taylor lost his eyesight temporarily due to a nervous condition, he returned home where he became an apprentice at the Midvale Steel Company. Midvale Steel was to Taylor what the Big Horn Mountains would be for future president Theodore Roosevelt, as his health was restored and life purpose defined. Of course, Taylor was no ordinary apprentice at Midvale, as he returned home at night to his family's residence in exclusive Germantown and he maintained his membership at the Germantown Cricket and Tennis Club.

At Midvale, Taylor would begin to formulate ideas that would later form the basis of scientific management. Scientific management, with an emphasis on efficiency and time and motion studies, sought to place within the purview of management the control of the work process, as the industrial engineer rather than the shop foreman or worker would direct the work process. At the heart of scientific management was a piece rate system, a "carrot or stick" approach that rewarded or punished workers depending on whether output matched or exceeded predetermined goals or fell short of them. In theory, scientific management proposed that there was one best way to do anything, from building a car to hitting a golf ball.[16]

The Genesis of Mass Production at Highland Park

The offshoot of scientific management — mass production — was put into practice for the first time around 1913. Only later in 1926 did Ford articulate it as "focusing upon ... the principles of power, accuracy, economy, system, continuity, and speed." How mass production fit in with organization and the market was further articulated by Ford in this way:

The interpretation of these principles, through studies of operation and machine development and their coordination, is the conspicuous task of management. And the normal result is a productive organization that delivers in quantities a useful commodity of standard materials, workmanship and design at a minimal cost. The necessary, precedent condition of mass production is a capacity, latent or developed, of mass consumption, the ability to absorb large production. The two go together, and in the latter may be traced the reasons for the former.[17]

The assembly line that followed, contrary to popular thought both then and now, was not simply the idea or the result of the efforts of Henry Ford alone. During a recent tour of Henry Ford's River Rouge Plant, I watched a film on the history of mass production that gave total credit to Henry Ford for both the concept and implementation of this system of manufacturing. The film, shown every day to thousands of visitors, perpetuates a lie, for there were many unnamed individuals who contributed to what became mass production at the Ford Motor Company.

Indeed, James Flink summarized the story as one in which mass production developed upward from the shop floor rather than downward from Henry, with key individuals that included skilled tool makers Carl Emde and staff members C. Harold Wills, Joseph Galamb, Charles Sorenson, Clarence Avery, William C. Klann, and P. E. Martin.[18] It was this group and others who, through experiment and trial and error, gradually perfected a way of making automobiles at the Highland Park factory. Fixed work benches, where the assembly of component parts took place, gave way to a series of positions along a moving line where one small component after another was added.[19]

Scientific management had an enormous influence on the nature of American life during the early twentieth century, and nowhere was that more obvious than at the Ford's Highland Park factory. It was there that by trial and error Ford and his team of engineers and mechanics developed the system of dragging a car chassis across the floor to stations where parts, brought by pulley, conveyor, or inclined plane, were bolted on. Unlike the Model T itself, the assembly line took time to develop to a level of perfection, as numerous improvements to the line were implemented during the T's 18-year production run. Ford applied four basic principles to increase efficiency: the work must be brought to the man; the work should be done waist high to eliminate lifting; waste motion, human or mechanical, must be minimized; and finally, each task must be reduced to utmost simplicity.[20]

The impact of the assembly line at Ford was staggering, as the volume of production was unprecedented and cost reductions unparalleled. Once governed by skilled mechanics, the shop floor was conquered by scientific management and the assembly line. This process was nearly completed by 1914.

Joyce Shaw Peterson has described the creation of the assembly line as a series of processes that began with arranging production in an orderly sequence and ended with the development of overhead conveyors. By 1913 an assembly line operated at Ford, and by 1916, helped by Ford's openness to journalists and visitors, it was institutionalized in various forms throughout the automobile industry. The gradual perfection of the assembly line inaugurated a second phase of automobile production between 1908 and 1925 and enabled production of the Model T in volume. It entailed rigid standardization, extensive division and subdivision of tasks, and progressive line production. It was an inflexible process, as opposed to a more flexible mass production system that emerged in the late 1920s. Under Fordism, semiskilled or unskilled workers operated highly specialized machines. In 1910, nearly 75 percent of all jobs were classified as skilled work, but by 1924 expert work declined to 5 to 10 percent.[21] The development of machine technology was crucial to control of the production process because it eliminated the need for strength or training. James Flink explained, "Fordism meant that neither physical strength nor the long apprenticeship required for becoming a competent craftsmen were any longer prerequisites for industrial employment. The creativity and experience on the job that had been valued in the craftsmen were considered liabilities in the assembly-line worker."[22] Furthermore, Flink lamented that "the American myth of unlimited individual social mobility, based on ability and the ideal of the self-made man, became a frustrating impossibility for the assembly-line worker."[23] Dexterity, speed, and concentration replaced craft and experience.

By 1913, a majority of workers were semiskilled or unskilled and operated a highly specialized machine that nearly eliminated the "human element." The process is evinced in Arnold and Faroute's observations in *Ford Methods and the Ford Shops*: "When the moving-assembly line was placed in work with 29 men, splitting the one man operations into 29 operations, the 29 men began turning out 132 magneto assemblies per hour, or 1,188 per 9-hour day, one man's time producing one fly-wheel magneto assembly in 13 minutes 10 seconds, a saving of 7 minutes time on each assembly or more than one-third of the best one-man time."[24]

In addition to descriptions of the production process, Arnold and Faroute took iconic photographs of Ford's workers, but their "classic" observations were about machines, not laborers. In a description of "Assembling the Steering and Front Axle," they wrote, "there are two operations to be performed: (1) to press the arm in its seat in the sub-axle hub boss; (2) to screw the nut on the threaded end of the steering arm."[25] No attempt was made to describe the three men in the photograph.

The assembly line initiated what scholar Harry Braverman has called the "degradation of work."[26] Braverman's thesis was subsequently modified and pursued by sociologist David Gartman in *Auto Slavery: The Labor Process in the American Automobile Industry, 1897–1950*.[27] Gartman asserted that the assembly line was born of class antagonisms rather than a technological rationality. Motivated by the "narcotic" of profit, capitalists wrestled production away from the craftsman. The craftsmen, having lost the ability to control pace and accuracy, became vulnerable to exploitation. Labor was reduced to repetitive, mindless motions. To vindicate his thesis, Garman distinguished between "repressive" capitalist and "non-repressive" natural controls of labor. Finally, bureaucracy and occupations were created to buttress the capitalist order, and gave birth to the modern corporation.

Marxist sociologists have enhanced the view of the assembly line, but historians have revealed that what happened at Ford's plants was a complex social process. The reactions of workers to monotonous labor defy simple Marxist explanations. Historian Joyce Shaw Peterson wrote:

> Scholars analyzing the labor process in capitalist industry have sometimes seen the progressive deskilling of jobs as synonymous with the degradation of labor. There is no question that deskilling characterized the development of the automobile industry during its successful emergence as a "giant enterprise." The question concerns how that deskilling was experienced by the workers themselves, whether as progress, or loss, or something else entirely. No single answer to this question is possible. Those workers for whom deskilling was experienced as degradation ... were those who personally lost the need for their particular skills and saw their pride in workmanship diminished as machines took over their jobs and their own autonomy was diminished by a division of skills and increased management planning. For these auto workers degradation was very real, diminishing their pride and status and undoubtedly con-

tributed to making them the most militant and union conscious of their fellows. Such workers comprised a minority of the workforce. Much more common was the experience of the auto worker for whom machine tending replaced simple heavy labor or the semi variegation of farm work. Not only could such workers make more money as automobile workers, but they also experienced their work itself as more modern and sometimes identified with the skill of their machines and indeed with their own skill in running them.[28]

Personal responses to working on the assembly line are difficult to assess historically, but whatever took place on the microscopic scale, Fordism transformed the social relations of the macroscopic work place. The individual became anonymous, and the division of labor reduced tasks to mindless repetitive actions. Peterson noted that visitors lamented at the monotonous labor, but the worker's response was "complicated, as it could not be a simple choice between monotonous, repetitive tasks, and challenging interesting work ... no such choice was offered."[29]

While the assembly line contributed to the "degradation of work," the opportunity to labor brought workers from Southern and Eastern Europe, the American South, and Mexico to the Midwestern United States. This opportunity was particularly powerful for Mexicans and African Americans.[30] In 1900, the population of Detroit was half native-born Whites, and half immigrants from Northern and Western Europe.[31] By 1913, the workforce included Russians, Poles, Croats, Hungarians, and Italians.[32] The workforce also came to include social outcasts. In 1919, "the Ford Motor Company employed hundreds of ex-convicts and 9,563 'substandard men'—a group that included amputees, the blind, deaf-mutes, epileptics, and about 1,000 tubercular employees."[33] In contrast to Gartman, Meyer argued that "between 1908 and 1913 Ford officials gradually discovered that workers required just as much attention as machines and the flow of materials."[34] The droves of workers were not "completely plastic and malleable," and "as Ford mass production became a reality, Ford officials and managers gradually uncovered a massive labor problem."[35]

To stabilize his workforce, Ford announced the $5 day. "This was not a simple wage increase," wrote Stephen Meyer, "but a sophisticated profit-sharing scheme to transform the social and cultural lives of immigrant workers and to inculcate the life-style, personal habits, and social discipline for modern factory life."[36] Ford used methods inspired by the Progressivism of the early twentieth century to stipulate how families should take care of their homes and how single men should take care of themselves.[37] From 1914 to 1921 Ford embarked on a social experiment steeped in a paternalism that aimed to "Americanize" the immigrant workforce. While immigrants were willing to work in coal mines, iron and steel mills, meatpacking plants, and tanneries, in addition to automobile factories, they lacked industrial experience. When World War I ended the flow of European immigrants into Ford factories, recruitment of Black and White rural Americans became the norm.

Ford aimed to eliminate the lackluster "dude employee," who talked and walked more than he worked. The application of scientific management to achieve mass production required a regulated "human element." From 1920 to 1923 the assembly line underwent a "speed-up." The pace of the assembly line was grueling, and in addition, smiling, laughing, and sitting were prohibited. But factories were safe, ventilated, and well lit. Nevins and Hill observed that, "as in all mass production industries of the time, they were the rules of an army, not of a cooperative community."[38] Joyce Shaw Peterson argued that while Ford was union free from 1903 to 1933, workers used turnover rates, absenteeism, restriction of output, and walkouts to convey disapproval.[39] Autoworkers accepted the high wages, adopted the new habits, and endured the degraded labor.

Historians have given a fair amount of attention to Black labor in the automobile industry.[40] The demographic shift inspired by Ford's factories provided reason for Blacks to migrate to Northern industrial centers. In 1917 Packard employed 1,100 Blacks, but Ford quickly overtook Packard and employed 5,000 Blacks in 1923 and 10,000 by 1926.[41] Despite Henry Ford's personal racial outlook that Blacks were racially inferior and should remain segregated, his factories were interpreted as places of inspired racial uplift. Ford felt that the superior race was obligated to facilitate the uplift of subordinate races with philanthropic services, and this earned him a reputation as a friend of the Black race. Yet, life for Black workers in Detroit remained mixed.

Joyce Shaw Peterson historicized the new Black industrial community forged in Detroit. Despite high wages, most African Americans were segregated at the plant and in life outside of it.[42] When Peterson inquired, "Apart from their existence inside the factory walls, what kind of life did black auto workers find in Detroit?" she answered with frustrating segregation, higher rates of disease, and overcrowded housing. In an industrial city the comforts of the home were paramount to the ability to endure monotonous and dirty work. Peterson noted that "migrants confronted the ironic situation of earning much better wages than they ever had before and still being unable to rent decent lodgings."[43] For Blacks, "segregated housing patterns ... not only were blows to comfort, pride, self-esteem and family life; they could also kill."[44] Peterson concluded that more racial tension existed in Detroit due to residential patterns and competition for housing than over jobs. Beyond the factory and housing, entertainment facilities, and recreational activities provided by the companies, such as sports leagues, were segregated. Peterson noted that, "by far the most important social institutions were black churches," which "became the most vital institution trying to both integrate rural blacks into the urban atmosphere and cement and develop a sense of racial community."[45]

In *Black Detroit* August Meier and Elliot Rudwick noted, "the income of Ford's Black workers was the cornerstone for the prosperity of the Black community's business and professional people."[46] Blacks "were employed in the laboratories and drafting rooms; as bricklayers, crane operators, and mechanics; and ... as electricians and tool-and-die makers."[47] James C. Price became an expert in purchasing abrasives and diamonds.[48] Eugene J. Collins became head of the die casting department in 1924, and was later named the first Negro foreman.[49] Meier and Rudwick point out that, "Ford established his own contacts among key black leaders, especially among the clergy."[50] Ford's paternalism extended to local African American communities. This won Ford praise from African Americans, so much so that "black workers at Ford felt themselves superior, and wore their company badges to church on Sunday."[51]

African Americans comprised a significant portion of Ford's workforce. James Flink pointed out, "Ford's black workers were concentrated at the Rouge, where by 1926 they numbered 10,000 and constituted about 10 percent of the work force." At the Rouge, African Americans were concentrated in "the most dangerous, dirty, and disagreeable jobs — chiefly in paint spraying and foundry work."[52] Blacks were employed in positions that required the greatest physical exertion, the highest accident rates, and most exposure to health hazards. Despite the racial victories of foremen like Eugene J. Collins, most Blacks were forced into hazardous jobs in separate parts of the factory.

Ford countered the critics of mass production in his own time in his 1926 article on the topic in *Encyclopædia Britannica*. He argued that

The need for skilled artisans and creative genius is greater under mass production than without it. In entering the shops of the Ford Motor Co., for example, one passes through great departments of skilled mechanics who are not engaged in production, but in the construction and maintenance of the machinery of production. Details of from 5,000 to 10,000 highly skilled artisans at strategic points throughout the shops were not commonly witnessed in the days preceding mass production. It has been debated whether there is less or more skill as a consequence of mass production. The present writer's opinion [Ford's] is that there is more. The common work of the world has always been done by unskilled labor, but the common work of the world in modern times is not as common as it was formerly.[53]

Fordism completed a revolution in the making of things that originated with the notion of interchangeable parts first proposed by Eli Whitney in 1798. Combining the practice of interchangeable parts as employed in nineteenth century armories with that of the moving disassembly line in the meat packing industry and techniques involving metal stamping from the bicycle industry, the assembly line led to what is called deskilling and monotony. But Fordism had its advantages. Fifteen million Model T's were produced by 1927, and profits exceeded $7 billion.[54] The following chart shows the actual production volume at Ford from 1903 through 1927.

TABLE 3: FORD ANNUAL PRODUCTION, 1903–1927[55]

Year	Number of Cars	Year	Number of Cars
1903	1,708	1916	734,811
1904	1,695	1917	622,351
1905	1,599	1918	435,898
1906	8,729	1919	820,445
1907	14,887	1920	419,517
1908	10,202	1921	903,814
1909	17,771	1922	1,173,745
1910	32,053	1923	1,817,891
1911	69,762	1924	1,749,827
1912	170,211	1925	1,643,295
1913	202,667	1926	1,368,383
1914	308,162	1927	352,288
1915	501,462		

Ford and the Ford Motor Company's accomplishments were more than simply making complex mechanical things in quantity, however. As Anthony Patrick O'Brien has demonstrated, beginning around 1910 or 1911 Ford also pioneered controls on mass distribution in the automobile industry.[56] "Telegraphic ten day reports" were sent by branch managers to Detroit summarizing current dealer stocks, production levels, and dates of customer purchases. Later data that also included the number of salesmen employed and live prospects on file came from dealers. This accounting system was in part responsible for Ford weathering recessions in 1910–11 and 1920–21 far better than its competitors. And contrary to the interpretation that it was General Motors that developed a tight connection between production and distribution by the mid- to late 1920s, it appears that Ford did it first. Ultimately then, GM's eclipse of Ford by the late 1920s was due not to a process control and distribution network advantage, but rather to the fact that GM offered more products in more price ranges. After all, while GM during the 1920s was trying to anticipate what customers wanted in a car, Henry Ford staunchly remained convinced that only he had the right idea about what a car should be.

By the early 1920s, there would be not just one Ford Model T assembly line, but many, in factories all over America. Surprisingly, perhaps, the factory with the largest output during the 1920s was not the Highland Park facility, but one located in Kearny, Nebraska. Large facilities were also located in Atlanta, Buffalo, Cambridge, Chicago, Cincinnati, Columbus, Dallas, Des Moines, Houston, Indianapolis, Kansas City, Louisville, Memphis, Milwaukee, Minneapolis, Oklahoma City, Omaha, Philadelphia, Pittsburgh, San Francisco, Seattle, and St. Louis.[57]

Henry Ford also demonstrated his genius by implementing the $5 day in 1914. While economists and industry experts asserted that Ford's $5 day would lead to his bankruptcy, Ford's motives were based on common sense mixed with a vision of the firm in which returns on investment were not maximized, but rather acceptable. It was both good business and an expression of concern for the common man. The assembly line in its early days had already led to an unacceptable labor turnover rate; in response, Ford raised hourly wages so that workers would stay despite the repetitive and exhausting nature of the job. And if a worker didn't like the conditions, there were many — Poles, African Americans, and other minorities — outside the gates waiting to replace anyone dissatisfied. The $5 day was just another reason why many viewed Ford as a hero. As Ford correctly recognized, the $5 day resulted in more business, not only as his own workers bought Model T's, but also for service industries that provided for line workers and their families. Ford had envisioned and then implemented a giant technological and economic feedback loop that accelerated his own profits while stabilizing his labor force.

The Flivver King

In 1937 Henry Ford's mass production methods, subsequent Prussification of the Ford Motor Company, and the everyday lives of his workers received a pointed social critique by Upton Sinclair. Reflective of the desperation of the working class during the depths of the Great Depression and penned in the tradition of *Oil* and *The Jungle,* Sinclair's *The Flivver King: The Story of Ford America,* portrayed Henry Ford as a despot possessing both a benevolent and an oppressive streak. Sinclair's central character was not Henry Ford, however, but the "everyman" Abner Shutt. Shutt experienced many of the vicissitudes typical of those working in the early automobile industry. He began his career as a machinist for the Perfection Tool Company, but left because he had no opportunities for promotion. Abner personally approached Henry Ford and asked for a job. He was put to work immediately. As Sinclair recounted, "Abner Shutt became a cog in the machine which had been conceived in the brain of Henry Ford," and Ford was "going to do the thinking, not merely for himself, but for Abner."[58] Abner was responsible for several tasks on the assembly line: he would roll two wheels at a time to a nearly finished car, push each wheel onto the axle and with a wrench screw on the "spindle nut." Additionally, he placed an alarm-bell and a lantern on the front of each car, finally carrying cushion seats to the car where he wiped the dust from them. For his work, Abner was paid seventeen and a half cents per hour. Sinclair concluded, "What more could a workingman ask for?"[59]

After Abner had mastered several assembly tasks, he worked up the courage to recommend to Mr. Ford the formation of a wheels department. His suggestion was well received, since it came at a time when Ford and his engineering associates were making process improvements. Soon two labor gangs were formed — one for the right wheel and another for the left. Abner was rewarded by a promotion to sub-foreman and a specialist in spindle nut-screwing. He was paid two dollars and seventy-five cents per day to make sure four men screwed nuts correctly. With the advent of the assembly line in 1913, Abner kept his sub-foreman position but now oversaw "a group of men, whose every motion had been calculated by an engineer."[60]

Shortly thereafter, Ford's implementation of the $5, 8 hour day marked a high point in his benevolent paternalism. After agents of the Sociological Department instructed the Shutts on proper domestic practices, Abner had "qualified" to receive the bonuses. Sinclair wrote, "it passed Abner's comprehension how any man or woman could fail to be grateful for such divine compassion on the part of Mr. Ford."[61] However, when Ford promulgated the $5 day the price of rent and goods rose and all gains were nullified.

While war raged in Europe, "It had occurred to Abner ... that it would be a nice thing to buy a Ford Car, and take the family for an outing in the country on Sundays."[62] With a new home and a new car, Abner's family was plunged into modernity. His wages rose to eight dollars and a quarter a day.[63] At the height of Ford's benevolence, Henry and his workers sought the same end, to win World War I, and "thanks to the efforts of Abner and Henry, America won the war."[64] From 1914 to 1920, Abner drove his Model T to work and gave fellow workers rides for a nickel each way. Later, Abner embodied the mythical common American man: he raised his family, went to church, and even joined the Ku Klux Klan.

Prompted by a harsh recession in 1921 and 1922, Ford shut down his plant and "reorganized." As Sinclair recounted, "Abner Shutt had been watching the work of five men, but now one foreman watched the work of twenty men — and Abner was one of the twenty ... they put him back on the line."[65] Now Abner was victim of the division of labor, and a chassis came to him with the spindle nuts screwed on. It was his job to put in a cotter-pin and spread it. After twenty-two years of service, a straw-boss who had been on the job for two years "rode" old Abner Shutt.

While Henry Ford had argued that the purpose of scientific management was to discover how much work each worker could do without strain, the "speed-up" and the "stretch-out" strained Abner's body to the limit. Sinclair described the now-divergent lives of Abner and Ford: "He [Ford] was going everywhere and doing everything except watching the assembly line of his huge factory.... With 200,000 slaves making themselves parts of machines — pick-up, push-in, turn, reverse — pick-up, push-in, turn, reverse, pickuppushinturnreverse, pickuppushinturnreverse."[66] Abner was one of 100,000 men laid off when Ford decided to build the River Rouge Plant. Five months later, the plant was completed and Abner Shutt was back at spindle-nut screwing, the work that he understood.

When the Depression worsened, Abner was laid off and later fired. S. S. Marquis had been replaced by Harry Bennett, Sinclair commenting that the transition was like "casting out Christ and putting Caesar in his place." Later Abner got a job as a supply runner at the Ford factory where his son was a machinist. In 1932, Abner marched with autoworkers on Ford's plant, but after bullets were fired, he quickly fled. In an act of desperation, he wrote a letter to Mrs. Ford, and a service agent investigated his file. Due to his long service with the Ford Motor Company, Abner received a job inserting small screws on the magneto assembly line two days a week, for $8. He kept this position for the rest of the novel, but alienation and destruction came to fruition in Abner's family. John, his son, suffered the same fate as his father — out of work and deeply in debt. Abner's second son Hank became a rum-runner and then worked in the Ford Service Department. His daughter Daisy went to college to become a stenographer with the hopes of working in an office and marrying a rich man. She married a bookkeeper, the Depression hit, and Sinclair coldly observed that "when poverty comes in at the door, love flies out at the window."[67] Abner's son Tom, a star high school quarterback, shunned sports for a college education at the University of Michigan. After Tom was radicalized by academe, he chose to work in the shops organizing unions. The novel ends with Tom being systematically beaten by Henry Ford's thugs. Sinclair morosely observed that, "From the lottery wheel of life, some boys draw lucky years and grow up in times of peace and have a chance for happy lives ... others grow up to find its war time; they are dragged from their homes, marched into battle, and shot to pieces."[68]

The Model T: What a Car!

Whether the Model T or A, or subsequent models, Henry Ford's cars did much to shape life in the twentieth century. For the farmer, county agents now made visits to even isolated farms and rendered scientific advice in an effort to improve crops and agrarian prosperity.[81] The automobile was now used to distribute the mail to rural areas, thus vastly improving communications. Farm folk had access to hospitals and other medical facilities. Families no longer had to rely on crossroad stores, but could shop in towns, and even do comparison shopping. For city folk, the changes were no less dramatic. The city became reconfigured, with the rise of new suburbs, and in more recent times, exurbs. Retail trade moved from center city to suburbs, which witnessed the rise of shopping centers and supermarkets. A number of key industries burgeoned due to the demand for materials used in automobile production: steel, glass, textiles, electronics, and rubber. Relationships within traditional family structures changed, as youth sought freedom behind the wheel.[82] And with the Ford automobile, America became a nation on wheels. Family vacations and trips to parks now became far more commonplace.

The highway was now a place for adventure, for both men and women, as exemplified in the journals of Rose Wilder Lane and Helen Dore Boylston. The pair traveled from Paris to Albania in a Model T Ford during the mid–1920s and left a remarkable written account. As they would assert, the hero of the trip was neither one of the women, but the car itself, named Zenobia. The maroon Ford was described as "a wonder. She went up all those frightful curving mountain roads like a bird."[83] It was an eloquent appraisal of a mass produced car whose very name implied that it was a living thing.

Despite all of the critiques leveled at Ford, his company, and mass production, his machine was simply remarkable.[69] Its dashboard had a gasoline gauge, speedometer, oil gauge (there was no dipstick) temperature indicator, and odometer. To start the car one put on the hand brake, got out of the car, reached below the radiator and turned the crank, and hopefully the engine would come to life after a cough and sputter. The car had two gears, high and low, and instead of a gear shift one had a foot pedal, which the driver pushed down for low and released for high. To go to neutral, one pushed the pedal halfway. To stop the car, one pushed the gear pedal halfway while at the same time pushing down on the brake. There was no accelerator pedal; rather, there was a lever on the steering column that when pushed, gave more gas. There was also a spark lever that often did little unless in the wrong position, which then caused a loud and embarrassing backfire. To engage reverse there was a third foot pedal; depress it with either foot, and one backed up. Steering was stiff, and the wheel itself abruptly snapped back to its original position when one released tension on it. One final note on the

Model T: the four-door version actually had only three doors, as what appeared to be the driver's door did not open. The contours of the door were merely stamped on the body at the factory. Entering the car from the left side required climbing over the fake door. In sum, with the Model T rural Americans no longer saw the car as a devil wagon, but rather as transportation technology that could meet and be modified for their varied needs.[70]

The Model T was also a machine that was unique to the individual who owned it, and thus a personal relationship invariably followed. John Steinbeck wrote this about a car that he did not name, but called "IT":

> I think I loved that car more than any I have ever had. It understood me. It had an intelligence not exactly malicious, but it did love a practical joke.... When I consider how much time it took to keep IT running, I wonder if there was time for anything else, and maybe there wasn't. The Model T was not a car as we know them now — it was a person — crotchety and mean, frolicsome and full of jokes — just when you were ready to kill yourself, it would run five miles with no gasoline whatever. I understood IT, but as I have said before, IT understood me, too. It magnified some of my faults, corrected others. It worked on the sin of impatience; it destroyed the sin of vanity. And it helped to establish an almost Oriental philosophy of acceptance.[71]

Simple and sturdy, with a high ground clearance, the T was easily repaired by any mechanic-farmer possessing only a few hand tools. If the radiator sprang a leak, you added an egg to stop fluid loss. The Model T was a car one generation removed from America's consumer society. At least in 1913, it was sold before there were many dealers with service repair facilities. Responsibility for maintenance and repairs fell to the owner, and in reviewing an early Model T owner's manual, it is astonishing to note what one was expected to perform on these vehicles.[72] For example, every 100 miles, the spindle bolt and steering ball should be oiled; at 200 miles, oil had to be applied to the front and rear spring hangers, the hub brake cam, and the commutator; other service had to be performed at 500 and 600 miles. The sophistication and difficulty of repairs was also a surprise to the modern automobile owner. Work described in the section "How to Run the Model T Ford" included valve grinding, carburetor overhaul, clutch adjustment, the removal of cylinder head and transmission bands, the removal of front and rear axles, and the adjustment of connecting rod bearings. It is no surprise then, that the Model T was responsible for the creation of a generation of do-it-yourself automobile mechanics. Also, it is quite a contrast to compare the 1913 manual to the Model A's 1931 *Instruction Book* that opens with the statement "Let experienced mechanics make repairs or adjustments. Your car is too valuable a piece of machinery to place in unskilled hands."[73]

The topic of many jokes, there was also a true admiration for this remarkable machine, early models of which had to be driven backwards over steep hills because of the gravity-fed fuel system. In 1915 the first of two volumes about the Model T, entitled *Funny Stories About the Ford*, was published.[74] The following are a few excerpts:

The Formula in Poetry
A little spark, a little coil,
A little gas, a little oil,
A piece of tin, a two inch board —
Put them together and you have a Ford.

The Twenty-Third Psalm
The Ford is my auto; I shall not want another.
It maketh me to lie down beneath it; it soureth my soul.

It leadeth me into the paths of ridicule for its namesake.
Yea though I ride through the valleys I am towed up the hill,
For I fear much evil. Thy rods and thy engines discomfort me;
I anoint my tires with patches; my radiator boileth over;
I repair blowouts in the presence of mine enemies.
Surely, if this thing followeth me all the days of my life,
I shall dwell in the bug-house forever.

Later Years: Hero or Anti-Hero?

In several important respects, the Henry Ford story was far from over in 1915, although by then he was 52 years old.[75] With the coming of World War I, Henry became involved in an abortive Peace Ship effort in 1916. Despite the railing of all of his critics, his pacifism was reflective of a life-long idealism and distrust of the elitist ruling classes. And while the Peace Ship chapter in Ford's life proved to be a failure, it shows us how complex and yet naïve the man was. He also was idealistic at the Ford Motor Company, at least initially, with his sponsorship of a Sociological Department in 1915 and the opening of the Henry Ford Trade School. His paternalism was perhaps born more out of a desire to control than a sense of compassion. Nevertheless, it was corporate paternalism practiced on a scale that differed little from that of John Patterson at the National Cash Register Corporation.

By the early 1920s, as Samuel S. Marquis chronicled, things changed.[77] Ford "Prussified" his company, and at the same time took an anti–Semitic position that was regularly written up in his *Dearborn Independent* newspaper.[78] According to Ford, Jewish bankers were responsible for World War I, and their power was ever-present in the Western world. A believer in the *Protocols of the Elders of Zion*, so much so that he had this forged work published, Ford proved inspirational in his anti–Semitism to none other than Adolf Hitler, who read Henry Ford's autobiography while in prison in 1924 as a result of the Munich Beer Hall Putsch. Indeed, there was an unsubstantiated rumor that Ford had funded the *putsch*! Later, when Hitler gained power in Germany, Henry Ford would be awarded the Nazis' most important award to a civilian, the Order of the Eagle.[79]

Despite Charlie Sorensen and others urging Henry to update his product due to changing consumer tastes, the Ford Motor Company would stick with the Model T until 1927, following a pattern of inflexible mass production. By the mid–1920s, however, consumer preferences were changing due to the very prosperity that the Model T had created.[80] Indeed, the desire for more colors, interiors, horsepower, and conveniences along with style demanded a more flexible production schedule, something that Alfred P. Sloan's General Motors would deliver. That did not mean that minor improvements were not made on the Model T. And despite what Ford said concerning his car only being available in black, in reality the car was painted in colors as early as the 1909 to 1913 period. By the 1920s, Model Ts were sold in blue, gray, and brown as well as black.

After 1921 Ford still had moments of brilliance, despite fading as an industry leader due to the Great Depression. First, in 1928 the Ford Model A was introduced. The Model A only stemmed the GM tide for one year, however. Then in 1932 a Ford V-8 was sold, the first mass-produced engine of that sophistication in the American marketplace. Like a number of natural product advocates who were active in the 1930s, Ford was a believer in chemurgical techniques, or the extracting of chemical products from agricultural materials. To that end, he owned many acres in and around Dearborn that were under soybean cultivation during the 1930s. Soybeans furnished the chemicals that were converted to plastics, and by the end of the 1930s plastic body panels that could withstand the onslaught of Henry Ford's axe were developed. Yet by the late 1930s it was chemical synthesis rather than extraction that proved to be the destiny of the chemical industry for the immediate future.

As Henry aged, he became more eccentric and more prone to harsh employment practices as exemplified by his hiring of Harry Bennett and other thugs to control union organizing efforts at Ford during the early 1930s. The tide of unionism could not be stemmed in the end, despite the loyalty of African American workers and the use of force, blacklists, and other forms of intimidation. Edsel, Henry's son, was in power in name only, although he would play an important role in the design of the streamlined Lincoln Zephyr during the 1930s. Edsel would die a sick and broken man in 1943; it remained for Henry II, Edsel's son, to remove Harry Bennett and save the company after 1945.

Gone in Sixty Seconds: Joy-Riders and Criminals

With Ford's "democratization" of the automobile and an explosion in the number of vehicles came an epidemic of automobile theft. Machines produced in mass quantities made easy prey for "joy-riders" and professional criminals. Moreover, the automobile was valuable, mobile, and its parts were interchangeable. Lucrative domestic and international markets for stolen automobiles and stolen parts yielded high profits. Interchangeable parts also gave thieves the opportunity to quickly reconstruct and disguise stolen automobiles. As evinced by thieves' ability to alter serial numbers, duplicate registration papers, switch radiators, and replace entire engine blocks, a nascent uniformity welcomed theft. Moreover, thieves sought out and stole the most ubiquitous automobile; popular, mid-priced models were most likely to be stolen, along with the easy-to-steal Model T. As early as 1910 joy-riding and automobile theft were problems for the automobilist. Major concerns centered on the unauthorized use of an owner's vehicle by a chauffeur or a parking attendant. To that end a number of devices were marketed, from a gear shift lever lock to recorders that kept tabs on when a vehicle was actually being driven.[84]

Until the introduction of the electric self-starter in 1912, automobiles employed a battery/magneto switch along with a crank.[85] The automobilist turned the switch to B (battery), got outside the car, cranked the engine, and then once it started, moved the lever to M (magneto) and adjusted the carburetor. On early Ford Model T's, the battery/magneto switch had a brass lever key, but there were only two types, with either a round or square shank. Later, in 1919, Ford offered an optional lockable electric starter, but only used twenty-four key patterns. To make things easy for the thief, each pattern was stamped with a code on both the key and the starter plate. Would-be joy-riders needed only a little luck to drive off with any unguarded Model T.

Unlike other stolen goods, the automobile enabled its own escape. As one author observed in 1919:

> Not only is the motor vehicle a particularly valuable piece of property ... but it furnishes at the same time an almost ideal getaway.... With the automobile there is no planning to be done. With a thousand divergent roads open to him and a vehicle possessing almost unlimited speed, escape is practically automatic.[86]

A New York police official commented in 1916 that "the automobile is a very easy thing to steal and a hard thing to find."[87] As early as 1915, 401 automobiles were stolen in New York and only 338 were recovered.[88] By 1920, it was estimated that one-tenth of cars manufactured annually were eventually stolen.[89] Astonishingly, perhaps, in 1925 it was estimated that 200,000 to 250,000 cars were stolen annually.[90] Table 4 provides theft data for major American cities.

TABLE 4. AUTOMOBILE THEFTS IN
MAJOR AMERICAN CITIES, 1922–1925

	1922	1923	1924	1925
New York	7,107	7,959	10,064	11,895
Chicago	3,636	2,334	4,946	7,587
Detroit	3,194	4,428	7,187	11,750
Los Angeles	4,802	4,218	7,326	8,392
San Francisco	1,960	2,154	3,257	3,746
Dayton	249	313	366	485

Source: *Automotive Industries*, 56 (February 19, 1927), 283.

Further, the automobile created new opportunities for criminals and confronted legal authorities with a myriad of problems. One author noted that, "as automobile thefts increase burglaries and robberies increase."[91] The automobile itself was stolen, but the automobile also played a central role in kidnapping, rum running, larceny, burglary, traffic crimes, robberies, and the deadly accidents of the "lawless years."[92] The Baltimore Criminal Justice Commission reported,

> In August, 1922, one of Baltimore's well known and highly respected citizens was held up, robbed of $7000 and brutally murdered in broad daylight on the busy thoroughfares of the city. The bandits perpetrating this carefully planned crime escaped in a high powered car bearing stolen license plates.[93]

In 1924, Arch Mandel of the Dayton Research Association observed, "The motor vehicle has ushered in a new era of crime and police problems, and apparently a new type of offender."[94] "To cope with this problem," Mandel wrote, "police departments have been obliged to detail special squads and to establish special bureaus for recovering stolen automobiles ... this has added to the cost of operating police departments."[95] Consequently, the increase in mobility was matched with a growth in government. The cost of police work in cities with populations over 30,000 rose steadily from approximately $38 million in 1903 to $184.5 million in 1927.[96] Automobile theft added new categories of crimes, and as a piece of technology cars became a central part of burglary and housebreaking. In Philadelphia, 8,896 people were arrested for assault and battery by the automobile.[97] In response, police began to patrol with the automobile. In 1922, Chicago police complained that their worn-out "tin lizzies" should be scrapped; they could not catch the high powered hold-up car that traveled at sixty miles an hour.[98] Even with the growth of government and the advent of patrolling, police forces were out-maneuvered by mobile criminals. Contrary to the iconic Prohibition image of police forces smashing barrels of alcohol, municipal police forces may have dealt with automobiles on a more regular basis.

Automobile theft was most acute in Detroit and Los Angeles. "Naturally Detroit is peculiarly liable to this trouble because it has such a large floating population of men trained in mechanical expertise in the various factories."[99] It stood to reason that Ford's workers stole

Ford's cars. In Detroit, in 1928, a total of 11,259 cars were stolen.[100] The same year in Los Angeles 10,813 automobiles were stolen.[101] By the 1920s, Los Angeles had the most automobiles per resident in the United States. Historian Scott Bottles pointed out, "By 1925, every other Angelino owned an automobile as opposed to the rest of the country where there was only one car for every six people."[102] Angelinos had more opportunities to steal cars. Baltimore, New York City, Rochester, Buffalo, Cleveland, Omaha, St. Louis, and many other cities also experienced major problems related to automobile theft. In an article published in *Country Life*, Alexander Johnson revealed the problem was not just endemic to urban America: "We who live in the country are not quite as subject as our urban brethren to this abominable outrage, but automobile stealing is carried on even in the rural districts."[103]

The cost of police work in state governments also rose from approximately $98 million in 1915 to $117 million in 1927.[104] To combat auto theft, state governments created license, registration, title, and statistical bureaus and urged the federal government to become involved. E. Austin Baughman, Commissioner of Motor Vehicles of Maryland, cited 1919 as "the climax of an epidemic of car stealing" with 922 cars stolen, 709 recovered, and 213 missing.[105] Baughman urged the country to adopt a Title Law which would assure all motor vehicles could be identified and located through the name and address of the owner on record.[106] The bureau helped Maryland to gather statistics:

> ... one can in a comparatively short time find anything from how many 1912 Cadillacs are still in existence in this state, to how many more Fords were stolen than Chevrolets in 1923 or 1922; and from how many six- and seven-ton trucks are still in use in Maryland and to what percentage of cars stolen in 1923 are still missing.[107]

In 1920, Massachusetts developed a similar program under the used-car department of the Department of Public Works.[108] States that did not pass title laws were a nationwide liability and became alleged "dumping grounds" by neighboring states.[109]

The interstate nature of automobile theft demanded federal intervention. The automobile nullified state boundaries and contributed to the nationalization of crime fighting. Arch Mandel wrote in 1924 that, "State lines have been eliminated by the automobile" and the "detection of criminals is becoming more and more a nation-wide task."[110]

In 1919, Congress passed the National Motor Vehicle Theft Act, which received the appellation of its sponsor, Senator Leonidus Dyer. The Dyer Act promulgated that thieves receive fines of $5,000 and 10 years in prison, or both. The American Automobile Association lobbied Congress to pass the Dyer Act.[111] Consequently, between 1922 and 1933 auto thefts were the most prominent federal prosecution of interstate commerce.[112]

During the first two decades of the twentieth century, auto theft was often blamed on owner negligence. A 1916 insurance company pamphlet entitled "Emergency Instructions" warned owners that "when dining in a public restaurant the driver of the car should be seated in such a position that he can observe his car."[113] Basic instructions also warned to "not leave your car unprotected on the street or any place at any time."[114] However, in 1922 many automobile owners left keys in their unlocked cars.[115] An article in *Popular Mechanics Magazine* observed, "Approximately seventy-five percent of all the cars that were not stolen were not locked at all."[116] One author chastised drivers for leaving automobiles unattended for an hour or more.[117] Beyond common-sense precautions, automobile owners were advised to take preventive measures to stop early car thieves. Owners were advised to lock their doors or "garage" their automobiles. In his 1917 article "Automobile Thefts," John Brennan proposed one countermeasure: "If owners would only take steps to put private identification marks on their cars, the problem of automobile thievery would be a simple one to solve."[118] It was suggested that the owner bore holes into the underside of the running boards, scratch their name somewhere secret, or tape an identification card inside the upholstery.[119] A 1926 article in *Popular Mechanics* passed on to readers one motorist's intricate plan of fake coils and pseudo ignition connections.[120] Other articles proposed that owners disconnect the magneto. In any case, the prevailing attitude of the day was that automobile theft was usually the owner's fault. In 1929, E. L. Rickards, manager of the Automobile Protective and Information Bureau in Chicago, stated: "A man or woman who leaves his car unlocked and unattended is committing an offense against society."[121]

Thieves were recognized as frauds, joy-riders, professionals, and gangs. They stole a range of models, but mostly low-priced Chevrolets, Plymouths, Chryslers, and Fords.[122] Furthermore, automobiles were most likely to be stolen in business or entertainment districts, where individuals parked the same models in the same place. Often a thief caught red-handed simply claimed that he had hopped into the wrong car. When interrogated by a judge, one thief explained why he was in the wrong Ford: "Because both cars are Fords, and all Fords look alike, not only to me but to their owners."[123] Charges were dropped. Despite preferences to steal commonplace vehicles, elite and unusual automobiles were not exempt from the threat of theft. Expensive cars were stolen, disassembled and repainted.

> Early automobile thefts were performed by owners who would, "steal their own car." To collect on insurance, owners would strip the car of accessories and move it to an out of the way location. The owner would work with a thief: ... the owner is in partnership with the thief. An auto, for instance, that is insured for $2,000 is reported by the owner as having been stolen. The machine is worth $1,500. So the owner, collecting his theft insurance, makes a clean profit of $500.[124]

Owners in debt often defrauded insurance companies as well: "an automobile owner, after using his insured car for nine or ten months, discovers that its market value is 40 percent lower than when first purchased; also the cost of maintaining the machine, oil, gasoline, tires, repairs, etc., is considerably in excess of the figure on which his first maintenance costs were based."[125]

Quite different in terms of criminal intent were the activities of the so-called joy-rider. Joy-riders stole for thrills. In 1917, Secretary to the Detroit Chief of Police George A. Walters estimated that 90 percent of Detroit's auto thefts were performed by joy-riders.[126] Joy-riders were often groups of young men in pursuit of fun, and had a "taste for motoring."[127] One author argued that joy-riders (in all cases male) had a sexual motivation, "Some young fellow with sporty tendencies and a slim pocketbook wants to make a hit with some charming member of the opposite sex ... he thinks an automobile would help him in the pursuit of her affections."[128] After a joy-ride, automobiles were often found damaged and out of gas. Historian David Wolcott has noted that in Los Angeles, "Boys approached auto theft with a surprisingly casual attitude — they often just took vehicles that they found unattended, drove them around for an evening and abandoned them when they were done — but the LAPD treated auto theft very seriously."[129] In the early period of automobility, authorities considered "joy-riding" a serious societal problem. Joy-riding was an action of a delinquent. Joy-riding was so serious that young boys were prosecuted under the Dyer Act of 1919. The federal government did not draw a distinction between joy-riding and professional auto theft until 1930.[130] Congressmen Dyer called for the repeal of his own law, and to convince the U.S. House of Representatives of the need for repeal, he read a letter from the superintendent of a penitentiary:

Of the 450 Federal Boys in the National Training School here in Washington, nearly 200 are violators of the Dyer Act, with the ages distributed as follows: Two boys 12 years of age, 6 boys 13 years of age, 19 boys 14 years of age, 31 boys of 15 years of age, 64 boys 16 years of age, 48 boys 17 years of age, 19 boys of 18 years of age, 1 boy 19 years of age, and 1 boy 22 years of age.[131]

Due to the capricious nature of theft for a joy-ride, policemen and journalists surmised that it could be easily prevented: "It is against this class of thief that the various types of automobile-locking devices and hidden puzzles are effective ... since the joy-rider does more than half the stealing it follows that car-locks are more than 50 percent effective in protecting a car."[132] However, more elaborate means would be necessary to stop the professional thief.

Writers who addressed auto theft from 1915 to 1938 admitted that the professional thief could not be stopped. Professional thieves employed an array of tactics to steal automobiles. Often chauffeurs, mechanics, and garage men became thieves. Even though locks supposedly prevented theft by joy-riders, thieves would simply cut padlocks and chains with bolt-cutters.[133] Often this was not necessary, since keys to early Fords were easy to obtain. In 1917, Edward C. Crossman described the naïve Ford owner:

Ford owners take out the switch key on the coil box and go strutting off as if they'd [sic] locked the car in the safe deposit box. The first half-baked auto mechanic who needs a Ford can slip in another key and depart via the jitney route without paying his fair.[134]

Crossman's solution was to lock a heavy metal band around the front wheel of the automobile.[135] In a May 1929 article "Tricks of the Auto Thief," *Popular Mechanics* described the array of tactics open to the automobile thief. Thieves stole accessories, unlocked and started cars with duplicate keys, "jumped" the ignition by placing a wire across the ignition coil to the spark plugs, ripped-off car dealerships, and towed cars away.[136] "Some thieves make a specialty of buying wrecked or burned cars as junk ... they receive a bill of sale, salvage parts which they place on stolen cars, and so disguise the finished automobile as a legitimate car for which they have the bill of sale."[137] One method called "kissing them away" involved an individual breaking into a car and, being unable to start the ignition, having a "confederate" push the stolen car with his car from behind. The car would be moved into a garage or alley and promptly dismantled.[138] Thieves used interchangeable parts to confuse authorities. In 1925, Joe Newell, head of the automobile theft bureau in Des Moines, Iowa, stated, "the greatest transformation that takes place in the stolen machine is in the clever doctoring of motor serial numbers ... this is the first thing a thief does to a car."[139] Automobiles were branded with a serial number that corresponded to a factory record, but thieves used several tactics to change the numbers. The "doctoring" of numbers involved filing down numbers and branding a new number into the car, or changing single numbers. In a detailed article entitled "Stolen Automobile Investigations," William J. Davis noted, "It is possible for a thief to restamp a 4 over a 1; an 8 over a 3 where the 3 is a round top 3; a 5 over a 3; to change a 6 to an 8, or a 9 to an 8, or an 0 to an 8."[140]

Apparently the joy-riding problem declined in the 1930s, but organized gangs emerged as a more serious threat to steal automobiles and, in the process, vex authorities. In *Popular Science Monthly*, Edward Teale noted,

the automobile stealing racket in the United States has mounted to a $50,000,000-a-year business. During the first six months of 1932, 36,000 machines disappeared in seventy-two American cities alone. In New York City, $2,000,000 worth of cars was reported stolen in 1931.[141]

Gangs developed sophisticated automobile theft operations from the expert driver to expert mechanic. Gangs even developed their own vernacular.[142] A stolen car was a "kinky" or a "hot short." The "clouter" actually stole the car and the "wheeler" drove it to the "dog house." The thieves were concerned with stealing the popular, mid-priced, widely-used makes. Gangs often specialized in a certain make or model. One New York gang "scrambled" the stolen automobiles: "a number of machines of the same make and model are stolen at the same time ... wheels are switched, transmissions shifted, bodies changed, and engines transferred from one car to another."[143]

At other times, gangs would use the "mother system." Under this system, thieves stole a certain make, had a fake bill of sale made, and changed all of the serial numbers to be identical to the bill of sale. Ultimately, four or five of the same car with the same serial numbers and bills of sale would exist.[144] In 1936, J. Edgar Hoover penned an article about gangster and international car thief Gabriel Vigorito (a.k.a. Bla-Bla Blackman), who had amassed a $1 million fortune from automobile theft.[145] "The 'hot car' depots of a dozen states dealt in his goods.... In Persia, Russia, Germany, Norway, Denmark, Belgium, and even China, the American car business included many automobiles stolen from the streets of Brooklyn." Authorities convicted Bla-Bla to ten years in prison. Historically, the point is poignant: the automobile trumped not only state lines, but national lines. The rise of an industrial and global industry also rose with a global theft ring. In 1936, the Roosevelt Administration entered a treaty with Mexico for "the recovery and return of stolen or embezzled motor vehicles, trailers, airplanes or the component parts of any of them."[146] The treaty prompted a convention with Mexico in 1937 to address the stolen automobile problem.[147]

To control rampant automobile crimes, authorities developed scientific means to fight crime. As early as 1919, a system of fingerprints to identify automobile owners was proposed.[148] Throughout the 1920s, law enforcement of automobile theft remained ineffective. By 1934, police developed sophisticated means to monitor a more mobile public. In 1936 it was urged that "every city join the nation-wide network of inter-city radio-telegraph service provided for by the Federal Communications Commission."[149] Police developed processes using chemicals and torches to identify fake serial numbers. Los Angeles police department officers departed the station for their shift with a list of stolen automobiles printed the night before.[150] Developments in communication aided police officers. "Chattering teletype machines and short-wave radio messages outdistance the fleetest car, while police encircle a fleeing criminal in an effort to make escape impossible."[151] Radio communication made auto theft difficult. By 1934, "auto thieves found their racket a losing one."[152] In response to mobile crime, governments at all levels grew more sophisticated. Insurance companies also grew more sophisticated: "In Chicago, a central salvage bureau, maintained by insurance companies is being established in an effort to wipe out a 10,000,000-a-year racket in stolen parts."[153] Automobile manufacturers invested in a "pick-proof" lock.[154] From 1933 to 1936, insurance companies and the government destroyed the market for stolen automobiles and stolen parts. In 1934 *Popular Science Monthly* reported, "figures compiled by the National Automobile Underwriters Association show that eighty-six percent of the cars stolen in 1930 were recovered while in 1931 eighty-two percent were recovered and eighty-nine percent in 1932."[155]

A definitive study of car theft during the Interwar years remains to be written. What the above paragraphs suggest is that the automobile placed unprecedented challenges before local, state, and federal government agencies, and in response the responsibilities and scale of government changed as a consequence. Indeed, the law itself changed, and that included the area of tort law during the 1920s, as sorting out negligence as a consequence of automobile accidents also posed new problems that demanded innovative structural solutions.

*   *   *

The complexities of the Ford story reflect the nature of life itself. At times, history turned on the elusive factor of personality, and clearly strong personalities, including Henry Ford, made a difference. Yet, the success of the Model T was also the consequence of American social values, social structure, and geography. The Model T is ultimately integral to the twentieth century story of the common man, but the Model T is also about technology. The emergence of mass production at the Ford Motor Company represented the accumulation of techniques rooted in the nineteenth century, refined and focused with unprecedented power. When all these strands came together, however, what resulted was more than just wealth creation; the Machine Age transformed the habits and everyday lives of virtually every American. Whatever America was prior to 1908, it now was on a different pace, and with a different sense of space.

3

THE RISE OF THE COMPETITION AND
THE CONSUMER DURING THE 1920S

Although General Motors has experienced a remarkable decline in market share and stock value, it was until recently (fall 2008) one of the most powerful corporations in the world.[1] Even as the giant struggles, hampered by health care costs and prior union agreements, one may still argue that "what is good for General Motors is good for America." Indeed, GM's financial resources are greater than those of all but a handful of countries. And while in many respects it has been characterized as a faceless corporation where decisions are made by committee and individualism is frowned upon, it is ironic that the firm was forged by a few strong individuals, among them William C. "Billy" Durant, Alfred P. Sloan, Charles Franklin Kettering, William S. Knudsen, Richard H. Grant, and Harley Earl. Perhaps its future will again be fashioned more by individuals than the organization itself, at least if current GM vice-chairman Bob Lutz has any say.[2]

Billy Durant and "Silent" Sloan

Chapters from Alfred Chandler's classic *Strategy and Structure* remain perhaps the most concise recounting of General Motors' early history.[3] General Motors' beginnings are intimately tied to the career and fortunes of the "dealmaker," Billy Durant.[4] In 1885 Durant, a 24-year-old insurance salesman living in Flint, Michigan, purchased a patent for $50 to make two-wheeled carts. Durant's partner in this venture was J. Dallas Dort, a young hardware salesman. The two began marketing their product nationwide, and as their efforts were successful, they first erected a manufacturing plant in Flint and set up specialized plants to make bodies, wheels, axles, and springs, to upholster interiors, and to apply paint and varnish. Durant's efforts to develop a high volume, integrated business made him a millionaire before he was 40, yet he was never interested in the operational details of the business. Accordingly, he moved his personal headquarters to New York, where in imitation of business titans J. P. Morgan and others, he began to look for new industrial empires to conquer.

By 1900 the automobile was clearly emerging as an entrepreneurial opportunity for many, and Durant recognized that it posed a threat to his existing carriage business. In 1904 one of the smaller firms in the America automobile industry was the Buick Motor Company, located in Flint, Michigan, and headed by Scotsman David Buick. Then in bankruptcy, the Buick firm was taken over by Durant, and it became the foundation for an auto empire. Durant redesigned the car, built large assembly plants, and set up a nationwide distribution network and dealer organization.

As sales volume increased, Durant encouraged the production of parts and accessories in Flint or purchased suppliers and moved them to Flint. Thus, he bought the Weston-Mott Axle and Wheel Company and moved it from Utica, New York, to Flint in 1905; in 1908 he bought Alfred Champion's spark plug company and moved it to Flint from Boston. Durant was following a strategy of backwards integration and in doing so he was eliminating uncertainties associated with outside parts suppliers.

As a result of Durant's leadership, Buick's output rose from only 16 cars in 1903 to nearly 8,500 units in 1908. This initial success with Buick convinced Durant that the automobile had a huge potential market in the U.S. Rather than expanding Buick internally and adding to capacity, Durant began to think of merging a number of existing companies into a conglomerate. To that end, on September 8, 1908, Durant formed the General Motors Company, which by the end of the year owned stock in Buick, Oldsmobile, and the W. F. Stewart Co., bodymakers located in Flint. Durant then followed a strategy of exchanging stocks to control Cadillac, Oakland, six other car companies, three truck companies, and ten parts and accessory companies.

While following both a vertical and a horizontal expansion strategy, Durant never prepared for a temporary decline in demand in the form of a business recession. He never considered building up cash reserves to weather an economic downturn. Ever-expanding through acquisitions, Durant made no attempt to collect information about output and demand in order to make adjustments in production that might compensate for temporary fluctuations in the economy. Further, Durant was not interested in management principles related to organization; he never focused on maximizing the economies of scale in purchasing or production that were possible due to his empire building.

In 1910 a slight recession took place, and Durant lacked the money to pay his employees and suppliers. He was financially rescued by bankers who took control of his company, and consequently, Durant was forced into a position where he had little to say about company matters. James J. Storrow was the leader of a group of bankers involved in saving General Motors. Storrow desired more organization and more control over what had been autonomous company operations. To that end, centralization took place at General Motors, and as a first step in that process Storrow moved headquarters from New York to Detroit. He set up three permanent offices at the main office, with the idea that the firm would be administered more effectively. A new purchasing office was established, so that economies would be achieved in volume buying for the various subsidiaries. An accounting office was also created, and accounting procedures were standardized throughout the company. Accurate information on costs, profits, and losses was now tallied. Finally, a new production office was set up. With Charles Nash as president and Walter Chrysler in charge of production at Buick, GM's sales rose from $85 million in 1912 to $157 million in 1915.[5]

Storrow's measures were all steps in the right direction, but in 1915, when he left General Motors, company operations were far from efficient. Storrow left because Durant returned through a complex financial arrangement. In that transition, the du Pont family was now in an important financial position at General Motors. With the support of the du Pont family, Durant encountered little restraint in expanding the firm in the years immediately after 1915. Increased volume was the focus of Durant's maneuvers, and he paid no attention to other needs or the demands of the market. Concurrently, he paid little attention to organization and strategies and policies where control and coordination would be exerted. Durant's expansion was exhibited in a number of different ways. First, he acquired several leading parts and accessory companies, including Hyatt Roller Bearing Co., Remy Electrical Co., Delco, and Pullman Rim Co. New products, including tractors and refrigerators, were also introduced. After World War I, this drive to expand accelerated, as Durant bought the Fisher Body Company; gear manufacturer T. W. Warner Company; and Buffalo Metal Goods, a producer of braking systems. Stock investments were also made in Alcoa, Goodyear, and General Leather, all major automobile suppliers.

The du Pont family — flush with money due to the profits made during World War I but conservative in their business strategies — was troubled by Durant's aggressive behavior and speculation in the stock market, but little was done until the economic downturn of 1920. By October, the automobile market had collapsed and General Motors stock took a nosedive. As a result, Pierre du Pont became president of General Motors and he acted decisively. One of his first acts was to approve Alfred Sloan's organizational structure for General Motors, a structure that remains to this day the company's basic organization. The multidivisional structure that was proposed and approved by Pierre and Irénée du Pont featured a central office that planned, coordinated, and appraised the work of a number of operating divisions and allocated to them the necessary personnel, facilities, funds and other resources. The executives in charge of these divisions had under their command most of the functions necessary for handling one major line of products or a set of services over a wide area, and these men were responsible for the financial results of their respective divisions. This new structure was designed to mobilize resources effectively, so that both short- and long-term demands were met.

Sloan's organization plan was implemented in 1921 and only slightly modified during the next four years. Up to 1921, competition existed between divisions. Boundaries between divisions were established based on market strategy. Furthermore, the company did not have a low-priced car to compete with the Ford Model T, but by 1923 GM product lines were redefined and readjusted. Cadillac sold in the highest price position, followed by Buick, Oakland, Oldsmobile, and finally Chevrolet. Chevrolet had the highest volume and the lowest price. In 1925 Pontiac was created, thereby filling a gap and enabling Sloan to achieve his goal of "a car for every purse and purpose."

The difference between the approaches of Durant and Sloan to the problems of administration reflected contrasting personalities, education, and experience.[6] Durant was a small man, energetic and personable. Almost everyone who knew him called him "Billy." Sloan, on the other hand, was tall, quiet and cool, and his increasing deafness heightened his reserve. Nearly everyone called him "Mr. Sloan," and when in company whom he did not know, he turned into "Silent Sloan." Durant had gone from high school into business, but Sloan was an electrical engineer with a degree from the Massachusetts Institute of Technology. Durant was a salesman and stock speculator, but Sloan was a very deliberate thinker and a production man. In 1899, with the assistance of his father, Sloan purchased the Hyatt Roller Bearing Company. It grew so rapidly that the company was sold to Durant for $13.5 million in 1916, at which time Sloan joined GM as a president of its parts subsidiary. Charles Franklin Kettering would join GM in a similar way as a result of the purchase of Delco.

Kettering, Earl, and "Keeping the Customer Dissatisfied"

Biographer Stewart W. Leslie has said this about Kettering and his technological style: "He made corporate bureaucracy work for him. Within the largest private organization of his time he fashioned a managerial role that proved technological entrepreneurship could flourish, and one man could still make a difference."[7] Kettering had remarkable personal qualities that distinguished him as one of the leading industrial scientists of his and any other era in American history. He was sharply inquisitive, and this trait led to an intimate knowledge associated with the problem at hand, the result of close observation and direct experience. Kettering was equally comfortable in both theory and practice, and he usually focused his attention on a commercial bottleneck where improvement seemed possible rather than striking out into completely unexplored areas. Yet he had little use for high-powered scientific theories and abstruse terminology that usually had little applicability in an industrial setting. He once said that "Thermodynamics is a big word for covering up our inability to understand temperature."[8]

Born in Loudonville, Ohio, Kettering attended the Ohio State University, majoring in electrical engineering.[9] Perhaps it was due to the strain of studies, but whatever the cause he temporarily lost his eyesight, only to regain it after working as a telephone line repairman. In 1903 he took a job at the National Cash Register Company (NCR), working in Invention Department No. 4, and was charged with the development of an electrical motor that would possess enough torque to operate a mechanical cash register. Dissatisfied with boss John Patterson, Kettering, along with Edward Deeds (then a vice-president at NCR), Bill Chryst and others, began work on an integrated automotive electrical system, a technology that would ultimately greatly improve the automobile as a form of transportation.

In 1908, on the eve of Kettering's involvement in the development of an efficient automobile ignition system, it was well recognized that ignition or providing the spark to ignite the fuel was a weak link. As Stewart Leslie has recounted:

> A proper ignition for such a variable, high-speed engine had frustrated inventors for decades. Continental engineers, led by Robert Bosch, had eventually worked out an acceptable magneto around the turn of the century. Americans still preferred dry cell battery ignitions, which were cheaper though less reliable. However, battery ignition had its own shortcomings. To provide a spark of adequate intensity from a relatively small bank of batteries, the dry cells were connected to an induction coil in such a way that the primary circuit was repeatedly interrupted by a master vibrator that created a shower of sparks, which then depleted the non-rechargeable batteries after a few hundred miles of driving.[10]

Kettering responded to this problem by drawing on his experience gained at NCR. He took a magnetic relay that he had used for a cash register design and used it to serve as a holding coil that would release the ignition contact only at the proper moment in the cycle and send one intense spark instead of a shower. He subsequently sold this ignition coil design to Henry Leland at Cadillac, and this success would not only form the basis of the Dayton Engineering Laboratories Company (Delco) but also further work leading to an integrated electrical system. That technology involved a self starter, generator, voltage regulator and lighting units, which were also first sold to Cadillac before being marketed to other companies.[11] By early 1913, Delco occupied three floors of a rented factory building in East Dayton, Ohio, employed 1,500 workers, and had sold a total of 35,000 starting, lighting, and ignition systems. Despite the catastrophic Dayton Flood of 1913, Delco continued to grow, and thus by the end of that year the firm tripled its annual output, to more than 45,000 units. Profitable and innovative, it would be purchased by Durant in 1916.

Kettering's successes at GM as head of research would far outweigh his failures. The two main areas of research at the laboratory were centered on studying the combustion process in

Bill Chryst (in passenger seat) and Charles Franklin Kettering (at wheel) testing the Delco self starting ignition system, Dayton, Ohio, 1913 (Dayton History).

engine cylinders and the nature of materials. In both cases, definitive answers to a scientific understanding of these important areas were not forthcoming. Yet, he once said, "You must learn how to fail intelligently, for failing is one of the greatest arts in the world." Indeed, it is instructive to look at his most notable failure, the copper-cooled engine. The story tells us much about the nature of engineering at GM, and how it was organized during the period between World Wars I and II.

In 1919, Kettering had become convinced that there was a great future for an air cooled, as opposed to a water cooled, engine. Light and maintenance-free in terms of freezing and adding coolant, the air-cooled engine had been developed in Europe and America, the most notable successes being the early Franklin engine and the designs of British automobile engineer Frederick W. Lanchester. Kettering and his research staff, including mechanical engineer Thomas Midgley, focused on the use of copper fins to dissipate heat emanating from cylinders. By 1920 a team of engineers and scientists had developed a technique to fix the copper fins to the exterior of cylinder walls. Pierre du Pont, at that time in charge of GM and trained as an engineer, saw the possibilities of this design, and encouraged Kettering to move forward on the project. What du Pont and other GM executives recognized was that this light and economical engine could be inexpensively manufactured in both 4- and 6-cylinder versions and be used in the low-priced Oakland and Chevrolet models. Especially with regard to the Chevrolet, it was thought that the copper cooled engine would provide the edge for Chevrolet to compete with the Ford Model T.

Despite the enormous resources that GM dedicated to this project, however, the copper-cooled-engine failed in the end. Kettering and his group could design and make small quantities of engines that worked in Dayton, where GM research laboratories were located. But in Detroit, manufacturing engineers could not or would not make engines that consumers were satisfied with. These engines often lacked power, pumped oil, threw fan belts, overheated, or just ran poorly. In sum, the research engineers and manufacturing engineers were at odds, and until GM in 1925 formed a technical committee to bring the two groups together, ventures like the copper cooled engine were doomed to failure.

Success would come to Kettering and Midgley related to tetra-ethyl lead, however. Around 1920 there was a fear that the world was running out of oil, and therefore leading automobile industry executives thought that engines had to be designed to run more efficiently. One way to do this was to increase the compression ratio of the engine, or the volume swept in the cylinder by the piston, but increased compression ratios led to pre-detonation of the fuel-air mixture, a phenomenon that was called knocking. Kettering initiated a search for an additive to prevent knocking, and after many trials, discovered an organo-metallic substance called tetra-ethyl lead, or TEL. There was one hitch with this project, however. Lead compounds had been known since Roman times to be notoriously poisonous, but it was claimed that in the ratio of 1:1300 in gasoline, the material was harmless. Industry leaders saw TEL as a "gift from God"; tests made by laboratories after 1925 indicated that TEL was safe for mechanics, gas station attendants and consumers.[12] Of course, as we know now, it was not. At low levels lead proved to be a neuro-toxin, but only in the 1960s did improved chemical instrumentation demonstrate the extent of the public health dangers posed by this substance. Beginning in the 1970s, TEL was phased out in the U.S., but only after two generations were exposed to relatively high amounts of lead that eventually entered the human body.

Kettering brought more to GM than just technical expertise: he brought talent that made crucial contributions to GM's efforts to surpass the Ford Motor Company during the interwar years. One of his closest associates at Delco was Richard H. Grant, who drew on his experiences at National Cash Register and the sales philosophy of John Patterson to teach GM to sell—first Chevrolets and then the entire product line. Known as "Dynamic Dick" and the "Little Giant," Grant was one of America's great salesmen. Born in Massachusetts and educated at Harvard, Grant learned to sell at NCR, became its general sales manager in 1913, later moved to Delco and Frigidaire, and in 1923 joined Chevrolet as sales manager. In 1929, Grant became a GM vice-president and was one of the top four or five executives of the firm during the 1930s, with memberships on six policy groups.

The "Little Giant" played a major role in reorganizing the distribution system at GM, eliminating distributors who previously held large territories and had control over local dealers. He was an orator and showman, but beneath the surface Grant was a careful, systematic thinker who implemented market research, accounting, and training procedures throughout the corporation. Grant had learned seven fundamentals of sales from NCR's John Patterson that were subsequently instilled into GM personnel:

1. Have the right product.
2. Know the potential of each market area.

3. Constantly educate your salesmen on the product, making them listen to canned demonstrations and learn sales talks by heart.
4. Constantly stimulate your sales force, and foster competition among them with contests and comparisons.
5. Cherish simplicity in all presentations.
6. Use all kinds of advertising.
7. Constantly check up on your salesmen, but be reasonable with them and make no promises you can't keep.[13]

Grant further refined Alfred Sloan's notion of using R. L. Polk Company's monthly state registration data to closely monitor subtle shifts in consumer demand. By the late 1920s, this information would be relayed to William Knudsen's production group, thus ensuring that the automobiles made would be the kind that customers would quickly buy off dealers' lots.

Closely related to Grant's efforts were those of the customer research group, led by Buck Weaver.[14] Weaver and his associates formulated a set of questionnaires aimed at asking the broad question of "What do customers want?" A large number of potential questions were mailed in memorandum books in which every aspect of design and engineering was queried. Among the questions asked were what should be the shape of the radiator; what designs are too conservative and too extreme; should there be running boards on cars; and most significantly, how should a car be sold. For buyers of the early 1930s, the results of the surveys pointed to their priorities for cars that were dependable and economical. For the average American, speed and the power of the engine seemed to be the least of their concerns.[15]

With the advent of Alfred Sloan's idea of a car "for every purse and purpose" and his choice of executive leadership in the likes of Kettering, Grant, and production genius William Knudsen, General Motors came to dominate the automobile industry. In the third phase of the production process, from the mid–1920s into the 1950s, Fordism was modified and intensified, thus evolving into what became known as "Sloanism." Sloanism can be thought of as an ongoing structural process by which an organization is shaped and decisions made in such a way as to facilitate effective positive change in the workplace and marketplace. By the 1930s, Sloanism translated into committees that set policies and decentralized operating divisions managed by individuals.

Sloanism was an idea at GM as early as 1925, first introduced on the shop floor in 1928, and fully implemented by 1932 and 1933. With machines that were flexible, rapid model change was now possible. Some assembly line positions were reskilled under Sloanism, as "vital maintenance and repair workers made up nearly 10 percent of the industry's labor force."[16] To fit machines to new models, a new class of mechanics was created. They were paid to think, solve problems and define the task that they had to accomplish.[17] Flexible mass production marked an important change for organized labor, but Fordism remained the productive motif for most Americans working in automobile assembly plants.[18] Stephen Meyer noted the continuity: "The Sloanist flexible production system retained the Fordist features of routinized work and work processes; it remained monotonous, repetitive, and machine paced."[19] For semiskilled and unskilled workers, the new machines furthered degraded skills and intensified the pace of the assembly line.

In the 1920s, managers and foremen aimed to increase output per worker to meet the insatiable demand for cars. Though the annual model change appealed to the American consumer, it frustrated the auto worker. "The annual model change meant several days or weeks of fussing and fumbling until they adjust to the new routines and rhythms of their work."[20] As Joyce Shaw Peterson indicated, early autoworkers sometimes opted to keep doing the same monotonous job in order to "space out" or daydream, rather than having to learn a new job.[21] The increased demand was met with a speed-up of the assembly line. James Flink noted that "Sloanism thus had the effect of intensifying the amount and pace of dehumanizing work in automobile manufacturing ... there was degradation of labor to lower skill levels and intensification of the production process."[22]

Flexible mass production persisted into the Great Depression. At General Motors, the process paid off; during the Depression they reported profits every year.[23] Indeed, by the late 1930s GM was no longer considered as "Big Business," but as "Colossal." Even during the darkest days of the Great Depression, the firm had over 250,000 employees working in 110 manufacturing plants located in 14 states and 18 countries.[24]

By the mid–1920s the GM strategy of a car for every purse and taste was markedly cutting into Ford sales. GM exemplified what the power of technology and organization, harnessed together, could do to dominate the American automobile industry. Chevrolet, the lowest priced of the GM models, was not only a key to GM's success, but emerged as the car for everyman by the end of the 1920s. Chevrolet was created by race driver Louis Chevrolet and Billy Durant before World War I. Originally an expensive automobile with a 6-cylinder engine, it later became a low-priced car with a smaller engine. During GM's financial crisis in 1920, discussions took place during which it was proposed that Chevrolet would be dropped as a product line, but in 1922 William Knudsen was hired to head production and Richard Grant to head sales. By 1927, Chevrolet had outsold Ford and become the largest customer for the various GM parts subsidiaries, like Delco-Remy, Fisher, Harrison, and Guide Lamp.[25] The 1929 Chevrolet, with features that included the reliable "stove-bolt" six (labeled so because of the stove bolts which held many of the engine parts together), set the benchmark for low-priced cars. As shown in Table 5, by the mid–1930s Chevrolet sales consistently outpaced Ford's, reflecting both GM's ascendancy and Ford's relative decline in the American, and indeed world, marketplace.

TABLE 5: FORD VS. CHEVY PASSENGER CAR PRODUCTION, 1928–1942

Year	Ford	Chevrolet	Year	Ford	Chevrolet
1928	713,528	786,670	1936	791,812	971,595
1929	1,715,100	856,384	1937	848,608	866,885
1930	1,261,053	647,520	1938	410,048	489,143
1931	626,579	623,901	1939	532,152	645,905
1932	420,824	323,100	1940	599,175	894,178
1933	334,949	486,378	1941	600,814	928,477
1934	563,921	556,666	1942	43,407	45,393
1935	942,349	793,106			

Source: Ray Miller, *Chevrolet: The Coming of Age, 1911–1942* (Oceanside, CA: Evergreen Press, 1976), p.319.

What was left to be done, in the words of Kettering, was to "keep the customer dissatisfied," and that largely would be the work of GM stylist Harley Earl, hired by Alfred Sloan in 1927 as head of the Art and Colour group. As a result of Earl's efforts, cars would become longer, lower, and more light reflective due ever-increasing amounts of chrome trim. Technological changes related to suspension, the engine, and drive train were incremental during the 1930s, but the looks of the vehicle became increasingly critical to the annual model change, in advertising copy, and consequently in attracting consumers.

Few television viewers could have understood the significance of the General Motors commercial made a few years ago that portrayed a flashy man in a broad hat who stated that he was Harley Earl. The commercial assumed too much, and gave more credit to the American consuming public for historical knowledge concerning their automobiles than they possessed. That said, perhaps no other single individual did so much to turn America into a consumer-driven society, one characterized by status, style, color, and planned obsolescence, as Harley Earl. From 1927 to 1958, Earl dominated design in Detroit, and by 1958 his legacy in the auto industry was one in which the stylist, and not the engineer, was supreme.[26] Excesses of flash over substance became the keynote of an American industry by the late 1950s that marked the beginnings of American auto industry decline that became evident only during the post oil-shock 1970s.

Earl was a big and burly Californian, who cut his teeth in the auto coach trade while working for a family firm during the 1920s.[27] He caught the eye of Alfred Sloan, and in 1927 made his first contribution to style at GM with a redesign of the LaSalle. Earl's cars were colorful, attractive to the ladies (who often made the family decision concerning which car to buy), longer and lower. GM cars of the 1930s continued along this line of evolution, with chrome trim increasingly employed in strategic positions and with beveling so that "reflective value" had its greatest impact. The culmination of Earl's efforts during the pre–World War II period was his 1938 prototype Buick Y Job, a stunning styling tour de force that presaged developments that were introduced into production cars after the war. Looking back on the pre–World War II era, Harley Earl was to jibe that "I have watched them spend upwards of $50 million since I have been here to drop cars three inches."[28]

While Earl exploited changing shapes and styles at GM, others within the organization did the same with color. Regina Lee Blaszczyk's important preliminary studies of the "Color Revolution" of the late 1920s highlighted the importance of the automobile and particularly GM's collaborative efforts with du Pont in introducing a host of new colorful finishes.[29] Prior to the early 1920s, automobile finishes could be classified as either the black, high-temperature hard enamel paint that was baked onto Henry Ford's Model T, or various coatings that required numerous applications followed by laborious sanding or rubbing down between coats. In 1922 du Pont chemists, working with GM, developed a lacquer named Duco that was tough and durable, chip- and fade-resistant, and easily applied to automobiles with a spray gun. This paint was first tried on GM's 1924 Oakland, where each vehicle would be painted two shades of blue. The "True-Blue" Oakland had been the idea of Alfred Sloan, who thought that customers might like a different colored car, and it turned out to be a big hit with customers, who subsequently demanded it. Accordingly, beginning in 1925 all GM vehicles were painted with Duco, and color, like style, became critical to GM employees who were charged with reading the market. In 1928 du Pont colorist H. Ledyard Towle was enticed to work for GM, and the same year automobile color codes and a system of standard colors were adopted. And while Towle's tenure at GM was short, his successor, Howard Ketcham, created the Automobile Color Index, which was a monthly analysis of consumer color preferences. Most significantly, during the late 1920s and early 1930s everyday cars became very colorful, with shades that included Bambalina Blue, Irish Green, Bantam Rose, Silver, and Lemon Yellow. And while black would remain a popular color, especially during the Great Depression, the car became a colorful object that reflected the desires and personality of its owner.

With the development and introduction of Duco, car color—and especially blue—quickly became embedded in American literary culture. For example, in 1926 Natalie Sumner Lincoln published *The Blue Car Mystery,* a tale about the murder of a prominent Washingtonian, two blue cars, a car thief, and a pretty young socialite.[30] More significantly, however, in 1930 the Nancy Drew mystery series began with *The Secret of the Old Clock,* and young Nancy drove a blue roadster in the first few titles as she unraveled puzzling crimes by following clues.[31] Scholars have interpreted Nancy's blue car as a symbol of her independence, a message that would be conveyed to millions of young women readers in the decades that followed.

The City of the Future and Dynamic Dayton of the 1930s

Just as the Buick "Y Job" was a final stylistic statement before the interruptions of a global war, so too the GM Futurama exhibit at the New York World's Fair of 1939 was of similar significance in terms of the highways that would carry these new forms of vehicles. Expressing rather naïve notions about what lay ahead and the role of technology in underdeveloped nations, GM exhibited the model of a road-building machine, a "factory on wheels," that was to cut through jungle forest and lay one foot of concrete road per minute, with service people installing lighting and other appurtenances shortly thereafter. Its models—some 1 million small scale structures—and mechanisms expressed the visionary ideas of designer Norman Bel Geddes, previously expressed in his *Magic Motorways.*[32] Bel Geddes envisioned a world connected by automated and elevated highways that reached into the far suburbs of large American cities, a futuristic environment of elevated broad expressways reaching out like ribbons into the hinterlands. More than a million visitors were transported in sound-equipped lounge chairs through the exhibit, and while developments that would turn this vision into reality were interrupted by World War II, it would be prophetic in terms of how American life would develop during the last half of the twentieth century.

The Futurama exhibit represented a vision of the future GM-shaped city, but at the same time GM had already had a profound influence on a number of urban areas. Next to Flint, Michigan, and perhaps Rüsselsheim, Germany, no city in America had been influenced by GM's success more than Dayton, Ohio.[33] With a history in agricultural implement manufacture and a place as the home of the National Cash Register Company, Dayton was home to a large number of skilled machinists who subsequently found employment in the rapidly growing automobile-related firms established by Boss Kettering and his associates. According to *Fortune,* in 1938 approximately 100,000 of the 200,000 residents of Dayton owed their economic livelihoods *directly* to General Motors. And not all of these activities were strictly involved automobile manufacturing, for Frigidaire employed 12,000 workers making refrigerators, beer coolers, air conditioners, electric ranges and water heaters. Nearby, in central Dayton, Delco Products made electric motors not only for Frigidaires, but also for Maytag washers, Globe meat slicers, and du Pont rayon spinners. It was estimated that some 10 million motors worldwide could be traced back to Dayton. Additionally Delco made coil springs and shock absorbers for GM, Nash, Hudson, Graham and Packard automobiles. Finally, Delco had a brake operation, making hydraulic brake assemblies and brake fluid while housed in perhaps the only flop to bear GM's corporate name, General Motors Radio. Often overlooked, GM's Inland Manufacturing in Dayton had its origins in World War I and the Dayton-Wright Airplane Co. After the war, its woodworking department formed the basis of an enterprise to make wooden steering wheels and later rubber-based ones. Product diversification followed, so that the firm made everything from rubber cement to running boards, motor mounts, and weather strips. To borrow a phrase from a book boosting the city during the 1950s, truly GM's Dayton operations were at the heart of "dynamic Dayton."

The Last of the Big Three: The Chrysler Corporation

Just as General Motors was best known for organization, Chrysler was known for its engineering and innovation.[34] Among early Chrysler innovations were the following:

1924 — Advanced design, high compression engine
1929 — Down-draft carburetor
1931 — Fully automatic spark control
1934 — Scientific weight distribution; unitized body; automatic overdrive; one piece curved windshield
1937 — Safety padding in back of front seats
1941 — Fluid drive (automatic transmission)
1949 — Key-operated combination starter and ignition switch; safety cushion dash
1950 — Electric window lifts
1951 — Hemispherical combustion chamber V-8; power steering
1955 — All-transistorized radio

During the first two decades of its history, the firm was the largely the product of the efforts of Walter Chrysler and a dedicated group of engineers.[35] Chrysler, a self-taught mechanic with roots in Kansas, began his career working for the railroad, and in 1908 bought a $5,000 Locomobile automobile. He promptly took the Locomobile apart piece by piece so that he could learn about it. Chrysler would later seek employment at Billy Durant's Buick Motor Car Company, where he would work as a foreman and production manager. While Henry Ford gets credit for mass production, partly due to his relentless campaign for recognition, at Buick similar kinds of manufacturing improvements were being made by Chrysler and associates, but in a slightly different way. Ford had started with ignition components, specifically the magneto, and had worked out the means of assembling it and then in turn other small parts. Ford worked his way forward to the final product, the Model T. In contrast, Chrysler began with the finished Buick and went backwards looking for improvements. Next to Ford, Buick was the most important marque of the World War I era, and its success was in no small measure due to the efforts of Walter Chrysler, the one-time sweeper of a Union Pacific roundhouse, farm hand, silverware salesmen and grocery boy. Ongoing disputes with Billy Durant, however, ultimately led to Chrysler's departure. After a one-year retirement, he landed the job of saving first a sinking Willys-Overland organization, and then Maxwell-Chalmers.

Chrysler was one of those rare breed of individuals who wanted to put his name on something. To that end, in 1924 he introduced a model named after him that was the most important car of the 1920s. As Walter Chrysler himself said about the 1924 Chrysler, "I gave the public not only quality but beauty, speed, comfort in riding, style, power, quick acceleration, easy steering, all at a low price." At the heart of the car's development were the efforts of three engineers who would contribute in big ways to the successes of the Chrysler Corporation for decades to come — Fred Zeder, Owen Skelton, and Carl Breer.

As Chrysler biographer Vincent Curcio has stated:

> It was a long time coming, but the new Chrysler automobile was made out of whole cloth by men who had no preconceptions of what a car should be, and because they were not burdened with a preexisting corporate culture dictating design and manufacturing traditions, they were free to burst onto the world with a brand new kind of car."[36]

The 1924 Chrysler was the product of scientific and technical research. It was said that it was a $1,500 car that could give $5,000 thrills. It was the first modern car made not for rural farmers, but for the now predominant urban America. And it drove like a modern car:

> On starting the engine, I was struck by the uncanny absence of those sounds so common to others. No clicks from the valve gear; no whine from the camshaft drive. Just a comforting tautness, as though each part was perfectly shaped to fulfill its function. The engine seemed to run with a freedom that suggested the total absence of friction. The controls were light and precise in action. Touch the brake pedal, and the perfectly equalized hydraulic system responded immediately. Touch the throttle, and response was instant.... Even gear shifting had been transformed from heavy drudgery to an act of swiftness and ease.... There was also a brand new kind of smoothness, so utterly lacking in effort it reached the senses in dynamic flow, backed by a torrent of power in reserve.... The modestly priced little Chrysler equaled our most costly machines in silence and smoothness, but added to this a sparkling new ingredient, mechanical effortlessness.[37]

While it was Walter Chrysler who had so perceptively recognized that American consumers were rapidly changing in their tastes and expectations, his engineering three musketeers — Zeder, Skelton and Breer — were most responsible for its introduction and subsequent success. With it came profits of more than $4 million in 1924, and in 1925 a transition in the name of the firm from the Maxwell Motor Car Company to the Chrysler Corporation. By 1924 the brief but deep post–World War I recession was over, and America was in the midst of a prosperity decade that witnessed the expansion of urban areas and key industries associated with the automobile, including steel, glass, and rubber manufacturing. Roads were getting better, and thus more Americans had a penchant for speed. New paints were introduced that resulted in more colorful cars, and as fashions became more widespread, so did fashionable cars for the middle classes. Closed cars were now "in," and cars began to be thought of as extensions of the home, with all its comforts, including the new communications device, the radio. And cash-poor Americans no longer had to wait for what they wanted, as installment plans were introduced so that one could get what one wanted when one wanted it. To be sure, the price to pay was that many American workers had to be subjected to industrial discipline and the pressures of time in this "Machine Age," but high among the car's benefits was the freedom to go wherever and whenever one pleased.

Chrysler's advanced engineering as expressed in its initial model ensured that the company would sell an excellent product for some years to come. For Walter Chrysler, the next major step in his drive to become a leading manufacturer and indeed take his firm to the level of what would become known as the "Big Three" involved simultaneous expansion and diversification. First, Chrysler established a luxury, top-of-the-line model, named the Imperial, in late 1925. By 1926 the firm sold 162,000 cars, with some 9,000 Imperials manufactured. In 1927, sales topped 192,000.

During the late 1920s GM began offering cars makes that were considered to be companion cars to established product lines. Thus, Pontiac was created as a companion to Chevrolet, and LaSalle to Cadillac. These cars served to fill in market gaps. To counter these moves and in response to the introduction of the Ford Model A, Chrysler began to think of adding new makes of his own to the Chrysler lineup. Chrysler first acquired the Dodge Brothers Company, and then created a new vehicle, the DeSoto.

Horace and John Dodge were born in the 1860s in Niles, Michigan.[38] The brothers, known for demanding perfection on the job and the consumption of liquor when not in the shop, were machinists who had built engines, transmissions, and axles for Henry Ford during the first decade of the twentieth century. They also built a large plant in Hamtramck, Michigan in 1910, and four years later struck out on their own in the manufacture of the Dodge automobile. According to Vincent Curcio:

> And what a car it was. At $785, it was 50 percent more expensive than a Model T, and worth every nickel. The Dodge Brothers Touring Car boasted a 35-horsepower engine, compared to 20 for the Model T: it had a sliding-gear transmission, rather than Ford's clunky planetary one, which required a lot of servicing: its pioneering all-steel welded body, designed by Edward Budd, was sturdy and less subject to vibration than the typical wood-based body; it sported a speedometer and a windshield, a Cadillac-style electric system (which included a self-starter and electric lights powered by a wet battery and generator), and demountable rims (which made possible for a motorist to carry a fully inflated spare).[39]

By the end of 1915, 45,000 Dodges had been sold. It was said that a Ford rattles, a Packard purrs, and a Dodge chugs. And these chugging Dodges quickly became legendary. They were used in Mexico by the U.S. Army to track down Pancho Villa. They were later driven by U.S. troops in Europe during World War I, one driver being none other than air ace Eddie Rickenbacker, who would later produce his own innovative car in 1924.

Despite the Dodge brothers' criticisms of Henry Ford's freezing of the production model once established, they did the same thing, advertising "constant improvements but no yearly models." At the zenith of their careers in 1920, the Dodge brothers' lives were cut short suddenly, due to pneumonia (John) and cirrhosis of the liver (Horace).

Under the guidance of John and Horace's widows, the Dodge Brothers firm continued to sell cars, with the able management of Frederick Haynes ensuring profitable years. Sold in 1925 to the investment firm of Dillon, Read & Company, Dodge Brothers declined gradually after 1926, as it entered a period of poor management.

It was then that Walter Chrysler came into the picture. He had recognized that the large and well-equipped Dodge facilities would add greatly to his own existing plant capacity, and that the Hamtramck site had the potential of allowing Chrysler to add new product lines and volume that he so desperately needed to keep up with GM.

In the midst of negotiations to purchase Dodge, Chrysler started with a ploy that turned out to be a new car product line, the DeSoto. The DeSoto was originally conceived as a way to devalue the Dodge so that it would be easier to purchase, but by early 1928 it turned into an operating group within the Chrysler Corporation. The car was named after a sixteenth century adventurer who discovered the Mississippi River, and the group offered Spanish-sounding models like Cupe Business and Roadster Espanol. A total of 1,500 dealers signed up to sell the car, which was introduced first as a 1929 model. The DeSoto was rather attractively styled, and equipped with a 6-cylinder engine, and Lockheed hydraulic brakes. Consumers quickly responded, as more than 80,000 DeSotos were sold during its first year.

The DeSoto was a 6-cylinder vehicle, and concurrent developments centered on a 4-cylinder vehicle, which would become the Plymouth. The Plymouth was initially envisioned as a parts bin car, essentially a patchwork of existing parts, and therefore inexpensive to build. A closely-guarded secret in 1927, it was named Project Q in early 1928 and began production in June of that year. On one hand, the car was loosely based on the old Maxwell, but it also had numerous features that the Ford and Chevrolet did not have. One of its main features was rubber motor mounts — the precursor to a Chrysler feature called floating power. This innovation isolated the car from the road and resulted in a far quieter ride. Additionally, the Plymouth had full-pressure lubrication, a waterproof distributor, and aluminum alloy pistons, along with hydraulic brakes. As an ad in the *Saturday Evening Post* proclaimed: "We have named it the Plymouth because this new product of Chrysler engineering and craftsmanship so accurately typifies the endurance and strength, rugged honesty, the enterprise and determination of achievement and freedom from old limitations of that Pilgrim band who were the first American colonists."[40]

Dillon, now controlling a Dodge Brothers firm that was dropping like a rock in value due to the introduction of these new Chrysler models, became desperate to make a deal. After extended negotiations and a complex stock exchange, the Dodge Brothers became the Dodge division within the Chrysler Corporation. With this merger, the new Chrysler Corporation had a capacity to produce some 750,000 cars, putting it firmly in third place behind GM and Ford with assets and capitalization of about a third of Ford and a quarter of General Motors.

The Dodge Brothers acquisition was reflective of broader changes taking place in the auto industry during the 1920s. The number of manufacturers gradually declined, and by the end of 1928 Ford, GM, and Chrysler were producing about 80 percent of all cars made in the U.S. Some 34 smaller car makers remained in business. With the coming of the Great Depression, a number of these would falter and fold, but Walter Chrysler's star would continue to rise, reflected in his construction of the Chrysler Building in New York City and his overtaking Ford as the number two manufacturer in 1934.

Key to Chrysler's success during the 1930s were changes in the design of the Plymouth. In 1931, an all-new Plymouth was introduced, the PA, which was longer and more powerful than the Ford Model A at a price that was sure to be attractive to Depression-era buyers: $535 to $645. It was said that Walter Chrysler took the third Plymouth PA off the line, drove it to Henry and Edsel Ford's Dearborn offices, sat for an hour with the two, then gave them the car and took a taxi home. By the end of the year some 94,000 units were sold, and Plymouth became the number three seller in America. With the success of minor improvements over the next two years, one out of every four cars sold in America was a Plymouth.

The Independents

To place the entire focus of the discussion on Ford, General Motors, and Chrysler would distort the nature of the automobile industry's history during the 1920s, for there were many other automobile manufacturers during the decade. In an industry that was not quite mature yet, entry was still possible, and a number of marques were both innovative and popular. A shakeout would take place with the onset of the Great Depression, but even during the grim 1930s a number of smaller companies hung on. The following chart lists a number of American car manufacturers.[41] There were also two electric car manufacturers — Detroit and Rauch & Lang — as well as other small producers.

Auburn	Ford	Packard
Buick	Franklin	Paige
Cadillac	Gardner	Peerless
Case	Hertz	Pierce Arrow
Chandler	Hudson	Pontiac
Chevrolet	Hupmobile	Reo
Chrysler	Jordan	Rickenbacker
Cunningham	Kleiber	Roamer
Davis	Lincoln	Star
Diana	Locomobile	Stearns
Dodge Brothers	Marmon	Studebaker
DuPont	McFarlan	Stutz
Elcar	Moon	Velie
Erskine	Nash	Wills Ste. Claire
Essex	Oakland	Willis Knight
Falcon-Knight	Oldsmobile	
Flint	Overland	

Given the complexity of the automobile market during the 1920s, it is impossible here to discuss the corporate histories of each of these firms. However, case studies of a few of these "orphan" marques may be instructive.

Innovation at the Periphery: The Cracker Jacker, Rickenbacker

The Rickenbacker automobile, advertised as "a car worthy of its name," was manufactured in Detroit between 1921 and 1927.[42] Named after Captain Eddie Rickenbacker, America's "ace of aces" during World War I and the commander of the "Hat in the Ring" squadron, the Rickenbacker was designed along the lines outlined by former auto racer "Captain Eddie's" specifications. In 1919 Rickenbacker decided that he would build a car that incorporated such race-proven advanced features as a rigid frame, 4-wheel brakes, and a high standard of construction. Envisioned as fitting in the market somewhere between the low-end Ford Model T and the far higher priced Cadillac and Packard, it was to be affordable to white-collar workers, prosperous farmers, and "women of taste."

Rickenbacker sold his ideas to Maxwell executive Harry L. Cunningham, who subsequently recruited an impressive management team. Among the new firm's executives were coach builder Barney F. Everitt and Walter E. Flanders, formerly the production manager at Ford. With Cunningham as Secretary and Treasurer and Rickenbacker as Vice President and Sales Manager, the Rickenbacker Motor Company was initially well positioned.

During 1921 a six-cylinder prototype was built and tested, $5 million worth of stock was sold, and a plant with a 12,000 unit capacity was acquired. Three Rickenbacker models debuted in 1922 — a Tourer, Opera Coupe, and Closed Sedan — and more than 3,700 cars were sold, resulting in a 5 percent stock dividend.

Rickenbacker 6- and 8-cylinder models gained a reputation for innovative technology and enhanced safety features. For example, while not the first American automobile to offer 4-wheel brakes, the Rickenbacker was the first moderately priced car to do so. Other advances not found in less expensive models included a low vibration flywheel engine, ignition and transmission locks, and an ingenious system to purify engine oil and avoid crankcase dilution, a carburetor air cleaner, and automatic windshield washer. The proud owner of a Rickenbacker could sing along to the popular tune "Merrily I roll along and there's nothing wrong ... in my cracker jacker, Rickenbacker."[43]

But in fact storm clouds soon passed over the fledgling firm, and it began to experience production and financial difficulties. By then, Walter Flanders had died the result of an unfortunate accident. Handicapped with small profit margins, Everitt cut prices without consulting dealers and stockholders. Marginal dealers went bankrupt, stockholders and management squabbled, and in 1926 Captain Eddie resigned. Everitt was now on his own and on borrowed time, and the company closed its doors in February 1927. Its machinery and engines were later sold to German industrialist J. A. Rassmussen, who used Rickenbacker engines in his Audi Dresden Sixes and Zwickau Eights between 1928 and 1932.

Like the Richelieu, Saxon, Dort, Flint, Winton, King, Jewett, Wills Ste. Claire and numerous other Midwestern automobile companies, the Rickenbacker could not survive competition from more highly capitalized and cost-efficient firms, even during America's prosperity decade of the 1920s.

The Jordan and Advertising the Dream

The Jordan automobile presents a different story but with a similar ending. The Jordan was the result of the vision and energy of Edward S. "Ned" Jordan. Born in 1881 and educated at the University of Wisconsin, Jordan's career included a stint in advertising at the National Cash Register Company in Dayton and in a similar position with the Jeffery Automobile Company, located in Kenosha, Wisconsin. In 1916, Jordan organized his own automobile company, located in Cleveland, Ohio, with the idea that the firm's vehicles would manufacture cars that cost not quite as much as a Cadillac but more than a Buick. Always relatively expensive and assembled from parts, engines, and bodies made elsewhere, about 80,000 units were sold between 1916 and 1931. Normally priced over $2,000, the Jordan was marketed at the well-to-do.

The Jordan was noteworthy for several reasons. Ned Jordan had an uncanny understanding of well-to-do American consumers from the point of view of color, and from the firm's origins, his cars could be ordered in a number of unusual shades, long before the color revolution of the late 1920s. Thus, as early as 1917 Jordan cars could be purchased in colors such as Liberty Blue, Pershing Gray, Italian Tan, Jordan Maroon, Mercedes Red, and Venetian Green. And when the "True Blue" Oakland was introduced in 1923, Jordan quickly followed with its 1923 Blue Boy model. Secondly, Jordan understood the post–World War I youth market and responded with the marque's most famous model, the Playboy. Supposedly, the Playboy idea was the result of Ned's dance with a 19-year-old Philadelphia socialite, who quipped, "Mr. Jordan, why don't you build a car for the girl who loves to swim, paddle and shoot and for the boy who loves the roar of a cut out?"[44] Ned would later refer to this as a million dollar idea, and the Playboy was born. Finally, Jordan was a flamboyant advertising copywriter, and it would be in his Playboy ad copy written in 1923, "Somewhere West of Laramie," that American automobile advertising would be transformed.

While there is little doubt that twentieth century advertisements serve as important cultural documents, there is considerable debate as to their meaning.[45] In his *Understanding Media* (1964), Marshall McLuhan asserted that "historians ... will one day discover that the ads of our times are the richest and most faithful daily reflections that any society ever made of its entire range of activities." This is especially true in a capitalist economy, where consumption and persuasion are so important. Raymond Williams insightfully labeled advertising as capitalism's "official art." With regard to advertising, the work of Judith Williamson, Roland Marchand and William O'Barr all significantly contribute to an understanding of its meaning. Williamson's *Decoding Advertisements: Ideology and Meaning in Advertising* provides the reader with a step-by-step guide in the dissection of an advertisement. Marchand's *Advertising the American Dream: Making Way for Modernity* is a powerful example of how a cultural historian can employ advertising to reconstruct the past. And O'Barr's work, while primarily aimed at using advertising to illuminate discursive themes in social history that include hierarchy, power, relationships, and dominance, has an excellent synthetic theoretical introduction. O'Barr follows along the lines of Marchand in arguing that social and cultural values appearing in advertisements are more a refraction than a representation. The two scholars also agree that audience response, while important to copywriters, is beyond the scope of the historian, and at any rate problematic. Past audience responses are simply impossible to accurately reconstruct. In the present, there is no simple way to ascertain meaning, for meaning involves the interplay of the naïve with the critical, and thus there is an ultimate variance among interpreters. The problems associated with the use of advertising, however, can be extended to many if not all of the various manuscript, textual, visual, and oral sources used by the historian.

In the early days of automobile advertising, the features of an automobile were often emphasized. For example an ad for the new 1917 seven passenger Oldsmobile claimed that

> This light weight, eight cylinder car combines power, acceleration, speed, economy, comfort, beauty, and luxury in a measure hitherto undreamed of in a light car. The eight-cylinder motor, developing 58 horsepower at 2,6000 rpm, with the light weight of the car — 3,000 pounds — presents a proportion of power to total car weight of approximately one horsepower to every 51 pounds — an unusually favorable ratio. The comfort of the car is beyond description. Long, flat, flexible springs and perfect balance of chassis insure easy riding under any kind of going. The seats, upholstered with fine, long grain French leather stuffed with pliant springs encased in linen sacks, increase comfort to the point of luxury.

This style of advertising was swept aside by the mid–1920s. In 1923, Edward S. Jordan created the most famous auto ad of all time to move his colorful Playboy Roadsters.[46] Jordan had a gift for writing advertising copy; in 1920 a Playboy ad suggested a visit to a local bordello:

> Somewhere far beyond the place where man and motors race through canyons of the town — there lies the Port of Missing Men.
> It may be in the valley of our dreams of youth, or the heights of future happy days.
> Go there in November when logs are blazing in the grate. Go there in a Jordan Playboy if you love the spirit of youth.
> Escape the drab of dull winter's coming — leave the roar of city streets and spend an hour in Eldorado.[47]

Jordan told the story that while he was traveling on a train across the flat and monotonous Wyoming plains, a tall, tan, and athletic horsewoman suddenly appeared, racing her horse toward Jordan's window. For a brief moment the two were rather close as the woman smiled at him; then she turned and was gone. Jordan asked a fellow traveler where they were: "Oh, somewhere west of Laramie" was the desultory reply. Within minutes he composed an immortal ad that later appeared in the *Saturday Evening Post* in 1923. Beneath an illustration of a cowgirl racing a sporty Jordan roadster against a cowboy straining to push his fleet-looking steed to catch up with her, there appeared these words:

> Somewhere west of Laramie there's a bronco-busting, steer roping girl who knows what I am talking about. She can tell what a sassy pony, that's a cross between greased lightning and the place where it hits, can do with eleven hundred pounds of steel and action when he's going high, wide and handsome.
>
> The truth is the Playboy was built for her.
>
> Built for the lass whose face is brown with the sun when the day is done of revel and romp and race.
>
> Step into the Playboy when the hour grows dull with things gone dead and stale.
>
> Then start for the land of real living with the spirit of the lass who rides, lean and rangy, into the red horizon of a Wyoming twilight.

The Playboy sold like hotcakes, and this ad galvanized the auto industry. Soon Chevrolet and Rickenbacker responded with ad lines "All outdoors can be yours," and "The American Beauty," respectively.[48]

Previously ads mentioned the features of the car, but with the Jordan ad new parameters came into play — freedom, speed, and romance. The practical Model T's life was coming to an end. Now art and color would be the key to auto sales.

The prosperity decade of the 1920s resulted in a remarkable restructuring of the American automobile industry and a drive towards consolidation as numerous small manufacturers dropped out of the marketplace. Given the drive towards efficiencies in production and distribution, intense pressures were placed not only on the workmen who assembled the cars, but also the consumers who bought them, increasingly on credit and after being exposed to more subtle and suggestive advertising. With more wealth and disposable income, consumers wanted more — more horsepower, more size, more colors and style, and more conveniences. The automobile was now an object of desire among all classes of Americans, and as such it transformed our personal and social habits, as well as the road and roadside.

4

FROM OUT OF THE MUD TO
ON THE OPEN ROAD

"O public road, you express me better than I can express myself."—Whitman[1]

In any careful analysis, the highway is inseparable from the automobile. While these two technological systems are quite different in terms of engineering expertise, materials and construction/production techniques, they intersect in critical respects. For example, the design of the modern automobile — in terms of power plants, suspension, and safety features — was largely determined by the highways on which it traveled. Automobiles are engineered either to transmit the "feel" of the road (a more recent American priority forced upon us by the Europeans), or eliminate it (the living room ride of Detroit iron during the 1950s, for example). Similarly, highway construction, in terms of width, grade, surface, drainage, and layout, is planned only after taking into account the nature of the vehicles that will traverse the land. Safety is a major point at the intersection of these two systems, although sadly that has not always been the case.

Which Came First: Good Roads or the Automobile?

The interrelated topics of adoption of the automobile and the construction of good roads in America have been the focus of a "chicken and egg" historiographical debate during the past twenty years. The central question is whether the coming of the automobile resulted in the development of improved roadways, or conversely, that existing roads in a number of cities were critical to the acceptance and growing popularity of the car. The interpretation that the car led to good roads was primarily the result of work done in the 1960s and 1970s by John C. Burnham, John Rae, and James Flink, whose interpretations corroborated reports written in trade magazines and popular literature dating back to the beginning of the twentieth century. Rae wrote in 1971, "When mass production of motor vehicles was introduced, it preceded any major improvement in the highway network. The historical principle that the highway is built for the vehicle, rather than vice versa, holds good for the automobile."[2] Later, these scholars were labeled by urban historians Eric Monkkonen and Clay McShane as "technological determinists." Monkkonen asserted that politics had a primacy over technology related to urban transportation when he stated that "good roads are purely political creations."[3] Monkkonen was settling scores with interpretations that were far more sweeping than those written by automobile historians. Yet to extend his analysis to the sphere of America both urban and rural, Monkkonen was traversing dangerous ground.

Clay McShane, whose previous work had been on urban infrastructures, followed Monkkonen's lead in *Down the Asphalt Path: The Automobile and the American City*. McShane also took a position contrary to Rae's, remarking, "The decision of American municipalities in the closing decades of the nineteenth century to adopt asphalt and brick pavements played vital roles in the emergence of the auto. Policy conflict over the regulation of vehicles and the provision of smooth pavements provides the crucial background for automobilization."[4] In particular, McShane, who has taken a position as a "social constructionist," argued that bicyclists and their influence on the improvement of urban highways should not be ignored, nor should the fact that the automobile had its roots in a number of cities, especially New York City. To some degree, this scholarly spat is the result of discussions concerning moving targets. One's answer concerning whether politics or technology drove road construction depends specifically on when and where. Circumstances were quite different in 1903 than in 1910 or 1920 or 1930, and what held for explanations concerning the automobile and the road in New York City is hardly similar to that what took place in Mississippi, Louisiana, or for most of America.[5] That said, it would be an egregious omission to avoid tackling the topic of the history of roads in twentieth century America in any serious study of the history of the automobile.

The Good Roads Movement

Dirt paths, rutted country roads, rocky inclines, and railroad right of ways were challenges that faced Horatio Jackson in 1903 on his transcontinental trip and then countless others in the years that followed.[6] Initially, these potential obstacles had little appeal for all but the most adventurous; if you wanted to go anywhere beyond the city limits, you faced the possibility of getting stuck in the mud, and to make things more tenuous, automobile tires were simply not very good in those early days.[7] For the automobilist, puncture repair was as important a skill as shifting gears.

The improved highway provided the common person with the unprecedented freedom to move beyond the narrow bounds of life, particularly for those living in the country. Without paved roads, the car would have had a limited impact on everyday activities, and a limited market appeal. The most discernible social impact of the automobile on American life took place along the highway, because it was there that gas stations, restaurants, auto camps, tourist cabins, and eventually motels were erected to serve ever-restless drivers and passengers.

Complex forces that emerged toward the end of the nineteenth century ultimately forced road construction in the U.S. Key pressure groups consisted of organized bicyclists, farmers, rural postal delivery advocates, and automotive enthusiasts. As mentioned previously, the bicycle created an awareness of how flexible and convenient travel by road could be. The bicycling craze demonstrated just how bad American roads really were. Thoroughfares outside of major cities were almost always dirt paths, unmarked, and rarely maintained. As a result of these difficult conditions, bicyclists spearheaded a campaign for improved roads. Their chief lobby group was the League of American Wheelmen, formed in 1880 in Newport, Rhode Island, "to ascertain, defend, and protect the rights of wheelmen, to encourage and facilitate touring." As part of this program, a good roads campaign was launched that in the end gained very limited success. In part, the campaign failed because the League of American Wheelmen had no national following, as a majority of its membership came from New York and Mass-achusetts and only 12 percent of its members lived in states west of New York. Also, while the bicycle was a boon to urban dwellers residing on flatlands, it had little utility for the farmer, and so initial attempts to create highway legislation were defeated.

A second stream of activism concerning good roads surfaced by the 1890s, and that involved rural farmers. During the 1890s, there was a wave of agrarian discontent in Amer-ica, in part fueled by railroad abuses that included high freight rates. Good roads meant more money for farmers transporting produce to the marketplace. Some populist leaders reasoned that perhaps highways could serve as alternatives to railroads, although at least in the south, the railroads recognized that roads fed into their transportation networks. Politicians clearly recognized their eroding population base and sought to arrest rural to urban migration. Fur-thermore, in southern states, patrician leaders argued that good roads could be constructed at minimal cost by employing convict labor. A booster in Virginia exclaimed, "History teaches that the best and most permanent roads constructed all over the world have been built by convict labor."[8]

As a result of this demand for more equitable transport, the National League of Good Roads was established in 1892. The group held a convention in Washington, D.C., a year later, and subsequently in 1893 the Office of Road Inquiry was established within the U.S. Department of Agriculture. This agency, with little funding to operate adequately given the task at hand, was responsible for collecting factual data on the nation's highway system. Its 1904 road census was most revealing. The U.S. had 2,151,570 miles of highway, of which 153,662 miles, or 7 percent, could be classified as improved. Of this total, some 38,622 miles had a small stone surface, 108,233 had a gravel surface, and the rest was covered with sand, shell, and even some plank. Only 141 miles of roads could be considered acceptable for vehi-cle traffic (particularly in the light of the unreliable and frail autos of that day)—123 miles of brick and 18 miles of asphalt.[9]

Additionally, to placate farmers who felt they were cut off in terms of communications, particularly since the postal system was so well established, the first successful Rural Free Delivery system was established in and around Charleston, West Virginia. Soon many other communities followed.[10] In sum, good roads were perceived by the politically astute as poten-tially slowing down rural to urban migration, possibly saving traditional folkways, and not incidentally, arresting the pace of shifts in voting patterns that this transition was causing.

Of far more significance than the political pressures of bicyclists or farmers was the appear-ance of the automobile. The motor vehicle added to the pressure for road improvement, and indeed was an even stronger incentive than the bicycle, since it was a lot harder to extract a car stuck in the mud than a bicycle. And the fact that the automobile was an expensive item initially motivated the most wealthy and politically powerful group of Americans in having a personal interest in the Good Highway Movement.

As automobile transportation grew rapidly in the decade after 1902, there were clear signs that farmers would embrace the automobile as much as city folk. The American Automobile Association was founded in 1902 to lobby for motorists. This group held a joint Good Roads Convention with the National Grange in 1907. It would be only a year later that the Model T appeared. Perhaps never was there a machine that did more to initiate change, both social and economic. If the automobile boom was to continue to flourish, surely good roads had to be constructed.

One example of the nature of early roads and road maps can be gleaned by reading the

Arizona Good Roads Association Illustrated Road Maps and Tour Book, published in 1913.[11] The tour book was a costly and time-consuming endeavor on the part of boosters to depict the new state as a progressive place with considerable economic opportunities. Detailed maps listed mountains and hills, crooked roads, grades, water, bridges, railroad tracks, buildings, telegraph, telephone, and power lines, rivers and washes, and most importantly accurate mileage between points.

A Transcontinental Link: The Lincoln Highway

With the increasing numbers of vehicles on the road, the level of talk concerning improved interstate roadways intensified. In 1911, Carl Graham Fischer, an Indianapolis businessman, promoter of the Indianapolis Speedway, and founder of Presto-Lite Company, first proposed building a hard-surfaced, coast-to-coast highway that he named the Lincoln Highway. The Lincoln Highway Association was organized in 1913, and its importance in both the short- and long run was significant. Travel literature concerning the Lincoln Highway appeared long before the highway was completed and certainly became influential in terms of encouraging the general public to hit the road and find adventure.

Effie Price Gladding's *Across the Continent by the Lincoln Highway* certainly was an early example of this genre of writing, a colorful travel account that curiously focuses on California while largely omitting much of the Midwest. For Price, the road trip had little danger and much romance. Price concluded that as a result of her trip, "We have a new conception of our great country; her vastness, her varied scenery, her prosperity, her happiness, her boundless resources, her immense possibilities, her kindness and hopefulness. We are bound to her by a thousand new ties of acquaintance, of association, and of pride."[12] And while automobile touring temporarily declined during World War I, it returned to Americans in 1919 who now had a "fever" to get back on the road. In fiction, Sinclair Lewis wrote of the adventures of Claire Boltwood in *Free Air*. Proper Ms. Boltwood escaped from her respectable life in Brooklyn by taking a cross-country road trip in a 70 horsepower Gomez-Dep roadster. Similar to Lewis's fictional account, Beatrice Larner Massey penned an account of her 1919 tour with the title *It Might Have Been Worse: A Motor Trip from Coast to Coast*. Massey and her husband leased their home, put family business affairs in order, and left New York City in a Twin-Six Packard. A total of 4,154 miles and about $1,000 later, Mrs. Massey concluded, "This trip can be taken in perfect comfort by two people for thirteen dollars a day, including everything, which means that you are traveling as well as living. Not bad, considering the 'H. C. of L.' today!"[13]

In a sense, the Lincoln Highway Association marked the emergence of the "road-gang," an effective lobby group that for the remainder of the twentieth century shaped federal highway legislation through political and economic influence. In addition to Fischer, who later made a fortune in Florida real estate while promoting the Dixie Highway, other leaders with automobile industry connections included Roy D. Chapin, John N. Willys, Henry B. Joy, and Frank Sieberling. With substantial funding from General Motors, the Lincoln Highway Association was a precursor to the efforts of Alfred Sloan's Highway Users' Conference of the 1930s. Its relationship with the U.S. military during World War I and then with the First Transcontinental Army Convoy in 1919 ensured that its arguments for federal road funding in Western states were duly heard. Between 1913 and 1920, more than 2,000 miles of Lincoln

Highway links would be built (U.S. 30 later on), but the cost and difficulties of local and state government jurisdictions led to the disbanding of the association once the landmark Federal Aid Roadway Act of 1921 was passed.[14]

Federal Legislation and the Gas Tax

This act had been preceded by the Good Roads Act of 1916, legislation that finally involved the federal government in road building. It remained an open question in 1916 whether efforts should be directed toward a system of arterial routes connecting major cities, or whether the farm population should be provided with better connections to surrounding communities. In the end, $75 million was appropriated for rural roads, only available if matched by the states. Since states like New York had previously raised $100 million through the sale of bonds, one can only conclude that this first piece of federal legislation was hardly adequate given the task at hand.[15]

A year later the United States was at war, and it quickly became apparent that roads were necessary for national welfare. The rail system became gridlocked in the Northeast because of the shipping of war materials, and as a result it became increasingly clear that a coherent network of trunk highways was necessary. Truck convoys carrying war materiel to shipping points quickly damaged the roads that had been built, and thus new approaches were critical, not only to meet future national defense needs, but for the burgeoning number of automobiles that were increasingly on the road.

Further measures were needed after World War I, since the 2 million vehicles of 1915 had exploded to 10 million by 1920. Federal action was forthcoming with the passage of the Federal Highway Act of 1921, which granted aid for the construction of both interstate and inter-county highways.[16] Matching funds were allocated to the states according to population, area, and mileage of rural and mail routes. State highway departments became responsible for much of the maintenance of these new roads, but benefited from federal monies that supported construction at $15,000 per mile.

Two Lane Black Top, or Concrete If There Is Money

The 1921 act resulted in employment for some 250,000 construction workers. Its most significant impact, however, was the transformation of road building techniques. Until the early twentieth century, best practice road building meant the construction of macadam surfaces, derived from the work of early nineteenth century English engineers Loudon Macadam and Thomas Telford.[17] Using small stones and the dust of these stones as a binder during a compaction process, road building had been gradually mechanized during the late nineteenth century with the introduction of steamrollers, rock crushers, graders and tractors. Macadam surfaces, however, while wholly adequate for bicycles, could not withstand heavy automobile and truck traffic. Attempts were made to tar the macadamized surface to improve its durability, but ultimately the widespread adoption of concrete and "black top" supplanted macadam roadways.

The first concrete road surfaces were widely adopted in California beginning in 1910. Headed by Austin B. Fletcher, the California Highway Commission pioneered banked concrete thoroughfares and curbing. A key innovation was the development of the paving train, where trucks and large drum mixers supplied materials to spreaders, levelers, and finishers pulled along on rails. And while concrete had its critics, particularly those who argued that it was too expensive for rural roads, in the end it became the material of choice in road building in heavily trafficked areas.[18] Alternatively, there was asphalt, and its plants also became larger and fed bituminous pavers that spread in lane widths a heated bituminous-aggregate mix.[19]

By 1923, the Bureau of Public Roads, under the direction of Thomas H. MacDonald, planned a tentative network of arterial highways that included all cities of 50,000 or more. Some 350,000 miles of highways were envisioned, in which even numbers were designated for east-west routes and odd numbers for north-south.

The question was how this ambitious internal improvements program would be funded, a critical one both in terms of future economic growth and national defense. As it turned out, the answer was to collect fees from registrations and license applications, and in part from gasoline taxes that began to be levied in 1919.[20] Road mileage doubled between 1920 and 1930 and then doubled again between 1930 and 1940.

Until the closed car became more popular in the mid–1920s, this pioneering stage of automobile and highway history was one of pure exhilaration, so well expressed by Drake Hokanson:

> The breeze rushing through the open windshield of an automobile was stronger than that on a boat or in a buggy, and the hiss of moving air blended smoothly with the sound of a powerful motor. It carried the perfume of motoring; the smells of rubber, oil, and gasoline, and the scents of woodland, river, prairie, and sage. It was this wind with the smell of someplace else in it that urged the traveler on, that made it clear that you were on the road for somewhere.[21]

By the mid–1920s, there were numerous interstate highways, although they were uneven in terms of surface quality and designated by name rather than by number. For example, the Dixie Highway, which connected travelers from Detroit to Florida, ended in Miami. Another road that ended in Miami was the Atlantic Coastal Highway, which began in Quebec City, Canada, and passed through New England, New York City, and Philadelphia. There was also the Capital Highway, starting in Washington D.C. and connecting the capitals of Virginia, North Carolina, and South Carolina. Another popular road was the Lee Highway, having its origins in New York City, passing through the District of Columbia, then running through Virginia, eastern Tennessee, Birmingham, Alabama, and then New Orleans, where it became part of the Robert E. Lee Transcontinental Highway that connected the southern states with San Diego and Los Angeles. Other routes went by names such as the Jackson Highway, the Jefferson Highway, and the Old Spanish Trail.[22]

This network of privately inspired interstate highways that crisscrossed the nation had become so complex that in 1924 the American Association of State Highway Officials (AASHO) petitioned the United States Department of Agriculture to systematize the situation by instituting some kind of numbering system. The following year, the Joint Board of State and Federal Highway Officials was created and within eighteen months came up with a solution. In November 1926, the joint board held a meeting at Pinehurst, North Carolina. In attendance were many prominent public officials representing national, state and local governments.

Soon a plan was publicly announced. It called for the designation of all east-west routes with even numbers and all north-south routes with odd numbers. U.S. highways 10, 20, 30, and 40 stretched westward across the northern states, and highways 50, 60, 70, 72, 74, 78, 80 and 90 ran east-west through the southern states. Generally, the numbers given to north-south highways were lower than fifty, but at times these highways intersected, and thus the previous older interstate routes did not acquire only one number. For example, the Capital Highway for the most part became U.S. 1; the Atlantic Coastal Highway U.S. 17; the Dixie Highway, with dual routes through the South, became U.S. 41, U.S. 27, U.S. 25, and U.S. 441.

Roads were standardized not only in terms of the signs that governed their use, but in their physical nature. The key agency in creating uniformity was the Committee on Standards of the American Association of State Highway Officials. In 1928 that group mandated 10-foot-wide lanes, 6-inch concrete pavement, 8-foot shoulders, and 1-inch highway crowns.

By 1927, a new classification for the nation's highways was in place, and the many routes that ran through the country were absorbed into the new national interstate network. National standardized black and white signs in the form of a shield emblazoned with the route number in the center replaced the colorful and regionally identifiable route markers that had at first marked the course of the many highways that had crossed the nation. Named highways, once so important, are now largely forgotten.

During the late 1920s, Louisiana was one state whose drivers finally climbed out of the mud (or "gumbo"), and its history illustrates not only the fact that the automobile preceded road development but also that politics proved critical to the story.[23] Like the rest of the nation, Louisiana witnessed an upsurge in car ownership beginning in the early 1920s. For example, in 1922, there were 122,000 motor vehicles registered in the state, but by 1924 that figure had risen to 178,000.[24] In 1920, a state highway commission had been established, but it was poorly funded and staffed, and the state's elite patrician leadership was conservative in raising the monies necessary to build a comprehensive state road system. Given the climatic and geographical difficulties associated with the state — for example, there were more than 5,000 streams and rivers in Louisiana — its citizens were limited in where they could take the new cars they had purchased. In Orleans Parish alone there were 43,000 vehicles, and yet there was no road to the east that connected New Orleans with the Mississippi Gulf Coast. The situation changed dramatically, however, with the coming of Huey Long to the governor's mansion in 1928. The "Kingfish's" clever political maneuvering resulted in first raising the necessary state funds to build good roads, and then the will to build them throughout the state. Long hired some of the best highway engineers in the country, raised the gasoline tax and floated state bonds, and put more than 8,000 men to work in the process. In a 1929 Louisiana Highway Commission report, it was asserted that "Power Creates Wealth," and that "Good Roads Throughout Louisiana Provide for a Wider Distribution of Power." Furthermore,

> The automobile has revolutionized transportation methods and eliminated distance. Combined with improved highways, the automobile has made friends and neighbors of us all, removed imaginary barriers and provided a sound foundation on which to build for happiness, prosperity, and permanent development.[25]

During the Long administration, thousands of miles of improved roadways were constructed, but three projects stand out. First, east of New Orleans, the Chef Menteur Highway connecting New Orleans to Mississippi was completed. Secondly, the Airline Highway connecting New Orleans to Baton Rouge shortened the driving distance between the state's major urban center of New Orleans and its capital of Baton Rouge.[26] Thirdly, a landmark achievement was the erection of a bridge across the Mississippi River at Jefferson, west of New Orleans. The Huey Long Bridge, with four lanes for motor vehicle traffic and railroad tracks in the middle, remains an adventure to cross today. Yet at its dedication in late 1935, the bridge provided a critical connecting point for the Jefferson Highway, Old Spanish Trail, Louisiana Purchase Highway, Colonial Highway, Mississippi Scenic Highway, and the Pershing Highway.[27]

Of all the highways with U.S. number designations, one, Route 66, truly stands out in American culture.[28] Spanning from Chicago to Santa Monica, the "Mother Road" was immortalized in John Steinbeck's *Grapes of Wrath*. Its road food, typified by the fare served by the Big Texan restaurant outside of Amarillo, and roadside architecture, like the Wigwam Village Motel in Holbrook, Arizona, has given Route 66 a mystique without equal. Route 66 was the idea of Cyrus Steven Avery, a businessman from Tulsa, Oklahoma, who became president of the Associated Highways Association in 1921 and State Highway Commissioner in 1923. He perceptively understood that highways meant business and tourism, and that the better the highways the better the business. To this day, with the rise of nostalgia about the "Mother Road," Route 66 is all about tourism. A journey down Route 66 takes one to a different time in American life, before McDonald's and fast food, before the homogeneity found on the interstate confronted travelers.[29]

Nostalgia for the open road of the past, however, should not blind us to its historical realities. For one thing, Route 66 was known as "bloody" 66, because it was so dangerous and so many died on that road. And as Steinbeck so astutely described, it was a road not only leading to the opportunities awaiting the beleaguered upon reaching California, but also a place where opportunism, exploitation, and disappointment occurred. With dilapidated cars and worn out tires, fear was at the hearts of drivers and passengers alike, who out of a sense of survival became one with their rides:

> Listen to the motor. Listen to the wheels. Listen with your ears and with your hands on the steering wheel; listen with the palm of your hand on the gear-shift lever; listen with your feet on the floor boards. Listen to the pounding old jalopy with all your senses; for a change of tone, a variation of the rhythm that may mean — a week here? That rattle — that's tappets. Don't hurt a bit. Tappets can rattle till Jesus comes again without no harm. But that thudding as the car moves along — can't hear that — just kind of feel it. Maybe oil isn't gettin' someplace. Maybe a bearing's startin' to go. Jesus, if it's a bearing, what'll we do? Money's goin' fast.[30]

Auto Camping and "Gypsying" Across America

A word might be said here about the "gypsies" that journeyed via the automobile during the first few decades of the twentieth century.[31] Beginning around 1915 or so, gypsies in their cars traveled throughout the U.S.A., setting up camp by the roadside. During summer nights, their campfires dotted main routes. They pitched tents on private property, often angering farmers who were typically far from hospitable. In an effort to maintain order and promote this inexpensive tourism, around 1920 communities through which many of these gypsies passed began setting up free camping facilities near towns. Enterprising individuals saw the commercial possibilities in all of this, and by the mid–1920s private campgrounds were established, along with the first tourist cabins.[32]

The tourist cabin, the size of a small shed with perhaps a cold water basin, bed, night table and dresser, characterized the American roadside before World War II. James Agee, writ-

Gypsy women and children and a man with an automobile, ca. 1925. Gypsying rarely involved gypsies, but the automobile took all kinds of families out on American roads during the 1920s (Library of Congress).

ing for *Fortune,* described these temporary domiciles as "curious little broods of frame and log and adobe shacks which dot the roadside with their Mother Goose and Chic Sale architecture, their geranium landscaping, their squeaky beds, and their community showers."[33] With a rate of perhaps $2 a night, and the fact that the owner cared little about names and who stayed in these structures, fears of the "hot pillow" trade surfaced.

The contemporary traveler on U.S. 40 or 66 has to look hard at the roadside to find these cabins, once a place of rest for those who had made 300 miles a day and were weary, hungry, and ready to stop for the evening. Later that night male travelers would gather outside the cabins and compare notes about road conditions and weather, while the women would congregate in one of the units and chat. Only recently married couples darkened their cabins at an early evening hour.

Fill 'er Up

Of all the roadside structures erected during the golden age of two-lane highways, perhaps the most significant was the gas station. Gas stations and their architecture and design developed in a competitive market with the hopes of attracting the consumer through brand association. Indeed, the architecture of the gas station played a vital role in attracting the consumer.

Initially, gasoline stations did not exist in the sense of featuring a curbside pump. Rather, workers filled gasoline containers and later transferred the gasoline to the automobile by hand. In 1905, a revolution took place in terms of gasoline dispensing as the Shell Oil Company opened its first true filling station in St. Louis, using a gravity-fed tank with a simple garden hose attached. In a few short years, the development of pumps made possible the first curbside stations. In their earliest years, these stations primarily existed in front of groceries, hardware stores, and other commonly-frequented businesses.

Following the early success of the curbside pump, the gas station evolved into a dedicated structure featuring a shed-like profile. The shed housed offices and supplies, but this was anything but an aesthetically pleasing structure, and a call went out by civic-minded citizens for a more pleasing building. In response, houses developed as a compromise.

These house-type stations, frequently prefabricated, were large enough to contain an office, storage rooms, and restrooms. They were made of brick, stucco, and galvanized steel, and thus were relatively easy to maintain. And they were very much characteristic of the new gas stations of the 1920s. For example, in 1922, more than 200 of the 1,841 Shell gas stations included common design aspects, and these 200 stations accounted for 40 percent of Shell's business.

During the 1920s the house and then the house with canopy style became popular. By 1925, most gasoline stations were equipped with grease pits and car washing facilities. These bays allowed the station to offer an increasing number of services, mainly minor repairs. Thus stations added to their business, and the filling station was transformed into a service station. Houses could easily be adapted to accompany one or several bays.

The house gas station design suggested a bond with the American family, and Pure Oil Company capitalized on

Rice's Gas Station, Powell County, Montana, ca. 1934 (Library of Congress).

Bonfield's Service Station, Montgomery County, Maryland (Library of Congress).

this notion. Pure designed a cottage-type station complete with a chimney, a gabled roof, and flower boxes on the windows.

Perhaps the most influential gas station design appeared on the scene during the Great Depression. This design, called the oblong box, developed as companies searched for functionality in station design. This layout gave the company the ability to sell tires, batteries, and accessories, referred to as the TBA line.

Generally, this design featured a flat roof, plate glass, and an inexpensive porcelain enamel-looking facing. The design was a loose example of the International style, inspired by Walter Gropius and his Bauhaus School in Germany after World War I. Most notably, Walter Dorning Teague, a designer hired by the Texaco Company, made the oblong box a feature found in virtually every corner of American life. *The Architectural Record* reported that Teague's stations featured "certain primary functional requirements [that] were obvious, such as trademark and color standardization, efficient layout for sales and servicing, adequate office and restroom space." In sum, the oblong box design met the physical need of adapting a structure to a variety of lots and the primary psychological needs of comfort and convenience to the customer. The house and oblong box gas stations characterized one facet in the development of roadside structures prior to World War II. Certainly the appearance of tourist cabins and then motels would reflect another view of changes in structures just beyond the highway.

Road Food

In addition to the camps, cabins, and gas stations, restaurants were also integral to life along the road. It was in these distinctive eateries where bad, good, and indifferent "road food" was served, often with regional flavors and dishes. Many hungry travelers during the 1920s and 1930s gobbled hot dogs (frankfurters was the term preferred by hot dog king Gobel), Bar-B-Q sandwiches, Good Humor ice cream and Popsicles. If ever there was a food that typified America and its restless citizens on the go, it was the humble hot dog.[34]

And while the hot dog remains a popular meal at truck stops across America, where one can purchase jalapeno, regular, ballpark, or corn dogs, with the rise of the divided highways slowly but surely the distinctive meal was supplanted by chain and fast food restaurants. How that transition from the two- to four-lane highway happened in America is an interesting story. During the interwar years, most construction consisted of two-lane highways like Route 66, as seldom were divided highways even thought of. But between the wars, innovators began to articulate ideas concerning the advantages of divided highway designs.

Divided Highways, Parkways, and Expressways

One such innovator was Englishman Hilaire Belloc, who in 1924 wrote a book entitled *The Road*. Belloc proposed great arterial roads joining main population centers that were to be wide, as straight as possible, with no intersections at grade, and finally having limited access. In a chapter entitled "The Future" Belloc stated,

> A very few great arterial roads joining the main centers of population would have far more effect upon our present difficulties than their mere mileage would seem to warrant. There

"Don't Kill Our Wildlife," a poster produced by the National Park Service, ca. 1936–1940. Studies of "roadkill," or the influence of the automobile on the living environment, began in the 1902s and continue to this day (Library of Congress).

could be no question of stopping the new form of traffic upon ordinary roads remaining, which might be twenty or fifty times those of the new roads. But it would be of such advantage for long-distance travel to use the great arteries that at the expenditure of greater mileage you would find the new traffic seeking them at the nearest point upon one side and clinging to them for as long as possible.[35]

Essentially, Belloc was envisioning the modern expressway, as were a few of his contemporaries such as Arthur Hale, who patented the cloverleaf in 1916.

Roads of this kind were built in Mussolini's Italy during the 1920s (the *Autostrade*) and in Hitler's Germany of the 1930s (the *Autobahnen*).[36] Adolf Hitler's highways were dramatically innovative roads that were perhaps the most publicized and visible products of the new regime. They have also proved to be the most enduring of the Third Reich's material legacies, still carrying traffic, and thus promising to fulfill Hitler's boast that "the construction of these roads will give the German people traffic routes for the most distant future." The *Autobahnen* were critical to Hitler's plan for the mass motorization of Germany, first announced at the Berlin auto show of 1933. Between 1933 and 1936 auto production increased five times. These roads were also important aspects of Hitler's plan to eliminate unemployment; by 1936 some 130,000 men were employed directly and 270,000 indirectly in industries like cement mixing and stone masonry. Construction workers, living under a military-like regimen, were housed in isolated camps near the work sites.

The autobahns of the 1930s amounted to beautiful works of civil engineering. They blended organically into the landscape; it was said that those who constructed them had a real concern for the environment. Autobahns were built not to disturb scenery and landscape unnecessarily, and they were designed to contribute to the driver's appreciation of the natural surroundings.

Even though most work went into conventional road building during the Depression years, the seed of the expressway system was sown at that time. Although federal funds went into two-lane projects, ironically perhaps, local funds were for the most part used to design high-speed motor traffic highways. This was especially true in Connecticut, with the opening of the Merritt and Wilbur Cross parkways. In Pennsylvania, where in 1937 a Turnpike Commission was created to build a toll road using an old railroad right of way, a mix of federal and state funds were allocated.

Some federal funds came from the Public Works Administration (PWA), and surveys had actually begun in 1936. Features of the new road included four 12-foot-wide lanes, a 10-foot-wide median strip and 10-foot side berms, and a limited access with 1,200 foot entrance and exit lanes. On October 13, 1940, 160 miles of turnpike between Carlisle (west of Harrisburg) and Irwin (east of Pittsburgh) was opened. It soon became the preferred way of truck traffic, since seven tunnels were used, the grade on the Pennsylvania turnpike had been restricted to 3 percent and thus fuel consumption was decreased considerably. Finally, the driving time between Harrisburg and Pittsburgh was cut from five and one-half hours to two and one-half. The Pennsylvania Turnpike had no speed limits until April 1941 when a 70 mph limit was set, although in tunnels one had to maintain a speed of 35 mph.

As successful as the Pennsylvania Turnpike became, across the country in Los Angeles similar developments were taking place that proved to be equally successful. Lloyd Aldrich, who became Los Angeles city engineer in 1933, became a principal champion of the freeway, and he was one of the first to perceive an essential element for a modern metropolis; namely, that the time required to complete the journey was far more important than the distance covered. In 1940 under Aldrich's direction the Pasadena freeway was completed, the first link in a proposed 300 mile web of urban freeway.

The first of the LA freeways was named the Arroyo Seco Parkway. This road had no number designation, and originally the speed limit was 45 miles per hour. With two lanes of traffic in each direction and a broad shoulder for emergencies, the route ran from downtown Los Angeles to Pasadena. At the time, it was considered an engineering marvel, although it is obsolete by today's standards. Indeed, most current-day drivers would consider the road dangerous; merging is almost immediate and right shoulders are narrow. Despite the fact that one must often stop before gaining access, it is a heavily used thoroughfare, with three lanes in each direction.

Thus, on the eve of World War II, America had taken critical steps in highway construction that would be instrumental to the explosion of interstate highways beginning in the 1950s. Regions were now linked together, tourism had become a part of middle-class life, and trucks were moving an increasing percentage of manufactured goods and agricultural produce.

5

RELIGION, COURTSHIP, SEX, AND WOMEN DRIVERS

The automobile and its relationship to society is a complex topic fraught with difficulties in terms of characterization and comprehension. As the quintessential technology of the twentieth century, the influence of the automobile upon everyday life was enormous. Yet even simple questions defy definitive answers. On balance, was the automobile a positive or negative in terms of the quality of life? Did we become slaves to a machine that we were to be masters over? Did the coming of the automobile lead to a new set of societal values? The paragraphs that follow explore three areas in which the car had profound social influence: religion, courtship, and the lives of women. In each case, issues centered on control and fundamental, traditional values. The automobile challenged traditional means of social control involving the church, parents, and male dominance in the family. Additionally, and in its broadest sense, the automobile gradually became an idol that demanded increasing amounts of attention, time, and money from the average American household.

An Answer to Prayer or Something to Pray About?

With the widespread sales of the Model T in rural areas of America after 1908, it was soon recognized that the automobile had a profound influence upon patterns of religious worship and beliefs. In terms of church worship, small rural congregations were displaced by the migration of believers to more central locations in larger towns and cities. More serious, perhaps, were the many sermons that called attention to young people who would forgo Sunday services for the joys of the open road. And then there were those who somehow lost faith due to the modernism that the automobile brought to American society.[1] For example, the following young woman's recollection took place either in 1919 or 1920:

> Our little Christian Endeavor flock of five high school boys and girls was returning for a religious retreat sheparded by our minister. The road home led up Pine Canyon from the Columbia River to Waterville [Washington]. It was a long steep grade of four miles or so. The day was hot. We were not yet halfway up when the minister's Model T balked. The radiator boiled and the motor failed. Our good minister suggested that we call for God's help so all six of us knelt in the road on the shady side of the car and prayed. The radiator soon ceased to boil, and we got underway again. Our prayers were answered but momentarily. Stops became frequent, and prayers increased in length. Three or four prayers later, the Model T topped the hill, and we were profoundly impressed with our convincing demonstration of the power of prayer.
>   Imagine the shock to my newly demonstrated convictions at what we learned from the owner of the service station in Waterville where we stopped to replace the radiator water

which had boiled away and for gas. On hearing of our difficulties on the Pine Canyon Grade, he commented that all Model T's behaved similarly on that hill. The customary and necessary way to get a Model T up that hill or any other which overheated the motor, he declared, was to stop at the instant the radiator boiled and wait to let the heated motor cool off as the Ford thermo-syphon cooling operated too slowly on hills to keep the motor at a safe operating temperature. When I learned that our prayers had merely provided the time for the thermo-syphon to overcome the motor heat, I was crushed. My faith in prayer suffered a mortal blow.[2]

Within Catholic and Protestant contexts, strands of serious discussion about the automobile and its social consequences can be traced back to at least the 1920s. Literature of that era contained a consistent thread of critical commentary related to automobile issues that included safety, organized labor, economics, and social justice. While this stream of articles often reflected topics similar to those voiced in the secular mainstream, what made the material in the Christian literature distinctive was that a moral and at times biblical voice was often injected into an ethical debate concerning what should be the proper relationship between technology and society.[3]

As shall be discussed, the Catholic viewpoint differed from that of the Protestant in both its emphasis on certain subjects at the expense of others, and surprisingly, perhaps, in terms of the intensity of its overall scriptural tone. Mainline Catholic literature tended to the practical and biblical; Protestant contributions were more idealistic while at the same time in language approached the secular. In both subcultures, however, authors attempted to solve difficult social problems created by the automobile during the Machine Age.

The automobile first became an issue for many American Catholics during the late 1920s, as the primary market shifted from rural to urban, and as city dwellers, many for the first time, began to contemplate purchasing vehicles. While the Catholic working class living in the largest of urban centers like New York City often would not purchase a car until after World War II, in the smaller cities and towns, the family car came home by 1929. That year Robert S. and Helen Merrell Lynd published *Middletown, a Study in Contemporary Culture*, which focused on Muncie, Indiana, as typical of these smaller cities, and highlighted attitudes of the time.[4]

To be sure, the automobile had been a topic in the Catholic literature of the first three decades of the twentieth century, but it was especially in the 1930s that it was frequently mentioned in the pages of *The Commonweal, America, Columbia, Ave Maria*, and *GK's Weekly*. Although these essays and commentaries reflected similar articles also found in the secular literature, they often paid scant attention to those issues that Protestants characteristically echoed in their Middletown interviews; namely, discourses on how the Sunday auto trip was now a threat to church attendance never appear in the Catholic literature. Seemingly, for Catholics, the car did not prevent parishioners from attending mass regularly. Nor was alcohol nearly as significant a topic for Catholic authors and editors as for their Protestant counterparts.

For example, an overwhelming number of articles appearing in nondenominational Protestant *Christian Century* during the 1930s railed against drinking and driving.[5] Prohibition had been repealed by the mid–1930s, and one commentator after another linked the rising national auto accident and fatality rates with the "almost complete absence of regulation of strong liquor traffic."[6] It was more than a shrill attack on drunkenness, for it was argued that the consumption of any amount of alcohol substantially increased the risks behind the wheel; therefore, for the responsible driver, the only safe course was temperance. Thus if it was sin, it was never mentioned in theological terms in these articles; rather, the evil was materially identifiable and liquid, with the simple remedy of abstinence. While far less frequently mentioned in the Catholic press, the practice of driving and drinking often resulted in an indignant diatribe despite the fact that Depression-era newspapers and secular periodicals normally ignored or hushed this type of news for a variety of complex reasons.[7]

Protestants and Catholics found common ground, however, on the issue of what speed was doing to Americans, subtly and psychologically. And while on the whole, much of what was said in the Catholic press dealt more with practical than spiritually abstract matters, the latter was occasionally dealt with in surprising fashion. Such was the case of Theodore Maynard's essay entitled "On Driving a Car" that appeared in a 1931 issue of *The Commonweal*.[8] The author fancied himself as a spirit-filled poet whose senses were now deadened by the automobile and speed. Sensing that his driving led to "a definite decrease in spirituality," coupled with an increase in "a hard, dry, positive frame of mind," Maynard had little or no inclination to learn about the technology he was saddled with, preferring to "think about it [the automobile] as little as possible." Indeed, he looked forward to a time when he could give up the car, since then he would be "set free from the tyranny of speed, [and] I can take my pipe and stick and walk again through the quiet fields." This tyranny of speed was part and parcel of the new world of the automobile. Increasingly, time and space were compressed. While technology had freed people from time-consuming chores and increased the pace of transportation, life was far more rushed and constrained than before. And this need for speed was apparently insatiable, as at times it was truly irrational, given the ever-increasing fatality statistics. Unlike Catholic writers who saw speed as an issue of personal responsibility and a moral decision, the editor of *The Christian Century* called for the installation of governors on all cars manufactured in Detroit. Clearly, responsibility was placed in the hands of the Big Three and the federal government, the latter acting as a countervailing force.[9] It was more than just horsepower and sheer highway speed, however. As one Protestant minister remarked in a *Middletown* interview, speed had resulted in demands for sermons that did not run over, so church could end no later than noon. High noon marked the time "to hit the road."

For all his acute insights, Maynard reflected a romantic strain of thought concerning the automobile, one in which it was thought that the car was a passing fad and that more eternal and simple values would ultimately prevail. According to this view, then, there was to be no American love affair with the car, for it was posited that the public would tire of accidents, and "a great ebbing of the tide of public interest in riding may set in. The novelty of speeding around in a car which has grown during the last thirty years into the great national pastime, may wear off, and people will stay at home more and tend gardens or otherwise occupy themselves in quiet and safety."[10] This writer, however, misjudged the power of the automobile over the individual; in contrast, as early as 1916 one astute priest remarked that "the automobile was here to stay."

Most of the Catholic literature of the early 1930s did not concern itself with deep matters related to human beings and their relationship to the machine, however, but rather the effects of the automobile on everyday, common lives, especially in terms of the alarming rate of fatal accidents. There was a sharp increase in fatalities during the 1920s, as automobile accident deaths rose from 15,000 in 1922 to 33,000 in 1930.[11] What most concerned Catholic writers about these statistics was the large number of pedestrians, especially the young and the old, who ranked disproportionately high on casualty lists. Authors made light of the fact that the automobile was killing more Americans than war, and that numbers were on a marked rise, despite the fact that the Great Depression had curtailed the number of miles driven.[12]

One essay equated the situation as akin to that of Herod and his slaughter of innocent children, for "It will suffice to face the central fact — that every day from one to a hundred little ones get in the path of speeding cars, are crushed to death or maimed for life. Such a toll summons to mind ancient and terrible images of gods to whom babes were tossed in sacrifice."[13] Apparently for some it was sport, according to G. K. Chesterton:

> Let me take the case of a very queer moral twist, about which this paper [*G. K.'s Weekly*] has often made protests; and often been practically alone in making them; the case of a motorist, clearly beholding somebody walking across the road, who drives straight at him, and knocks him down in a way that is more than likely than not to kill him.[14]

Statistics aside, the topic of accidents was dealt with either by an exploration of causes — drivers, speed, the vehicles themselves, or highways — or remedies that included driver education and stricter licensing laws, better enforcement of speed restrictions, the construction of walking paths and better roads.[15] Above all, it was a discussion about responsibility, and here fingers were pointed at mothers, manufacturers, government, but above all inexperienced or dangerous drivers. In the Lynds' follow-up to *Middletown*, *Middletown in Transition*, published in 1937, the complaints concerning the automobile and its threats towards child pedestrians were quite similar to those mentioned in Catholic articles, but with one important difference — responsibility and moral matters were never grappled with.[16]

One article from the secular press that held sway in Catholic circles was Curtis Billings' "The Nut That Holds the Wheel," published in the *Atlantic Monthly* in 1932.[17] Billings argued that many drivers were unprepared for the faster speeds now experienced, and that one needed to be properly taught to drive and maintain the car. He concluded, "It is time for us to learn that the automobile is no longer a novel toy, that it is a tremendous social force, mainly for good, but certainly for terrific evil unless it is sanely used."[18]

Between the 1930s and the 1950s, the frightful nature of automobile accidents remained a central theme. However, one issue quickly gained importance during the second half of the 1930s — the tensions between organized labor and the Big Three. Until 1935, it was totally absent from the *Catholic Periodical and Literature Index* and *Readers' Guide*. But between then and the coming of World War II, a substantial number of articles in both the Catholic and Protestant press demonized capitalists while sympathetically portraying the plight of the working classes. One Catholic author who railed against capital and management was Fr. Paul L. Blakely, S.J., who characterized the condition of autoworkers as "differing little from that of slavery."[19] Blakely righteously blasted the automakers, asserting that

> this huge and inhuman industry has grown up within the last thirty years, is sad evidence of the world's inability to understand the message of Leo XIII in his Labor Encyclical. But the message was simply the message of Jesus Christ, and his name is not in reverence in our modern world. Decidedly, there is something rotten at the heart of our alleged civilization, something that cannot be healed or excused by the forces which have been at work in the body politic for more than a quarter of a century.[20]

Blakely followed with an essay on spies that had infiltrated the unions, assigning to management the name of Satan.[21] Clearly, a wing of American Catholicism had taken on matters of social justice and there was no better stage than that of Detroit auto factories during the mid- to late 1930s. Given the ethnicity and class of many churchgoers of the decade, and in the wake of such horrific episodes as the "Battle of the Overpass" involving bullies from Ford and the Reuther brothers, labor relations in Detroit was one topic that apparently was of interest to many readers. And indeed at least until the 1960s labor-management relations would form one important cluster of writing that appeared in the Catholic literature.[22]

Protestant literature also covered union-management issues during the 1930s and beyond, but with little of the fierce intensity and biblical ire that characterized Catholic writing.[23] Indeed, Protestant reporting was coldly analytical, with the only bit of emotion coming when describing the life of the first UAW president, Homer Martin, a former Baptist minister from Kansas City. Martin, "who was forced out of that Church in Kansas City has by his change of pulpits become a kind of Paul, who has taken away some of the profits of Demetrius and the Ephesian silversmiths, who has been in jail for his convictions, but whose cause is so just that not even the wealth of Dives can prevail against him."[24]

In sum, Church literature reflected sincere and sensitive concerns about the automobile and human purposes. The numerous essays and editorials revealed that Catholic writers recognized that the automobile possessed a Janus-like double face, and that despite all of their conveniences, cars not only could maim and kill, but also subtly alter the human spirit. Thus, these writings mirrored a struggle that was associated with the rise of automobility during the first half of the twentieth century. It was serious stuff to debate thoughtfully, and profound questions concerning contemporary culture surfaced. Would a technology become the master of a society rather than a mere utilitarian tool subordinate to human purposes? Were humans somehow less important than machinery? In what ways were we inwardly changing to accommodate patterns of automobile use? These and more tensions were a part of a dialogue that was never fully addressed then or now, as evidenced by the fact that most people remain entranced by and dependent upon a machine that changed the world, both for better and for worse.

Sex in the Back Seat

Although no other twentieth century innovation has so intensely influenced manners, customs, and living habits, the nature and scope of the automobile's influences are far from being fully understood. As early as the first decade of the twentieth century, the automobile was equated with adventure, including and perhaps especially sexual adventure. It liberated riders from social control and allowed men to pursue women (and women to pursue men!) in a manner that was to change patterns of courtship and sexual behaviors.

Music of the day reflected the romantic possibilities and opportunities now afforded by the coming of the automobile. In 1899, Alfred Dixon published "Love in an Automobile," and a year later at least six song titles featured the theme of a charming young woman riding in a car. That same year, Rudolph Anderson wrote the following song about a male persuading a female to take a romantic drive:

> When first I proposed to Daisy on a sunny summer's morn,
> She replied, "you must be crazy" and laughed my love to scorn.
> Said I, "Now I've hit on a novel scheme, which surely to you may appeal.
> Say wouldn't you go for a honeymoon in a cozy automobile?"
> When she heard my bright suggestion, why, she fairly jumped for joy.
> Her reply was just a question, "Oh joy, when do we start dear boy?"
> Said I, "You will take 'bout half an hour to pack up your things and grip.
> And then 'round the corner we'll married be, and start away on our trip.
> We'll fulfill your dreams, marring mishap of course."[25]

The famous song of this era, "In My Merry Oldsmobile" sold between 600,000 and 1 million copies of sheet music. It ran:

> Come away with me Lucille
> In my merry Oldsmobile.
> Over the road of life we'll fly,
> Autobubbling you and I.
> To the church we'll swiftly steal,
> And out wedding bells will peal,
> You can go as far as you like with me,
> In our merry Oldsmobile.[26]

Other early titles included:

"The Automobile Girl"
"My Automobile Girl"
"My Auto Lady"
"The Motor Girl"
"The Auto Show Girl"
"Motor Maid"
"Let's Have a Motor Car Marriage"
"Automobiling with Mollie"
"In Our Little Lovemobile"
"An Auto Built for Two"
"Riding in Love's Limosine [sic]"
"On an Automobile with a Girl You Love"
"The Auto Kiss"
"The Automobile Honeymoon"[27]

Previously, "calling" was the traditional means by which couples were brought together. "Calling" was a courtship custom that involved three central tenets of middle class American life: the family, respectability, and privacy. Calling admitted the male into the young woman's private home, where he could engage in conversation with the girl under the watchful eyes of her mother. Tea was often served, and perhaps the girl would display her musical talents and play the piano as light entertainment. All of this took place in the parlor. Mothers, the guardians of respectability and morals, decided who could call on their daughters and who could not. Daughters could request a certain male visitor, but the mothers made the final decision as to his acceptability. Family honor and name, along with class boundaries, were to be respected.

The calling ritual as practiced resulted in giving middle class mothers and daughters a measure of control. How much of this was real and actually practiced is certainly open to question, particularly since horse-drawn carriages, the woods, and the haystack were also options for young couples. But community controls and prevailing rituals and beliefs certainly have power. Yet it is undeniable that the emergence of the automobile and dating caused the loss of some of that control as power shifted from women to men. Under the calling system the woman asked the man; but in dating, the male had the car and invited the female out beyond the sphere of the parental domain. Cars took young couples off porch swings, outside of home parlors, and far away from concerned mothers and irritating brothers and sisters.

This transition in coupling habits was well described in a racy and imaginative 1927 song entitled "Get 'Em in a Rumble Seat." The so-called rumble seat was an extension of the trunk, open and separate from the automobile interior.

It certainly was a little tight in a rumble seat. Despite the space constraints, social commentators feared the thought of young people getting together unsupervised. There were also concerns over promiscuity and premarital sex. Initially, cars were open and seats were uncomfortable. But by the mid–1920s, most vehicles were closed, and heaters were soon available. Seats became wider and more luxuriously appointed. And as historian David Lewis has remarked, "Many cars were also equipped with long, wide running boards, and starting in the mid–1920's increasingly long, sloping fenders," which when covered with pillows and blankets provided impromptu settings for romance.[28] By the 1920s, manufacturers designed beds into the front seat that folded into the rear seat cushions to assist in romance. The 1925 Jewett slept two people in comfort, as long as the couple did not stretch out more than six feet. Other car companies followed with "sleeper" cars, convenient for both auto-campers and illicit lovers.

As Frederick Lewis Allen recounted in his *Only Yesterday,* the 1920s brought a revolution in terms of sexuality among young people. While the automobile was one venue for sexual activity, it was far from the cause of this shift in moral values that was perhaps brought on by World War I and the disillusionment and modernist thought that followed.[29]

Every community had its lovers' lane and makeout point. After World War II, and despite the intention of drive-in owners to make their businesses attractive to families, drive-ins were often seen as "passion pits." In-car shows were often better than what was transpiring on the screen. If a speaker was not in the car window, there were credible suspicions that something had to be happening inside.

In an interesting study published in 1953 by Alfred Kinsey and the staff of the Institute for Sex Research at Indiana University, 983 women were surveyed concerning the places where they had premarital coitus. While a marginally greater proportion of liaisons took place in the homes of the male or female than in automobiles, the data suggested that sex in automobiles, outdoors, or in hotels and rented rooms occurred in nearly equal numbers, and only slightly less than in a home.[30] Kinsey concluded that "the importance of the car has more than doubled in the thirty years covered by the sample. In earlier generations in both European and American history, the buggy or other horse-drawn conveyance appear to have served the function which the automobile now serves."[31]

Those Women Drivers!

The topic of women and the automobile is a rich and complex one that attracts interest from various angles. As James Flink wrote in *The Automobile Age,* "Despite the traditional association of the automobile as a mechanical object with men and muscularity in American culture, automobility probably has had a greater impact on women's role than on men's, and the women have been enamored with the motor car from the onset of its diffusion."[32] Indeed, the automobile provides the scholar with a powerful handle to explore issues related to women's and family history. To that end, Virginia Scharff's *Taking the Wheel: Women and the Coming of the Motor Age* is the key monograph in starting one's exploration of this important anthropological and historical topic.[33] Unfortunately, Sharff's analysis ends with the 1920s, and thus a significant amount of material and themes remains to be examined.

Significantly, the automobile appeared at the same time that women were striving for freedom in the home and in politics. During the late Gilded Age many women were chafing to break through the separate spheres of home and vocation that had characterized them as weak, frail, and biologically incapable of sustained effort, either physically or on the job. At first, they were almost exclusively passengers, although there were rare exceptions when they got behind the wheel. It was the electric automobile, however, that gave upper middle class women the freedom to leave the home and break free of the control of their husbands. The automobile not only took them shopping, but in the case of a few intrepid pioneers like Alice Huyler Ramsey, carried them across the continent. Despite the obstacle of crank-starting, a number of women did get behind the wheel of early gasoline-powered vehicles, and with the introduction of the self-starter and the Model T, a social revolution began that progressed one ride at a time. Scharff carefully traces the role of the automobile and the suffragettes in the regional and cross-country campaigns that led to women's gaining the right to vote in 1920.

World War I provided many opportunities for women, not only to drive ambulances and taxis, but also to demonstrate their abilities to organize, manage, and assist combat troops in France and at home. By then the suffrage movement was well underway, and to prove themselves, women participated in numerous acts of civil service for their country. During the war, women drove alongside men, and, for the time being, equality was the norm rather than the exception. Women had to "replace" men in almost all aspects of life, including servicing vehicles and taking on the role of a skilled mechanic. By necessity, they were forced to learn to repair vehicles, including military trucks. In a 1918 article titled "Women Motor Mechanics for War-Time Work," a photograph of a woman working on a truck engine bore the caption, "Not Exactly a Woman's Job, Perhaps, but These Patriotic Sisters Stop at Nothing When They Have Once Entered the Work."[34] To guide them in their repair activities, in 1918 a popular handbook was made available for women, *The Care and Management of the Modern Motor-Car*. Virginia Scharff concluded that "Although its tone was jocular and patronizing, it praised 400 female graduates of a YMCA school for mechanics who were as apt as men in 'mastering the mechanical and technical details of a car' and warned professional chauffeurs, all men to expect an invasion of women drivers."[35]

After the Armistice and Versailles Treaty the nation would "Return to Normalcy," but of course nothing was normal during the decade of the 1920s. War, especially a global conflict like the one just ended, brought with it enormous social changes. According to Scharff, younger women took to driving with a confidence that their mothers never had. It was the age of the flapper, a woman characterized as impulsive and interested in self-gratification. Yet, in the everyday lives of common American women, an increasing number of women drivers not only found new freedom and pleasure behind the wheel, they also somehow reconciled themselves to meet their domestic responsibilities.

While men working in Detroit and elsewhere were in charge of making cars, industry executives, including ad men, clearly recognized that women not only bought cars, but played a powerful role in purchasing decisions within families. Thus, while a "new woman" was in the making during the 1920, the automobile advertising industry was blossoming as well, and the convergence of the two strands played out in a remarkable way.

As Laura L. Behling has argued, gender roles and expectations were reflected in the automobile advertising of the 1920s.[36] Her findings suggest that despite the image of the flapper and her joy-rides, the majority of advertisements reinforced more traditional representations of male dominance.[37] When women were featured in automobile ads, the message usually

A U.S. government-owned Pierce-Arrow at the Union Station, Washington, D.C., ca. 1915. The military was often slow to adopt new technologies, and to a degree this was certainly true during World War I (Library of Congress).

focused on safety, dependability, security and comfort, beauty, or fashion. It took several generations before nineteenth century stereotypes of the American woman would substantially change. However, women were now behind the wheel, and while some argued that she did not belong there, in retrospect there was no turning back. The automobile allowed women to gain employment in areas once totally closed to them. It offered broader opportunities for association, but also added to the responsibilities of the home. Ruth Schwartz Cowan characterized this tension:

> These various individual and corporate decisions were spread out over two decades, but they all conspired in the same direction—to shift the burden of providing transportation services from the seller to the buyer. By the end of the 1930s, the general notion that businesses could offer lower prices by cutting back on services to customers was ingrained in the pattern of business relations. The growth of suburban communities in the postwar years did little to alter the pattern: as more and more businesses converted to the "self-service" concept, more and more households became dependent upon "herself" to provide the service.[38]

Given these tasks to transport and acquire, it is no surprise that the middle class American mother had a range of needs for the automobile to meet. For the husband, the car may express individuality, but the woman of the family must deal with children, pets, and schedules. For the woman, the car—or sport utility vehicle—also provides solitude in addition to efficiency. The drive time is perhaps the only time the woman is alone.

Thus, for a woman the car is a place of safety and security, and thus women desire features that may not have the same priority for a man: climate control, seating comfort, pleas-

A young woman at the steering wheel of an automobile, 1921. The automobile liberated women in manifold ways (Library of Congress).

ing colors and safety. The lines of the vehicle, its horsepower and status of make are perhaps not as important to the middle class woman.

Despite the image of the woman driver putting on makeup while driving 65 mph on the interstate, statistics indicate that women drivers are safer. In 1994 males accounted for 67 percent of total fatalities and 68 percent of all pedestrian fatalities. Additionally, 22 percent of male drivers involved in fatal crashes were intoxicated compared to 11 percent of female drivers.

Cars as Homes

Since the 1920s, the home and the automobile have been inextricably linked.[39] Perhaps a word should be said at the outset about the psychological meaning of these two things. The word home — clearly very different than house — has a meaning that is distinctive in American culture and in the English language. For example, home is not exactly translatable in the Italian, French, or Hungarian languages. It is a sacred place to many, a sphere in which inhabitants shape a material environment that is essentially reflective of self. For many individuals, the home is a place of relaxation, comfort, and intimacy with others. The walls and roof of a home provide safety from the elements and hostile others. The home is also a place of special objects. In some cultures, the Middle East for example, the car dashboard contains numerous trinkets. A generation ago, St. Christopher medals were attached to many American dashboards. Not only did my parents always have a St. Christopher medal in the car, they also had other non-essential gadgets from time to time. For example, my cousin had a 1950 Oldsmobile with a vacuum-assisted pop-up bird on the dash that responded to increases and decreases in acceleration. It was like having a bird in a cage in the living room.

In any case, typically for men, that special object attached to the home is often the auto-

A man sits on an automobile reading a newspaper in Waco, Texas, November 1939. Obviously, during the 1930s fenders were made with such a thick steel that one could comfortably sit on a car and read a paper, and just watch the world go by (Library of Congress).

mobile, a possession that conveys status; for women, the things that mean the most in a home are usually connected with loved ones or special people. According to Mihaly Csikszentmihalyi and Eurgen Rochenberg-Halton, the home "brings to mind one's childhood, the roots of one's being."[40] I can certainly attest to this with regards to the car as an extension of the home, as some of my first memories center on the dashboard, radio, ashtrays, lighter and upholstery of my father's 1948 Chevrolet.

For the car to be an extension of the home, it had to be closed rather than open, unlike the pre–World War I roadster or touring car. Thus, the first and undoubtedly most important step in creating personal space in the automobile was the closed steel body. Historian James J. Flink has called this development "the single most significant automotive innovation."[41] Almost immediately after World War I, public demand increased dramatically for a closed car that would no longer be a seasonal pleasure vehicle, but rather all-weather transportation. The few closed body cars built before World War I were extremely expensive and the work of custom coach builders. This rise in demand during the 1920s, coupled with a remarkable number of concurrent technical innovations in plate glass and steel manufacture, resulted in a revolution in production methods, productivity and economies of scale. William J. Abernathy has carefully characterized the transformation that took place on the shop floor and assembly line, the first fruits of which occurred when in 1921 Hudson first mass-produced a closed car. The transition away from rag tops (the word convertible was first used in 1927 and officially added to the Society of Automotive Engineers lexicon in 1928) was rapid: In less than a decade the ratio of closed cars to open cars virtually reversed, as depicted in Table 6.

TABLE 6. TRANSITION FROM OPEN TO CLOSED CARS

Year	Open Cars (%)	Closed Cars (%)	Year	Open Cars (%)	Closed Cars (%)
1919	90	10	1924	57	43
1920	84	16	1925	44	56
1921	78	22	1926	26	74
1922	70	30	1927	15	85
1923	66	34			

Source: John Gunnell, *Convertibles: The Complete Story* (Blue Ridge Summit, PA: 1984), 129.

Significant improvements in the quality of sheet steel were certainly part of this story, but so too were developments in welding technology, the development of sound deadening materials, and construction of the single unit body. All of these innovations and far more were pioneered by the Budd Manufacturing Company. Typical of the Budd All-Steel ads of the mid–1920s was one that appeared in the *Saturday Evening Post* in 1926, with the headline "Put the Protection of All-Steel Between You and the Risks of the Road."[42] Like the safety inherent in a home, the steel body protected its occupants, especially women and children. The ad continued, "Self preservation is the first law on Nature. Today, with 19,000,000 cars crowding the highways.... With the need for safer motoring more urgent than ever before.... America is turning to the All-Steel Body. It is the greatest protection ever devised to prevent injury in the case of accident. See that your next car is so equipped!" A second 1926 Budd ad, like the first mentioned, depicted a closed car traveling down a busy city street but in its own clear lane, separated on both sides by huge sheets of steel that prevented the masses of cars on each side from touching the car and harming its occupants. The headline for this ad read in part, "The protection which it [the all-steel body] brings to you and to your families is priceless — yet the cars which have it cost no more than those which do not."[43] Clearly, the message was that Budd-engineered closed body cars were worth the money spent.

The rationale Budd used in ads published during the 1920s continued during the 1930s in the General Motors ads touting the "Turret-Top" design with such sentences as, "The instant feeling of security you get ... is beyond price."[44] The pitch toward safety was far more prevalent in ads of the 1930s than one might think, although ironically during the early 1930s convertibles were the center of many ads, even when closed cars were pictorially featured![45] On the eve of World War II, however, the theme of the home and the car was clearly brought together, as reflected in a Hudson advertisement featuring a beautifully attired woman sitting in a plushy upholstered rear seat. The ad touts the availability of "a wide selection of interior color combinations that harmonize with the exterior colors ... at no extra cost!" This ad has clear-cut similarities in terms of an emphasis on color and comfort to paint ads of the same period, as exemplified by the Sherwin-Williams Paint and Color Style Guide of 1941.[46]

> In automobiles, up to now, one upholstery color has usually done duty with every body color. Carpets, floor mats, steering wheels, and trim have introduced still other assorted colors and tones.
>
> Now Hudson's Symphonic Styling gives you, in your 1941 car, the kind of color that permit a wide variation in the details and equipment of each individual car, without interfering with orderly, efficient mass production. Symphonic Styling is the climax of this long-time development.[47]

With the widespread adoption of the closed body car by the late 1920s, automotive engineers next turned their attention to the suspension system.[48] To the uninitiated, suspension system engineering involves very complex mechanics and geometry.[49] One area of concern focused on shock absorbers or dampeners. In addition to mechanical and hydraulic improvements, the use of air springs, or the insertion of an inflatable inner tube inside a coil spring, was one strategy developed during the 1920s and 1930s to improve ride. A second involved driver control of the shock absorber system, and in 1932 Packard pioneered a Delco-Remy unit in which a cable mounted on the dash vastly enhanced ride quality and handling.[50] The most important innovation, however, was the introduction of independent front suspension.[51] First used by Mercedes in 1932, independent front suspension was installed in Cadillac, Buick, Oldsmobile and Chrysler vehicles in 1934, with Ford adopting this technology only after World War II. Prewar Pontiacs and Chevrolets employed a much less effective Dubonnet design that did not fully realize the potential advantages of independent front suspension.

The closed body style was designed for all-weather driving, as previously mentioned, but it took several decades before climate control within the personal space of the automobile became efficient and widely introduced. Beginning around 1925, aftermarket manufacturers began to sell hot water type heaters for American automobiles.[52] The problem of heating the car was more difficult than what one might initially think: proper controls and the mixing of heated air coming from a heat exchanger with ventilated fresh air did not take place until 1937, when Nash introduced its WeatherEye system. Variants of the Nash system were introduced by Buick in 1941 and Ford in 1947 (Magic Air).

Air conditioning and the development of an integrated heating/cooling system lagged by perhaps only a decade or so behind hot water heater technology.[53] From its inception, air-conditioning was touted as a feature that would exclude noise from the outside. During the late 1930s Packard pioneered an early system. An early Packard ad proclaimed "you can step OUT of summer heat—when you step INTO your stunning new Packard." The air-conditioned Packard created a private, personal place.

> And—don't shout, they can hear you! In the superbly comfortable air-cooled Packard, you ride free from open-window traffic noise and the rush of the wind which so often carries away one's words with it! In this greater silence front and rear passengers converse with ease and complete audibility. You enjoy a ride that is infinitely more restful than you have ever experienced.[54]

One final technology that transformed the car into a home-like environment was the radio. Commercial radio broadcasting began around 1920, but radios in cars would not exist for several years. Surprisingly, perhaps, there is not one scholarly essay that explores how the two dynamic technologies of radio and automobiles were brought together beginning in the 1920s.[55] Early on, the main technological bottleneck centered on multiple battery power supplies that were compatible with existing tube grid and filament voltage requirements. In 1929, based on the work of William Lear, the Galvin Manufacturing Corporation introduced the first successful car radio, the Motorola Model 5T71. A year later, other manufacturers entered the fray; for example, the Crosley Corporation introduced its first car radio, the "Roamio." In 1932 Mallory and other manufacturers produced several new power supplies, and four years later Ford was the first to install a radio tailor-made for the dashboard. It was claimed that among other advantages, the radio in a car would ensure that one could listen to favorite shows without missing them. "When it's a quarter before Amos 'n' Andy or Lowell Thomas and you're in the ol' bus, far, far, from home and radio, is it a tragedy? Or you can tune in right where you are?"[56] Thus the home was again extended to the car. This was also one theme among several that was employed in advertising. For example, a 1934 Philco auto radio ad asserted, "Enjoy Philco in your car ... as you do at Home! You wouldn't be without a radio at home — why be without one in your car? Just as a PHILCO brings you the finest radio entertainment in the comfort of your living room, a PHILCO Auto Radio gives you the most enjoyable radio reception in your car."[57] Contrary to other technologies discussed above that stressed the safety angle, in 1939 psychologist Edward Suchman argued that listening to the radio distracted the driver from the road.[58] Suchman's applied psychological study was a response to a long-standing criticism of the radio in cars, for several states initially refused to register vehicles with radios, although apparently the prohibition was never enforced.

6

THE INTERWAR YEARS: THE GREAT DEPRESSION, AERODYNAMICS, AND CARS OF THE OLYMPIAN AGE

In late October 1929, the Prosperity Decade of the 1920s came to an abrupt end. Stock prices collapsed, banks failed, businesses closed their doors, unemployment lines grew, and some ruined investors committed suicide. There have been many explanations of why the Great Depression took place, including analyses that point to excessive stock speculation, depressed agricultural prices, and adverse monetary policy. Certainly the automobile industry figured prominently into this event. James Flink, in his *The Automobile Age*, squarely places the automobile at the heart of the reasons for the downturn, stating that "mass motorization played a key role in creating the most important necessary conditions underlying the Depression. The steep decline in aggregate spending evident by the late 1920s then, can be shown to have resulted from the economic dislocations that were an essential ingredient of the automobile boom, and from the inevitable drying up of that boom."[1] Said another way, the industry had over-expanded, the market had become saturated, and, as it contracted, this leading sector pulled the economy downwards.

The impact of the Depression on automobile production can be gleaned from Table 7, which shows General Motors annual production figures:

TABLE 7. GENERAL MOTORS UNIT SALES BY DIVISION

Calendar Year	Buick/Marquette	Cadillac/LaSalle	Chevrolet	Oldsmobile/Viking
1926	267,991	27,340	692,417	57,862
1927	254,350	34,811	940,277	54,888
1928	218,779	41,172	1,118,993	86,235
1929	190,662	36,698	1,259,434	101,579
1930	121,816	22,559	825,287	49,886
1931	91,485	15,012	756,790	48,000
1932	45,356	9,153	383,892	21,933
1933	42,191	6,736	607,973	36,357
1934	78,327	11,468	835,812	80,911
1935	106,590	22,675	1,020,055	182,483
1936	179,279	28,741	1,228,816	186,324
1937	225,936	44,724	1,132,631	211,715
1938	175,369	28,297	655,771	94,225
1939	230,088	38,390	891,572	158,005

Source: Alfred P. Sloan, *My Years with General Motors* (Garden City, NJ: Doubleday & Company, 1964), 446–7.

Of more than 1,000 automobile manufacturers that had been active between 1900 and 1930, only 19 were in business in 1931, selling about 40 models of cars.[2] At the bottom rung were the cheap cars — Ford, Chevrolet, and Plymouth — selling for about $600. One step up were makes that included Pontiac, Dodge, Oldsmobile, Essex, Willys, DeSoto and Graham. The middle market segment was led by Buick, followed by Chrysler, Nash, Studebaker, Hudson, Hupmobile, Oakland, Willys-Knight, and REO. Upper-middle-class vehicles, which were priced between $1,800 and $2,500, were sold in much smaller numbers. For example, it was estimated that LaSalle would add only 6,400 new registrations in 1931. Other cars in this class included Marmon, Franklin, Cord and Peerless, with Jordan and Kissel already in receivership. Finally, Packard led the sales of the very highest-priced marques, with Cadillac in second place, Lincoln in third and Stutz and Duesenberg minor players. By the end of the decade of the thirties, this list would be considerably pared down, as times were so hard that the replacement cycle of the 1920s was significantly extended. For many drivers, their only option was a used car.

In 1931, Boss Kettering thought that the Depression was due to "boredom." In his opinion, not enough new products had entered the market. That insight was ironic, perhaps, given that Kettering was the chief of a large research laboratory that was a part one of the world's most powerful firms, and that its task was to develop new "new thing." There may well be truth, however, to Kettering's perceptions. According to James Flink, the drop in demand due to over-production and market saturation was bad enough, but during the 1930s the industry entered a phase of technological stagnation that led to few major changes in the product or how it was made. In sum, the technologically dynamic industry of the 1920s gave way to a conservative one with no real gains in productivity. Flink claimed,

> By the late 1920s no manufacturing innovation was in sight of comparable importance to the continuing strip mill for rolling sheet steel or the continuous process technique for manufacturing plate glass, much less anything that could have the impact on investment in new plant and equipment that the moving assembly line had had a decade earlier.... Increasingly into the 1930s new investment in the automobile and ancillary industries was being stimulated more by the demands of planned obsolescence and the dictates of style than by basic innovations in automotive and manufacturing technologies.[3]

Flink's argument centered on the premise that 1930s was a decade characterized by continual refinement of the automobile as a technological system rather than radical changes. One may challenge this assertion, however. In terms of engine design, for example, Henry Ford's flathead V-8, introduced in 1932, certainly revolutionized automobile power plants of that era. And there were dramatic changes at the top of the product ladder. Yet, only in a few rare cases did these innovations trickle down to the cars of the common person, and their cheap Fords, Chevrolets and Plymouths.

Olympian Automobiles of the 1930s

The Great Depression was replete with many ironies, none more obvious to those living at the time than the magnificent, extravagant automobiles that were being produced for a privileged few during a time of enormous dislocation. At the very top end of the American automobile market Packard was the sales leader, with Cadillac second. Other prestige cars included Cord, Duesenberg, Franklin, Lincoln, Marmon, and Pierce-Arrow. These marques reflected an Olympian Age in automobile history. The best of these makes included the Cadillac V-16, the Pierce-Arrow Silver Arrows, the Auburn boattail speedster, the coffin-nose Cord, and perhaps the most publicized vehicle of that type and era, the Duesenberg SJ and SSJ.[4] They were opulent, shiny, large, and stunningly beautiful. And they performed. Unlike today, where performance is measured in 0–60 acceleration times and top speed, cars like the Cadillac V-16 were judged by their ability to accelerate in high gear from 5 to 25 mph. It was performance criteria that weighed the most with luxury buyers, who were unconcerned with the V-16's top end of 87 mph or its 9–10 mpg.[5]

The Duesenberg Models J, SJ, and SSJ were the most glamorous cars that one could own during the early 1930s; the cheapest J sold for 20 times the price of the least expensive Ford Model A, with prices typically between $13,000 and $20,000 when custom bodywork was added to the powertrain and chassis. The phrases "He drives a Duesenberg" and "The world's finest motorcar" said it all during the Great Depression. Duesenbergs were long, low, powerful, beautiful, and often open. One wonders what a displaced sharecropper thought when standing beside the road and seeing one of these cars passing by. It was the car that many Americans, no matter how down and out at the time, aspired to own. The Duesenberg was the ultimate idol in a culture that increasingly worshipped things, especially the automobile. Right or wrong, they were one important scene in the American dream of that era, much like a Lamborghini, Ferrari, or Bentley today.

And appropriate to the American dream, the Duesenberg came out of Midwest farm soil. The Duesenberg brothers, Fred and August (Augie), were born in Lippe, Germany, during the 1870s and grew up in Iowa. They first made a reputation in bicycle racing between 1897 and 1899, briefly made bicycles, and added a motor to one of them. They moved to Des Moines, where they founded the Iowa Automobile and Supply Company and modified cars for country fair races. Their success with a two-cylinder engine named the Marvel gained the

Jean Harlow and her Auburn Speedster, 1932, in Los Angeles (Auburn Cord Duesenberg Automobile Museum, Auburn, Indiana).

Clark Gable with his 1935 Duesenberg (Auburn Cord Duesenberg Automobile Museum, Auburn, Indiana).

attention of local attorney and financial backer Edward R. Mason. In 1904, the brothers then began making the Mason car, "The fastest and strongest two-cylinder car in America." Later, the Maytag family purchased the company, moved it to Waterloo, Iowa, and changed the name of the car to Maytag-Mason. Regarded as poor businessmen but mechanical geniuses, Fred and Augie were gradually marginalized at Maytag-Mason. In 1913 they moved to St. Paul, Minnesota, where they made small, high-speed engines, eventually producing marine engines for the Navy during World War I. In 1920, the operation moved to Indianapolis, where shortly thereafter, the first Duesenberg car, the Model A, was manufactured. In a 1922 ad, the Duesenbergs proclaimed that the Model A was "Built to outclass, outrun and outlast any car on the road." The Duesenberg quickly developed a reputation for racing prowess. It was the only car ever to win the French Grand Prix, doing so in 1921, and it won the Indianapolis 500 in 1924, 1925, and 1927.

The Duesenberg models that followed were not only the reflection of Fred and Augie's genius, but the result of a heated rivalry between the brothers and perhaps America's most talented automobile engineer ever, Harry Armenius Miller.[6] Miller, one year younger than Fred Duesenberg, was also a product of the Midwest, in this case Wisconsin. Like the Duesenbergs, Miller would also prove to be a poor businessman who entered the automobile industry via the fabrication of racing bicycles. During the 1920s, Miller, based in Los Angeles, made major innovations in racing engine design, including the use of the supercharger and front wheel drive. Racing pushed both groups towards bankruptcy, but before the decade ended, Miller cars won four Indianapolis 500s and set a land speed record of 171 mph.

In 1926 Errett Lobban Cord acquired Duesenberg, and plans were soon underway for what became the Model J, a car that was to be better than anything the Europeans could make. The Model J finally appeared in 1929, and its debut resulted in many superlatives. Above

A 1935 advertisement claimed, "He Drives a Duesenberg" (Auburn Cord Duesenberg Automobile Museum, Auburn, Indiana).

Another 1935 advertisement for Duesenberg: "She Drives a Duesenberg" (Auburn Cord Duesenberg Automobile Museum, Auburn, Indiana).

all, it was rolling sculpture. The J was nearly 20 feet long, with a prominent radiator and a sensuous rear. Its exterior hid what was the heart of this vehicle, a huge 7-liter double over-head cam straight 8, with four valves per cylinder and numerous aluminum components. The J was the car of the moneyed and mighty, the ultimate status symbol. It has been claimed that the phrase "It's a Duzy" was coined in its honor, connoting anything superb. (Careful scholarship, however, suggests that the term, with a slightly different spelling, was in use prior to the Duesenberg's appearance on the automotive scene.[7]) Perceptions and desires related to the Duesenberg, however, are beyond question. Two of Hollywood's greatest stars of the era, Clark Gable and Gary Cooper, bought short wheelbase Duesenberg SSJ roadsters in 1935, and their photographs standing next to their cars belied the immense suffering of many Americans during those desperate times.

The J was produced between 1929 and 1936, and it was complemented by the Model SJ, introduced in 1932, a supercharged version that contributed to the approximately 36 speed records Duesenbergs achieved, including the 24 hour world's record run of 1935 in which a 400 horsepower car averaged 135.47 mph, with one lap timed at over 160 mph on a 10 mile oval at the Bonneville, Utah, salt flats. Duesenbergs were a prime example of the technological sublime, and remain one of the most desirable of all collectible cars in America.[8]

The Duesenberg was only one of Errett Lobban Cord's ventures during the 1920s and 1930s.[9] A one-time used car salesman, Cord rose meteorically during the early 1920s to become one of America's leading business figures (he was twice on the cover of *Time*), and directed companies that manufactured, in addition to the Duesenberg, the Auburn Boat-Tailed Speedster and the Cord 810 and 812.[10] Despite Cord's contributions to the introduction of some of the most innovative automobiles of the twentieth century, he cared and knew next to nothing about automotive engineering. Perhaps this is key to developing an understanding of why his influence was short-lived, but he did correctly perceive that style and innovation were most significant to car sales once the Model T had had its run. As a stock manipulator, he had little interest in his cars once they were introduced. Indeed, in his drive to release startling new designs so as to whip up consumer interest, insufficient time was spent in ensuing product quality. Consequently—and it should be no surprise—his automobile empire crumbled in 1937.

While Cord's business success increased Auburn sales during the 1920s, like many others of that day he wanted to put his name on something of value. He did so in 1929 with the introduction of the Cord L-29, America's first front wheel drive car made in substantial numbers. In a brochure authored by Cord to entice customers, Cord wrote "The Cord car is a specialty car, different from others.... Being the very latest automotive development however, it creates an entirely new place never before occupied by any other car."[11] The Cord L-29 drew on the innovative technology developed by Harry Miller and allowed the body of the car to be significantly lower than comparable models that employed rear wheel drive. It was introduced in the summer of 1929, however, absolutely the wrong time for an unproven design to hit the marketplace given what would happen to the American economy later that year. Despite weak sales of the L-29 after 1930 and the fact that the Auburn Automobile Company never profited from the sales of this model (approximately 5,600 were manufactured between 1929 and 1932), Cord was undeterred in building an empire that included not only automobile manufacturing but also Lycoming engines, Century Air Lines, Century Pacific Airlines and Spencer Heater Company.

In 1934 Cadillac and Pierce-Arrow introduced aerodynamic coupes, and in response, Cord charged a small group of underfunded designers to respond. What crystallized was the

Cord 810 (a supercharged version would later be manufactured, the Cord 812). Compared to the common cars of the era, the Cord 810 had the appearance of a vehicle from Mars.[12]

Designed by Gordon M. Buehrig, perhaps the most talented American automotive designer of the twentieth century, the "Coffin Nose" Cord 810 was a brute with personality.[13] Among the innovations of the 810 were front wheel drive, the first practical independent front suspension, an "alligator" hood free of chrome trim, fingertip shift, concealed headlights, step down frame and body arrangement, V-shaped windshield, smooth, aerodynamic back, and pontoon fenders. The 810's aircraft-like instrument panel was stunning, made even more attractive by its soft lighting. Buehrig had taken the many cutting-edge contemporary styling ideas and combined them in what can only be regarded as a remarkably beautiful car. Further, to develop this design, Buehrig, working with Dale Cosper, designed and built clay modeling equipment at Auburn that was used for the first time in making a one-quarter scale model that was extremely accurate. It made the scale-up to working prototype possible in a shorter period. This table-top device would become the industry standard to at least the 1950s.

More than two thousand Cord 810s were made during the mid–1930s, and the car could perform. Its 175 horsepower engine would propel the 810 at more than 112 mph, a stock car record until 1954. It was described as "decidedly unconventional and "born and raised on a highway," but by 1937 its production run ended with the closing of the doors at the Auburn Automobile Company. Years later Gordon Buehrig would reminisce and attempt to answer the question of why the Cord 810 ultimately failed. He claimed that it was such a radical design that more time was needed to develop and refine it before it was introduced to the market. However, E. L. Cord impatiently rushed the car into the market, displaying the car at the New York Auto Show only five months after the prototype was built. Just as people can fall in love with a car, so too can they fall out of love, especially when that car lets its owner down on the side of the road. As Buehrig recalled, the Cord's steering shimmied, its front whitewalls were often covered with grease (due to the improper application of grease to the universal joints), its engine overheated, the transmission would jump out of gear, and few mechanics were bold enough to work on the car. The Cord 810 was cutting-edge technology not taken to completion.[14]

Streamlining and the Chrysler "Airflop"

Streamlined styling represents another exception, or counterargument, to the notion of technological stagnation during the interwar years. James Newcomb has argued that in terms of shape and design, the 1930s "represent a period of the most pronounced transition in automobile styling."[15] Newcomb argues that beginning with the 1931 Reo Royale and the 1934 Chrysler Airflow, rounder, smoother, and more flowing shapes gradually were introduced, and that this was due to cultural constructs that emphasized security and togetherness at the expense of individualism. In sum, it was a shift in values tied to a Depression-era culture in transition that became expressed in the way cars looked. Consequently, the automobiles of 1940 in no way resembled the automobiles of 1929, just as the America of 1940 was far different from that prior to the Great Depression.

One prominent example illustrating Newcomb's argument is the story of the development of the Chrysler Airflow and work in streamlining and aerodynamics in general that occurred in the automobile industry. Throughout the 1920s and 1930s, there was considerable enthusiasm for aviation, some of which spilled over into automotive areas. Indeed, the relationship between the automobile industry and aviation remains to be studied beyond superficialities. As previously mentioned, the dashboard of the Cord 810 resembled that found in aircraft of the day. Supercharging, developed at Wright Field in Dayton, Ohio, was installed in 1930s Mercedes and Auburn-Cord-Duesenberg models. But the rise in interest in automobile aerodynamics was also due to increases in engine size and horsepower, coupled with improved roads. The drag of a vehicle was responsible for both lower top speeds and higher fuel mileage.

One of the first individuals to explore the aerodynamics of the automobile beyond a theoretical discussion was Edmund Rumpler, who constructed his Tropfenwagen (a car the shape of a water drop) in 1921.[16] The Tropfenwagen can be translated as teardrop car, or raindrop car. Rumpler's idea was that a falling drop of liquid was nature's perfect airfoil design. As a drop fell, it would react to the pressure around it, and in so doing, its contour minimized wind resistance or drag. Only a limited number of these vehicles were built in 1921 and 1922, and then Rumpler sold the patents to the Benz firm. A surviving example of this historical curiosity can be found in the Technical Museum in Munich.

It is unclear what if any influence Rumpler had on the thinking of American automobile engineers, but technical articles appearing in the 1930s suggest that Paul Jaray's work was noticed and carefully studied in the U.S.[17] The Hungarian-born Jaray was chief of the development department of the Zeppelin Airship works between 1914 and 1923. During the spring of 1921 he studied air flow passing around car bodies by using one-tenth scale wood models at the Zeppelin facility in Friedrichshafen, Germany. Jaray concluded that the vertical longitudinal section of a car was most important, and that it must be designed in such a way as to guide the air flow up and over the car in the front and down in the rear in such a manner as to minimize turbulence.

Others were thinking along similar lines during the late 1920s, and certainly one important figure was Carl Breer. As previously discussed, Breer, Owen R. Skelton and Fred Zeder were known as the Three Musketeers at Chrysler Corporation during the 1920s. The three had formed a consulting engineering firm in 1921 after working for a time at Studebaker, and it was then that they caught the attention of Walter Chrysler. In 1924 they were instrumental in designing the Chrysler Model 70. As the story goes, Breer conceived of the Airflow concept while driving to his summer home in 1927. Traveling near Selfridge airfield, he spotted what he first thought was a flock of geese flying overhead, only to find it was a squadron of Army Air Corps planes on maneuvers. Aviation was on the minds of many Americans in 1927, as it was in May of that year that Charles Lindbergh flew solo across the Atlantic, and a new era of commercial aviation was just beginning. At any rate, this insight and his playful inquisitiveness involving the forces of air resistance to an arm extended outside his car's window led Breer to ponder ideas that were being discussed much of the time, namely that of form following function that had roots in the writing and architectural work of Louis Sullivan and his famous pupil, Frank Lloyd Wright. The question that remained in 1927 was "Why were aircraft becoming more streamlined while cars remained little more than boxy carriages?"

Approaching the problem scientifically, Breer went to William Earnshaw, an engineer at a research laboratory in Dayton, Ohio, and provided him with a car for making measurements of air-pressure lift and distribution. He also talked with Orville Wright, who assisted Earnshaw in designing a small wind tunnel where Breer subjected various scale models consisting of blocks of different shapes to aerodynamic analysis. With the addition of smoke, airflows passing around the models could be studied in the wind tunnel. As Earnshaw discovered from these experiments, areas of lower pressure formed behind the model, and higher pressures in the front. By rounding the front of the design and tapering the rear, streamlining was achieved.[18]

Before long, Walter Chrysler became interested, and approved construction of a much larger wind tunnel at Highland Park, Michigan, where over the next three years researchers tested hundreds of shapes, plotted eddy curves, noted turbulence, checked wind resistance, and calculated drag numbers.[19]

In addition to Chrysler engineers, there were others working on streamlining at this time. Most significantly, Amos E. Northrup, who worked for the Murray Body Company, designed the 1932 Blue Streak Graham with its enclosed fenders and radiator cap under the hood. A few others had more radical solutions, especially Buckminster Fuller with his Dymaxion car.[20]

Fuller, one of the true design geniuses of the twentieth century, is better known for his geodesic dome structure that was first proposed in 1949. In 1928, during a period of intense study, Fuller wrote a 2,000 page essay he called 4-D, and it was from the ideas articulated in this essay that the Dymaxion car emerged. Fuller designed his streamlined automobile in an abandoned Locomobile factory located in Bridgeport, Connecticut. The first Dymaxion was produced in 1933 from plaster models, and demonstrated at the Chicago Century of Progress World's Fair. It was a gleaming, aluminum bullet-shaped object powered by a standard Ford V-8, and it was capable of going 115 mph. It brought together submarine and dirigible shapes, and there was nothing like it on the road. In this car the driver sat in the front, and there was no long hood. Shatterproof aircraft glass wrapped around the front, and sticking through the roof was a rear periscope. It was a low-slung vehicle that resembled a wingless fish and rode on just three wheels, two in the front and one in the rear. The two front wheels provided traction and braking and the rear steering. So many new ideas went into that transport: front wheel drive, air-conditioning, recessed headlights, and a rear engine. But an unfortunate accident killed the novel vehicle, even though it was not its fault, and its major idea, streamlining, was captured by the 1934 Chrysler Airflow.

In the six years that Breer and his team spent on the Airflow project, many trial and error experiments were performed that discovered some of the practical the rules of aerodynamics. One of the conclusions suggested a modified teardrop shape that allowed for a windshield and hood.[21] The Airflow was an "engineer's car," with a conventional front engine rear and drive layout, but with some important modifications. Its engine was moved some 20 inches ahead of its normal position. The body featured front end styling characterized by a short curved nose and an integral trunk. The fuel tank and radiator were now concealed. Inside the center latch doors were chair-height seats in a vast, spacious interior. Riders sat at almost the center of the car's balance, producing an effect described in one brochure as "Floating Ride." Indeed, "Floating Ride" was the consequence of Breer's insights concerning the natural rhythms of the human body and the periodic oscillations that automobiles developed because of spring height. "No matter whether you are sitting in the front seat or the back, you can relax completely and utterly ... you can ride comfortably amidships ... experience no bumping, bouncing or vibration of any kind. The bumps seem to flow under the car without reaching you." Also missing from the Airflow was the typical wood and steel composite body common to virtually all other cars of the period. In its place was one complete unitized steel unit "built like a modern bridge." Streamlining was thus achieved not only on the outside of the car, but structurally as well. Box girders ran longitudinally up from the front and were joined with vertical and horizontal members to create an exceptionally strong structure, supposedly 40 times more rigid than the conventional frame and body. With the rear seat moved 24 inches inward and the engine now positioned immediately above the front axle, driver and passengers no long experienced the same levels of fatigue as those riding in traditionally designed vehicles.

For all of the Airflow's virtues, its new shape proved too different for the general public to accept. Controversial elements included the rounded snout with its waterfall grill, slabbed sides and the spatted rear wheel openings. After its introduction in 1934 and public criticisms, modifications were made to the 1935, '36 and '37 designs, including changing the shape and size of the grill to the point that by the end of the production run, it had taken on a conventional appearance.[22]

Despite these attempts to earn public acceptance, the critics were unforgiving and unrelenting. Industrial designer Henry Dreyfuss claimed that the Airflow was a "case of going too far too fast." Frederick Lewis Allen, editor of *Harper's Magazine*, described it as being "so bulbous, so obesely curved as to defy the natural preference of the eye for horizontal lines." Because of lengthy retooling delays, the car was late coming off the line and there were rumors of it being a lemon. GM didn't help by orchestrating a smear campaign and introducing its own turret-top all steel roof automobiles in 1935. And certainly early models were plagued with flaws, as line workers had difficulty making this very new kind of car.

Chrysler responded with publicity stunts like that of Citroën where a car was dropped off a 110-foot cliff. The Airflow's doors opened easily; it then started under its own power and was driven away. Beginning in 1935, Chrysler made outward design changes and entered the car in various endurance motor sport events. But the damage was done, and the cars would not sell. Beginning with only 12,000 units sold in 1934, the numbers continued to slide though 1937 before it was discontinued after 1938. More conventional models and a conservatively revised Airflow design called Airstream saved the company, but the whole episode is a case study in what rumors will do to undermine a technologically advanced product. From innovative leader to conservative follower, Chrysler emerged from the Airstream episode badly shaken, reluctant to take on major changes given what could happen. Throughout the 1940s, and indeed into the 1950s, Chrysler was content to follow GM designs, the third of the Big Three. Chrysler's executives were well aware that it could be trampled by the large paws of GM if it went in too bold a technological direction.

The story of aerodynamics and the automobile industry during the 1930s had a happier ending at the Ford Motor Company. It was at Ford during the late 1930s that John Tjaarda, a Dutch-born designer who had studied aerodynamics in England and served in the Dutch air force, designed the Lincoln-Zephyr. The Lincoln-Zephyr's drag coefficient was lower than that of the Airflow, as was its weight. Dr. Alexander Klemin, one of the designers of the Airflow, had miscalculated and made the Airflow's body twice as strong as it had to be.

Drag and aerodynamics were for the most part ignored in the U.S. even after World War II, the one exception being the abortive Tucker of the late 1940s. In Europe, however, car companies that included Citroën, Volkswagen, and Fiat did pay attention to aerodynamics. It was only after the 1973 fuel shock that computer-aided design and computer-aided engineering were harnessed to improve the streamlining of autos, since fuel efficiency is intimately connected with drag. Thus, it was 40 years after Carl Breer at Chrysler had made the bold move to study aerodynamics at Chrysler that the industry caught up.[23] In the process, the engineer and the stylist were now together in terms of their functions, and thus the stylist of old, artists the likes of Harley Earl, gave way to a new type of professional in the auto industry working in the 1980s.

Sitdown, the Coming of the United Auto Workers, and the Battle of the Overpass

The Depression exacerbated labor woes. James Flink wrote, "Labor unrest in the automobile industry spread with massive unemployment and the deterioration of working conditions as the Depression deepened."[24] The crisis was compounded by technological stagnation, and since workers were more flexible than machines, human labor was pushed to increase productivity.[25] Work on the assembly line was characterized by the "speed up" and "stretch out" of the workforce. "Too many men competed for too few jobs and automobile manufacturers took advantage of the glut in the labor market."[26] Autoworkers of the 1930s had manifold complaints, but the foremost grievance was the speed-up. Workers argued bitterly that the speed of the line was unbearable, that annual earnings were inadequate, and that methods of payment were too complicated. They also complained about the seasonal unemployment created by the industry's insistence upon an annual model change and upon shutting down during the model changes (at Ford); the practice of hiring workers, regardless of skill, at the starting rate; management's refusal to recognize seniority; the difficulty workers over 40 found in remaining employed; the substitution of female labor to replace male labor; and the espionage networks and the Bennett regime of Ford.[27] Mounting complaints would give impetus to a fledgling union movement.

Under the auspices of the New Deal, Congress passed the Wagner Act and created the National Labor Relations Board (NLRB). The original agreement was admittedly weak; it only stipulated requirements for worker representation, and automobile companies continued to resist unionization. The promises of the Wagner Act eventually came to fruition. "In only ten years," noted historian Richard Oestriecher, "the Wagner Act led directly to an increase in union representation from approximately one worker in ten in 1934 ... to more than three out of 10 by 1945, and strong unions forced corporations to raise wages at roughly the same rate that the economy expanded."[28] Concurrent with the Wagner Act, the American Federation of Labor (AFL) chartered the United Automobile Workers of America (UAW).

Even under the aegis of the Great Depression and the New Deal political climate, the "Big Three" were able to thwart workers' attempts to organize. Unionization of the automobile industry was not concluded when the ink of the Wagner Act dried. Ford used a police regime to prevent violence; General Motors, Chrysler, and other firms embarked on campaigns of espionage. It was said at the time that one out of ten workers was a company informant. To unionize the auto industry, American politics had to be moved to the left. In *Management and Managed* Steven Jeffreys argued that the external political environment was crucial in shaping the limits of unionization. He observed that the Roosevelt labor coalition had left the "business community exposed."[29] Jeffreys' thesis is also important because it recognized that "different patterns of managerial authority developed in different plants."[30] Labor unrest is a microcosm of larger political effects on the American social fabric. The historical experience of unionization was complex, and thus different in every company, and then every plant within that company. A high number of automobile strikes followed Franklin D. Roosevelt's 1932 election.

Companies battled to maintain Detroit's reputation as an open shop city. Historians have noted several reasons for the auto industry's ability to resist unionization. First, both the AFL and communist organizations bungled opportunities to organize autoworkers. A proper political mechanism was not realized until a group within the AFL created the Congress of

Industrial Organizations (CIO), which intended to jettison the AFL's craft principle to organize workers in the mass production industries. Second, the racial and ethnic composition of the workforce made organization difficult. Third, management pursued deliberate strategies to make unionization difficult. Ford's initial benevolence was a subtle attempt to assuage unionization, and his regime of violence under thug Harry Bennett was an overt strategy to stop unions. General Motors had a spy racket. In addition, politics within the unions were brutal and divisive. Even with mounting complaints and the automobile industry's speed-up, racial and ethnic differences proved difficult to overcome.

Collective bargaining was made a reality by historical actors who were catalyzed by the Great Depression and energized as a part of the New Deal political coalition. Franklin Roosevelt's charisma forged a new political bloc that embraced class-based politics and sided tentatively with labor. Workers also began to overcome their differences, and as Ronald Edsforth and Robert Asher pointed out, "no matter what their race, ethnicity, or gender, automobile workers found themselves confronting similar problems ... between 1935 and 1941 deeply felt resentments about what these workers called "the speedup" or "the stretch out" brought diverse groups of auto workers together in the successful organizing drives of the United Automobile Workers Union."[31] Leaders such as Homer Martin, Walter and Victor Ruether, Richard "Dick" Frankensteen, George Addes, and others organized a motley gang of laborers into the United Autoworkers (UAW). In a pivotal moment at the 1935 South Bend Convention, Dick Frankensteen's Automotive Industrial Workers Association (AIWA) joined the UAW.[32] Arnold Bernstein noted, "In the summer of 1936 the now more or less 'United' Automobile Workers confronted the major task of organization, which, given the extreme oligopolistic structure of the more industry, necessitated a frontal attack upon one of the big three."[33]

The opportunity for a "frontal assault" came in 1936 with the sit-down strike at General Motors plants around the country. Irving Bernstein noted that the youth of the autoworkers made the sit-down strike "democracy run wild."[34] The autoworkers used the innovative sit-down strike tactic to prevent the removal of dies and to obstruct the importation of strike breakers.[35] After a 44-day period of intense negotiations, the UAW gained the right to bargain with General Motors. The moment was unique in American history; both Michigan Governor Frank Murphy and President Franklin Roosevelt declined to forcibly remove strikers. The UAW's conquest of General Motors quickly exacted contracts from Hudson, Packard, and Studebaker, along with numerous parts producers. In the wake of the strike, the union had "256 locals, 400 collective bargaining agreements, and 220,000 dues-paying members."[36]

The union won several victories and had growing numbers, and in the summer of 1937 began to take on the Ford Motor Company. The assault on Ford was concomitant with vicious union factionalism. Dick Frankensteen led a progressive caucus while Walter Reuther headed up a Unity caucus. Perhaps the most dramatic moment of UAW–CIO's campaign to unionize the automobile industry was the "Battle of the Overpass," a brawl between Harry Bennett's thug regime and UAW leaflet distributors led by Walter Reuther and Richard Frankensteen. *Detroit News* photographer Scotty Kilpatrick captured the beat-down, generating iconic images of the fight to unionize the auto industry. Irving Bernstein described the attack:

> The UAW people were attacked unmercifully. Reuther was beaten, knocked down, lifted to his feet, and beaten again. Four or five men worked over Frankensteen. They skinned his coat up his back and over his face and two men locked his arms while others slugged him. Then they knocked him to the concrete floor.... A separate individual grabbed him by each foot and

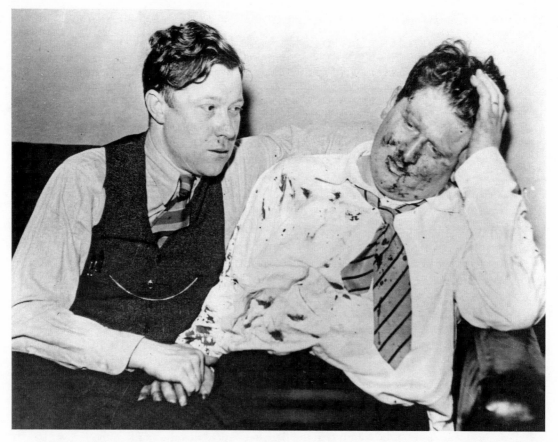

Walter P. Reuther and Richard T. Frankensteen after the Battle of the Overpass, May 26, 1937. Harry Bennett's Service Department caught Reuther and Frankensteen on an overpass near the Rouge plant and severely beat the union organizers in an attempt to thwart unionization efforts at Ford (from the Collections of The Henry Ford).

by each hand and his legs were spread apart and his body was toward the east ... and ten other men proceeded to kick him in the crotch and in the groin, and around the head and also to gore him with their heels in the abdomen.[37]

That attack, and the public revulsion that followed, ultimately forced Henry Ford to give in to union demands to organize, which occurred on the eve of World War II. After several organizers and workers were fired in the spring of 1941, a walkout occurred in the foundry, which spread to the entire plant. Unionization was called to a vote, and a majority approved of the UAW–CIO. Much to the dismay of a senile Ford, the "UAW received over 70% of the vote, won recognition in all Ford plants, and obtained a favorable collective bargaining contract."[38] The contract set limits on the arbitrary authority of management, established grievance procedures, and stopped the use of steward systems to mitigate disputes.

The Poetic Response to the Automobile

The automobile evoked emotional responses, both at work and in leisure. Poetry is most significant in understanding a culture at any moment in time, since poets aim at expressing the latent meanings of life. In the era before World War II what poetry was written about automobiles rarely, if ever, contained verse about human relationships, let alone sexual themes or glimpses. Instead, poetry was largely bifurcated into two subsets, either celebrating the freedom and the physical and psychological exhilaration of the ride, or criticizing changes in the human condition that had resulted in a loss of peace and harmony.[39] Exceptions to these two views were few and far between, particularly with regards to human relationships and sex.[40] One such exception was e.e. cummings' "XIX," written in 1926, the last year of the Model T's production run. A second notable exception was Karl Shapiro's poem "Buick," written at the beginning of America's involvement in World War II. Shapiro, later poet laureate and faculty member at Johns Hopkins University, had written this as a love poem to the car itself, a vehicle he had seen during the time he was in the army.

The emotion and intensity, the feeling between human beings and automobiles, would not quite reach the same heights in American poetry until the late 1970s and beyond, when this time it was women poets who would share more latent feelings with their readers.

Singing the Blues about Automobiles and Life

In the 1920s and 1930s, blues artists — often coming from humble and racially restricted worlds — recognized the car as being symbolic of freedom and unrestricted mobility. As Blacks living in a world of very limited freedom in the Jim Crow American South, their artistic expression — the blues — contained the message that the car was liberating in terms of personal privacy and social and financial emancipation. It was a message of hope to those living in the Mississippi delta, connected as it was by U.S. Highway 61.

Post–World War I blues singers often sang about Fords, especially the Model T. It was a hard working and durable machine, built by workers who included those who were Black. It was a car ignored for its virtues, as were the African Americans who were working the cotton fields in the vicinity of Greenville and Natchez, Mississippi. One musical example expressing the notion of neglect was Blind Lemon Jefferson's "DB Blues," released in 1928. One lyric proclaimed that a Ford was preferable to a Packard. Seven years later, Sleepy John Estes echoed a similar theme about the Model T in his 1935 "Poor Man's Friend." Indeed, while a Cadillac might have been in their dreams, it was more than likely a Ford that was the friend of African Americans living in the Delta who were fortunate enough to purchase any car before World War II.

As E. C. Widmer has pointed out, there were strong sexual innuendoes in blues songs, and that included tunes referring to cars.[41] In 1926 Virginia Liston lamented that her "Rolls Royce Papa" had a bent piston rod. A year later Bertha Chippie Hill, in "Sports Model Mama," claimed to receive punctures every day. The most important car-related song of the period was the 1936 Robert Johnson hit, "Terraplane Blues," in which Johnson pushed the car-human being metaphor to the limit.

Johnson's songs served to lift the spirits of those oppressed and downtrodden during the bleak Depression years. It would be after World War II, however, with unparalleled prosperity and automobility, that music would take a broader societal significance to a far broader audience. And it would be the blues tradition, drawn on by both Black and White artists after the war that would set the stage for the birth — in the back seat of an automobile, so to speak — of rock and roll.[42]

Program, Legion Ascot Speedway, August 26, 1931. One of the great dirt tracks in America, it was located in southern California. Action from Legion Ascot was depicted in the film *The Crowd Roars*, 1932.

NO. 1—THE CLIFF DURANT TROPHY—To be awarded to the driver winning the most points in racing in 1931. Two points are given for each mile of racing, divided among the winners,, in the same ratio of prize money paid. The trophy carries with it the **Championship** of **California, Arizona** and **New Mexico.**

NO. 2—THE AMERICAN AUTOMOBILE ASSOCIATION TROPHY—To be awarded to the driver finishing second in the **Championship** standing of **California, Arizona** and **New Mexico,** 1931.

NO. 3—THE CRAGAR CORPORATION TROPHY—To be awarded to the driver who with his pit attendants makes the most attractive and neatest personal appearance and has the highest degree of pit organization.

NO. 4—THE HARRY HARTZ TROPHY—To be awarded to the owner of race car showing best all around appearance in 1931.

NO. 5—THE EDWARD WINTERGUST TROPHY—To be awarded to the driver, car owner, or mechanic performing the most sportsmanlike act during 1931. The referee will make a complete and detailed report to **The American Automobile Association** of any act or acts that are of a meritorious nature.

Racing Trophies, from the program of the Legion Ascot Speedway, August 26, 1931. During the 1920s and 1930s, with few exceptions, racer drivers risked their lives for very little material reward.

Filming on the Race Track and Soundstage

Filming the automobile in motion during the 1930s was much less involved than it is today, primarily because many of the scenes featuring cars were produced on a sound stage. One of the most interesting films dealing with auto racing during the 1930s was *The Crowd Roars* (1932), directed by Howard Hawks and starring James Cagney. Hawks, who had a personal interest in auto racing at that time, shot a number of remarkable racing scenes at Ascot Park in California and Indianapolis. Duesenbergs, Millers, and modified Ford speedsters are featured in this film about two brothers, a faithful friend, their women (played by Ann Dvorak and Joan Blondell), a fiery accident, fear, and redemption. *The Crowd Roars* provides a rare glimpse into the world of racing and the cars of the 1930s. According to one recent reviewer, footage from *The Crowd Roars* was removed and inserted in a later Warner Brothers film, *Indianapolis Speedway* (1939). Later, when the footage was reinserted, it contained some 1939 scenes, including automobiles, racing announcers and an ambulance that were not in the original version. Despite its weak plot and at times cheesy acting, this film contains an important historical record, including scenes with Indy winners Billy Arnold, Fred Frame, and Lou Schneider.[43]

The serial was part and parcel of American moviegoing during the Depression era, and one serial adventure that prominently featured racing cars and automobiles was the 1934 *Burn 'Em Up Barnes*, starring Jack Mulhall, Frankie Darro, Lola Lane and a host of evil characters that included Jason Robards Sr. Viewers watched 12 episodes filled with crashes, chases, races, and treachery, as two capitalists and their henchmen attempt to swindle the heroes out of land that contains a bonanza of oil underneath it.[44] The 1930s brought out not only the best in Americans, but also the worst, if this film is at all a true reflection of everyday life and human motives and needs.

One immensely powerful film about the American automobile that was not seen in the local cinema during the 1930s was *Master Hands* (1936). Produced by the Jam Handy Organization, a firm that specialized in corporate-funded public relations, *Master Hands* used innovative cinematography similar to that of Leni Riefenstahl's much more famous *Triumph of the Will* to portray the men and machines that made quality Chevrolets in Flint, Michigan. Opening with a score from Richard Wagner's *Die Walküre*, it contained little narrative and many powerful images. After viewing this film, the question is "which was more important, the hands of factory workers or the machines which they work with?" The human beings in this film are portrayed as intense and almost devoid of emotions, like the machines they are charged to operate. Scenes from the foundry as fiery, molten metal is being poured into sand molds to cast engine blocks are both stunning and a reminder of the harsh work environment that many automobile workers faced back in those days. *Master Hands* is perhaps the single best example of cinematography depicting what assembly line work was like in the era before World War II.[45]

Both film and the automobile would change dramatically after World War II, and their influence on American life would be attenuated. Ironically, given his pacifism, Henry Ford's plants played a critical role in the war effort, although he had wildly exaggerated what his factories could produce. Ford would live to see the end of the conflict, but with greatly diminished mental capacities. In 1947 Henry Ford died quietly, but the world was anything but at peace. Whatever America had been before the Model T, it was profoundly changed by the mid-twentieth century, thanks to Ford and others in the automobile industry. After 1945 America and the American automobile industry were ascendant, but both were about to face both internal and foreign challenges.

7

WORLD WAR II AND THE RECONVERSION ECONOMY: NO TIME FOR SERGEANTS OR ASPIRING AUTOMOBILE MANUFACTURERS

With the advent of World War II the automobile industry was converted into the "arsenal of democracy."[1] From 1942 to 1945 companies manufactured no cars or auto parts; instead, the industry produced tanks, trucks, jeeps, bombs, steel helmets, planes, and small arms ammunition.[2] This episode has been well studied, but the period immediately before the conflict and the transition to wartime production has been comparatively neglected. The automobile industry's conversion to the production of war materiels was neither voluntary nor expedient.

Barton J. Bernstein has argued that the automobile industry resisted the transformation into democracy's arsenal.[3] According to Bernstein, the industry was still on the defensive from the Depression, suspicious of the Roosevelt government, and wished to avoid the World War I epithet "merchants of death." Instead of wartime responsibility, "auto producers contended that their equipment could not be used for armaments and that partial conversion was impossible."[4] This was particularly true of Henry Ford, who initially refused to produce airplane engines for the British Royal Air Force. In 1940, with the specter of Nazism on one side of America and Japan's aggression on the other, President Roosevelt called for increased production of armaments with a goal of 50,000 airplanes. On May 28, the President appointed General Motors chairman William S. Knudsen to the newly created National Advisory Defense Committee (NADC), but this did little to hasten the conversion. Knudsen moved slowly, defending partial conversion of the industry as sufficient for war production. John Rae observed that automobile companies had no need to change from production for an emerging civilian market to war materials for the government. Both government and industry assumed that with "the continuation of depression conditions, there was ample excess plant capacity and labor, so that wartime needs could be met without disturbing the normal course of the economy," and when World War II arrived, "both government and industry had to learn their production roles from scratch."[5] Just a month before Pearl Harbor, the industry was barely restricted — only thirteen auto manufacturers held defense contracts.[6] And of those who held defense contracts, only part of their production power was dedicated to the war effort. "Even after Pearl Harbor," wrote Bernstein, "the industry continued to resist conversion to war production."[7]

On February 22, 1942, the production of automobiles ceased, and American industry conducted total war against the Axis powers. When conversion was accomplished, the results surpassed expectations. John Rae noted that as the world's greatest concentration of capital, "the American Automobile industry outstripped all others in the total volume of production

Applying automobile production methods to machining of 40 mm anti-aircraft gun barrels in a Chrysler Corporation plant, Highland Park, Detroit, during World War II. Five cutting instruments work at the same time. Under the old single-operation methods of gun making, only one of these could work at one time (Library of Congress).

and the diversity of its output."[8] Instead of cars, automobile factories accepted government contracts to produce "completely novel and uniform products; artillery and shells, gun mountings, machine guns, fire-control systems, small-arms ammunition, fuses—all the complex equipment of twentieth century war."[9]

By December 1942, the industry had formed the Automotive Council for War Production to organize the resources of the automobile firms and maximize efficiency and production. Larry Lankton has pointed out that "working together, the auto manufacturers and the military struck a delicate balance between producing the best weapons and producing the most weapons."[10] General Motors, Ford, and Chrysler all contributed to the war effort in different ways. Chrysler produced 22,000 tanks (to Germany's 24,000), Ford 288,000 of the novel Jeep, and General Motors assigned 120 plants to defense work.[11] At the end of 1943, General Motors reported that every defense contract was in production, on schedule, and yielding more output than the government had considered possible.[12] The company delivered approximately $12 billion worth of military materiel during the war years, and they had never made two-thirds of the items before.[13]

Ed Cray, in his history of General Motors entitled *Chrome Colossus,* concluded that "if the corporation ever had a supreme moment, a period of unqualified contribution to the com-monweal, it was during the war years of 1940 though 1945."[14] Small companies such as Packard, Studebaker, Bantam, Mack, and Willys-Overland also contributed to the war effort. James Flink summarized that "before the war had ended the American automobile industry had pro-duced for the military 4,131,000 engines, including 450,000 aircraft and 170,000 marine engines, 5,974,000 guns and 27,000 completed aircraft."[15] Automobile makers and the mil-itary created a feedback loop of innovation and production. The military would suggest improvements, and auto companies would make changes in production. A 1950 work on the Automotive Council for War Production, *Freedom's Arsenal*, reported: "Ingenuity on the part of the automotive engineers was outstanding ... to cut down on welding operations one com-pany adapted huge presses — formerly used to stamp out automobile body panels — to the forming of armor plate. These presses eliminated 64 inches of welding in two places on the tank hull."[16] Flink concluded that "American superiority in mass-production techniques — techniques developed in the automobile industry — was indeed the main reason for the Allied victory."[17]

In May 1940, Franklin Roosevelt challenged American industry to produce fifty thou-sand airplanes. The production of airplanes proved to be the automobile industry's most for-midable wartime operation. Airplanes, wrote Rae, were "items that few automobile men had ever seen, let alone manufactured."[18] Further complications arose because the airplane indus-try opposed any foothold for potential competitors, and the industries had divergent philoso-phies; the airplane industry aimed for quality, and the automobile industry aimed to produce in quantity. Nevertheless, "these difficulties caused less trouble than might have been expected especially because both industries were staffed by men who realized that there was a vital job to be done."[19] The automobile industry began by producing Rolls-Royce engines. By the fall of 1940, the industry produced fuselages, wing sections, and various airplane parts.[20] Output for 1942 alone was 47,000 aircraft. Chief in this effort was Ford's Willow Run Plant near Ypsi-lanti, Michigan. Built distant from any labor force, the plant became a "social disaster." Makeshift shacks were built to house the workforce. In addition, Ford experienced a short-age of materials and trained labor. Willow Run became known as Will-it-Run. "As late as September, 1943," wrote Rae, "the Air Force was seriously considering asking the government to take charge of Will-It-Run."[21] During the dispute, Walter Reuther suggested that idle plants be devoted to aircraft manufacturing that included government, the automobile companies and the UAW. He claimed that five hundred airplanes could be manufactured a day. The provocative suggestion never materialized. Finally, by late 1943, Willow Run began to pro-duce between four and five hundred B-24 bombers a month.

"Little Bo Peep Has Lost Her Jeep..."

Despite inevitable hang-ups and bottlenecks, the overall record of World War II indus-trial history suggests that automobile manufacturers and their military consumers created an institutional matrix that resulted in innovation and production. The outstanding example of this process was the Jeep. In June 1940, the army's Ordnance Technical Committee called for a "low-silhouette scout car."[22] The army invited 135 manufacturers to develop a prototype, but due to short deadlines, only two companies responded — American Bantam and Willys-Overland. The chief engineer and vice-president of Willys-Overland, Delamor Roos, had championed the light automobile for years.[23] Bantam developed the original prototype, and Willys-Overland added a number of improvements. The Willys-Overland design was accepted, and Ford agreed to mass-produce the Jeep. In total, 660,000 Jeeps were constructed for the war effort.[24] The Jeep came to symbolize mechanized total war. It was unlike any other automobile. Herbert R. Rifkin noted that beyond performance, "In appearance, too, the jeep was radically different."[25] He wrote, "Soon well-known to every school-boy on the street were its squat, rectangular, utilitarian shape and its coat of olive-drab, lusterless enamel that had been developed shortly before; its low silhouette; the flat fenders on each of which an additional man could be carried if necessary; the heavy brushguard protecting the front; the folding windshield and detachable folding top or canopy, the pintle [sic] and towing hooks; the heavy duty mud-and-snow tread tires, and the front and rear blackout lights."[26]

Beyond the Jeep's military significance are several less notable social and cultural influences. The outpourings lavished on the Jeep resulted in this machine becoming an indelible part of war-time culture. In *Hail to the Jeep,* A. Wade Wells wrote, "The Jeep possesses the American flair for getting around."[27] During the war, like many other mass-produced

Actor Joe E. Brown driving a Jeep loaded with American GIs in China, 1942 or 1943 (Library of Congress).

machines, the Jeep was perceived as a liberator. After entering Paris, the Allies paraded along the Champs Elysees in Jeeps four abreast. In rural Sicily, the Jeep liberated a rural town from the malfunctions of water power. At the mill, GIs carried a Jeep up a flight of stairs and connected the motor to a failed olive crushing machine, saving 88,000 pounds of olive oil. The Jeep was heralded as "a top flight ambassador of good will."[28] Soldiers individualized their Jeeps and became attached to them. One author speculated, "The practice of naming vehicles, especially if the soldier had a free choice of names, was a great factor in developing this personal attachment."[29] Jeeps were named after women (*Alice, Donna, Aloha Betty*); terms of endearment (*Angel Face, Babe, Honey*); men (*Jack, Joe, Tony's Tank*); virtues (*Duty, Honesty, Vigilant*); cartoon characters (*Bambi, Batman, Wizard of Oz*); music (*Back Beat Boogie, Jumping Jive, Sinatra*); functions (*Surge-on, Buckets o' Bolts, Low Gear*); military terms (*Attack, Cannonball, Salute*); war locations (*Argonne, Berlin Bound, Geneva*); and obscenities (*Cherry, Hot, Pussy*).[30]

During the war, the Jeep became an icon of American technology, representing the superiority of mass production techniques and a centerpiece of poems, songs, movies, and books. The Andrews Sisters sang "Six Jerks in a Jeep" in the 1942 film *Private Buckaroo*. In 1942, Jerry Bowne and Frank De Val wrote "Little Bo Peep Has Lost Her Jeep."

In 1944, children's book writer Henderson Le Grand penned *Augustus Drives a Jeep*. The plot of the novel centered on Augustus' discovery of his neighbor's Jeep and the subsequent adventure that ensued. To the awed schoolboy Augustus, the Jeep was a conveyance of adventure. Augustus drove the Jeep off road, delivered a sick man to a hospital, and even used the Jeep to replace an obsolete mule in the plowing of a field. The reader wonders whether Augustus or the Jeep is in control: "The jeep adjusted itself to its uncertain driver and rolled easily over the bumps and hollows of the field with a motion like a small boat in a heavy sea."[31] In 1944, actress Carole Landis published *Four Jills in a Jeep*, a memoir of her five-month tour of Europe as a member of the Hollywood Victory Committee.[32] With actresses Martha Raye, Mitzi Mayfair, and Kay Francis, Landis moved about the front in a Jeep and entertained troops.

In 1944 artilleryman and newspaper correspondent Fairfax Downey wrote *Jezebel the Jeep*, a tribute to the Jeeps he drove in the war. Even in the process of mass production, Jezebel was born an individual:

> The chief inspector himself took Jezebel off the line. He slapped her on the steering wheel button, and she squawked lustily. He turned her lights on and she wink at him. He twisted on her ignition, and she warmed to him; in fact, she fairly purred at him the second he touch the self-starter. There was nothing backward about Jezebel but her reverse gear.[33]

Jezebel lavished her affection upon a Johnny, an artillery officer. She saved his life in the Tunisian campaign and helped him invade Sicily. After the war, Jezebel and Johnny went on hunting and fishing trips, and she served him as the ultimate peacetime utility. Downey concluded that Jezebel, the machine, was as much a wartime survivor and veteran as Johnny, the human being.

To sum things up, *Smithsonian* writer Doug Stewart noted, "The jeep became the personification of Yankee ingenuity and cocky, can-do determination."[34] After the war, the Jeep became an important utility vehicle for American farmers, and later, with a return to smaller cars from large gas-guzzlers, a preferred automobile of American consumers.

Wartime Labor: Sacrifices and Selfishness

Factories and shop floors, though they provided major impetus to the war effort, were hotbeds of conflict and endemic to labor problems. Change began, as John Barnard noted, when "more than a quarter of a million UAW members left the factories for the armed forces."[35] Their places were filled with women, African Americans, and teenagers. The war created conditions where racial and sexual divisions of labor were challenged. Up to World War II very few women had worked in the automobile industry.[36] Ruth Milkman pointed out that the proportion of women employed in the auto industry "swelled from only 5 percent just before Pearl Harbor to 25 percent just two years later."[37] At the end of the war, it became apparent that management believed female employment was a temporary exigency of war, and in a deliberate "defeminization" of the industry women were laid off against their will. While the industry was defeminized, African Americans were hired en masse. "Plentiful jobs at good pay, with more opportunities for advancement into machine-tending and assembly work assignments previously closed to them, exerted a strong pull, drawing blacks already resident in Detroit as well as migrants from the southern and border states."[38] This engendered racial tension and conflict. In 1943, a major race riot erupted in Detroit. Many wildcat strikes erupted because White workers refused to work alongside Blacks, in an attempt to protect jobs deemed "White." During the struggle for democracy abroad, the shop floor became a home of racial angst.

The new labor force of wartime Detroit was composed of fresh wartime recruits. Nelson Lichtenstein wrote, "While this great influx of new workers was taking place, the conversion of the auto industry ... set the stage for a substantial decline in factory discipline."[39] The wartime shop floor was characterized by lax discipline. The industry hired a stratum of young and inexperienced managers who lost control of the shops. Absenteeism was rampant, and wildcat strikes became frequent. During the war labor gained the upper hand against management. Barnard wrote, "The equation of wartime supply and demand for labor reconfigured to the workers' advantage created an environment in which wildcats could flourish."[40] Despite a no-strike pledge, wildcats were frequent. For example, the June 4, 1941, wildcat strike at North American Aviation defied agreements made by the National Defense Mediation Board (NDMB) and the UAW met the strike with swift action. Richard Frankensteen, then in charge of the UAW's aircraft division, flew to California and fired the local leadership. President Roosevelt dispatched 2,500 soldiers who broke picket lines and prevented public gathering. The strike ended and workers returned to the plant.[41] "By 1944, one of every two workers in the auto industry took part in some sort of work stoppage, up from one in twelve in 1942 and one in four in 1943."[42] With government largesse covering company's losses and labor's advantage over management during the war, the "arsenal of democracy" played host to labor conflicts.

Gas Rationing

Lifted out of the Great Depression by the war in Europe and a resurgent consumerism, Americans renewed their appetite for automobiles and driving. In his analysis of American culture during the war, John Morton Blum noted, "By stimulating the economy, the war did wonderful things for the American people.... There were plenty of jobs. Business and farm profits were rising, as were wages, salaries, and other elements of personal income."[43] After Pearl Harbor, Americans spent their disposable income and sought new economic opportunities. Using mass transit, public transportation, and automobiles, "Americans moved faster and in greater numbers than before."[44] As a result of this renewed affluence, Americans needed to buy more gasoline. Harold Williamson observed, "Between 1939 and 1941 the annual domestic consumption of all petroleum products rose by approximately 242 million barrels — an increase of slightly over 20 percent."[45] Perhaps with some irony, however, global war limited the supply of petroleum to the American market, dashing consumers' hopes of an open road. The commitment to send oil tankers to Great Britain, coupled with the toll that German submarines took in the North Atlantic and Caribbean, reduced petroleum supplies available on the East Coast. To further complicate things, Japan invaded East Asia in late 1941 and with the fall of Singapore controlled 90 percent of the world's rubber supply.

Americans resisted gas rationing from its inception. Government officials' wartime policies concerning the conservation of critical commodities were often at cross purposes to a rising consumerism among those Americans active on the home front. Economists James Maxwell and Margaret Balcom explained: "The inspiration for the debate was not simply the high esteem in which the American motorist held his car. A babel of voices arose which left citizens unclear as to what was necessary. Some oil companies feared the effect of gasoline rationing on their businesses, automobile associations feared a loss in clientele and State gasoline tax officials feared a loss in revenue."[46]

In an attempt to provide East Coast Americans with gasoline, government officials pursued a strategy of "opening the valves." Pipelines were constructed, railway transportation increased, and domestic refining of crude oil increased. The pipelines "Big Inch" and "Little Big Inch" were built by War Emergency Pipelines Inc. to transport crude oil from east Texas to New York and Philadelphia. But government and industry efforts did not meet military and civilian demand for gasoline. The urgent situation led to the creation of the Office of Defense Transportation, which was given the task of coordinating all domestic transportation for the successful prosecution of the war.[47]

By early 1942, the transportation bottleneck and burgeoning industrial, commercial, and civilian demand for petroleum products began to put pressure on supplies.[48] Before rationing was instituted, government agencies attempted to limit consumers' access to gasoline. In February 1942, the Petroleum Administration for War (PAW), whose function was to allocate necessary gasoline to subcommittees, recommended a reduction in the amount of time service stations would remain open. In March, the War Production Board (WPB) ordered a 20 percent reduction in the normal deliveries of gasoline to service stations and bulk plants in District I and the Pacific Northwest.[49] Concomitantly, the PAW launched a public information campaign to encourage drivers to economize in the use of gasoline and heating oil. "But the public failed to respond," a PAW official lamented, "because it could not understand why the statements of abundance of a few months before should suddenly be reversed to claim of shortage."[50]

As the amount of gasoline allocated to the war effort increased and the amount allocated to the citizenry decreased, it became apparent to officials that gas would have to be rationed. Americans still needed the automobile to get to work, for recreation, and to maintain familial and community relationships. Many Americans, whose work was essential to ensure victory in the war, needed to drive to their places of employment. Bradley Flamm wrote, "Private cars had to remain the principal form of transportation ... and they had to be used as efficiently as possible."[51] Rationing aimed to *control* the use of gasoline, and urged citizens to draw a distinction between essential and non-essential travel. Since the automobile had become a necessity in American life, a semblance of the structure of everyday life had to be maintained to allow victory in Asia and Europe. Public transportation was not sufficient, and during the war trolley tracks and rail lines were worn to a nub.

Individual travel and disposable income combined to create what *The New York Times Magazine* called "The Taxi Driver's Golden Age."[52] With gas rationing, and the number of taxicabs reduced, New York cabbies found themselves "one of the most popular forms of life."[53] Beyond the urban environment where cabs could transport individuals, government officials faced unprecedented transportation challenges.

On December 1, 1942, the Office of Price Administration (OPA) made gasoline rationing a policy in District I, and later that year a national policy. The Office of Defense Transportation (ODT) was created to keep essential passenger cars and commercial vehicles fueled. In his analysis of the ODT, Flamm pointed out, "the system of rationing evolved extensively over time."[54] Beyond reduction of supplies, Flamm wrote, "it quickly became a more complex system based on ration books and coupons that were administered by thousands of War and Price Rationing Boards."[55] In theory, rationing was to be executed through a complex system. Economists James A. Maxwell and Margaret N. Blacom described the process:

> Rationing is a process of controlling demand for a scare commodity. Therefore, the first step in the function of a rationing program must be placing of ration evidences (representing the right to buy) in the hands of the right consumers and in the right quantities.... In order to control effectively the use of that currency, and the distribution of the commodity it represents, supervision must be exercised over the industry engaged in distributing the commodity ... the principal control was the flowback system.[56]

At the top were state-licensed distributors, then the intermediate wholesaler, and then a retailer who sold to customers. A card-based system was put in place temporarily while officials developed a system based on coupons.[57] The system depended on the discretion of local administrators. The local boards gave citizens, depending on circumstances, either "A," "B," or "C" coupons. Government officials assumed that all cars averaged 15 miles per gallon.[58] "A" coupons were the standard ration: 150 miles for occupational purposes and 90 for miscellaneous family driving. This amounted to an annual 5,250 miles per vehicle. "B" and "C" coupons included additional miles for those whose work was seen as necessary in wartime America.[59] Boards also provided rations for hardships, furloughs, fleets, and transports.[60] Drivers in preferred categories received what they needed. "Rural teachers are limited to 5,400 miles and prospectors for strategic minerals to 11,800."[61] For obvious reasons, American citizens chafed against rules implemented by their local boards.

In 1943 Joe M. Dawson, a board member in his community wrote, "We are about as popular as tax collectors."[62] He noted, "in the gasoline and fuel-oil rationing ... there is the most discretion, and much depends upon the judgment of the board members."[63] Doctors, traveling salesmen, and businessmen lobbied Dawson to give them more gasoline. When he did not grant their requests, Dawson would often be "cussed out."

The ODT used several methods to control American's gas consumption. "The most important method of controlling travel demand was to simply limit the amount of gasoline that civilians could buy by rationing supply."[64] Methods also included a national 35 mph speed limit, bans on pleasure driving, and a requirement to carpool. The ODT also had suggested cooperative methods such as the coordination of business and travel schedules.[65] The

ODT used posters, radio programs, newspaper articles, and advertisements to influence Americans to drive less. They often linked their propaganda with patriotism, and they still encouraged Americans to travel. Flamm explained, "keeping up morale and ensuring that productivity remained as high as possible depended, in part, on ensuring that some purely social and personal travel was permitted."[66]

A July 1942 survey, "Do Americans support gasoline rationing?" revealed that 70 percent of Americans approved and recognized the necessity of the government program.[67] Americans recognized the necessity of rationing during wartime, but still disagreed with the decisions of local boards and yearned for the open road. When local boards turned down requests for additional gas, Americans had no difficulty in acquiring "black gasoline," and a widespread black market for gasoline quickly developed with the coupon system, which threatened to upset the war effort. Maxwell and Balcom estimated that 8 percent of oil was purchased illegally, and Williamson estimated that in 1944, up to 125,000 barrels a day were illegally procured.[68] The PAW wrote that black markets "drained millions of gallons of sorely needed gasoline from legitimate users" and "time after time threatened to upset the entire gasoline distribution system," particularly on the East Coast.[69] Bradley Flamm asserted that the amount could not be quantified, but that "demand for fuel, and the personal mobility it permitted, remained high."[70]

When the bureaucrats responsible for the flowback system first generated statistics on gas use, they reported that the market was full of unused coupons.[71] The buying and selling of additional coupons enabled Americans who wanted to travel in automobiles during the war to do so. Beyond surplus coupons, many were counterfeit. Highly organized rackets developed to take advantage of the ease of theft and the lack of punitive risk. The coupon system welcomed a "Who's Who" of criminals from bootlegging, counterfeiting, white slavery, kidnapping and murder to the world of oil. A March 27, 1944, *Newsweek* article noted the ease and profitability of racketeering: "the risks are fewer, the work is clean and not unpleasant, and the operating costs are not nearly so prohibitive ... the profits are unbelievably high: 1,000,000,000 a month."[72] Racketeers supplied the demand of American consumers for gasoline and enabled automobility. Racketeering was a part of American culture, and the anonymity of car culture provided opportunity for illegal profit.

In the 1944 movie *Jitterbugs*, comedians Stan Laurel and Oliver Hardy were a traveling two-man jitterbug band.[73] The movie opens with the comedians in their broken down Ford with just an "A" card. Suddenly, a debonair salesman played by Bob Bailey arrived and sold the duo magical gas pills. The gas pill, sold in 5- and 10-gallon packets, transformed water into gas. They were marketed by Bailey as the answer to the "rationing problem," which in *Jitterbugs* was stated to be the "world's greatest problem." The con man convinces a naïve Laurel and Hardy to play a concert at a local carnival and sell the pills to the crowd. They con a small American town for $223. The trio moves on to engage in other plans to swindle real-estate racketeers and other fortune seekers. In *Jitterbugs,* trust or good feelings were absent in wartime America.

The Black Market: "Chiseled Gas"

Consumers, gasoline dealers, and distributors gave the black market a tacit approval. Beyond approval, many American consumers purchased from the black market. In 1943, *Col-*

liers writer Mike Miller traveled on "chiseled gas" from the Mexican border at Brownsville, Texas, to the Canadian boundary at International Falls, Minnesota. A chiseler, defined during the war, was one who drove to gas stations and attempted to "finagle" a tank of gas. Some gas stations refused Miller service, but many were willing to sell gasoline at the regular market price. He also discovered that truckers reported they used gas, but still had gas in the tank, and received more tickets to sell. Miller noted that retailers were permitted to build surplus in their tanks. He wrote, "No one had stopped me to ask if the trip was necessary or to examine my ration books. There was an A card sticker on the windshield."[74] Miller's trip might have been more difficult if he traveled from Florida to Maine, but his journey exposed the OPA's inability to prevent a black market.

By 1943, the black market threatened America's successful prosecution of the war. The *Senior Scholastic,* in a call to "Smash the Black Market Menace," wrote, "the general public has been too tolerant, or ignorant, of the activities of the black market."[75] The article blamed ignorance and called for teamwork. It linked American's driving directly with the war: "The Nazis know that a breakdown in our gasoline rationing program would seriously hamper the American war effort."[76]

By 1944, the Office of Price Administration recognized the black market as a serious threat to the American war effort. Chester Bowles, an OPA administrator, wrote, "every gallon of gasoline bought in the black market is an overdraft on our precious war stock: gas that is diverted from legitimate users."[77] In 1944, even with limited manpower, the OPA began to thwart the black market. First the OPA launched a public information campaign to warn the American people of "black gasoline." Second, the OPA appealed to car owners to endorse their coupons. Beginning March 1, all "B" and "C" stamps were issued with serial numbers to make stolen and counterfeit coupons easier to trace.[78] The Petroleum Industry War Council created a Black Market Committee and paid for $500,000 in newspaper ads. By the summer of 1944, a majority of the American public was informed of "black gasoline."

In 1943 the OPA cracked down on the black market. Chester Bowles declared, "We must smash the racketeers, if we are to save soldiers' lives."[79] Before the war ended, more than 4,000 stations had lost their selling licenses, and 32,500 drivers lost their ration coupons due to illegal gasoline transactions.[80] In 1944, Congress convened to address the problem.[81] Despite a diminished black market, more oil was dedicated to military use. In the latter years of the war, Americans hoped for more gasoline, but the prospects were bleak. A September 1943 *Business Week* article noted that the "PAW considers civilian supply seventh on its list of important jobs."[82]

Business Week explained that rationing was more of a problem than a solution, because "car owners turned out to be rugged individualists."[83] In June 1943, more gas came to America by barge, but the Army and Navy demanded more gasoline,[84] so much so that "Good Humor's jingling ice cream trucks were swept off the streets," and made stationary outlets.[85] By summer 1943, rationing became more stringent. Gasoline supplies for civilian use were pressured between military demands for both aviation gasoline and all-purpose gasoline.[86] *The Nation* declared, "Maybe We'll Get More Gasoline, but Outlook's None Too Bright." Civilian supply remained lowest on the PAW's triage list even with crude production oil reaching a peak in 1944. Americans supported the war effort and wanted to defeat the Nazis and the Japanese empire abroad, but the war revealed an American dependency on gasoline for the operations of daily life and a car culture of individual anonymity that permitted ease of theft and widespread complicity in a black market. Gas rationing also revealed the masterful effort of various government agencies to control automobile travel. In his final analysis, Bradley Flamm asserted that "had the American public been able, they would have used the money they were finally earning after the lean years of the 1930s to get in a car and go," and thus the efforts of the ODT to control American desires was "a remarkable accomplishment."[87]

Rubber was also necessary for the prosecution of war, while at the same time critical for life on the home front as well. The overwhelming use of rubber was in the tires of the nation's 30 million automobiles. "In 1941," wrote historian Michael J. French, "nearly 30 million passenger cars were registered in the United States, and their existing tires were both the largest reserve of rubber and a potentially disastrous drain on current stocks."[88] Approximately 75 percent of America's rubber was used in automobiles. When Japanese expansion in the 1930s threatened America's supply, the government presciently began to stockpile rubber. The stockpile reached a zenith of 634,000 long tons at the beginning of 1942, a number equal to America's consumption in 1940.[89] Concurrently, rising consumer use drained supplies. In early 1942, Japan seized British Malaya and the Netherland Indies, cutting off 97 percent of America's — and thus the allies' — rubber supply. The war effort demanded rubber for an array of conveyances and armaments, notably trucks, jeeps, tanks, and airplanes; but also rubber footwear and rubber-soled boots, millions of feet of hose, and bulletproof fuel cells for B-24 bombers.[90] Civilians whose mobility was necessary to aid the war effort needed rubber for their aging automobiles. The prospect of a debilitating rubber shortage threatened the war effort during the critical years of 1942 and 1943.[91] A Senate report confirmed military and export demands would exhaust stocks of crude rubber and that tires on civilian cars were being worn down eight times faster than they were being replaced. B. F. Goodrich's President John Collyer inquired in a wartime pamphlet: *Will America Have to Jack Up its 29,000,000 Automobiles?*[92]

Similar to what happened in automobile industry, the wartime transformation of the rubber industry became difficult and at times slow. An absence of presidential leadership and conflicts between government and industry threatened wartime operations. On June 21, 1941, with the War Production Board's Order M-15, rubber became the first controlled commodity. In addition to control, the U.S. government took several measures to increase America's rubber supply. Initially, America imported rubber from Ceylon. The U.S. government subsidized a South American rubber program, created a guayule plantation in California, promulgated a national speed limit, called a scrap-rubber drive in July 1942, and controlled and rationed rubber consumption. The Ford Motor Company attempted to develop a rubber plantation.[93] Of the patriotic scrap-rubber drive, one author wrote, "the U.S. woke to realization that it had accumulated a great national resource scattered among the basements, barns, and family discard heaps of the land."[94] The drive produced 454,000 tons, nearly a year's supply, but not enough to satisfy war demand. In 1942, the critical year of home front mobilization, the government instituted, "tire and gasoline rationing as twin weapons to enforce driver conservation of scarce rubber resources."[95] Gasoline rationing was designed to reduce the expenditure of rubber, especially in the Midwest. Lack of rubber threatened the war effort, and also threatened free use of the automobile. Americans could not perceive the need to ration. William Tuttle wrote, "Americans were beginning to believe that it was the stupidity of officialdom, rather than the exigency of war, that was threatening their free access to their automobiles."[96] Civilian use of natural rubber was reduced in 1943 to approximately one-tenth of 1941 consumption.[97]

In 1940 and 1941, the government demonstrated foresight in planning for war, but by the end of 1942 the depletion of rubber supplies was in sight. Government efforts were insufficient: "the United States had to supply not only its own military forces, but also those of its allies.... To fulfill these requirements as well as meet critical civilian needs, the country had to develop a synthetic rubber industry."[98] The need to maintain a total war effort expedited the invention of synthetic rubber. In 1940, industry and government reached an agreement to produce 108,000 tons of synthetic rubber per year.[99] Scientists and engineers developed synthetic rubber and alleviated the American need for scrap or plantation-based raw materials. In 1943, several synthetic rubber factories were constructed, and production began soon after. Firestone, B. F. Goodrich, the United States Rubber Company, and Goodyear, among others, joined the arsenal of democracy.[100] After initial bungling, "the combined know-how of production men, industrial engineers, technicians, scientists, purchasing departments, transportation experts, top executives, middle management personnel, and a host of rank-and-file employees faced each situation, found answers, and kept production in full swing."[101] The invention and mass production of synthetic rubber was a major wartime victory. William Tuttle noted, "Rubber consumption in 1942 had been 96 percent natural and 4 percent synthetic; in 1945, the totals were 15 and 85 percent, respectively." Synthetic rubber was essential to the war effort, and became a booming postwar industry. Headed into the Cold War, "the mass production of synthetic rubber thus greatly reinforced public recognition of the value of science and technology."[102]

The Reconversion Economy and a Man's Dream

World War II has been labeled the physicists' war, although chemists also made important contributions, as in the case of the Emergency Synthetic Rubber project. But we remember the physicists' contributions more, for their work led to the Atomic Age. In August 1945, World War II ended suddenly with the dropping of two atomic bombs over Hiroshima and Nagasaki, Japan. American policy makers and economic planners had anticipated an allied victory beginning in mid–1944, however, and discussions concerning the reconversion of the economy to a peacetime footing began to take on more substance and significance after the Battle of the Bulge.[103] For the American automobile industry, meeting the pent-up demand from consumers who had not been able to buy new cars since early 1942 was an unprecedented opportunity. And, not surprisingly perhaps, new players wanted to get in on the act. With huge wartime production plants empty and the federal government eager to assist those at the margins rather than the center of the economy, entrepreneurs, including Henry Kaiser, Joseph Frazer, Powel Crosley, and Preston Tucker formulated ambitious plans to enter the marketplace and challenge the Big Three.[104]

Until recently, the reconversion economy has been largely neglected by historians, although auto "buff" historians have been writing marque histories that focused on this period for some time. Of all the postwar figures, perhaps the most interesting and controversial was Preston Tucker, a name resurrected in more recent years due to the 1988 film on his life directed by Francis Ford Coppola. Coppola's interest in the Tucker went back to his childhood, when his father ordered but never received the car. Later, the younger Coppola would research the firm and collect Tuckers. Two of his cars, along with twenty others, were used in the film. With meticulous detail and a final script written by Arnold Schulman and approved by

Tucker's three sons after several rewrites, Coppola rescued the man and his car from the mists of time.[105]

Born in Capac Michigan in 1903, Preston Tucker had "gasoline in his blood" at an early age.[106] He worked as an office boy at Cadillac, then briefly at the Ford Motor Company before selling Studebakers, Stutzs, Chryslers, and Pierce-Arrows. A visionary, by the early 1930s he had become involved in an aviation engine firm, the takeover of the bankrupt Marmon Company, and the Miller-Tucker Company, a builder of racing engines. On the eve of World War II, Tucker was living in Ypsilanti, Michigan, where he designed a "tank"—a war vehicle that was capable of going over 100 mph, a design apparently rejected by the military for going too fast. However, his Plexiglas rotating gun turret was a success, and was employed on numerous military aircraft during the war. The turret gained Tucker considerable recognition. During the war, Tucker partnered for a time with another charismatic businessman, New Orleans boat builder Andrew Jackson Higgins. After the war, he moved forward with his dream to build the world's finest performing and safest automobile.

Initially, Tucker's chances to succeed were good, and since the War Assets Administration made factories available first to independent entrepreneurs, Tucker acquired a wartime plant used by Dodge and located in south Chicago. But Tucker, like others who were attempting to break into the automobile business at that time, failed to realize just how much money was required to do so. To raise money, Tucker had to sell dealer franchises, and that sent him on a collision course with the Securities and Exchange Commission (SEC). SEC investigations resulted in a decline in investor confidence, which, coupled with opposition from Michigan senator Homer Ferguson and the Justice Department, by 1948 put a dark cloud over the entire effort. Despite this adversity that some have suggested was technological suppression on the part of powerful interests that included the Big Three, some 51 Tucker '48s were produced, and these highly innovative cars remain among the most sought-after collectible cars in America.

The Tucker '48 was designed by Alex Tremulis, who had previously worked at Auburn during the 1930s and served in the Army Air Force during the war. This innovative car had a rear engine, was streamlined with doors that curved into the roof, and was capable of a top speed of more than 100 mph while getting more than 20 mpg. It was a safe car as well, with a padded dash, a "crash basement" for its front seat passenger, tubeless tires, independent suspension and a pop-out windshield. But because of the roadblocks raised in obtaining supplies like steel, SEC investigations, press leaks, and a well-orchestrated rumor campaign, the company shut down in August 1948. In his disappointment, Tucker published an open letter in June 1948 concerning the obstacles he was facing. He wrote:

> But there is another group—a very powerful group—which for two years has carried on a carefully organized campaign to prevent the motoring public from ever getting their hands on the wheel of a Tucker. These people have tried to introduce spies in our plant. They have endeavored to bribe and corrupt loyal Tucker employees.... But it hasn't stopped there.
>
> They even have spokesmen in high places in Washington. As a direct result of their influence, Tucker dealers all over the country—men of character and standing in their communities—have been harassed and grilled by agents of the government and Congressional Investigating Committees.
>
> When the day comes that anyone can bend our country's laws and lawmakers to serve selfish, competitive ends, that day democratic government dies.[107]

In a publicized trial Tucker was acquitted of fraud, but the damage was already done, and all that was left for him was to go to Brazil and attempt to build his last dream vehicle,

Henry Ford II driving the first 1949 Ford off the assembly line at Rouge Plant, April 27, 1948. Henry Ford II literally saved the Ford Motor Company from ruin by pushing for this new model, and more importantly hiring the "Whiz Kids" to implement managerial and accounting controls at the firm (from the Collections of the Henry Ford).

the Tucker Carioca, a kit car that supposedly could be assembled with only one wrench. Tucker may have been victim of powerful forces, or he may just have been a bad businessman. His experience may well have been reflective of life in America during the early Cold War. Whatever the case, the dream for a truly revolutionary post-war automobile was gone.

Incremental changes coupled with annual style makeovers would lead the American automobile industry down the road that would end in the appearance of the dinosaur in the driveway by the end of the 1950s.

8

THE GOLDEN AGE OF THE AUTOMOBILE: THE 1950S IN AMERICA

No one, I imagine, escapes the authentic involvement with this gathering symbol of our pervasive materialism. But the 50th annual Auto Show, it seems to me, gives the lie to surveys ... and to motivation researchers who suggest that at the root of America's disproportionate reverence for automobility there is something profoundly sexual. Few people give ultimate devotion to sex; their really ultimate devotion goes to religions like this one.[1]

In his essay "The Altar of Automobility," a young Martin Marty, later destined to be one of America's preeminent theologians, recorded his observations after visiting the 1958 Chicago Automobile Show. Marty argued that the enthusiasm and passions surrounding the automobile had created a true, universal, and practical religion that was directed towards the "dinosaur in the driveway." For Marty, passions for automobiles in America were fueled by more than just sex; rather, the automobile was worshiped by true believers. And during the 1950s the church of the automobile, like the Protestant Church in America, had an unprecedented number of followers. Only later would allegiances begin to wane.

The 1950s proved to be a golden era for the automobile in America.[2] Particularly after 1955, it was a time characterized by cars featuring tailfins and chrome, high horsepower V-8 engines, and numerous accessories. The car influenced culture as no other technology of the day.[3] Yet was it really a golden age, or an era so complex that it defies any simple characterization?

This complex interaction between human beings and this machine was reflected in contemporary literature, music, and film. While these cultural manifestations of automobility — or at least the ones scholars tend to focus on — often dealt with troubling matters like alienation and rebellion, the average family preferred to drive on without much thought concerning the larger issues raised by concerned observers, the Beats, and critics of the new lascivious rock and roll music. Despite the uncertainty and anxiety of the period, for many it was an era of smooth rides and good times.[4] Or so our faded memories want us to believe.[5]

During the 1950s, and indeed in previous decades as well, the family car was more than transportation. It was part of the family, and like children in the family, nurtured and cherished. Perhaps it was a substitute for a lover or girlfriend, as in the case of the tale Stephen King spins in *Christine,* where a 1957 Plymouth Fury both is loved and loves (to the death). This passion between person and machine was well expressed in Henry Gregor Felsen's *Hot Rod,* published in 1950. The book's key character is Bud Crayne, a 17-year-old high school student. Crane is a loner and often alone, as his parents died long ago. Only a fickle girlfriend, approval from school mates, and especially a car he built from the ground up keep Bud going.

No matter what his mood or his feeling, his trouble or his joy, it made everything right and good to be guiding his car, the car he had built, that belonged to him, that owed everything it was to him. Not a day passed without Bud's taking time for a spin. It was more than a ride; it was more than speeding; more than killing time. In some ways these daily sessions on the road were his hours of meditation, of true expression, the balm for his soul and the boast of his spirit. In these flying hours he had sought himself out, molded himself into what he was, and found his creed.

Bud's car, variously called his baby, hop-up, strip down, roadster, heap, hot rod, jalopy or set of wheels, was like Bud himself. In a way he had built a mechanical representation of his life, and its oddly-assorted parts could be likened to his patch-work past.[6]

There were many Buds in America during the 1950s. The typical family car (perhaps like my own family's 1954 blue and white Chevrolet Belair) often had its exterior lovingly waxed for protection with Simoniz, and its interior protected with plastic seat covers. More than occasionally the car was accessorized with steering wheel spinners, fender skirts, and continental kits. Interestingly enough, when in 1958 *Life* featured a young man living in Wichita, Kansas, purchasing his first car, the things done after bringing the 1951 "Merc" home were: (1) remove chrome on the front and hood, and (2) buy an imitation shrunken head to hang from the rear view mirror![7] Thus for a large number of young men (how many women is less clear), this interest in car care and the improvement of looks and performance became a hobby. Hot rods, sports cars, or customs captivated many who during this prosperity decade had increased leisure time and disposable incomes. In a world of increasing conformity (punch cards and time cards, for example, were prevalent) brought on by the stresses of the Cold War and competition with the Soviets, these vehicles gave their owners a distinctive individuality, and, if desired, entrance into a subculture of fellow enthusiasts. It was also a sexy hobby, unlike another popular pastime during that day, stamp collecting. Cars were sex objects, and it was perceived that working and riding in cars enhanced one's sexiness. A colored piece of paper could never be loved quite like a car. As social critic John Keats argued in 1958, "automobiles were love objects from the start. Venerated, called friends, lovingly polished and assigned the virtues of ponies, veterans, and dogs."[8]

The tailfin of a 1960 Desoto (author photograph).

Despite critiques concerning the automobile and its design, place, and purpose in American society, this intense love affair with the car was unparalleled. Perhaps, as David Gartman has suggested, the two-toned, V-8 powered car of the era was nothing more than an opiate for hardworking Americans during the Cold War era. According to Gartman, the automobile, no matter what model, was essentially the same. It served to lessen the rather harsh realities of a competitive capitalist system with its class

1957 Cadillac Eldorado Brougham. During the heyday of fins and chrome, this car was the best of the best. GM lost money on every car made, but it was the ultimate symbol of excess and success (author photograph).

structure, repetition, dehumanization, and repressive impulses. In sum, it was at the heart of a "contradictory system."[9] Therefore, during the 1950s, the car was a symbol and an expression of freedom at a time in American life when autonomy was in retreat.

The Automobile and Civil Rights

Abstractions concerning freedom aside, the car was a real vehicle of freedom for Blacks living in the South during the civil rights struggles of the decade. Thomas J. Sugrue has written that the automobile enabled Blacks to escape "the insults of Jim Crow." More specifically, Sugrue states that, "the car provided southern blacks a way to subvert Jim Crow. Driving gave southern blacks a degree of freedom that they did not have on public transportation or in most public places."[10] And Warren Brown, writing in *The Washington Post*, recalled that in 1955,

> Long before the legendary Rosa Parks defied a white Montgomery bus driver's order to move to the back of the bus, the city's blacks had grown weary of such assaults on their dignity. Perhaps it was an accumulation of those frustrations that prompted Parks, on that fateful Thursday, December 1, 1955, to refuse to give up her seat near the front of the bus to allow a white man to sit down. Whatever the cause, she did what she did and blacks in Montgomery supported her by refusing to ride the city's buses until they could sit wherever they wanted to sit.

During that boycott, blacks used personal cars to create what was called a "private taxi" system. They shared rides, carried one another to work and to school — and to churches. Black churches bought station wagons to help support the "private taxi" operation.[11]

Outside of Blacks living in the South, few of us living at that time recognized that we were becoming more like the enemy we were attempting to defeat, or that automobiles were soothing the angry emotions brought on by work routines as well as class and wealth distinctions. Whether it was the Rosenberg case or McCarthyite investigations, these repressive events in American life seemingly did not affect or disturb the common American. Gartman's Marxist analysis has limited explanatory power in reconstructing an era that was inherently complex. Further, those who drove the cars of the 1950s would dispute his claim that all car models were essentially the same, and that only minimal differences existed between them. Indeed, driving a 1955 Cadillac was quite different from driving a 1955 Plymouth. It was not just chrome strips and more cylinders that distinguished the makes of that era — it was build quality, materials, performance, and engineering. No single explanatory model can tell the automobile history story, with its inevitable twists, turns, chance circumstances, and irrationalities.

As a distraction from the possibilities and fears of destruction wrought by the atomic

Detectives examine a burned out police car in Brooklyn during riots, 1964 (Library of Congress).

bomb, Americans were encouraged to consume.[12] British economic historian Avner Offer has provided a number of interesting points related to the American consumption of automobiles in the 1950s, tying purchases to notions of well-being, satisfaction, pleasure, and comfort.[13] To begin with, auto companies during the 1950s offered a large variety of models to protect themselves from rapid shifts in consumer tastes. Secondly, model change demanded a rapid retooling process and new product turnaround, and this was accomplished during the decade. This time compression resulted in increased prices to consumers, as the retooling costs rose nearly eight times per car between 1952 and 1957. Additionally, and as one might expect with the enhanced competition to court new customers, advertising expenditures on the part of both manufacturers and dealers sharply increased, as did depreciation with which owners were ultimately saddled. Finally, quality commensurately decreased; the notion of "American Made" as standing for products of the highest quality for the price certainly was more myth than reality by the end of the decade, at least in the automobile business. Due to these and other factors, an interesting purchasing dynamic was taking place among American consumers as the decade of the 1950s unfolded. Namely, Americans became less loyal to automobile brands, and tended to buy down rather than up. For an example, upon trade-in, a Pontiac owner would buy an accessorized Chevrolet rather than a plain Pontiac, as somehow the accessories conveyed more status than the marque. This new pattern of consumer behavior was the result of the strategy formulated by Ford executive Lewis D. Crusoe.[14] It took him eight years to fully execute, but in 1957 Crusoe finally succeeded in blurring product lines with the widespread acceptance of accessorized Ford models. His approach led to Ford eclipsing Chevrolet in sales in 1957, and concurrently diminishing the purchases of mid-sized Buicks and Pontiacs. Ironically, however, the expansion of the low-priced car segment also weakened demand for the Edsel a year later, although there were other reasons that contributed to the hasty demise of the horse-collar designed disaster from Dearborn. Edsel Ford's legacy surely deserved better.

Who purchased all of these automobiles during this time of unprecedented prosperity and social mobility? In terms of new car purchases, the top two income quintiles of Americans purchased approximately 70 percent of all new cars. The lower ends of the income spectrum bought used cars, a phenomenon yet to be explored by historians.

And while homes and neighborhoods were key signifiers of class and income, the automobile was more than that, for it was status on wheels. It was the ultimate symbol of personhood, yet ironically often bought on time and with marginal financial resources to back up the loan. And despite what was not in the bank, what one wore and drove was often interpreted as being an accurate reflection of class. For example, in *American Graffiti,* Toad, the goofy but tragic nerd, acquires cool wheels (a 1958 Impala hardtop) and expects his problems in attracting girls to be over. To a degree, that does happen to Toad for one night in the film. In real life, however, did cool wheels have the power to attract pretty girls? Or was it nothing more than a deceitful delusion? Can the automobile really cause us to escape from the dark side of ourselves?

Whether it was actually true or not, children living in the 1950s believed that what your father drove told everyone in the neighborhood quite a bit about your family. Unlike today, where so many of our cars appear similar due to aerodynamic design considerations, every major brand had its own distinctive look. Virtually every boy became a car spotter, one who could pick out a DeSoto from a Plymouth at 500 yards. Each car model had a distinctive grill or face, a huge bumper with bullets or "Dagmars," easily distinguished set of rear tail

lights, and an overall profile that included for much of the decade a chromed hood orna-
ment.[15] It was only after safety issues surfaced that the pot-metal ornaments depicting birds,
rockets, jets, Indians, or sleek women sadly disappeared. At least in the 1950s, there was no
confusion concerning the branding of automobiles.

Hot Rod

The car hobby grew to be quite complex by the mid–1950s, and it involved both engine
and body modifications along with creative painting techniques. Pre–World War II antecedents
included the organization of dry lakes racing at Muroc, California, in 1931 under the leadership of speed equipment manufacturer George Riley and sponsorship of the Gilmore Oil
Company.[16] Racing at the lakes continued to 1941. Hot rodding took off after World War II,
however, and it is clear from reading early issues of *Hot Rod Magazine* that the phenomenon,
while focused in Southern California and dry lakes racing, was really nationwide in scope.
By 1948 numerous dirt track activities in the Midwest (at Columbus, Indiana, and Dayton,
Ohio, for example) featured designs similar to Southern California cars.

One example of the diffusion of hot rod culture from west to east involved the Granatelli
brothers of Chicago. During the late 1940s, Joe Granatelli, who had constructed a hot rod in
Chicago, drove it to the West Coast, where he picked up parts to stock the family speed shop,
Grancor.[17] The rise of this postwar phenomenon on a national scale led to the remarkable
success of publisher Robert Petersen, whose *Hot Rod Magazine* was first published in January
1948 and distributed at the Los Angeles National Guard Armory Automobile Equipment Display and Hot Rod Exposition. After an initial experiment with the inclusion of fiction in the
first issue, readership demands focused the periodical on two major topics: technology and
pretty girls. In fact, the remaining eleven issues of *Hot Rod Magazine* in 1948 featured a photo
of a very pretty Hollywood
model holding a car part!
Pretty girls attract young
men, and at its core hot
rodding was all about
autonomous technology —
young people tinkering
on limited budgets and
working in their garages.
These hot rodders and custom car builders, using trial
and error methods, made
significant improvements
in engine horsepower and
chassis design. It was all
about going fast and looking good, first on the streets
and the lakes and then later
more on drag strips and

A classic 1950s hot rod (author photograph).   custom car shows.[18]

The tensions of this era relating to rodding were encapsulated in Henry Gregor Felsen's *Hot Rod*, a novel directed to early 1950s youth but that became so popular that it remained in print to the mid–1960s. The central figure of the story is Bud Crayne, with an accompanying cast of half a dozen high school students from the small town of Avondale. As mentioned above, Bud is a car builder and street racer, and while a social outsider, also has as his girlfriend the pretty but mercurial cheerleader LaVerne. Overconfident of his driving skills and easily manipulated by his girlfriend and rivals, Bud sets a record driving from his town to another. In the process, he leads the police on an exciting chase. Bud escapes the consequences of his actions, however, as he strikes a bargain with the local police and a school teacher, agreeing to participate in a test in driving skills, a so-called roadeo. The concern of authorities is street racing and "teenacide," and their hope is to use Bud to convince others that driver's education is of value. Since he did not take lessons, however, and despite his prowess behind the wheel, Bud does not place first in this event. Nevertheless, due to a tragic accident in which several teens in his town, including estranged girl friend LaVerne, are killed while imitating Bud's driving, Bud gets to the state competition. The carnage aside, the story has a happy ending, as Americans of the 1950s would like, for Bud, now much wiser, goes to engineering school to improve the modern motor car. His past somehow now forgotten and forgiven, he nonetheless left a wreckage not only of cars, but of lives. The assumption — which was that of educational leaders of that day — was that education can cure teenage driving impulses, and that properly directed, rodding can be a healthy way to let off steam. However, the author does acknowledge toward the end of this book that risky behavior was "a question of glands."[19]

Felsen's writing about hot rodders and the police took a very different turn four years later in his *Cup of Fury*. In this story, the reader is introduced to a young hot rod enthusiast, Link Aller, not terribly different in character from Bud Crayne. Unlike the understanding policeman in *Hot Rod*, however, in *Cup of Fury* there is a new sheriff in town, and he teaches young Link a brutal lesson in obedience and respect at their first meeting. After Link is caught spinning tires in the school parking lot, policeman Kern introduces himself this way:

> The cop didn't say anything. There was a click and before Link could set himself, the door of the police car was hurled open, and smashed against him. It seemed to hit him all at once, from his head to his knees. He was stunned where it hit against the side of his face, and bruised where it hit his chest and legs.... Holding his light inches away from Link's eyes, Kern used his wrist to push Link's chin up, and his head back. Link's eyes were glassy. Except for the hold Kern had on him, he would have fallen. His mouth was open and he was fighting for breath. Kern pressed against him, choking him a little. Link's left eye was beginning to swell and change color. Kern maintained his pressure as Link sucked air into his throat in long, noisy, tortured gasps. His eyes cleared and his limp body became rigid. He stared into the light that was being directed into his eyes, trying to remember what had happened.[20]

Most likely, the police of the 1950s in reality treated young men more like Link Aller than Bud Crayne. It was an era before such issues as police brutality and human rights were public concerns.

In addition to Felsen's fiction, the hot rod was also the subject of songs — actually many of them by the early 1950s. The seminal lyrics of many versions that followed was that written by George Wilson and performed by Arkie Shibley and his Mountain Dew Boys in 1950. "Hot Rod Race" proved to be the precursor of many future songs, including "Hot Rod Lincoln," the best-known versions of which were performed by Johnny Bond in 1960 and Commander Cody & His Lost Planet Airmen in 1972. Initially, the song told the story of a family trip from San Pedro in a Ford that turned into a race with a Mercury. Surprisingly, at the end both the Ford and the Mercury are blown off the road by "a kid, in a hopped up Model A." Later, the Ford and Mercury were replaced by a Cadillac and a Lincoln, but the continuity through the long chain of versions is obvious.[21]

As one might expect, numerous B-grade films featured teens and hot rods during the 1950s—Hot Rod (1950), Hot Rod Rumble (1957), Drag Strip Girl (1957), Hot Rod Gang (1958), The Ghost of Drag Strip Hollow (1959), and finally, perhaps the best known of the group, Hot Rod Girl (1956). Following Felsen's story line, Hot Rod Girl was about an attempt on the part of authorities to co-opt teen hot rodders by getting them off the street and onto the drag strip. Its actors and actresses are teens who look more like they are in their mid- to late 20s and early 30s. Starring Lori Nelson as the "hot rod girl," the budget for the film was so tight that Nelson drove her own 1955 Thunderbird to save money. With Chuck Conners playing the role of a sympathetic policeman and Frank Gorshin as the character "flat-top," the highly unlikely and often silly plot involves a confrontation of "chicken," several fatal accidents, and a happy ending. The message of the film seemed clear: in the war between good and evil that takes place in the minds and lives of teens, understanding elders know best and incorrigible rebels meet with an untimely demise.[22]

Shifting from cultural manifestations to the technology that made the hot rod possible, perhaps the best example of this tinkering that led to cutting-edge technologies was the work in Southern California of Stuart Hilborn, who worked as a chemist in a paint laboratory during the day and raced in his spare time. Using scientific logic on one hand and primitive machine tooling methods on the other, Hilborn moved from using an arrangement of Stromberg carburetors injecting fuel into each cylinder to true mechanical fuel injection. Hilborn's system was relatively simple, so much so that the shade-tree rodder could employ a state-of-the-art technological system that rivaled that of Mercedes Benz 300SL. He was a true pioneer in developing a technology that is now universally used as a fuel delivery system in automobiles, although this technology now employs computer controls and a vast number of sensors.[23]

The hobby demanded not only new technology and expertise, but also equipment suppliers, and Hilborn marketed his fuel injection apparatus by the 1950s. Other prominent equipment manufacturers included Vic Edelbrock, Ed Iskenderian, and Phil Weiand, who ported, polished and in other ways modified Ford flathead V-8s in Los Angeles area speed shops. Body shop men like George Barris and Ed "Big Daddy" Roth chopped and channeled old 1932 Model B and 1928–1931 Model A and 1908–1927 Model T bodies and began lowering and cleaning up the chrome from late '30s and early '40s convertibles. Trial and error methods were even extended to the formulation of car paints, as colors like candy color red came out of southern California body shops during the late 1950s. Using these new paint formulations, Von Dutch (Kenneth Howard) earned a reputation for the finest in pinstriping and flames.[24]

Sports Cars on American Tracks, and The Red Car

Other popular car magazines of the 1950s included Car Craft, Rod & Custom, Road and Track and Motor Trend. Mechanix Illustrated had perhaps the most influential automobile writer of the post–World War II era, "Uncle Tom" McCahill. A Yale University graduate who later owned a large black Labrador named Joe, McCahill loved dogs but had little success with his three wives and despised children. "Uncle Tom" pulled no punches concerning his road tests and his preference for the better-handling European models that were just making it to American shores. In his 1954 *The Modern Sports Car* McCahill wrote,

> The typical Detroit product is designed for tender-bottomed dowagers and weak-backed Certified Public Accountants. Detroit is reaching for a ride that would simulate floating in a bubble-filled tub on the Queen Mary in a gentle sea, which, if developed at a Cadillac Square, will be like the invention of Penicillin, splitting the atom, and little boys-finding-out-about-little-girls, all rolled into a ball.
>
> These Detroit disciples of pogo-stick springing have gone a long way toward accomplishing this aim. They have induced our larger tire companies to build super-super balloon tires to complement their foam-rubber seats. They've pushed the engine of the car so far forward into the nose to get the passengers off the rear axle that all resemblance to balanced weight distribution between the front and rear has ceased to exist.
>
> It is amazing how millions of aging Americans spend a goodly part of their lives worrying about future financial security, while every day they live the life of a clay pigeon on a skeet field—driving the family hack to the grocery store. In automobiles, the intelligent human animal likes to know—as he drills down the turnpike at eighty—if he has to make a fast swerve to avoid a crash, or to compensate for a blow-out, he has the equipment under him to meet these situations without fear.[25]

Not beholden to the automobile companies who paid for advertising, McCahill had the largest following of his generation. And if something was wrong with a design, McCahill was quick to point that out, using his gift of glib humor in an unforgettable way. For example, McCahill, in his road test of a Jowett Javelin, commented that the ashtray "looks like it was invented by Lord Whiffenpoof after he was shot in the rump during the Boer War. Like the cup your favorite dentist tells you to spit your teeth into, it hinges out but spends most of its time just rattling."[26]

With journalists like McCahill expounding on the virtues of good automobile handling and design, sports car enthusiasts became more prevalent during the decade, especially encouraged by the importation of British sports cars that included the MG-TC, -TD, -TF-1500, and -A. With the UK home government setting incentives to earn export dollars and to help pay for World War II debts, Jaguar, Austin-Healey, Rootes (Sunbeam) and Triumph all came ashore to meet the demand of those who wanted more handling agility than power. Key to this story were New York City dealers Max Hoffman and Fergus Motors, both of whom who did much to forge relationships with a number of European manufacturers. The market consisted of middle-class enthusiasts and above. Soon accessory suppliers entered a marketplace that included MG Mitten, Moss Motors, Paxton Superchargers, and Wilhelm B. Haan of Beverly Hills.

A number of tracks became popular weekend haunts for the sports car crowd, including Watkins Glen in New York and Sebring in Florida. Sports car racing moved from road courses to airports and finally to dedicated facilities. Major events were reported in *Road and Track* and *Sports Car Graphic*. The premier races early in the decade were the Pan-American road races, where Mercedes, Porsches and Ferraris dueled with factory modified Fords, Lincolns and Hudson Hornets.[27]

Just as Felsen's *Hot Rod* stimulated a generation of young people to build their own customized coupes and roadsters, Don Stanford's *The Red Car*, first published in 1954, whetted the appetite of many a young person to own a two-seated imported sports car. These vehicles, typically small and by American standards often underpowered — unless one was talking about higher-end Austin-Healeys, Jaguars, or Aston Martins — and were the antithesis of the dinosaur in the driveway. Driving a sports car was for the most part a top-down and noisy experience, but above all the driver was an uncommon individual in an era of conformity. Perhaps that is why during the Cold War *The Red Car* became the best-selling car book of all time, with more than two million copies sold, many purchased by teenagers who bought 45 cent paperback versions from Scholastic Book Services.

At the heart of *The Red Car* was a red MG-TC, rescued from a junk pile by a Colorado rancher's son with the assistance of a French-born mechanic with a troubled past. Young Hap Adams was taken by a wreck that had "looked almost alive. It had a personality all its own — an arrogant, insolent, challenging way of looking you right in the eye and saying, "Drop dead!"[28] And indeed, with the help of Frenchy Lascelle the car is rebuilt and later successfully raced. While the pair experiences a hair-raising crash after which Hap holds on to a fender as Frenchy steers the car to the finish line, it is the life-changing experience for Hap that is both striking and enduring:

> As Hap moved off to meet his parents he cast one last fond glance at the little red car. Battered it was, and dirty, and weary and worn; but still with that arrogant cocky "drop dead!" way of carrying itself. It had been a long hard day, and the little car looked a happy tired athlete after a game well played, but she still looked ready to go anywhere, with anybody, to do anything.
>
> And that, thought Hap with deep satisfaction, is what a real sports car is. Not just a specially bred racing machine, useless for any other purpose; but a car you could race all day and win with, and then wash a bit and proudly take your mother to dinner or your girl to the movies that night. A car you could live with, and could love; a luxury, yes, but the best of all possible luxuries to own.[29]

Filmmakers used sports cars as the centerpiece of their plots. For example, an early Corvette was Mike Hammer's (played by Ralph Meeker) mode of transportation in the murder mystery *Kiss Me Deadly*, released in 1955. A second example was Roger Corman's 1955 *The Fast and the Furious*, starring Dorothy Malone and John Ireland. The weak plot focused on a wrongly-accused fugitive and a pretty hostage, who incidentally owned and raced a Jaguar XK-120. *The Fast and the Furious* was all about sports cars, the types who drove them, and the skills needed to keep rpm's up while road racing through tight curves. With a happy conclusion, the movie suggested that sports car types need not be well-to-do, well-bred, and wear fashionable clothing.[30] The photographic record of the decade suggests otherwise, however. Racing then and now involves cars that are "money pits," and only the wealthy elite could afford the expenses of racing and the social scene that was a part of this lifestyle.[31]

The influence of the Jaguar XK-120 on American life went beyond B-grade movies. At GM, Harley Earl had paid considerable attention to the Jaguar, and it was not coincidental that the new 1953 Corvette had the same 102-inch wheelbase. The Corvette was a truly innovative vehicle, however, particularly in terms of body construction.[32] Consisting of plastic and reinforced fiberglass panels, the Corvette had jet-age taillights and a toothy grill. When it was introduced at the New York Waldorf car show in January 1953, public acclaim was so great that GM quickly moved into production, but performance was initially lacking. Ed Cole's engineering group tweaked its six-cylinder "Blue Flame" engine with a three carburetor setup, but it lacked in power and by 1955 was in jeopardy of being cancelled due to the remarkable success of the Ford Thunderbird. In response, a new 265 cubic inch V-8 was installed, and that was the start of a performance legend. Key to this transition was the figure of Zora Arkus-Duntov.[33] Duntov was in attendance at the Corvette's introduction in 1953, and three months later was hired by GM. It was Duntov who pushed for the Corvette to enter racing, and who designed the Duntov cam that enabled the intake and exhaust valves to be open far longer, making for a better breathing and more powerful engine. With this and other performance enhancements, a team of four Corvettes successfully raced at Sebring in 1956. The GM board could not have been happier, and any notion of canceling the Corvette program was put aside. From then on the Corvette was America's sports car, made easier by Ford's decision in 1958 to increase the size of the Thunderbird and to make it a luxury model. Its equation with sexuality (and perhaps a vagina) was later immortalized in Prince's breakout hit, "Little Red Corvette," released in 1983, in which the artist tells of a one night stand with a beautiful but promiscuous woman.

The Thunderbird was the result of a crash program to counter General Motors' Corvette.[34] In the fall of 1952, chief Ford designer Frank Hershey learned of the GM project, and with the assistance of William Boyer began work on a car that was to have a distinctive American and Ford appearance. Initially, the car was named after Henry Ford's estate, Fair Lane, but subsequently, and after an employee contest, the name Thunderbird was assigned to a car that was to be ten to fifteen miles per hour faster than a full-sized American car. From the beginning it was to be quite different from the Corvette. The Thunderbird was to have a V-8 rather than a six-cylinder engine, both manual and automatic transmission options in contrast to the Corvette's Powerglide automatic, and a level of comfort that included power steering, brakes, seat, and windows. The spartan Corvette, fitted with side curtains instead of roll-up windows, simply could not match the Thunderbird for luxury and comfort.

The concept for the Thunderbird reflected the automotive passions of the early 1950s, an era during which there was significant interest in V-8 engines and performance, European sports cars, and California customs. As a result, the style of the first Thunderbirds mixed a touch of European influence with such hot rod features as a hood scoop, "frenched" headlights, and dummy fender louvers. Despite occasional references to it in advertising literature as a sports car, Ford maintained that it was a personal rather than sports car, and therefore quite different from its primary American rival, the Chevrolet Corvette.

Clark Gable could be seen in his '55 cruising Hollywood; Marilyn Monroe owned a '56 model painted in Sunset Coral. With its introduction, the Thunderbird, named after a mythical bird of great power and beauty in Indian lore, became the trendsetting automobile of the 1950s. Initially a two-seater and then in 1958 extended to four seats, the Thunderbird was the definition of a personal, luxury car during an age of excess.

Songs about the T-Bird invariably followed. In 1957, Gene Vincent & His Blue Caps released "Pink Thunderbird." Vincent crooned that his pink Thunderbird had a raked front seat, and that along with other things he owned, it was all yours "if you say I do, I do, I do."[35] Two years later, the Delicates sang "Black & White Thunderbird," employing rather moronic lyrics exclaiming that cruising in this car led them to be "happy as we can be." Looking back, songs like these seem astoundingly simplistic, considering the sophistication of the cars and the complex psychology of the teenagers who were supposedly in them.[36]

Some Critics Surface: Safety and the Environment

While songs of the 1950s praised the car for what it could do for one's image and spirits, the decade also witnessed negative diatribes against the automobile and its influence in

American life. In his *The Automobile Age*, James Flink discusses the most visible of those voices of dissent.[37] In particular, John Keats' book *The Insolent Chariots* represented this perspective, as did Vance Packard's *The Hidden Persuaders*. Other thoughtful commentators included S.I. Hayakawa and Lewis Mumford. On the more grass-roots level, however, the Consumers Union and monthly articles in *Consumer Reports* tell a more critical story of the automobile in American life that balances the ever-present accolades that one finds in the mountain of "buff" literature. The topics of automobile safety, performance, economy, and product quality were found in virtually every issue of *Consumer Reports* during the 1950s.[38]

During the 1950s, however, in addition to issues concerning styling, much of this questioning of the place of the automobile in American society was due to the horrific toll that automobile accidents had taken in America. In 1952, automobile writer Ken Purdy remarked,

> The U.S. makes, crashes, and junks more cars than any other nation. Every 15 seconds or so, we smash a car into some unyielding surface, haul it away, mop up the blood, and hurry on.... The automobile is here to stay, but half of the fun has gone out of it. It was not necessary that the American car grow 500 pounds heavier than it need be. It was not absolutely essential that it develop a huge prairie of a hood for the poor driver to peer across.[39]

Automobile accidents are still an issue today; fatal accidents occur almost daily in every area of the U.S., and typically the scene is swept up and sanitized within hours, with the only reminder of the incident being the occasional cross and flowers on the side of the road.

During the decade of the 1950s, fatal accidents were particularly devastating in terms of human lives taken per capita, the consequence of a lack of safety features on automobiles and the fact that brakes did not keep up with the horsepower generated by the new V-8 engines. Yet, as the decade unfolded, per capita statistics belie the notion that the carnage was getting worse over time. Table 8 lists accident statistics for the 1950s.

TABLE 8. AUTOMOBILE ACCIDENT DEATHS, 1950–1959

Year	Number of Deaths	Estimated Number of Vehicles (Billions)	Estimated Vehicle Miles (Billions)	Estimated Number of Drivers (Millions)
1950	34,763	49.2	458	62.2
1951	36,996	51.9	491	64.4
1952	37,794	53.3	514	66.8
1953	37,956	56.3	544	69.9
1954	35,586	58.6	562	72.2
1955	38,426	62.8	606	74.7
1956	39,628	65.2	631	77.9
1957	38,702	67.6	647	79.6
1958	36,981	68.8	665	81.5
1959	37,910	72.1	700	84.5

Source: National Safety Council, "Motor-Vehicle Deaths and Rates," *Accident Facts* (1988), p. 104.

The accident was a favorite scene in film and theme in fiction. For example, in a 1953 issue of *Esquire*, Robert Switzer told a story through an eyewitness to a "head-on," the consequence of speed and poor judgment. The scene was described as follows:

> There was only one person in the Buick and she wasn't exactly in it. She was three-quarters through the windshield. The crash through the glass and the rolling dive down the embankment had pulped her. There was a good moon and he could see teeth glistening in the brown mess.... He went on to the other car and found three people. The driver was a small man, so the steering shaft had come through at the base of the neck ... he turned the woman's head so

she would not drown in blood and then he removed the little girl.... It could be worse.... Just two dead. One to a side. An even break.[40]

Despite this carnage, until the 1950s Americans, and particularly the car companies, paid little attention to the problem of automobile safety. The typical American automobile had dashboards with numerous hard protrusions, no seatbelts, poor brakes and tires, non-collapsible steering columns, doors that opened on impact, soft seats and suspension systems, and windshield glass that shattered easily. These features were the consequence of manufacturer neglect, consumer preferences, the psychology of driving, and the failure of the government to further public interest in this matter.

Despite obvious evidence to the contrary, industry representatives maintained that drivers and their behavior, not automobile design features, caused accidents and injuries. Nevertheless, several forces for change converged during the late 1950s and the early 1960s. Indeed, by the end of the 1960s, the previously unassailable industry was brought to its knees by the rising tide of public opinion, regulatory legislation, and a newly created federal bureaucracy.

One major reason for the new emphasis on auto safety was enhanced technical knowledge about the "second crash"; that is, the collision of the automobile's passengers with the interior after the initial exterior impact. Wartime studies conducted on aircraft cockpit injuries at Wright-Patterson Air Force Base in Ohio and Cornell University Medical College in New York were subsequently extended to similar phenomena inside automobiles at the Cornell Aeronautical Laboratory. Evidence from these studies, coupled with the work of the Detroit plastic surgeon Claire Straith on "guest" passenger injuries, clearly suggested that relatively simple design modifications could save lives and prevent serious injuries. In 1955 and 1956, the industry was confronted with these facts and failed to respond with enthusiasm. The industry thus lost any chance to remain autonomous with regard to safety and design, and federal legislation addressing design safety passed a decade later.[41]

A similar situation took place during the 1950s with regard to automobile emissions. In this case, the story centered on Los Angeles, not only because the region had witnessed the growth of automobile use from a little over 1.1 million cars in 1940 to 2.3 million vehicles in 1954, but also because of the area's unique geophysical and meteorological conditions. Incomplete combustion caused some 850 tons of hydrocarbons to enter the atmosphere every day in Los Angeles County in 1954. Eye irritation and damage to vegetation were commonplace. Lawrence White has recounted the various institutional obstacles that emerged after World War II to ensure that the automobile industry dragged its heels on the issue of smog and atmospheric pollution that had its origins in automobile exhaust.[42] By the mid–1950s, it was clear from studies done by California Institute of Technology chemist A. J. Haagen-Smit and others that automobile exhaust was responsible for ozone formation, the release of solid and liquid aerosol particulates, and lead compounds. Their story is remarkable in terms of the science and technology employed in motoring and analysis. The conclusion was obvious: "automobiles should be equipped with devices which will curtail the exhaust content of hydrocarbons by 60%."[43] Yet it took federal government intervention a decade later to address this serious situation. What is so remarkable about this story is that while the Automobile Manufacturers Association continued to sponsor more and more fundamental studies on automobile exhausts, engineer Eugene Houdry, better known for his work on catalytic cracking during the 1930s, developed a relatively inexpensive catalytic converter that could have reduced at least 80 percent of the hydrocarbon emissions by 1958.[44]

In 1959, the Automobile Manufacturers Association announced that in 1961 cars sold in California would have a crankcase ventilation device. It was hoped this device would allow manufacturers to avoid government intervention, but with the election of 1960 and the presidency of John Kennedy, big government was here to stay, and the auto industry's complacency was soon shattered during the far more turbulent sixties.

Dealers, Good and Bad

While the design, economic wastefulness, and safety features of automobiles were at the heart of the critique, some of the anti–Detroit criticism during the period was brought on by dealer practices. Until recently, the automobile dealer in America has been a neglected subject.[45] Dealers were an important aspect of the overall automobile business, however, and a critical function in the long chain between raw materials used in making cars and the consumers who ultimately purchased them. With every new model year, the dealership became a place of great excitement. Windows were covered with paper to hide the new cars, and often hundreds of would-be consumers stood outside, trying to get a peek at the new autos before the paper was taken down and the showroom floor opened to the public. It was a major community event, particularly in smaller towns.

The price of a car was and still is rarely set, and that opens the door to deceit and unethical business behavior. At a flea market one is taught to be wary and bargain, and the same type of game is played on a car dealer's lot. However, the stakes and the consequences of purchase are much higher. In short, the seller, or dealer's salesman or sales manager, knows far more than the typical buyer, so a game is played in which the buyer rarely wins. Where else do you buy a product that depreciates to the extent a car does once it is driven off the lot? According to some economists, federal regulation concerning fixing sticker prices, first implemented in the late 1950s, did little to make things better for the consumer. Two recent films highlight the car buyers' dilemma and the arrogance of those who sell cars — *Slasher* and *Suckers*.[46] The point of both flicks — and they are highly amusing — is that consumers are stupid sheep and car salesman are rarely honest.

Between 1946, when new cars became available again after World War II and 1953, the end of the Korean War, there were far more buyers than cars, and thus dealers could charge full price or even above that for cars whose price was inflated with needless and costly accessories. But beginning in 1954 the situation was reversed, as the market became a buyer's market, and as dealers were getting squeezed by manufacturers to take far more cars than they wanted or else risk losing the franchise. Unscrupulous sales methods tended to follow.[47] One tactic, still used today, is the "bait and switch," in which an advertised good deal on a desirable car is simply impossible, since it is no longer on the lot when one gets there. Other cars, less desirable and more costly, are substituted. Additional abuses, forms of which persist today, included the "finance pack," where inordinately high finance rates are applied to the car purchase; additional charges for fabric and paint protection; deceptive masking of the real value of a used car trade-in, and the slow return of an owner's car from appraisal ("unhorsing the customer"). Such tactics made for a totally unpleasant experience in the showroom. Yet, facing little alternative, Americans returned time and time and again to face this situation at the dealer.

Sales personnel at dealerships are often organized in a complex manner, with inexperienced salesmen and increasingly women sales personnel showing features of the car to the potential buyer and then taking them for a ride. These sales folks are everyone's friends, and rarely disagree with the potential buyer about anything related to the car or for that matter, the world in general. Behind these nice guys and women are the "hard ballers" and finally the sales manager, all with experience and cunning. The situation led to federal intervention in 1958 when the Automotive Information Disclosure Act (also known as the Monroney Act, after the key senator who worked on this bill) mandated the use of stickers on new cars to clearly indicate prices and options. To this day, there is controversy and confusion over invoice prices and rebates that make the game difficult for the average consumer to follow.

The story is far from negative, however. An example from the Mid-South serves to illustrate both the entrepreneurial spirit and integration into the social life of the community that characterized the late 1940s and early 1950s automobile boom. In 1946, Carlos Bryant Garten, already a successful local businessman in Summers and Raleigh counties, West Virginia, obtained one of the first postwar Ford Motor Company dealer franchises.[48] Clearly, for Ford Motor Company the period immediately following the war was a make or break time. Henry Ford II himself spent portions of 1945 and 1946 traveling to visit dealerships around the coun-

Employees of Garten Motors Ford, Hinton, West Virginia, ca. 1954. An automobile dealership was one way to not only become a valued and respected member of the community, but also do quite well financially (Edward Garten).

try. Ford wanted to meet established and new dealers personally, wander showrooms and listen to concerns.[49]

Meeting Mr. Ford in one of those forays outside of Dearborn was Carlos Garten, who in late 1945 built a small dealership to Ford Motor Company specifications and later in 1946 took delivery of some of the first new Fords to be shipped to dealers since the end of wartime production.[50] Given demand, those first two Ford coupes pushed off a C & O railcar at Hinton, West Virginia, were driven to Garten Motors Ford a few miles away and already had a dozen potential buyers standing in line. Over the next decade, Mr. Garten would sell hundreds of new Ford and Mercury cars in addition to taking extensive orders for profitable mine and timber trucks. By the mid–1950s, Garten had become among the wealthiest businessmen in the community.

While Chevrolet, Dodge, and Pontiac dealerships were established later, in the early 1950s in Summers Country, Garten's dealership became a trusted mainstay within an Appalachian community of 5,460. Garten Motors Ford, not unlike many new small town dealerships in the postwar period, was a family affair. Garten's son Magee was vice-president, son-in-law Damon was senior salesperson, son Johnny drove the company's wrecker and man-

Hinton, West Virginia, Ford dealer Carlos Garten hands over the keys to the first drivers' education car (a 1948 Ford) in the county. Small-town dealers proliferated in America during the period to the 1960s, and were important members of the local community (Edward Garten).

aged the parts department, and the women in the family were often called upon for secretarial services and advice in ordering paint colors and upholstery trim options on the assumption that females heavily influenced their husbands' car selection!

Like many of the post-war new small town "mom-and-pop" dealers, Garten Motors Ford became a fixture in the community, a place where men and their sons would sometimes go simply to hang out and talk cars with like-minded folks. As in many communities, early September of each year brought the new model year launch and Carlos Garten was never one to let that opportunity go by. Each year in the early '50s he would sponsor a parade through town with grandsons on horses and banners waving to advertise the new vehicles. From dealership sponsorship of little league softball teams to playing Santa Claus in the annual Christmas parades to chairing fund-raising projects to better the area, Garten quickly became influential within the social and political life of his community. As a strong supporter of education, Mr. Garten built trust within the community through such generous acts as contributing to the Board of Education its first drivers' education car, serving as president of the Board of Education, and leading numerous civic organizations. Such community leadership was not unlike hundreds of other 1950s car dealers who, at the time, simply viewed the cultivation of strong community relations as part of good business.

The UAW, the Big Three, and Pattern Bargaining

Between 1945 and 1972, the UAW and indeed all of America experienced "golden years" economically. Under Walter Reuther's astute politics, internal unity was maintained. The main priorities of the Reuther cadre were to raise the standard of living and create economic security. During the "fat years" a highly centralized UAW exacted concessions from the Big Three. Reuther and the UAW fostered a new philosophy about laborers, one that connected production and consumption, as Ronald Edsforth and Robert Asher noted:

> UAW leaders understood the organic character of worker consciousness. Auto workers and other wage earners were both producers and consumers. No matter how much they enjoyed the security of home ownership, pensions that would enable them to have consumption security in their own age, and the purchase of consumer durables ... workers were deeply concerned about being treated with dignity in the workplace.[51]

Reuther and his cadre developed a highly effective strategy called pattern bargaining that exploited competition among manufacturers, maximized the effectiveness of union negotiations, and reduced the frequency of costly strikes. First, the UAW would target a specific company that would give what it most wanted. Then the union would threaten a strike to halt production that allowed competitors to continue. Having exacted the desired benefits, the union would use that bargain to "set the pattern." It would then use the pattern to talk to other firms, and force them to conform. The automobile industry never developed a sophisticated countermeasure. The novel tactic was first applied to General Motors, and resulted in a wage raise and increased vacation time. Into the 1950s and 1960s, the wages of automobile workers rose and so did the profits of the Big Three. But the era was not without conflict. There were many strikes in the 1950s and 1960s; management and workers were in constant tension.

Even in a political atmosphere of increased conservatism from the Cold War and the Taft-Hartley legislation, wages and living standards rose dramatically: "measured in constant dollars the 1947 average wage in the industry of $56.51 had doubled by 1960 to $115.21, and tripled by 1970 to $170.70."[52] By 1960, the Big Three paid better wages and offered their workers better benefits than any other industry in the nation. The vision of the union rank-and-file differed markedly from the goals of new president Martin Reuther. Nelson Lichtenstein argued that Reuther saw the challenge as "to reshape the consciousness of millions of industrial workers, making them disciplined trade unionists, militant social democrats, and racial egalitarians."[53] The union's "fat years" were characterized less by Reuther's vision of militancy and more so by increased leisure and generated by postwar posterity. John Barnard wrote:

> A generational change had clearly taken place. Many of the UAW's early leaders and rank-and-file activists shaped by capitalism's 1930s crisis, had a philosophical-political outlook as liberals, socialist-democrats, independent leftists, Socialists, Communists, Trotskyists or Catholic labor activists that gave motivation, direction, and meaning to their actions.[54]

The workers of the 1950s seemed concerned with attainment of a middle-class status and the consumer culture of American life that came with it. Sociologist Ely Chinoy's *Automobile Workers and the American Dream*, a study of "Auto town," revealed the daily life of autoworkers as aimed towards a quick entrance to the middle class and an enjoyment of its various benefits, rather than any concern with a particular philosophical-political outlook.[55] Chinoy's study also acknowledged management's preference for youthful workers and the lack of opportunity for social advancement.

Labor in the 1950s and 1960s was characterized by increased mechanization of the production process. Beginning in 1947, at the Brooks Plant in Cleveland, Ohio, Ford introduced the concept of automation, mechanizing the process of handling materials. Stephen Meyer wrote that automation "eliminated worker intervention as castings moved between machines on the huge transfer lines.... An operator loaded rough stock onto the transfer line's first automation device and the piece moved from machine to automation device to machine until another operator removed the completely machined casting at the end of the line."[56] Automation, it was thought, threatened workers' jobs. Automation reoriented worker classifications, but still required that workers load materials into machines. Thus, the workers remained, but the result was more control for management and increased degradation. Flink wrote, "Even where automation displaced human operators, there was degradation to lower skill levels and intensification of the production process."[57] He provided the figure that in the mid–1970s approximately "75 percent of jobs in automobile manufacturing remained semiskilled or unskilled, versus only about 10 percent for the rest of American industry."[58] As Stephen Myer pointed out, "Reuther and other top UAW leaders moved slowly to address the complex problems of automated production."[59] The UAW pursued Keynesian policies that linked American automobile worker's production with consumption.

The Cars of the Golden Era

In general terms, what were the cars of this era like? The 1950s was the age of excess, and in Detroit, a decade of complacency regarding foreign competition.[60] As the decade unfolded, cars became longer, lower, heavier, and more powerful. Aviation motifs were prevalent in terms of styling, from fins and spinners to jet hood ornaments and spacecraft-like dashboards. It was the era of the overhead valve V-8, and thus as the decade moved forward and engines became ever larger, cars of the 1950s used more fuel of higher octane and increased tetraethyl lead content, much to the delight of the petroleum companies.[61]

In general, the mentality in Detroit was not to think in reasonable ways, but rather to build cars large, because there was far more profit per unit in a large car loaded with accessories than in a smaller vehicle. Those accessories included everything from the very useful to the frivolous. Heaters, radios, and turn signals were installed on many vehicles, where they had been options or not available before World War II. Automatic transmissions, power windows, push-button controls, unreadable speedometers and power steering and brakes were marks of luxury, found only on the heavier, higher-priced cars. Traditionalists decried the use of "idiot lights" rather than gauges on the dashboard. Air conditioning remained for the most part a dealer-installed under-the-dash option, superior to window swamp coolers found in the Southwest. Automatic headlight dimmers, a GM innovation, were installed on a number of select models.

Particularly in the period to 1953, whatever was made, whether was stylish or functional, sold due to the post–World War II car shortage. In addition to the Big Three, the market-place was populated by the independents, whose market share during the first half of the decade was around 15 percent. In 1955, the top seller was Chevrolet, closely followed by Ford, and then Buick, Plymouth, and Oldsmobile. The independents accounted for 12 to 19 percent of the market.

Two important aspects concerning the independents should be mentioned, given that for the most part these firms were out of the marketplace by the end of the decade. First, *Consumer Reports* reliability surveys noted far more expensive and frequent repairs than average on independents including Kaiser-Frazer, Studebaker, and Nash.[62] To what degree quality as opposed to styling contributed to the demise of these businesses remains an open question. Secondly, trade-in value for independents' vehicles was quite low. One former Studebaker dealer told me that GM dealers in Dayton, Ohio, told prospective buyers of independents that if they purchased a Studebaker, they should not expect the vehicle to be accepted as a trade-in later on.[63]

Studebaker, the best selling of all the independents, featured its Raymond Loewy "Coming and Going" design of 1948, and then the absolutely beautiful 1953 Champion Starliner coupe. The venerable Packard Car Company attempted to broaden its market base beginning in the 1930s, and its postwar models looked like bulbous, pregnant elephants. It is hardly surprising, given Packard styling during the 1950s (with the exception of the 1955 Caribbean convertible), that the company would close its doors in 1958, although its final coffin nails were not its cars but the debts incurred by merging with Studebaker.[64]

Powel Crosley, Jr., best known for taking Henry Ford's mass production techniques and applying them to radios during the 1920s and '30s, and then being the visible owner of the Cincinnati Reds, took over a wartime plant in Richmond, Indiana, in 1949 and marketed a series of inexpensive cars. Prior to the war, Crosley had produced a limited number of cars, but it was he saw his greatest opportunity after 1945. Unfortunately, Crosley aimed his Hot Shot, Super Sport and station wagon at consumers who, for the most part, wanted more luxurious vehicles. Crosley thought in terms of simple technologies and simple tastes, and believed he could change the preferences of American consumers. He once said, "We are probably the most extravagant nation in the world but this extravagance must end. Economic conditions make it essential that we give some attention to mileage per gallon and operating cost and possible economies.... Why employ 3,000 lbs. to carry a person around when 900 lbs will do as well."[65]

Hudson cars beginning in 1948 featured a "step-down" design with a lowered floor, and most notably the powerful Hornet engine that dominated the early NASCAR series. While aesthetics on the Hudson were a shortcoming, the fact that passengers sat between the frame rails and the design's superior handling characteristics set the step-down Hudson apart from its competitors in terms of safety. Indeed, the Hudson anticipated safety concerns and the designs of the 1970s.[66]

In the aftermath of World War II, successful entrepreneur Henry J. Kaiser entered the market with a number of models, some of which were quite innovative while others were more conventional. Kaiser's Henry J, which sold also in a version at Sears under the nameplate of the Allstate, was an economy car that entered the marketplace at simply the wrong time. His Darrin Roadster, named after designer Dutch Darrin, was perhaps the most beautiful American sports car of the decade, but sold only in small numbers. Entrance into the automobile industry was costly, and compromises had to be made at Kaiser. To keep up with annual model style changes, the development of a V-8 was postponed, and perhaps that was the death knell of the company in 1955 when the last models were introduced to a public hungry for more power.[67]

Finally, the Nash Motor Car Company featured aerodynamic styling (the Airflyte look) that resembled inverted bathtubs along with one of the most innovative autos of the era, the Nash-Healey roadster. With their hidden wheels and limited turning radius, the other Nash designs were called "Perhaps the unloveliest production cars ever built."[68] Innovation can be pushed only so far, and despite the $39 option of a twin bed conversion, the Airflyte was as unsuccessful as the Chrysler Airflow design that had preceded it. In a fresh way, Nash also produced the Metropolitan, a two-seat Austin powered urban commuter car whose sales were second only to the Volkswagen among imported cars during the 1950s. Yet it was these unappealing designs that led to the death of the Airflyte cars; even Superman and his early 1950s TV show, which used Nash cars, could not save a car profile that the masses perceived as unattractive.

After 1953, however, the automobile market became far more unpredictable, and no one knew what the public really wanted. This was a time of different styles and the rise to center stage of the stylist in Detroit. The great stylists of the era were Raymond Loewy, whose 1953 Studebaker was a styling tour de force; Harley Earl and disciple Bill Mitchell, who at GM were responsible for a number of remarkable design prototypes that included the Firebird I and II; Virgil Exner at Chrysler and finally Frank Hershey at Ford, whose 1955 Thunderbird quickly outstripped the Chevrolet Corvette in the sales of personal, sports car models.[69]

Automobiles changed not only in shape during the 1950s, but also in terms of color, as two- and even three-tone paint schemes became popular. Innovations in paint technology allowed colors to become more vibrant and varied. For example, in 1955 Ford offered such unique colors as Regency Purple Iridescent and Tropical Rose; Pontiac offered two-tone models with Avalon Yellow and Bolero Red combined with Raven Black; and Oldsmobile enticed customers with Turquoise Iridescent and Bimini Blue Iridescent.

Just as the appearance of automobiles was dramatically altered, so too were several key auto technologies. For much of the 1950s, Detroit manufacturers engaged in a horsepower race, a competition that began with the introduction of the Oldsmobile Rocket V-8 engine in 1949. Gradually, straight 6- and 8-cylinder engines were displaced by overhead V-8 designs. At Chrysler, hemispherical chambered V-8s, or "hemis," gained in popularity. In 1955 Chevrolet introduced its small block V-8, which quickly became a favorite among the hot rod crowd.

A 1955 Dodge passes through a small town in the west during the 1955 Mobilgas Economy Run. The Economy Run was a popular event, and the single largest corporate promotion during the 1950s (Joseph Freeman).

By 1956, some 80 percent of buyers purchased cars with V-8s, which is perhaps appropriate given that during the same year the interstate highway system became a reality. While in 1957 the Automobile Manufacturers Association banned factory-sponsored racing and discouraged the preoccupation with speed in auto advertising, horsepower and engine size continued to escalate through the early 1960s.

Concurrently, automatic transmissions became increasingly popular with consumers, including pushbutton-on-the-dash versions in Chrysler and Packard products. In fact, automobile interiors began to be filled with home-like conveniences. Power windows and color coordinated plush seats, outside and day/night mirrors, automatic dimming headlights, transistorized radios, and air conditioning were options in higher-priced models by mid-decade.

The 1958 Recession and European Competition

The decade so simplistically characterized as one of "Happy Days" ended on a turbulent note. To begin with, in 1958 America experienced a short but painful recession, one in which unemployment reached more than 7 percent. It was during this downturn that Ford introduced the ill-fated Edsel, Chevrolet's models were featured without fins, Packard ceased production, and car sales dropped more than 30 percent for the model year.

Yet Detroit manufacturers continued to build large, heavy, and expensive-to-operate cars, ignoring the fact that sales of import models had increased tenfold from 1951 levels. In addition to Volkswagen, Volvo, Mercedes, Renault, Fiat, MG, Triumph, and Austin were all making inroads into the American market. In response, Detroit automakers in 1959 released models with soaring upward fins, like those found on the Cadillac, outward extensions on the Chevrolet, and a delta-wing design found on the Buick. Only after a year of record import sales did the Big Three counter with economy cars — the Corvair, Falcon, and Valiant.

The Volkswagen Bug

Of all of the imports of the 1950s, the model that had the most impact on the American scene was undoubtedly the Volkswagen (VW). Like all manufactured objects, the VW Beetle represented more than a successful design, past and present. It was a material reflection of the human beings who conceived it and then made it in large quantities. The author of one of the first of several fine studies on the VW, Walter Henry Nelson, got it right when he opened his *Small Wonder: The Amazing Story of the Volkswagen* with the assertion that

> the story of the VW is not primarily a technical, nor even industrial story, but a human one. I wrote about the things which interested me — a man's long dream and his hard work to realize that dream, the nightmare of seeing that dream shattered, and the near miraculous fulfillment of it after World War II. I wrote for those who are more interested in men than machines, and for all those who have been amused, bemused, or puzzled by this strange little car which so many people have taken to their hearts.[70]

The Volkswagen success story in America has been told many times since the late 1950s, but a few points bear emphasis here. First, the high resistance to the car in terms of its looks and its heritage as "Hitler's Car" was overcome by common-sense business practices, although few in Detroit followed such practices then or now. Customer service and high quality dealerships were integral to Heinz Nordhoff's sales strategy in the U.S. Beginning in the early 1950s, technicians traveled in vans from dealer to dealer, teaching mechanics the right way to service these vehicles. And restrictions were placed on dealers to carry adequate supplies of spare parts, so much so that on a number of occasions mechanics put together complete cars from dealer parts inventories. Secondly, a unique advertising campaign initiated in 1959 based on honesty and understatement struck a chord with buyers who tended to have above-average education and were tired of the Big Three ads that could be viewed as downright silly.

Finally, the car itself was of remarkable quality. Every VW received four coats of paint, with sanding in between, producing a luster that was unmatched in production cars at three times the price. More than 3,000 inspectors scrutinized vehicles on the line. In short, the VW Beetle became legendary for its feats, particularly those in which the car floated in the wake of storms and floods, but also as the result of publicity feats. Any car in which you had to open a window to close a door was a striking contrast to the sloppily-constructed behemoths born in Detroit.

During the late 1950s and early 1960s, VW owners were a different breed than the typical American car consumer. Their cars were practical and excessive, not accessorized or flashy. The VW was a status symbol of a different kind, for it told those around you that you held different values, such as thrift, sensibility, honesty, practicality, and modesty, that were traditional in American life. The car appealed to the highly educated and those who had not bought into the culture of suits and ostentatious affluence. It was a statement that transcended time, perhaps going back to the Model T era, before longer, lower, and more colorful (and perhaps superficial) vehicles characterized American life. The VW was the antithesis of Harley Earl's creations at GM.

1957 Plymouth Belvedere. Perhaps the best of Virgil Exner's "Forward Look" designs of the 1950s, the 1957 Plymouth served notice on Chrysler's competitors that the smallest member of the Big Three no longer built stodgy vehicles (Chrysler LLC).

Just like the Model T, the Beetle had its day in the American market (1968 was its best sales year). It was gradually phased out in the late 1970s, due as much to changing safety and emission standards as to its timeless design. Once Nordhoff stepped down, VW temporarily lost its way, first with the water-cooled Dasher, and then in an abortive attempt to build vehicles in Westmoreland, Pennsylvania. But the design would not die, as it continued to be made in Mexico and Brazil, and of course now in a modified form again for the American import market in our own time. Ironically, while Hitler's 1000 year Third Reich lasted only twelve years, his people's car is as popular as ever.

The Volkswagen story was exceptional in terms of the success of imports in the American market during the period. In contrast, take the case of Renault Dauphine.[71] Dauphine sales in the U.S. were far from inconsequential; for example, by 1959 some 95,000 units had been sold. Unlike the VW Beetle, however, the Dauphine's quality was so bad that it tarnished the company's reputation in America for decades to come. It was said that tow truck operators were afraid to pick up the Dauphine, for the undercarriage was so inherently weak that it collapsed when raised. Little issues that existed with this car, like door handles breaking off when one opened the door, were minor in comparison with stability issues, especially when the vehicle was caught in cross winds. With its most powerful engine, the Renault's 0–60 time was between 34 and 36 seconds, hardly acceptable to American drivers who increasingly were using interstate highways.

Cars and Rock and Roll

It is not surprising that the automobile was at the center of artistic enterprise during the 1950s, given its place in popular thought, its presence throughout our society, including in everyday life, and its importance economically. Particularly significant in the emergence of the new music of the 1950s, rock and roll, it was also integral to the plot and backdrop of many films, and as the stage upon which literary drama and self-discovery were played out. However, no form of popular artistic expression celebrated the automobile and the highway with more *feeling* than rock and roll. This vast body of music, difficult to define and ever-changing over time, often featured themes derived from the automobile. Furthermore, even a cursory examination of record jackets starting with the 1950s reveals an astonishing number that feature photographs of "cool" cars.[72] Rock music praised the car, and its performers drew on the wealth that followed success to buy cars that were excessive and extravagant. These materialistic values characterize popular music performers today, as witnessed by those featured in MTV's series "Cribs."[73]

For rock and roll performers who had beaten the odds and had "made it," much like Hollywood film stars of the 1920s and 1930s, cars and fame went hand in hand. Just as love from the opposite sex followed famous musicians who had become famous, so too cars became the object of artists' love. Loving women and loving cars could be convoluted together in a confusing and complicated way in this new music of the 1950s, as exemplified in the words of Chuck Berry's "Maybelline."[74]

It was at the mid-point of the decade, the year of the Chevy V-8, Chrysler's Forward Look styling, and the introduction of the Ford Thunderbird, that rock and roll began to influence American life in a profound way. With its energy, rock moved listeners, as did the automobile, in ways that intimately touched the soul. Rock conveyed messages that could be individually interpreted, as did custom cars and hot rods.

Richard A. Peterson provides a deft explanation of why rock music emerged when it did in an article entitled "Why 1955?"[75] Peterson diminishes the importance of the appearance of such individual artistic geniuses as Chuck Berry and Elvis as well as the role of the Baby Boomer generation in his analysis. Rather, he stresses legal, technological, and organizational changes, without dismissing the role of historical continuity between earlier blues and country and western forms of music and rock.

The introduction of new technology was a part of the rock and roll and automobile story of the 1950s. With the transition away from 78 RPM records made of shellac to 33⅓ RPM vinyl discs, and especially the 45 RPM, the format for music changed dramatically after World War II. The immensely popular and inexpensive 45 RPM record shortened the length of a recording to approximately three minutes or less.

New automobile radio designs were integrally connected to the new length of musical performances. Pushbutton radios, introduced in the late 1930s but popular by the 1950s, enabled listeners to switch from station to station as they made choices while sitting at a traffic light.[76] Since red lights are generally set for 100 seconds and green lights for 60 seconds, the pause enabled riders to listen and switch songs with minimal distractions. Indeed, the pushbutton and signal-seeking auto radios of the 1950s were like juke boxes on wheels.[77]

Finally, the transistor radio was introduced as a portable car radio in the mid–1950s and made optional equipment in cars beginning in 1955. Lighter, generating less heat, incorporating improved automatic volume control, and with fewer electronic components to go wrong, car audio began its ascent in importance in American culture.

With the FCC greatly increasing the number of AM radio licenses after 1947, stations rapidly doubled in number. Previously, radio had been dominated by the national networks, and these network-affiliated stations had used their own bands and orchestras, rather than recorded music. Now the airwaves were open to any musician who had recorded his work. An all-popular music format was first adopted at KWOH in Omaha, Nebraska, in 1949, and the same station went to a "Top 40" format in 1953. These programming ideas caught on elsewhere rather quickly. In sum, all the prerequisites were in place for a revolution in modern music directed at an emerging youth culture.

Beyond broadcasting changes and a transition that took place in the material culture of the music industry, another important technological development was the introduction of the electric guitar. Beginning in 1946, Leo Fender improved the electric guitar in terms of eliminating feedback.[78] His Telecaster was later replaced in 1954 with the Stratocaster. Competition came from Gibson with the Les Paul guitar, first produced in 1952. With either guitar, the artist could now play high frets with emotion, and in the process exude sexuality while on stage. One cannot imagine rock and roll, with its pace and tones, without the electrification of musical instruments. The electric guitar enabled artists to break new ground and become showmen in the process.

While the origins of modern rock are somewhat nebulous and remain controversial, it is clear that its form and content had roots in the work of several blues artists, including Robert Johnson. Historian E.L. Widmer and others suggested that Jackie Brenston and the Kings of Rhythm's "Rocket 88," produced on March 5, 1951, in Memphis on the Chess label, was the first to bring together the various elements now associated with modern rock.[79] Later, Ike Turner would receive credit for its words. The Oldsmobile 88 was a new kind of postwar automobile, one with an overhead V-8 engine, yet light and usually stripped down, closer to a Chevrolet than an Oldsmobile 98. For its day, the 88 was fast and clean. An advertisement in 1950 exclaimed, "you've got to *drive* it to believe it."

The fuzzy guitar in the song, the consequence of the amplifier's having fallen out of the trunk of a car before the recording session in Memphis, was one distinctive aspect of "Rocket 88" that made it unique. And the pace of the piano segment in the song foretold the performances of Jerry Lee Lewis.

Chess Records' Sam Phillips, who was known for his discovery of both Elvis Presley and Jerry Lee Lewis, would later assert that the recording of "Rocket 88" marked the birth of rock. Bill Halley and his Saddlemen played it as well, a reflection of the lack of color lines that was characteristic of rock and roll, ironic at time when the color line was perhaps drawn tighter than ever in American life.

The success of "Rocket 88" was followed by many similar songs, including a follow-up number by Brenston himself called "Real Gone Rocket" (July 1951) that flopped. As E. L. Widmer has so adeptly chronicled, Chess Records followed with Betty Love's "Drop Top" (November 1951), Rosco Gordon's "T-Model Boogie" (December 1951), Howlin Wolf's "Cadillac Daddy" (January 1952), Johnny London's "Drivin' Slow" (March 1952), and Joe Hill Louis's "Automatic Woman" (September 1953). "Cadillac Daddy" was one of many songs about Cadillacs written during the post–World War II era, but down deep in the lyrics, one can discern a fearful and subservient tone, so prevalent on the part of Blacks towards Whites along Route 61 in Mississippi.

The Blues tradition was an important, and indeed a necessary, precursor to a song that undoubtedly is the first true rock and roll tune — "Maybellene," performed by the great Chuck Berry in 1955. Berry, borrowing from the old song "Ida Red," spun the tale of a car chase and a troubled love affair. The song has been carefully dissected and analyzed by Warren Belasco on a level that is undoubtedly far deeper than Berry was ever thinking while he penned the lines to the music.[80] Driving a modified Ford V8, our hero pursues his woman who is riding in a Cadillac. For a time the focus is on the woman, then it shifts to the car, and which is more important is a serious question. The song alternates between describing the vehicle and the woman. Berry invents a new word — "motorvating" — which he is doing in his Ford before he sees his two loves, the woman and the Cadillac Coupe de Ville. A chase follows, ending only after a shower cools the Ford, enabling the hero to catch the female and the car. "Maybellene" merged Black and White musical traditions, as perhaps only a St. Louis performer like Chuck Berry could do. It is suggestive in terms of sexuality, but leaves much to the imagination. Somehow, if we are to believe Berry, a Ford can keep up with a Cadillac. In sum, "Maybellene" was energetic and happy, unlike the typical Blues fare of the day.

In "Maybellene" and the other songs that followed relating to automobiles, Berry conveyed to his audience the joy of driving. A later (1964) popular hit, "No Particular Place to Go," continued to extol the sheer exuberance of riding, without purpose or specific goals. Berry's artistic genius — apart from the humor that is embedded in his lyrics — was that he somehow knew what Americans were all about: restless and seeking a kind of happiness that only the automobile and the highway could provide. It might not last, but escape from our environment and ourselves was part and parcel of the 1950s and beyond.

Film: The Rebels

Just as the automobile played an important role in shaping music during the 1950s, its place in cinema was also significant. In this survey, I will focus on only two films from the decade, *Rebel Without a Cause* (1955) and *Thunder Road* (1958), although the topic in general is almost limitless in scope. In particular, cars were significant props in many of the films of that day, and their meaning varied from film to film. I cannot help but think that in films like Alfred Hitchcock's *Vertigo* (1958), *A Touch of Evil* (1958) *and North by Northwest* (1959) the cars that are used are more than props; their colors, shapes and styles contribute to the tone of the scene, and are integral to the overall meaning of the film.

Film industry advances have often resulted from the introduction of new cinematographic techniques. For films in which the automobile plays an important role, the jobs of cameramen and editors become especially complicated due to the many camera angles employed and the limited working space. Realism in a film sequence poses many challenges for both producers and editors. What camera angles are necessary so that all the views of a scene are covered? This often involves interior and exterior shots of the car or cars involved, as well as shots of the people inside the car. Once these are taken, it becomes the editor's responsibility to arrange the scenes in a particular order to faithfully reconstruct the scene. Continuity from angle to angle and from interior to exterior and car to car needs to take place with a realistic yet also imaginative and aesthetic flow. This is accomplished by the tedious work of cutting and splicing.

The job of the cameraman in filming these driving scenes can be considered just as difficult, primarily because of the lack of space the cameraman has to maneuver. Three basic angles are used when filming: a side or frontal view of the people in the vehicle from outside the vehicle, an interior shot taken from inside the vehicle, and an exterior shot of the vehicle. Especially in more modern films, no one particular shot is used and usually a mix of all three are blended together for the full effect of the scene.

Little changed in the filming of cars from the 1930s to the late 1950s. It was still clear that interior shots were produced primarily on sound stages, as evidenced by films like *Rebel*

Without a Cause and Robert Mitchum's *Thunder Road.* The one noticeable advance made in cinematography during the fifties was the use of much closer exterior shots of the automobile in motion; cars as filmed driving right up to a single camera lens or to the side of the lens.

Much has been written about James Dean and his character in *Rebel Without a Cause.* It is generally acknowledged that the film is reflective of the rebelliousness of the mid–1950s youth culture. It is also of interest in terms of its portrayal of mid–1950s middle class American parents. Dean, an All-American boy from Indiana who had previously won an Academy Award for his role in *East of Eden*, would make one more film, *Giant*, before his untimely death at age 24 in 1955. Recently Katie Mills, in her *The Road Story and the Rebel*, places Dean and the film in a broad cultural context.[81]

In *Rebel Without a Cause*, Dean co-starred with Natalie Wood and Sal Mineo. The film is a brilliant portrayal of the pain associated with adolescence, and an equally scathing criticism of their parents. This movie ripped away layers of hypocrisy and societal untruths, exposing a far darker, and perhaps more representative side of middle class American life than that usually depicted in the media. It was also a car film — James Dean's everyday driver is a 1949 chopped and customized Mercury. From then on this car model was enshrined as the ultimate in 1950s cool. As an aside, the famous "chicken" scene purportedly employed two stolen cars. While the film was fictional, in real life car theft had become an epidemic in 1955. There were 227,150 stolen vehicle cases that year, followed by 263,720 in 1956. It was considered a juvenile problem, as the "joy ride" resulted in the arrest of almost 5,000 sixteen-year-olds, 5,500 fifteen-year-olds, and 5,600 children under the age of fifteen for this crime. Clearly, *Rebel Without a Cause* exposed a dark side of American life that to this day we refuse to admit about the decade of the 1950s.[82]

In real life Dean would be killed in late September 1955 when he crashed his 1955 Porsche 550 Spyder head-on into another car while driving to a car race in Northern California. The extremely light Porsche was no match for the Ford coupe that it encountered. Dean died on the way to the hospital, although his fans refused to believe it. For years it was rumored that the cult figure was not dead, but horribly disfigured. Dean's tombstone was stolen in 1983 and a second marker was disfigured in 1985. Grant County, Indiana, makes the most of Dean's hometown origins, with a memorial service every September 30, a gallery, and memorial theater.

Associated with Dean's death is the bizarre fate of his Porsche. After the accident, the car was sold to a used car dealer who put it on display supposedly as a campaign for public safety. Next, customizer George Barris bought the car to sell it for parts, and as it was unloaded from a truck, it rolled off and broke a mechanic's legs. Troy McHenry, a Beverly Hills doctor, bought the Dean engine and installed it in his Porsche. The first time McHenry took the car out, he died in a fiery crash. A second doctor bought the transmission, and subsequently he would be injured in another crash. Next, a New Yorker bought two of the tires from Dean's wreck and he too had an accident when both ties blew simultaneously. Additionally, as the shell of the car was being transported to a road safety exhibition in Salinas, California, the transporter crashed and its driver was killed. Finally, the shell of the car was stolen and never recovered. Do you believe that some cars are cursed? Whatever the cause, Dean's fatal accident created a mystique about Porsches, an attraction that has caused celebrities like Jerry Seinfeld to assemble collections of them, and this author to work for years on raising one from the dead.[83]

Thunder Road was another popular film of the decade that featured a rebel and a defiance towards authority, but the setting was quite different from that of *Rebel Without a Cause*.[84] Robert Mitchum played the role of bootlegger Luke Doolin, and Gene Barry was cast as a federal agent hot on his trail. The film was shot in the vicinity of Lake Lure, North Carolina, and Mitchum drove modified 1950 and 1957 Fords, each with a special tank installed in the rear. Supposedly based on a real incident in which a bootlegger crashed into an electric substation near Knoxville, Tennessee, in April 1954, the film predictably takes Mitchum's character to a tragic end. The film was low budget and not particularly well made, but it led to Mitchum's release of the song "The Ballad of Thunder Road," which made the pop charts at number 62. The film became a minor cult classic, played at drive-ins throughout the Southeast during the 1970s and 1980s, and was the inspiration for Bruce Springsteen's 1975 *Thunder Road* album. Most significantly, the film's theme was about freedom, and in the words of Luke, a freedom to do whatever one wanted on one's own land. In this case it was erecting a still and making whiskey despite the federal government. The consequences for Luke and other "transporters" in pursuing that freedom, however, was death at worst, imprisonment if lucky.

A Night at the Drive-In

For every film classic like *Rebel Without a Cause*, there were ten shot on low budgets, largely now forgotten by all except film buffs and those who watch Turner Classic Movies while killing time at the nursing home. Yet, a number of these films have become cult favorites and several, like *Thunder Road* or *The Blob*, starring an up-and-coming Steve McQueen, gained new significance in more recent times. Many of these marginal films became the staple for the drive-in of the 1950s and 1960s, a time when youths were anxious to remove themselves from parental control and search for self-identity. Drive-ins have become an endangered institution, the consequence of changing mores, suburbanization, and a migration to the exurbs. In 1958, there were more than 4,000 drive-ins in America, but by the early 1990s, the number had fallen to about 870. They were a place to meet friends and to find entertainment, passion if one was lucky, and cheap but often bad food. But on a hot summer's night, what better a place to spend some time and money? And what if it rained?

The longest running drive-in can be found in Orefield, Pennsylvania, north of Allentown. Shankweiler's Drive-In was the second drive-in established in America.[85] It opened during the summer of 1933, after its founder stopped at Richard M. Hollingshead's theater in Camden, New Jersey, on his way back from the Jersey Shore. Hollingshead had opened his operation on June 6, 1933, to 600 people who paid 25 cents per person to see the film *Wife Beware*. Back in Orefield, Shankweiler hung up a giant sheet between two poles, set up a giant speaker, and was in business.

Soon others would follow, but Hollingshead, who had patented his drive-in idea, would be mired in court for years over infringement suits. Technical innovations, including RCA speakers that would be hung on car windows and in-car heaters for use during the winter months, were incorporated after World War II. American life was never the same with the viewing of such films as *The Hideous Sun Demon*, *I Married a Monster from Outer Space*, *Cat Women on the Moon*, and *The Texas Chain Saw Massacre*.

On the Road

No discussion of rebels of the 1950s could be complete without at least briefly mentioning Jack Kerouac's *On the Road* (1957), one of the most important works of twentieth century literature.[86] A reflection of the social and cultural ferment of the early Cold War era, *On the Road* marked the apex of 1950s Beat literature, far surpassing the writings of fellow Beats Allen Ginsberg, William Burroughs, and Neal Cassady. Incidentally, it redirected the American road narrative as well, and interpretations of its meaning and significance remain a hot scholarly topic to the present. Looking back to that time, Bob Dylan remarked that "I read *On the Road* in maybe 1959 — it changed my life like it changed everyone else's." It is a story about Americans on the margins of society — transients, disaffected intellectuals, farm laborers, racial minorities, and far more. *On the Road* also takes us into the world of the 1950s that was far removed from middle class suburbia of the day — bop music, spontaneity, recklessness, drugs, and promiscuous sex. It seems unlikely, however, that Kerouac was just aiming in *On the Road* to describe a dark underworld populated by fascinating characters, the composite of which is one snapshot of America usually not taken. Is the road trip merely a mindless adventure or escape? Certainly *On the Road* is infected with youthful optimism, far different from the negativity displayed in Henry Miller's *The Air-Conditioned Nightmare* or John Steinbeck's *The Wayward Bus*. It also is far removed from the dark tale of a road trip gone bad, best exemplified in the classic 1945 film *Detour*.[87]

One can interpret *On the Road* as a tale of self-discovery and a search for God. In his narrative, Kerouac speaks of life being "holy," and he stops to reflect,

> So in America when the sun goes down and I sit on the old-broken down river pier watching the long, long skies over New Jersey and sense all that raw land that rolls in one unbelievable

Park and Shop Shopping Center, one of the first auto-oriented complexes in the District of Columbia. The widespread use of the automobile led to a move from the center of cities to suburbs and finally exurbs (Library of Congress).

huge bulge over the West Coast, and all that road going, all the people dreaming in the immensity of it, and in Iowa I know by now the children must be crying in the land where they let children cry, and tonight the stars'll be out, and don't you know that God is Pooh Bear?[88]

Many other passages and phrases suggest that Kerouac's Catholicism was never far from his writing.

The Coming of the Interstates

Initially Kerouac's Sal Paradise had planned to take U.S. 6 across America, but things changed and other routes were taken as he made his way to Denver to be reunited with his Beat friends. Ironically, just a year before *On the Road* was published, the interstate highway system was established, and the way Americans traveled across the country would be dramatically changed in future decades. Writers that included William Least Heat Moon and Michael Wallis waxed nostalgically about travels along the two-lane black top, but beginning in the late 1950s limited access, divided highways became the preferred mode of travel for most folks traveling to far destinations, and even in and around densely settled urban areas.[89]

For those driving in the period before World War II, two lane highways certainly had their limitations, both in terms of safety and traffic flow. For example, U.S. 1 connecting Baltimore and Washington, D.C., was only some forty miles in length, but it was intersected by approximately 1000 driveways, as motels, hamburger joints, clubs, used car lots, and occasionally a home were located along the highway's edge. Since one could make a left turn across traffic through its entire length, lanes were only 10 feet wide, and trucks were ever-present, collisions were inevitable. Yet this road, despite its many limitations, typified the best thoroughfares that one could take in 1939.

The first impulse to transform interstate highways took place during the Depression, but in 1938 the Senate rejected an $8 million bill, despite its obvious employment benefits. A year later, Thomas MacDonald, chief of the Bureau of Public Roads, began to promote a plan for constructing 30,000 miles of expressways.[90] A few years later, FDR appointed a seven member Interregional Highway Committee. From their deliberations, MacDonald drew up a proposed interstate highway map that closely resembles what was actually built. From that map one can clearly see the outlines of what became Interstates 15, 25, 35, 55, 75, and 95, along with 10, 40, 70, and 80. Some important links are missing, but MacDonald's 1941 preliminary effort proved prescient.

After World War II, a number of states began building toll roads, including Maine, New Jersey, and West Virginia. But it was only after the Korean War and the election of Dwight David Eisenhower, that a strong nucleus of leaders, including Francis du Pont, emerged to politically forge a bill that overwhelmingly passed Congress in 1956. The Federal Highway Act promised something to virtually every constituency, including trucking interests, on which high taxes would not be imposed. Financing came from taxes on gasoline, rubber, buses, trucks and trailers. The federal government was to pay for 90 percent of all the construction costs, and the states had the right to determine where to locate the routes. While some thought that the money would merely improve existing U.S. highways, in the end these routes, like U.S. 40 passing north of Dayton, Ohio, would become used only for local traffic.

Indeed, these new interstates were quite different from all other American highways except the few toll roads built immediately after World War II. To begin with, these thoroughfares cost far more than undivided highways, approximately $1 million per mile, compared to $60,000 per mile for the construction of U.S. 1. The older highways had pavement 5 to 6 inches thick, but the new interstates had concrete 9 to 10 inches in thickness on a carefully prepared roadbed that sometimes went down 50 inches. Earth moving was done on a heroic scale in building the interstates, with new designs of pavers, excavators, dump trucks, graders and concrete plants located on site.

There was no golden spike ceremony to commemorate this effort, as work continues on the interstate system to this day, as is so apparent every spring with the reappearance of the orange barrels. Its benefits for some were enormous, with a dramatic rise in property values and the development of new tourist sites, numerous new motels, truck stops, and fast food restaurants.

The interstates made travel between major cities within a region fast and much safer than previously experienced. But they also damaged the cities they went through, often dividing urban areas racially and economically. Some cities, like San Francisco and New Orleans, would stop freeway development and save historic views, but many others were far worse because of them. With White flight and the development of exurbs, further divisions in the nation's fabric resulted.

Summing Up the Glorious 1950s

In sum, what can be said about the place of the automobile in America during the 1950s? As many commentators have stated in previous writings, the '50s was the Golden Age of the automobile in America. But in many respects, careful study of this crucial period remains to be done. True, the surface has been scraped time and time again, and the familiar story has been retold many times. But we still know relatively little about a great range of important topics, including African Americans and their cars, automobile theft, the sale of used cars, cars and sex, and the meaning of the automobile as reflected in film, music, and literature. If it is true that our everyday lives were radically changed by the automobile, then we need to search hard for answers to that important topic. True, there has been much "buff" literature written on makes and models. And scholars of business history have made a good start. But how society contributed to the automobile design process, why certain technologies were introduced — indeed the social construction of technologies associated with the automobile — remains to be written.

9

THE GO-GO YEARS, 1959–1973

Americans who lived through the 1960s typically look back at the decade with either great enthusiasm or a decided negativity. For the "flower-power" children or "red diaper babies," the 1960s was a turning point in history that failed to turn, as America afterward regressed socially and politically.[1] In contrast, the evangelical right characterize the decade as one in which Satan largely had his way, ushering in an era of free love, the widespread use of drugs, and the theological subversion of mainline Protestantism. The continuing fear of conservatives was and is that the arrested revolution will regain its lost momentum in the early twenty-first century and transform America into a country with more liberal "Western European" values. In truth, there is a little "hippie" in almost all who lived through the era, and among other things, it has influenced decisions concerning the cars we drive.

This binary view of a most complex era undoubtedly awaits further, more sophisticated interpretation. To date, the history that has been written has focused either on social unrest and politics or the Vietnam War. Economic and cultural history, and in particular the history of the automobile industry, remains largely unexplored, yet it is hardly insignificant,[2] for it was during the 1960s that decline was first evident. The Big Three's gradual slide was symbolically reflected in the Detroit race riots of 1967 and the inability to the city's elite to reverse what became an urban death spiral.[3] This was ironic perhaps, given the spectacular successes of Motown music, and went largely unperceived, as automobile profits and sales soared in 1968 and 1969.

The Microbus, Cars, and the Hippies

What *is* of particular interest is the overlap of worldviews that took place between a car culture in America that had reached its zenith during the 1950s and the counterculture of the subsequent decade. Both car culture and hippie ideology espoused freedom; however, one had its origins in standardization and industrialization, while the other was based on transcendentalism, shamanism, free love, and drugs.

One contemporary view of hippies and the automobile is that it was hippies who ultimately "killed the car," or at least killed the kinds of cars that people once loved during the 1950s and early 1960s, but any discussion of hippies is bound to be superficial unless one incorporates obvious social complexities.[4] Hippies were mobile, and some hippies did own cars, vans, buses, or motorcycles.

A keen observer of the hippies during the late 1960s, sociologist John Robert Howard not only dated the appearance of the term "hippie" to sometime in the fall of 1966, but also classified hippies into four various distinct groupings — visionaries, freaks, midnight hippies, and plastic hippies.[5] According to Howard, the visionaries articulated a coherent ideology that was opposed to the automobile. Visionaries inverted the values of their parents and substituted voluntary poverty for wealth and status. In contrast, freaks were druggies who did not figure much in the automobile story, with the exception of their hitchhiking up and down California's coast highway 101 and catching rides in battered vans. A *Newsweek* reporter described one such van as having an "interior green with a purple dashboard and curtains and rugs strung throughout. A set of copper bells jingles intermittently."[6] Midnight hippies, however, undoubtedly owned cars, and perhaps are most relevant for our discussion. Midnight hippies were older, typically in their 30s, and bridged a world between the straights and the hippies. Often they were academics, working in a world of tolerant ideas, but they still had functions in everyday life and a steady paycheck. Finally, Howard labeled a group of hippies "plastic." These were individuals who joined the movement without a deep commitment, ostentatiously wearing beads but without committing their lives to "transformation by example."

Although not "true believers," midnight and plastic hippies undoubtedly drove cars that were different. These cars tended to be older, unusual, and often decorated. Little has been written on this topic beyond commentaries on the VW Kombi or Microbus. Painted in psychedelic colors, often fitted with a mattress in the back, the Type 2 or Transporter was produced as a split window VW bus from 1950 until 1967, then replaced by a second-generation model with a one-piece windshield. Hippies often replaced the VW logo with the peace symbol.[7] One former hippie remembered that

> From 1964 until the mid–70s, there were an assortment of unusual cars that came into my life. I think back on these as "hippie cars." They were acquired as part of dope deals, abandonment, and other unorthodox means and never really belonged to anyone in the sense of title, insurance, etc. A major consideration was the amount of unexpired time on the license. The first was a Saab Station wagon with a 2 cycle engine. One of those Saabs that you poured a quart of oil in the gas tank to make a 2-cycle mix. I think it made about 8 trips from Ohio to San Francisco, northern California and back. Then came a baby blue Nash Rambler 2 door coupe, a 1954 Hudson Hornet and a 52 Buick Special. The Buick was dark brown and called the "Roach." The Hudson had more room in the back seat than any car ever, was green, and of course was called the "Green Hornet." I also owned collectively a Volkswagen bus with 2 hinged doors on both sides....
>
> It's easy to see what this assortment of vehicles had in common. They were 10+ years old when cars lasted five and were undesirable in a pre-energy crisis 70 mph interstate world. The little Nash and Volvo were the epitome of automotive counter culture.... The Volkswagen van went to California and back on the interstate and was passed by every other car on the road. The Hudson was in that automotive limbo of being a car that wasn't made anymore and the Buick—well it was Buick.
>
> These things became part of the lifestyle with constantly changing affects. The Nash Rambler ended its days covered with concert posters from the Avalon and Fillmore Ballrooms. The Hudson's swan song was a short stint as a demolition derby car since no one could get a title for it.[8]

A similar sense of the cars that hippies drove was described by Peter Jedick in his fictional account of hippie culture and life in Kent, Ohio, during the late 1960s:

> Everything back in the 60s was kind of communal: our weed, our food, our albums, even our automobile. The vehicle of choice was purchased the previous spring from Murph's older brother for $25, $6.25 apiece. Not bad, huh?
>
> So what if it was a huge rusted out '59 Chrysler New Yorker. The price was right even though its V-8 engine sucked up gasoline like elephant drinks water. What the hell, gas was only a quarter a gallon.

The Chrysler did look a little out of place on a campus filled with hippie vans, Corvairs, and Volkswagen beetles. We tried to compensate by decorating it with those yellow plastic stick-on flowers that were in vogue at the time. We put them on the floor panels, the trunk, the hood, even the roof, but all it did was make it look even more obscene.

Did we care? Hell, no. We were the trendsetters, not slaves to the fashion dictates of the age. We were confident that once our contemporaries saw the advantages of our ride they would want one themselves.

After all, the Chrysler seated six comfortably, ten if necessary, started on a dime and best of all, no car payments. What more could a college kid ask for?[9]

Perhaps the quintessential vehicle associated with the hippies was Ken Kesey's 1939 International school bus that he converted into a camper for his "Merry Pranksters." One observer described it as "the original psychedelic bus, the precursor of the wildest transit system ever unloaded on the world's roadways of rainbow colors and blaring music and long-haired men and women packed together with their necessities...."[10] The "Bus" reflected hippies' high priority for sound, as described by Tom Wolfe in his classic *The Electric Kool-Aid Test*:

Kesey gave the word and the Pranksters set upon it one afternoon. They started painting it and wiring it for sound and cutting a hole in the roof and fixing up the top of the bus so you could sit up there in the open air and play music, even a set of drums and electric guitars and electric bass and so forth, or just ride. Sandy went to work on the wiring and rigged up a system with which they could broadcast from inside the bus, with tapes or over microphones, and it would blast outside over powerful speakers on top of the bus. There were also microphones outside that would pick up sounds along the road and broadcast them inside the bus. There was also a sound system inside the bus so you could broadcast to one another over the roar of the engine and the road.... There was going to be no goddamn sound on that whole trip, outside the bus, inside the bus, or inside your own freaking larynx, that you couldn't tune in on and rap off of.[11]

Hippies not only drove cars, they also owned tools and fixed them. Perhaps the most significant development in do-it-yourself automobile repair after World War II was the consequence of an engineer-turned-hippie's efforts to teach everyday folks to repair their VWs. In 1969, the first edition of John Muir's *How to Keep Your Volkswagen Alive: A Manual of Step by Step Procedures for the Complete Idiot* appeared, and its 5,000 copies quickly sold out. By the 1990s this clearly-written and well-illustrated repair manual had gone through 16 editions and become the first of a series of eclectic publications from John Muir Publications. Muir's intentions were simple: to enable those who had previously thought of themselves as mechanically challenged to perform everything from regular maintenance to the rebuilding of a VW engine. Muir, educated at California-Berkeley in civil engineering, had held a series of technical jobs for much of his working life, but found himself in Taos, New Mexico, in the late 1960s as the owner of John's Garage. Beginning with the writing of simple instructions for a woman to grind valves, Muir and his third wife Eve compiled a manual that featured the remarkable illustrations of artist Peter Aschwanden. Throughout the narrative, Muir inserted bits of philosophical wisdom like the following:

While the levels of logic of the human entity are many and varied, your car operates on one simple level and it's up to you to understand its trip. Talk to the car, then shut up and listen. Feel with your car; use all of your receptive senses and when you find out what it needs, seek the operation out and perform it with love. The type of love your car contains differs from you by timescale, logic level and conceptual anomalies but it is "life" nonetheless. Its karma depends on your desire to make and keep it — ALIVE![12]

To this day, no automobile repair manual is as clear or as easy to use for the shade-tree home mechanic as *How to Keep your Volkswagen Alive.*

The Cadillac and the Establishment

A stark contrast to hippie values and their cars can be found in the place of the Cadillac in American life during the 1950s and 1960s.[13] Paradoxically, perhaps, the one Cadillac hippies did embrace was the Cadillac hearse. And with 90 percent of all hearses being Cadillacs, it is a foregone conclusion that most Americans take their final ride in a Cadillac. The marque has appeared in popular song like no other—BMI has registered more than 1,000 songs with Cadillac in the title.

Indeed, at the same time that Haight-Ashbury was at its peak as the epicenter of the counterculture and Vietnam War protests were raging across America, the Cadillac reached its apex in terms of sales and social presence. In 1967, the Cadillac blotted out its competitors, posted record profits, and introduced a new 472 cubic inch engine, the largest production engine for passenger cars in the world. The typical Cadillac buyer had an annual income of more than $25,000 and had a median age of 53.[14]

Throughout the twentieth century, Cadillac was a distinguished American marque, although like almost all American cars, its luster was diminished by the early 1970s. It was only one of a number of cars that were purchased by the wealthy elite in America before World War II. Other makes of the so-called "Olympian Age" of the 1930s included Duesenberg, Cord, Auburn, Pierce-Arrow, Packard, and Lincoln. The Depression era forced these manufacturers one by one to either close their doors or change their pricing strategies. But even then Cadillac had a mystique, a name—"the standard of the world." It was a symbol of hard-earned success.

Under the leadership of German-born mechanic Nick Dreystadt, during the late 1930s Cadillac emerged as a force to be reckoned with. The division invested heavily in new and efficient production facilities and sleek designs that foreshadowed the post–World War II era. However, after the war Cadillac moved to center stage in America with new designs featuring gently upturned fins, a bathtub profile, and an influential advertising campaign. The Cadillac was more than flash, however, for it was a true technology leader; its high compression engine, power accessories, and hardtops far outstripped the competition in the early 1950s. It was a machine superior to anything else built, but more importantly, it became a symbol to the increasing numbers of well-to-do in post–World War II America. Jewish businessmen drove Cadillacs as a result of their desire to enjoy the good life. African Americans, often unable to live in affluent neighborhoods during the 1950s and 1960s because of covenants, saw the Cadillac as the symbol of the end of Jim Crow, and the rise of a Black middle class. They too could be a part of the American Dream.

The architects of Cadillac's success were advertising executives from the Bloomfield Hills, Michigan, agency of McManus, John & Adams. Jim Adams' copy lines fostered an intangible spiritual desire for something that was more than a car. In a 1955 article published in *Fortune*, author William H. Whyte, Jr. summarized Adams' advertising campaign by bringing together a number of the latter's copy lines:

> *Let's say it was thirty-one years ago, on a beautiful morning in June. A boy stood by a rack of papers on a busy street and heard the friendly horn of a Cadillac. "Keep the change," the driver*

OFFICE OF
GENERAL SALES MANAGER

1580 EAST GRAND BOULEVARD
DETROIT 32, MICHIGAN

July, 21, 1955

Mr. Otis C. Brannock
473 S. Salina St.
Syracuse, New York

Dear Mr. Brannock :

In America, today, the automobile a man drives
is often regarded as outward and visibile evidence of the station he has achieved in life ...
and a mirror of his taste and judgement as well.
You drive a fine car, and you have undoubtedly
encountered this reaction.

It also seems that the appeal of a fine car is
universal. That is why we are sure you will be
interested in this Portfolio of Fine Cars from
Packard as interpreted by Alexis de Sakhnoffsky.

The Studebaker-Packard Corporation is proud that
Alexis de Sakhnoffsky, one of the foremost automobile illustrators in the world, selected Packard to typify his conception of America's finest
motor car.

Superior design and creative engineering has been
a Packard heritage for more than a half century,
a heritage that enables us to invite you to "Ask
The Man Who Owns One."

Sincerely yours,

Dan O'Madigan, Jr.
General Sales Manager

O'M:ljs

Letter from Dan O'Madigan, Jr., Sales Manager, Studebaker-Packard, to Mr. Otis C. Brannock, July 21, 1955. The first paragraph explains how what one drives reflects who one is as a person. The Port-folio mentioned was a beautifully illustrated book of Packard designs and color schemes (The Citizens Motorcar Company, America's Packard Museum, Dayton, Ohio).

grunted, as he took his paper and rolled out into traffic. "There," thought the boy, as he clutched his coin, "is the car for me."

And since this is America, where dreams make sense in the heart of the boy, he is now an industrialist. He has fought— without interruption— for a place in the world he wants his family to occupy. Few would deny him some taste of the fruits of his labor. No compromise this time! The papers are all in order ... and the car of his dreams is waiting for him. It's his!

It's Junetime— and the top is down— and he's going halfway up the hill, to a spot where a lane strays into the wildwood and he can glimpse the top of a fieldstone chimney above the trees. The family rushes out with the final voice of confirmation. "Hi there neighbor, isn't it a lovely day?"

There's the first trip to the office with a waiting delegation to admire his choice. He'll get those quick glances of approval that tell him the dream he dreamed for so many years is still in the heart of others.

Let him arrive at the door of a distinguished hotel or a famous restaurant ... and he has the courtesy that goes with respect. "Here is a man," the Cadillac says— almost as plainly as the words are written here— "who has earned the right to sit at the wheel."[15]

The Cadillac is no longer the symbol of success in America that it once was. Now the Lexus, BMW, Mercedes and Jaguar are more popular in county club parking lots, although of late, Cadillac has experienced a resurgence of sorts. Yet it had its place in twentieth century history, as it was a proud product at a time when "American Made" was the standard of the world.

An Age of Ambivalence

One might argue that the decade of 1960s began not on January 1, 1960, but rather sometime during 1957 or 1958. Using the same kind of historical reasoning, one might posit that the conclusion of this most tumultuous decade in American history took place not on December 31, 1969, but during 1973 or 1974.

The year 1957 witnessed not only the publication of Jack Keroauc's *On the Road*, but also the successful launch of the Russian artificial satellite Sputnik. To many, Sputnik was proof positive that Americans were distracted and complacent, and their institutions largely ineffectual in keeping up with the Soviets in terms of science and technology. As a brief recession led to serious economic difficulties by November 1957 and hit depths unmatched since the Great Depression in February 1958, Eisenhower's America seemed to be a wasteland inhabited by organization men, naïve consumers, and spend-happy and rebellious youth.[16] Similarly, the curtain on this era was closed between the Mideast War of October 1973, the subsequent "Oil Shock" I, and the August 1974 resignation of Richard Nixon. As rising energy prices shifted demand to small cars and increasing government regulations took effect, Detroit's long decline in the American market began in earnest.

The automobile industry was certainly implicated in these perceptions of general economic, political, and social failure. The hubris of its executives related to consumer needs, an obsession with big cars, garish designs coming from its studios, the neglect of safety and air pollution matters, and rising prices all played into the hands of critics who succeeded John Keats, and who now were heard by the public and politicians.[17] As economist Lawrence J. White demonstrated in his *The Automobile Industry Since 1945*, the industry was largely complacent, fattened by high rates of return of investment.[18] With little incentive to develop new technologies, automobile executives turned a deaf ear during the 1960s to matters related to both safety and air pollution. It was only after the government intervened as a countervailing force that the automobile industry responded at all to pressing issues, and initially it did so halfheartedly. A new vision concerning individual mass transportation was clearly called for, but was not forthcoming from Detroit. In time it would come from our former World War II enemies, the Germans and Japanese.

The unparalleled prosperity of the 1950s shifted the concerns of many Americans away from the economy to issues that were once considered secondary. Beginning in the late 1950s, grass roots movements connected to politics, the consumers' movement, public health, and race all emerged. Traditional authority, conventional wisdom, and trust in institutions and professions were now all challenged by a relatively small but highly educated, vocal, and influential minority. In Baltimore and New York City, public health officials questioned the use of lead paint for interior applications and expressed concern over flaking paint that was being eaten by children, resulting in childhood lead poisoning. The widespread application of pesticides by aerial spraying was seen as being problematic to the natural order. In the West, the Sierra Club voiced opposition to the damming of wild rivers. And in the South, African Americans were no longer content to live with the insults of Jim Crow racism.

One can push the argument too far, however, that America's love affair with the automobile was coming to an end in the early to mid–1960s. Writing at the tail end of a remarkable period of social transitions, James Flink asserted in 1972 that the "era of uncritical mass accommodation to the motor car has ended...."[19] Flink pointed to the mid–1960s as a watershed of change for both the automobile industry and American society, and perhaps that was true for the highly educated middle classes. If we are to believe Tom Wolfe, a Yale-educated Ph.D. with his feet on the ground in America during the early 1960s, culture was being created from the bottom up, and the vast majority of American remained as much in love with their automobiles as during previous generations.[20] In his *The Kandy-Kolored Tangerine Flake Streamline Baby*, Wolfe featured customizers George Barris and Ed "Big Daddy" Roth, demolition derby promoter Lawrence Medelsohn, and moonshine runner and NASCAR hero Junior Johnson. Clearly, the rank and file in American life was not particularly concerned with either the fate of the American city, the quality of the nation's air, or the plight of the powerless consumer. Regardless of the region of the country, good old boys and their women were more representative of American life than effete Eastern intellectuals wearing horn-rimmed glasses.

Harry Crews and the "White Trash" in His Novel Car

This ambivalence surrounding auto-mobility during the late 1960s and early 1970s was perhaps best represented in the fiction of southern writer Harry Crews. Crews's "white trash" novel *Car* was published in 1972, and its strangeness reflected the era. The focus of the novel is one unusual family in the junkyard business, one of whom takes it upon himself to eat, piece by piece, a 1971 Ford Maverick. The local Ford dealer envisions this absurdity as a spectacle, with the car, the diner, and a "throne" for bodily evacuation all under glass for the public to witness. The novel is at the same time gross and sexy, with the Maverick-eater's sister portrayed in leather, enjoying getting her breasts massaged from time to time as a prerequisite to back seat lovemaking, and a frustrated prostitute supposedly in charge of our dreamer-hero. A bigger question emerges than this bizarre happening in Jacksonville, Florida. Are we consuming the car or is it consuming us? Were we shaping the automobile to our societal needs, or was the automobile literally shaping us as human beings? The lead character in the novel, Herman Mack, dreamt the following as he was about to eat his first piece of the Maverick:

> Filled with terror and joy, he tried to wake up. But he was not asleep. His eyes were filled with cars. They raced and competed in every muscle and fiber. Dune buggies raced over the California sands of his feet; sturdy jeeps with four wheel drive and snow tires climbed the Montana mountains of his hips; golden convertibles, sleek and topless, purred through the Arizona sun of his left arm; angry taxis, dirty and functional and knowledgeable, fought for survival in the New York City of his head.
>
> And his heart. God, his heart! He felt it separate and distinct in his chest. Isolated and pumping, he knew its outermost limits. And every car that raced and roared in his vision of himself finally ended in his heart. An endless traffic of Saabs and Fords and Plymouths and Volkswagens and modified buggies of every sort and Toyotas and cars from all over the world lined up and entered his pounding heart.
>
> He watched, amazed and stupefied, as he filled up with cars tighter and tighter until finally he was bumper to bumper from head to toe. His skin stretched. His veins and arteries blared with the honking of horns, jammed with a traffic jam that would never be over because it had no place to go. Cars, cars everywhere and no place to drive.
>
> But at the last moment, when he was gasping and choking with cars, truly terrified that they would keep multiplying until the seams of his skin split and spilled his life, a solution — dreamlike and appropriate — came to him in his vision. He was a car. A superbly equipped car. He would escape because he was the thing that threatened himself, and he would not commit suicide.
>
> If he needed more air he'd turn on the air-conditioner. If he needed more strength, he'd burn a higher octane gasoline. If he needed more confidence, he'd get another hundred horses under the hood. If the light of the world bothered him, he'd tint his windshield. And his immortality lay in numberless junkyards....[21]

Ralph Nader and Unsafe at Any Speed

The Crews story is only one snapshot of a complex set of impressions concerning the car and society during this time of inordinate introspection. A holistic account demands the consideration of intellectual impulses and politics at the top as well a social customs and mass movements at the bottom, for just as modern corporations came under suspicion after Rachel Carson's *Silent Spring* was published in 1962, so too did the professionals associated with universities and chemical companies. And as much as Ralph Nader attacked GM for its Corvair in his *Unsafe at Any Speed*, he also broadened his critique to include the engineers who worked in Detroit. Perhaps more than anyone else since Thorstein Veblen, Ralph Nader focused on the shortcomings of engineers and the flawed institutional arrangements that existed where they worked. Published in 1965, *Unsafe at Any Speed* accused automotive engineers of disregarding ethical principles and ignoring public safety. The publicity given to his critical analysis and Nader's own crusade spurred the consumer movement and the work of trial lawyers, both of which have led to powerful social changes since the early 1960s.[22]

At the heart of Nader's early work was his attack on the safety of General Motors' Corvair. In Nader's opinion, "the Corvair was tragedy not a blunder." The tragedy was a consequence of engineers who cut corners to shave costs. This was a common occurrence in the auto industry and indeed all manufacturing, but with the Corvair it happened in a big way. Fatefully, during the late 1950s, General Motors, under the leadership of engineer Ed Cole, developed the Corvair, in part the consequence of the unexpected success of the Volkswagen Beetle, but also the result of two decades of engineers' fascination with the concept of a vehicle with its engine placed in the rear. While the Corvair had its supporters who argued that the car got a raw deal by consumer advocates, it was generally regarded as one of a number of Detroit products of the era that were egregiously unsafe and based on flawed designs. It was hubris, economics, and blind obedience on the part of engineers working in a flawed institutional environment that led to the Corvair tragedy. The Corvair was the wrong car at the wrong time in American history.

The tragedy can be translated into human terms. For example, in August 1961, Mrs. Rose Pierini of Santa Barbara lost control of her new Corvair while driving 35 mph. The car flipped on its top, and Mrs. Pierini was trapped underneath, blood gushing from a dismembered arm that was lying in the street. She would later receive $70,000 after being worn down by GM attorneys and deciding not to go any further with her lawsuit. In a similar fashion, GM Truck and Bus Vice-President Calvin J. Werner, living in Dayton, Ohio, purchased a Corvair for his daughter. She was afraid to drive the car, but her brother was not. That brother would die in a low-speed accident, the consequence of the vehicle's inherent instability. The Werner family's plight is reflective of just how little the public, and indeed even GM insiders, knew about the inherent design flaws of the Corvair during the first few years after its introduction. There was a conspiracy of silence about unsafe vehicles before the era of recalls.

Indeed, during the 1960 to 1964 model years, the Corvair could go out of control at 22 mph with a turning radius of 50 degrees and front rear and tire pressures of 26 psi. Ford engineers quickly discovered this fact, when in 1959 two of them lost control of an early Corvair on the Dearborn, Michigan, test track.

The tragedy began with conception and development of the Corvair by leading GM engineers — Edward Cole, Harry Barr, Robert Schilling, Kai Hansen, and Frank Winchell. Cole, a long-time devotee of rear-engined cars, saw a market as early as 1955 for a small, compact car, and in 1956, after rising to the head of the Chevrolet Division, put his finest engineering talent to work on the project. By 1957, the program was given a full go-ahead, even though executives knew that several design obstacles had yet to be overcome.

As early as 1953, GM executives were aware of the main problem that was associated later with the Corvairs. In that year, one of the GM's brightest engineers, Maurice Olley, wrote a technical paper, "European Postwar Cars," that contained a sharp critique of rear-engined automobiles with swing-axle suspension systems. He called such vehicles "a poor bargain, at least in the form in which they are at present built," adding that they could not handle safely in wind even at moderate speeds, despite the tire pressure differential between front and rear. Olley went further, depicting the "forward fuel tank as a collision risk as is the mass of engine in the rear."[23]

Despite these warnings, GM went ahead, with its primary aim being a target rate of return on investment. The 1960 Corvair came off the assembly line at two-thirds the weight of a standard Chevrolet, with a selling price $200 lower than standard models, but to keep costs down and profits high, compromises had to be made. Suspension stabilizers were left off, and a peculiar kind of swing axle was used that created "oversteer" or instability when deviating from a straight path. To compensate for oversteer, Corvair engineers recommended that owners maintain critical tire pressure differentials between front and rear wheels. This whole design, confessed one GM engineer, was based on lower cost, ease of assembly, ease of service, simplicity of design, and the desire to create a soft ride.

The biggest problem with the Corvair was that GM was slow to react to a known problem — the large number of accidents due to loss of control. The company was silent when questioned on the matter. Until Nader gained a wide public audience, GM did little or nothing. The moral of the story is that the corporations of the early 1960s faced the consequences of their actions only when threatened with government sanctions, expensive litigation and court judgments, or public hostility on a massive scale. Indeed, it took GM four years and 1,124,076 Corvairs to correct the problem.[24]

The convergence of forces for change took the industry by total surprise in the months immediately after the 1964 presidential election. The Johnson administration's willingness to sponsor social reform legislation and the appearance on the Washington scene of Ralph Nader, Abraham Ribicoff, and the American Trial Lawyers' Association are all part of the story. Significantly, a 1966 landmark case, *Larsen vs. General Motors*, marked a new trend in automobile liability decisions.[25] Manufacturers were now held responsible for inadequate designs that resulted in injuries due to a collision. Other cases followed *Larsen*, but it was this case, involving the dangerous design of the Corvair steering column, that made possible an additional recourse for consumers. With agencies like the Department of Transportation often influenced by industry, the judiciary was a second route to ultimately enhancing automobile safety.

Government Regulation: Safety and the Environment

The Corvair was at the center of a consumer firestorm on auto safety that peaked by the end of the 1960s. In absolute numbers, traffic fatalities had risen from 34,763 in 1950 to 39,628 in 1956 to 53,041 in 1966 and 56,278 by 1972. During those years, every Christmas and New Year's resulted in the death of approximately 1,000 Americans. The rise of the interstate highway system beginning in 1956 and the marked increase in younger drivers contributed to the alarming trend. Design also played its part; along with horsepower gains, cars of the mid–1960s possessed poor handling characteristics and abysmal braking capabilities.

The seminal legislative action that set in motion strict automobile safety regulations was the 1966 Vehicle National Traffic and Motor Safety Act. Beginning in 1968, this act mandated seatbelts, padded visors and dashboards, safety doors and hinges, impact absorbing steering columns, dual braking systems, and standard bumper height in all new autos sold in the United States. Critics, however, argued that these measures would do little to save lives and prevent injuries. History has proved them to be somewhat correct.[26] As economist Sam Peltzman demonstrated in the mid–1970s, automobile safety devices resulted in "off-setting behavior" on the part of a number of motorists who engaged in more risky behavior as a result of the introduction of features that were designed to increase their chances of surviving a crash. And while seatbelts, soft interiors, and improved glass did reduced driver fatalities, risky behavior increased the chance that a bicyclist or pedestrian would be killed or injured.

With regard to the safety issues that followed, the most significant problems centered on drivers and passengers actually using their seatbelts and the development and introduction of the airbag. In the former case, the federal government initially tried to force compliance with the mandate to install seatbelt interlocks on all cars beginning in 1974, but due to public outcry, this measure would be repealed in 1976. However, it was federal pressure on the states to enforce the use of seatbelts after 1990 that has led to tough seatbelt laws in which local traffic officers can ticket offenders. With the automobile becoming increasingly safe, the current issue with SUVs — high bumper height and reduced visibilities — remains to be solved. Additionally, with each decade from the 1930s forward, more emphasis was placed on drinking and drunk driving, as operator error superseded vehicle design limitations as causes of accidents. A key advance was the widespread use of the breathalyzer, a device that was pioneered first in Britain and only later used in traffic enforcement in the United States.[27]

A second area where government had to step in and force manufacturers to take responsibility was the environment, particularly air pollution. Air pollution and haze first became an issue in Southern California, and it was California that first responded legislatively to the problem, with the federal government subsequently following the state's lead.[28] For years, manufacturers had claimed that devices to reduce the level of pollutants would take considerable time and research to develop. Industry's hand was forced, however, in terms of technical feasibility, by the California legislature. In 1964 California certified four emissions control devices designed by aftermarket companies, and then mandated that devices of these types be installed on 1966 car models. In 1966, of an estimated 146 million tons of pollutants discharged into the atmosphere in the United States, some 86 million tons could be attributed to the automobile. The major chemical culprits were carbon monoxide, hydrocarbons, nitrogen oxides, and lead compounds.

As in the case of safety, a seminal federal act related to automobile emissions was passed and enacted in the mid–1960s, the Motor Vehicle Air Pollution and Control Act. This act set limits in terms of carbon monoxide and hydrocarbons, and was amended in 1971 to include evaporated gasoline. Additionally, the Federal Clean Air Act (1970) and emissions stipulations further reduced allowable pollutants with the newly created Environmental Protection Agency as the enforcer.

In the wake of this legislation, however, Detroit showed shameless disregard for seriously tackling the issue. Rather than make substantial investments in a new generation of cleaner cars, the Big Three merely added stopgap devices to existing engines, thus minimizing their costs while producing autos with very poor performance and drivability characteristics. Devices that included PCV, Decel and EGR valves and air pumps resulted in engines that were difficult to tune and unreliable. Finally, by the mid–1970s catalytic converters were introduced, which had the beneficial side effect of forcing tetraethyl lead off the market, though they sidelined development of more viable lean-burn engines for the long term. Fuel injection systems, first mechanical and then computer regulated, were certainly feasible and often installed on European cars, but they cost more than carburetors, which when connected to emissions controls were simply inefficient and troublesome.

The federal government tried to tackle several other automobile issues during the 1960s, but not with the same degree of success as with matters of safety and the environment. In December 1968, a Senate Judiciary subcommittee held hearings on the automobile repair business and heard testimony about rising repair costs, prices for parts, abuses of the flat-rate system, and improper repair practices.[29] Nothing came of these hearings, or of efforts to reform the automobile insurance industry, whose premiums rose markedly throughout the decade.[30]

The oil shocks of 1973 and 1979 more forcefully influenced Detroit's direction in the manufacture of more fuel-efficient automobiles than federal Corporate Average Fuel Economy (CAFE) standards and the 1978 Gas Guzzler Tax. Indeed, the shortage of petroleum products and the rise in the cost of gasoline, along with foreign competition, carried more weight in transforming automotive technologies than consumer demand or government regulation.

From a Brief Affair with Economy Vehicles
to the Emergence of the Muscle Car

The tragedy of the Corvair notwithstanding, America's love affair with the automobile continued through the 1960s. The Corvair, the Ford Falcon and the Plymouth Valiant were the Big Three's first response to consumer dissatisfaction with tailfins and chrome that had resulted in the first wave of the import invasion of the late 1950s. These compacts were introduced in the fall of 1959 with only short-term success, however.

When introduced, the Valiant possessed all of the qualities that the "dinosaur in the driveway" that preceded it had lacked. Indeed, designer Virgil Exner, who a few years earlier made fins the hallmark of the American automobile with his "Forward Look" Plymouths, DeSotos, and Chryslers, now penned a car that had no real fins.

In a speech introducing the Valiant, Chrysler vice president William C. Newburg pointed out that the Valiant design had resulted in low production and operating costs, high fuel efficiency, good handling, and ample luggage space. It was claimed that the Valiant was a car "that was totally new and different."[31] Its slant-6 engine was coupled to a newly-designed 3-speed automatic transmission. Its body was unitized, dipped, and sprayed several times to prevent corrosion and deaden sound, and the car's electrical system featured an alternating current alternator rather than a direct current generator. In contrast to the innovative features of the Valiant, the Falcon was a totally conventional vehicle that initially sold well — more than 435,000 cars its first year! Falcons were cheap, and for the most part you got what you paid for, as they frequently rusted away in a few years, to be thrown away by their owners. Perhaps they were one of the first truly discardable vehicles, in a society where discardable was to take on a new meaning to include what was considered as durable goods. A year later, the GM divisions Pontiac, Oldsmobile and Buick introduced their own import-fighters, the Pontiac Tempest, Olds F-85, and Buick Special. As a true innovative economy vehicle, the Tempest was in production only between 1961 and 1963. Its unibody design, incorporating a long torque rope and flexible driveshaft with the transmission and transaxle located in the rear, gave way to a conventional frame layout beginning in 1964 that was rugged enough to support the larger engines and longer wheelbase designs that followed. The 1961 Oldsmobile F-85 was also a unique car, for it had a 215 cubic inch aluminum engine. And the 1962 Buick Special, a compact car using an old nameplate, featured the first V-6 engine in America. Given these new directions, it was no surprise that the 1961 Tempest was named *Motor Trend's* car of the year, and similarly, the Buick Special won the same award the following year.

Detroit's reaction to the rising presence of the Volkswagen in America, along with other lesser-known imports like French Simcas and Renaults and British Triumph Heralds and MG Magnettes, was transitory. Or perhaps it reflected the fact that the real cost of gasoline in adjusted-for-inflation dollars reached its lowest point during the 1960s. With low fuel prices and the rise of the new interstate highways, why should status-conscious Americans drive a compact when a high compression accessorized car offered so much more in terms of comfort and status? Perhaps the prosperity of the times began to erase those memories of the 1930s and the "depression psychology" that embraced thrift as a primary virtue. Consequently, the compact car fad fizzled by 1963, and Detroit reacted quickly by scaling up its "economy models." By failing to maintain a commitment to this market segment, however, American manufacturers would be unprepared to fill the needs of American consumers after 1968, when the small car market exploded from approximately 10 percent of the market to nearly 50 percent in 1974.

A series of important questions beg to be answered. What was the focus of research and development at the Big Three during the last 40 years of the twentieth century? In his path-breaking book on the post-war automobile industry, Lawrence J. White traced many of the innovations that were to be found on modern cars to suppliers of materials like aluminum and fiberglass and components that included disc brakes, power steering, electrical systems and suspensions.[32] Did the Big Three possess no interest in long-term trends shaping the future? Why were serious alternatives to the internal combustion engine — turbines, rotary designs, electrics, steam — given serious study, only to be dropped as unfeasible? Key to understanding this inertia is a 1969 public relations booklet published by General Motors promoting their research into alternative power plant systems.[33] Indeed, a number of fascinating studies were done at GM in the 1960s in areas that included steam propulsion, hybrid vehicle designs, and electrics. Yet in the end it was an exercise in futility, and perhaps the tip-off was the first chart in this publication, which traced the history of fears concerning petroleum shortages and a subsequent response that led to new oil field discoveries and an abundance of reserves. It is ironic that at the same time that the U.S. was reaching peak oil production GM concluded that oil supplies would be abundant for the foreseeable future.

On another level, how could sophisticated psychological and market research groups repeatedly either misread the market or ignore potential threats outside the United States? What were Big Three corporate leaders doing with the expertise, gained from decades of global industry leadership, to lose an edge they had gained from the innovations of pioneers like Henry Ford and Charles Franklin Kettering? And finally, in a broader national sense, why were so many Americans so jaded and materialistic in their wants? Had the car become such a signifier of status and self-worth that excesses were justified by manufacturers who claimed that all they were doing was meeting the demands of the market?

From the Plymouth Valiant were later derived larger, sportier models, the Barracuda and Duster; the former evolved into a true muscle car by 1970. The humble and boxy Ford Fal-

1970 Dodge Coronet "Super Bee." One of the last of the true muscle cars, the Coronet "Super Bee" exuded masculinity (Chrysler LLC).

con formed the basis for the far more successful Mustang. Available with six- or eight-cylinder powerplants in coupe and convertible forms, by the end of the 1960s, the Mustang had morphed into the unrecognizable shape of a Ford Torino. Indeed, the fuel efficient and light economy cars beginning with the Pontiac Tempest and Olds F-85 were for the most part transformed by mid-decade into the muscle cars Pontiac GTO and Oldsmobile 4-4-2.

The compacts were among the first poorly made products produced by the Big Three. Prior to the 1958 recession, "American Made" meant something worldwide. Americans who were tempered by the harshness of the Great Depression developed a work ethic that their children working on the line 20 years later simply did not have.

During a transitional period between 1962 and 1973, the muscle car emerged as a dominant icon in car culture America. Yet in reality, for every Chevy 409 or Camaro Z-28 of the period, there were ten cheaply constructed Chevy IIs or four-door Biscaynes driven by blue-collar workers who were more prosperous than ever, yet still at the lower end of the multidivisional marketing spectrum. The high horsepower, high fuel consumption vehicles competing for the young man's segment of the market — the Chevy SS models; Pontiac GTO; Olds 4-4-2, Plymouth Barracuda and Roadrunner; Dodge Charger and Challenger; Shelby Mustang — were all high profile automobiles of that era.

Of all the makes and models from the 1960s, two models stand out — the Pontiac GTO and the Ford Mustang. It took Detroit market analysts and auto executives nearly a decade after Chuck Berry and Elvis to figure out that the same youth market responsible for 45 RPM records and rock and roll could also stimulate automobile sales if the product was made properly and also attractive. At Pontiac, the key figures were "Bunkie" Knudsen, Pete Estes, and especially John Z. DeLorean.[34] In 1956, Knudsen inherited a product line that was languishing, and through his leadership and vision it was revitalized by 1959 as an automobile that exhibited the "wide track look." Knudsen moved up the organizational ladder at GM in 1961, leaving Estes and DeLorean at the reins of the Pontiac division. It was market savvy and engineering prowess that contributed to the upgrading of the lowly Tempest in 1963 to a larger vehicle named the Le Mans. With a 326 cubic inch V-8 engine, the juiced-up and redesigned Tempest was only one big step away from the remarkable high-performance GTO of 1964. With a standard 325 horsepower engine, optional tri-power performance, and a Hurst 4-speed, this light, fast, and inexpensive car resulted in a thrill with every ride.[35] Although GM executives with offices on the fourteenth floor were taken by surprise, the success of the GTO was hardly surprising given the large number of young people with money in their pockets who were looking for excitement. Thus, the relatively inexpensive ($3,200) GTO was a hit from the beginning, with sales of 31,000 in 1964, 64,000 in 1965, and 84,000 in 1966. And advertising contributed to the GTO's success: the car was depicted as a tiger, with "tiger paws" for tires. According to one advertisement, by driving a GTO could you distinguish the "tiger" from a "pussycat?"

Lee Iacocca is often given credit for the marketing insights that led to the Ford Mustang, yet, as Iacocca recounts in his autobiography, the Mustang story was far more complex than simply the genius of one executive.[36] In the wake of the Edsel debacle and a false start with an economy car named the Cardinal, later to be sold only in Europe, the Mustang captured the imagination and pocketbooks of many young or youthful-thinking Americans beginning in 1964. Inexpensive, sporty, with a long hood and a short trunk area, the Mustang was so accessorizable that it could be found with small 170 cubic inch six or a 289 cubic inch V-8 engine. More and more options were made available with time, and as the decade progressed the once lean machine, based on a Ford Falcon wheelbase, became a rather heavy but high-powered muscle car, if so optioned. What is so important about the Mustang, however, was that despite its phenomenal initial sales, Ford's overall market share remained nearly the same. Thus, what the Mustang did was take buyers away from other Ford product lines, rather than from GM, Chrysler, or the imports.[37]

California Dreaming

With the automobile fixed in our culture in an unprecedented manner, rock and roll music brought to daily consciousness the California car culture, as epitomized in the songs of Jan and Dean and especially the Beach Boys with their "Little Deuce Coupe," "409," and "Little Old Lady from Pasadena."

Before they were the Beach Boys they were the Pendletones. Five good-looking young men, three of them brothers, they could sing, but initially had little stage presence. They sang the California Dream to young people living hundreds to thousands of miles from the surf. Their first serious effort was "Surfin' Safari," but by the spring of 1963 "Surfin' U.S.A." was a top ten hit. It was all about life in Southern California, with its sun, hot rods, high schools, and pretty girls. As rock historian Jonathan Gould recounted concerning the Beach Boys, "They sang with a deadpan bass at the bottom, a whooping falsetto on top, and in between, a kind of epic Californian nasality, so calmly enthusiastic that they sounded like the sons of NASA personnel."[38] On the flip side of "Surfin' Safari" was "409," describing a Chevrolet with a 409 cubic inch V-8, a "family car" that when equipped with a four-speed transmission, two four-barrel carburetors, and a posi-traction rear end could go 0–60 in less than 5 seconds. As the Beach Boys sang, "nothing could catch her." In fact, none of the cars mentioned in Beach Boys songs could be kept up with. In 1963, Beach Boy Brian Wilson coauthored with Roger Christian "Little Deuce Coupe."

Christian also wrote songs for two friends of the Beach Boys, Jan and Dean. Jan Berry and Dean Torrance grew up together in West Los Angeles and after a number of hits including "Jenny Lee" and "Linda," they moved in late 1962 into surfing and car music. Subsequently, they released the humorous "The Little Old Lady from Pasadena," a song about a granny who drove a super stock Dodge. More significant, however, was their "Deadman's Curve," ominously foreshadowing in 1964 Jan's close brush with death in an April 1966 accident in Beverly Hills. Indeed, the car songs of Jan and Dean encapsulated the two faces of the automobile that were a part of 1960s car culture in America, for the automobile could both bring delight and destruction, and it was a capricious machine at best.

Oil Shock I

In October 1973, OPEC (Organization of Petroleum Exporting Countries) placed an embargo on oil shipped to the United States as a result of American support for Israel during the October 1973 Yom Kippur War.[39] Gasoline, already in short supply since the United States had reached its peak of oil production in 1970, suddenly became very scarce and more costly. Lines formed at virtually every gas station that had gas. At a number of stations, color-coded signs or flags indicated availability. Eventually, even-odd license plate rationing took place, as did a federally mandated reduction in the interstate highway speed limit to 55 miles per hour. Gas station customers, once accustomed to service that included the washing of windshields and oil checks, now waited three hours or more. The situation led to shortened tempers and fist fights, even in laid-back southern California.

OPEC thus used oil as a weapon, and it was a weapon used well. The embargo not only brought the United States to its knees in terms of unemployment and inflation, but also increased the profits of OPEC members nearly seven-fold between 1972 and 1977. Gas prices, responding to a nervous market, climbed 70 percent. Along with the embargo and further price increases, OPEC announced a cut in oil production. Leonardo Maugeri recounted, "Total Arab oil production in September 1973 had reached 19.4 million barrels per day; in November, 15.4 million."[40]

Conspiracy theories abounded as the price of gas ran up. Were the Arabs or the oil companies at the heart of the problem? As studies subsequently demonstrated, it was neither. Rather, the decrease in supply wasn't the chief cause of Oil Shock I and its impact. Looking back to that time of fear and confusion, Maugeri claimed that "considering as well additional output from other parts of the world, there was never a shortfall in supply. It was not loss of supply, but fear of possible loss that drove up the price."[41]

Federal government action in response to the oil embargo of 1973 and 1974 was largely ineffectual, and indeed even made things worse. In response to the inflation that followed, the Federal Reserve Board attempted to contract the economy by raising interest rates, and in so doing only deepened the recession. President Nixon, already facing a crisis in confidence over Watergate, called for a $410 billion "Project Independence," based on American efforts to develop synthetic rubber during World War II. Nixon's proposal sought to make America energy independent by 1985, a worthy goal that none of the energy experts in Washington thought possible. Nixon's successor, Gerald Ford, emphasized supply rather than a curtailment of demand on the part of Americans, and thus encouraged the development of nuclear power plants, an initiative that that hit a brick wall after the Three Mile Island accident in 1979. Politicians were averse to placing blame for the energy crisis on those who were most responsible, namely the American consumer, who used a disproportionate percentage of the world's petroleum supplies and owned more automobiles per family compared to other developed nations.

What Oil Shock I meant to the auto industry, however, was far-reaching, for Detroit responded by making what were undoubtedly the worst cars in its history, while at the same time Japanese manufacturers made high quality and very reasonably priced products that consumers grew to love.

Prior to the first oil crisis and following a whimsical cycle of trying to meet consumer needs, Ford introduced a new "world" economy car, the Pinto, and GM similarly rolled out the Chevrolet Vega. The Pinto was particularly interesting in terms of manufacturing processes, as it was perhaps the first modern "world car," the result of a global assembly line that included engines and transmissions from Great Britain and Germany. It had only 1,600 major parts, as compared to anywhere between 3,500 and 9,000 in a full-sized car. These cars could be fixed by a novice mechanic with a handful of tools, making it a do-it-yourself car. Light and fuel efficient, the Pinto, however, was subsequently deemed dangerous as its gas tank was prone to rupture in a collision from the rear, while occupants would be trapped by doors that had jammed shut upon impact.[42]

The Vega was also a light, four-cylinder economy design. From the beginning, however, it was built at a new state-of-the-art GM facility in Lordstown, Ohio, where worker dissatisfaction soon boiled over, leading to deliberate worker sabotage of cars coming off the line — one such example being Coke bottles being placed in doors prior to final assembly. Also, Vega engines were based on a new aluminum block design and quickly proved to wear and burn oil far sooner than they should have.

The American automobiles made between 1974 and 1979 were generally of poor design and poor quality. For example, the author's father's 1979 Chevrolet Malibu mated a V-8 engine to a small metric THM-200 automatic transmission, an arrangement that led to repeated transmission failures. One of my coworkers during this period, an African American proud of his ability to purchase a new Oldsmobile, soon discovered that it had a Chevrolet engine. Emissions controls that included smog pumps, decel and exhaust recirculation valves, and a maze of vacuum lines under the hood resulted in day to day drivability problems that included dieseling and hard starting.

It was no surprise, then, that within this void a new global competitor emerged: Japan.

Japanese Automobiles Come in a Big Way to America

As James Flink states, the keys to the success of the Japanese auto industry were organizational structures, policy programs and conscious planning.[43] At the heart of the success story is the Ministry of International Trade and Industry (MITI), created in 1949 to protect certain industries from foreign competition so that home industries could be competitive abroad. This was done by eliminating foreign competition from the domestic market. To this day, American cars in Japan are more curiosities than staples of transportation. Competition among Japanese firms was discouraged, and thus economies of scale resulted. With low wages and union cooperation after 1953, the Japanese had a key initial advantage in their quest to penetrate American shores. But given their reputation for shoddy products, could they make cars that Americans would buy?

While the Japanese made mostly military vehicles before World War II, the first seeds of its future growth were linked to supplying the American military during the Korean War. The emergence of the Japanese automobile industry is elegantly traced by David Halberstam in his *The Reckoning*.[44] His story features a host of remarkable and powerful personalities, but perhaps two Americans were as critical as any in creating the Japanese automobile. Prior to World War II, American engineer William R. Gorham played a key role in setting up the first factories and promoted a distinctive manufacturing philosophy; after 1945 quality control expert W. Edwards Deming instilled a passion for quality at a time when American automobile executives seemingly cared less.

Deming's 14 Points, articulated in *Out of the Crisis*, served as management guidelines that were embraced by the Japanese.[45] The application of these points resulted in a more efficient workplace, higher profits, and increased productivity. They included the following:

- Create and communicate to all employees a statement of the aims and purposes of the company.
- Adapt to the new philosophy of the day; industries and economics are always changing.
- Build quality into a product throughout production.

- End the practice of awarding business on the basis of price tag alone; instead, try a long-term relationship based on established loyalty and trust.
- Work to constantly improve quality and productivity.
- Institute on-the-job training.
- Teach and institute leadership to improve all job functions.
- Drive out fear; create trust.
- Strive to reduce intradepartmental conflicts.
- Eliminate exhortations for the work force; instead, focus on the system and morale.
- Eliminate work standard quotas for production. Substitute leadership methods for improvement.
- Remove barriers that rob people of pride of workmanship
- Educate with self-improvement programs.
- Include everyone in the company to accomplish the transformation.

While the 14 Points made for great publicity during the 1980s, statistical analysis was the key to Deming's management methods. It was this merging of the quantitative with quality that made Japanese production methods so effective, with the result that "Made in Japan" meant goods of the highest precision and quality. But the Japanese have to be given credit for their efforts as well. At Toyota, lean manufacturing was pioneered after World War II. A complex system of ideas that is well described in James Womack, Daniel Jones, and Daniel Roos's *The Machine That Changed the World*, lean manufacturing involved production, supply, and distribution principles that included continuous improvement with just-in-time inventories.[46] This powerful new way of making cars was first recognized by California consumers during the mid–1960s, when Nissan pickup trucks never quit, and just kept going and going with minimal service.

Beginning in 1958, both Datsun and Toyota began to import vehicles into the U.S., but the few early models were underpowered and technologically primitive, but beginning in the late 1960s, both quality and performance improved dramatically. The models that exemplified this transition to competitiveness were the 1965 Toyota Corona, 1970 Datsun 240Z and the 1973 Honda Civic.

To fully understand the rise of the Japanese industry and its subsequent transitory stagnation after 1990, one must fully explore the complexities associated with international economics and monetary policy. The split-commodity tax, floating yen to dollar values, tariffs, and import quotas all contributed to Japanese competitiveness in the American marketplace, along with the inability of American manufacturers to export to Japan.

The Corona proved to be remarkably well built at a time when the quality of vehicles coming from Detroit was lagging. The Datsun 240Z became a favorite among sports car enthusiasts, especially displacing British Triumphs and MGs, and the Honda Civic offered no-nonsense, reliable, efficient, and environmentally clean transportation.

James Bond, Steve McQueen, and the Action Thriller

While Japanese cars were successful in penetrating the American market, they were far less successful in becoming a part of contemporary American culture. In film, high horsepower and elegant body lines, not unlike those of the actresses in the cast, were featured. The 1960s introduced a completely new film genre, the action thriller.[47] These were mostly big-budget films that starred some of the biggest names in Hollywood, including Steve McQueen, James Garner, and Sean Connery. These films employed a fast-paced sequence of action scenes, impossible stunts, and fiery explosions. It was also during this period that the automobile moved to center stage as a major part of film and the film industry. Cars, often unusual and expensive models, became a requirement for any action film, as it was necessary for a "real" action film to contain at least one major chase scene that culminated in a major crash or explosion. The true pioneers of this sort of film were Harry Saltzman and Albert "Cubby" Broccoli, the creators of the James Bond film series.

The James Bond films set the stage for all the films of the action genre that would follow. Bond is perhaps the most enduring character in the history of the screen, with a résumé spanning more than 45 years and, at this writing, 22 films. No fewer than six actors have assumed the role of the secret agent. James Bond films are famous for their exotic locations, beautiful and often willing women, and stunning scenes. Over the long film career of Bond, his films have contained some of the most memorable car chases and stunts that have ever been brought to the screen, as well as some unforgettable "modified" cars that have almost become icons of car culture. The impact of the James Bond series on the industry is unquestionable.

Perhaps the most memorable of all Bond films was the third installment in the series, *Goldfinger*. In the film, Bond (Sean Connery) is equipped with an Aston Martin DB5 with modifications that included revolving license plates, bulletproof front and rear windscreens, a homing device on the dashboard, left and right front fender machine guns, two battering rams, and a device under the tail lights that sprayed oil, nails and a smokescreen. A passenger ejector seat was the most unforgettable of the DB5's accessories, and a feature that actually worked. As the plot unfolds, Bond trails Goldfinger to Switzerland, where he uses nearly all of these gadgets while trying to escape Goldfinger's henchmen. The silver Aston Martin again made a brief appearance in the next Bond film, *Thunderball*, and Pierce Brosnan can be seen driving it briefly thirty years later in *GoldenEye*. This car is certainly the most memorable of any Bond car, and perhaps the most memorable car in any film.

Though among Bond fans *Goldfinger* is most revered, many of the other films in the series provided memorable chase scenes, stunts, and unforgettable cars. Featured cars included a Lotus Esprit that turns into a submarine after Bond (Roger Moore) dives into the sea to avoid an attacking helicopter in *The Spy Who Loved Me* and a BMW 750iL that Bond (Pierce Brosnan) drives via a remote control (*Tomorrow Never Dies*). These cars were occasionally overshadowed by death-defying automobile stunts. One such stunt was performed by Bumps Willard in *The Man with the Golden Gun*, and has since become one of the most celebrated scenes in film history. While Bond (Moore) is chasing Scaramanga (Christopher Lee), the film's antagonist, from the opposite side of a river, he spots a fallen bridge with only the two ends remaining intact. Bond then does the unthinkable by jumping the river across the fallen bridge, while doing a 360-degree spiral jump in midair. Willard had previously performed this spectacular jump at a stunt show in the Houston Astrodome. It is the classic cars and stunts such as these that have made the James Bond series endure over the years.

Though Bond films are considered to be the true pioneers of the action film and chase scene, the film that truly set the stage for all future Hollywood chase sequences was the much celebrated scene from the film *Bullitt*. This chase featured all of the essential components that would become a necessity for all future chases: high speeds, fast turns, and of course, plenty of destruction. The cars involved in this classic were McQueen's 1968 Ford Mustang GT390 fastback (the Mustang was among the most popular of cars to be featured in films of this era, and this has probably contributed to the iconic status that these original Mustangs carry) and a 1968 Dodge Charger R/T 440 Magnum. McQueen, playing the character of a San Francisco detective in a plot that is far from clear at times, senses that the Charger, carrying two bad guys, is following him. He quickly turns left while the Charger is caught in traffic, doubles back, and closes in on the Charger from behind. Realizing this, the driver of the Charger tries to outrun Bullitt. What follows is two cars flying through the streets of San Francisco at speeds upwards of 110 mph, leaving hubcaps, wrecked cars, and an injured motorcyclist in their wake (the stuntman who drove the motorcycle in the scene was actually the same person who performed most of the driving of the Charger). The Mustang eventually catches the Charger, shotgun blasts follow, and finally McQueen rams the Charger off of the road, where it explodes spectacularly. McQueen, who had earlier received accolades for his motorcycle driving in *The Great Escape*, did his own driving in the chase, setting the standard for all similar scenes that followed.

The cinematography in *Bullitt* was unique, since it was the first film to use a new Arriflex camera design exclusively during production.[48] Specific camera placement resulted in unprecedented realism. A Chevrolet camera car, named the "Bullittmobile," took close-up shots of the actors and stunt men at high speeds. Additionally, a camera mounted on the Mustang resulted in the perception of high speeds without having to break away to a speedometer shot. Cameras were also placed on the sides of the cars, as well on the street.

McQueen's love affair with automobiles went back to his childhood.[49] At age 13, along with a friend, he built a dragster using a Ford flathead V-8 and a Model A frame. Once he became established as a leading actor, his interest in automobiles turned to sports car racing, and between 1959 and 1970 he participated in at least twenty races in all classes and on all types of tracks, including Sebring. Invited by *Sports Illustrated* in 1966 to test eight exotic sports cars, McQueen said of himself that "I'm not sure whether I'm an actor who races or a racer who acts."[50] His car collection included a 1961 Austin Mini Cooper S, a 1963 Ferrari Lusso Berlina and a 512, a Jaguar D-Type XKSS, and three Porsches — a 356 Speedster, a 917, and a 908.

McQueen followed *Bullitt* with the *Le Mans* in 1971, a remarkable film in its own right, but popular only among a small group of racing and Porsche devotees who appreciated the attention to detail that was taken in the film. Cast as Michael Delaney, an American driver who was severely injured in an accident at Le Mans the year before, McQueen is drawn to Lisa Belgetti (played by Elga Andersen), widow of a Ferrari driver, who was killed in the same accident. Delaney's chief racing rival is Erich Stahler (Siegfried Rauch), who is driving a Ferrari. With spectacular cinematography and a sensitive portrayal of the French countryside and fans, *Le Mans* was undoubtedly the best film depiction of European racing of that era. For McQueen, it proved to be an obsession that never paid off, a docudrama that failed to resonate with American audiences since it had no dialogue during the first forty minutes of the film. In addition, character development was poor and the dialogue deadening. But for McQueen, it was the ultimate racing film that he always wanted to make.

John Frankenheimer's *Grand Prix* (1966) was another European racing spectacular of this period, but was far more slow-moving than *Le Mans*. What Frankenheimer contributed to the genre, however, was technical; his use of NASA–developed cameras and microwave systems, monster camera cars that were capable of 150 mph, and helicopters was imitated in other films, and set a benchmark in terms of realism.[51]

Mobile Lovemaking

Music of the 1970s and early 1980s related to the automobile was significantly different from the rather mindless lyrics of early Beach Boys tunes. On one hand, it reflected society's increasing openness concerning sexual matters and the fact that sexual revolution had been realized. Despite higher gas prices as a result of Oil Shock I, vans became increasingly popular. As David Lewis has pointed out, it was the locus for mobile lovemaking. The van enabled young people to break away from home, but at the same time, because of all its comforts, remain tied to the home. Typically, a van owner was between 20 and 35 years old and often would decorate the vehicle with popular murals and slogans. These "love making machines" were often furnished with soft lighting, shag carpeting, mirrors, wine racks, and refrigerators. An emerging young guitarist from Charlotte, North Carolina, Sammy Johns hit the charts for the first time in 1975 with his memorable "Chevy Van." The song had a rhythm as flowing and free and easy as the man who picks up a young woman while on the road. In an age when no-strings-attached love became all too frequent, the lyrics struck a chord with a generation caught up in the freedom brought on by the hippies from a previous decade and a machine that it fostered.

Summing Up the Sixties

In sum, the 1960s marked a transitional period in the history of the automobile and its influence on American life. On one hand, the love affair with the automobile was maturing but for the most part still intense, at least until 1969 or 1970. Sales were at record levels, but cars were getting smaller towards the end of the period. Reflected in popular culture, the automobile was initially celebrated as never before in the music of the Beach Boys and others, but as popular culture turned to deeper and darker matters, the car seemed almost superficial to the realities of life. With government now restraining the automobile industry, the big bumpers required of all 1974 models signaled a new era of compromises and ambivalence.

10

The Automobile World Upside Down, 1980s to the Present

In the period since 1980 the structure of the automobile industry, its geographical locus, assembly line processes, government oversight, market dynamics, and the products themselves have all changed dramatically. Car culture is as significant as ever, however, if perhaps more diffuse than in the past. Automobiles powerfully influence contemporary literature and music and shape the lifestyles of Americans from all classes.

Our selective study of the automobile and American life has pointed to a number of significant discontinuities that affected ordinary people and their everyday lives, but perhaps none had more impact during the post–World War II era than the Oil Shock of 1979.[1] The years 1979 and 1980 are watershed dates in the history of the automobile in America. During the 1960s U.S. industry, despite its complacency and products, manufactured about half of all the world's vehicles. Yet by 1980, the Japanese automobile industry, once the butt of Detroit auto executives' jokes, surpassed the United States in the global market. Furthermore, more than one-quarter of the cars purchased by Americans in 1980 were made elsewhere.[2] The decline had an enormous effect on the American economy, as the automobile industry was at the core of the American economy and critical to national prosperity. For example, some 4 million Americans had jobs that were directly connected with the industry. And the manufacture of automobiles used 60 percent of the synthetic rubber, 30 percent of ferrous castings, 20 percent of the steel, and 11 percent of aluminum produced in the United States.

"Oil Shock II" resulted in record Big Three deficits. In 1980, Chrysler lost $4 billion, Ford $1.5 billion, and GM $8 billion. Job losses followed: some 200,000 workers lost their jobs in the auto industry, and unemployment in this sector rose from 3.9 percent in 1978 to 20.4 percent in 1980. These developments led MIT industry analyst Martin Anderson to state that the changes in the auto industry "constituted the largest shift in technological, human, and capital resources in U.S. industrial history."[3]

In response to this economic catastrophe, automobile executives began massive capital investment initiatives to regain their competitive advantage. Among other things, they bet that robots could replace assembly line workers. The implementation of these robotic devices resulted in the shop floor being radically different than those associated with mid-twentieth century Fordism. Presses, while still in use, no longer were central to the auto manufacturing process; rather, images of robotic arms stretched over unitized steel shells that were moving rapidly down the line represented the changing industry. The threat from robots at that time was so significant in our culture that one scholar has suggested that the popularity of the film *The Terminator*, released in 1984, was a consequence of fears concerning the automated assembly line. It was perhaps satisfying, then, that at the end of this movie Sarah terminated the Terminator and sent what was left to the melting pot.[4] However, in the real world automobile workers were experiencing an irreversible transition where global competitiveness demanded lower labor costs.

By the end of the twentieth century, the power of the unions was severely diminished. Several reasons exist for the union's contemporary impotence. The 1979 Oil Shock redoubled a consumer shift from gas guzzling autos to smaller, more efficient vehicles. Global competition ended both management's and workers' era of the "American Dream," and foreign competition encroached on the industry's profits and workers' jobs. Global events combined with advances in robotics and the advent of the "team concept" also eliminated positions so that the industry's workforce had fallen by as much as half by 1985. In addition, a conservative political atmosphere — evinced by Ronald Reagan's immediate firing of striking air traffickers — abolished the dwindling clout of the labor bloc. Most importantly, both labor and capital enjoyed the gluttony of postwar American prosperity. The days of conflict had passed, and unions began to tacitly accept the dictates of management. Steven Jeffreys noted, "The UAW was now a junior partner with Chrysler management. It shared the same goal as Iacocca — the economic survival of the company — and was committed to cooperation to attain it."[5] Perhaps more poignant was the prescience of a worker interviewed in Michael Moore's documentary *Roger and Me,* who stated, "the union is getting weaker, we are losing power. Too many union guys are friends with management."[6] He chided the auto industry and stated, "some people know what time it is, some don't."[7] By the 1980s the union had lost its clout, and the impotence continues in the twenty-first century. When the Flint, Michigan, Fisher Body plant, famous for sit-down strike of 1937, was shut down in 1983, the UAW promised to stage a major demonstration. Rather, it was a pathetic gathering — only four workers showed up, and they were relegated by security to the sidewalk. Dodge Main also quietly closed in 1980. As Emma Rothschild suggested a decade before all this happened, the auto industry auto industry was now *Paradise Lost.*

Rivethead *and the Quality Cat*

Certainly paradise was hard to find for those working the line. In 1991, Ben Hamper's *Rivethead: Tales from the Assembly Line* was published, a memoir of his time toiling at the General Motors Flint Truck and Bus factory. Hamper was a factory worker with a remarkable ability to write with humor and sensitivity. His partnership with muckraker Michael Moore earned him a national reputation as a cutting edge blue-collar writer.[8] Hamper was a third-generation "shop rat." His grandfather had moved from Springfield, Illinois, to Detroit in 1925 and worked at Chevrolet. During World War II, his grandmother built machine guns at the AC Spark Plug factory, and then worked in an aircraft factory. His uncle worked for 45 years at the Buick Engine Plant. Hamper's father, a womanizer and drunk, floated in and out of the factories. An early memory recounts the day that the Hamper family visited the father while he was working on the line. Ben watched his father install car windshields over and over. That night he observed, "Car, windshield. Car, windshield," and thought, "Do something else!"[9]

Yet Hamper sees his life as largely predetermined, and for him, that unfortunately meant the same assembly line work that his father had detested. Hamper grew up in a broken home and a sense of inevitability hung over his future. After a drug-ridden high school experience and an unplanned pregnancy, Hamper painted apartments. When the recession of the 1970s began to lift, his sister-in-law scored him an application to work at General Motors. Claiming his "birthright," Hamper was ushered to the Cab Shop, known by workers as "the Jungle," and "began to install splash shields with a noisy air gun in the rear ends of Chevy Blazers and Suburbans."[10] Within a shift and a half, Hamper had conquered his assignment.

For leftist intellectuals, the degradation of labor is lamentable; for Hamper, the degradation of labor is something to revel in. To Hamper, labor in the automobile industry was enjoyable because it was mindless, and at $12.82 an hour, lucrative. After he mastered his initial job, Bud, a linemate, convinced Hamper to "double-up." This setup required that one worker do two jobs at the same time, while the other worker rested. Hamper read novels, newspapers, drank at local watering holes, and occasionally wandered through the factory. When Bud left, Hamper convinced Dale, a new worker, to double-up. Hamper's pen revealed the insanity created by the line as many workers drank and took hard drugs. A worker named Roy took acid and vomited all over the line. A few nights later, Roy incinerated a pet mouse with a brazing torch, of which Hamper wrote, "The money was right, even if we weren't."

Even with the layoffs of 1979, Hamper continued to receive money — a comfortable $268 a week. When his grandfather commented that he was getting a free ride, Hamper thought, "indeed I owed a tremendous debt to my grandfathers and uncles and to all those who bravely took part in the historic sit down strikes of 1937 ... but hold on, we worked damn hard also." Hamper continued, "some things never did change ... the factory was still a shithole, comparisons be damned." Hamper concluded that the generations of shoprats could not relate to each other's era.

When Hamper came back from his layoff, he was in the cab shop, this time with a scheme to produce tailgates faster than they came off the feeder line. For his efficiency, he earned 45 minutes of free time. This glory quickly ended with another set of layoffs. After a few weeks of debauchery, Hamper was back at GM, this time on the rivet line.[11] Hamper began working the "pin-up" job. This position riveted a cross bar, a four-wheel-drive spring casting, a muffler hanger, and another cross bar to the vehicle's underbelly. The worker aligned the holes and then drove the rivet in with a gun. Compared to his earlier placement in the cab shop, the rivet line was in constant motion and Hamper was in relative solitude. He used a myriad of strategies to conquer the monotony of the assembly line:

> Desperation led me to all the usual dreary tactics used to fight back the clock. Boring excursions like racing to the water fountain and back, chain-smoking, feeding Chee-tos to mice, skeet shooting Milk Duds with rubber bands, punting washers into the rafters high above the train depot, spitting contests ... [and] pretend that my job was an Olympic event.[12]

After a few weeks, Hamper was laid off and then called back. Both Hamper and General Motors indulged in the gluttony of the postwar automobile industry. Both the machines and the workers were interchangeable. Hamper recalled an incident where a woman was knocked unconscious by a rivet gun, and a fellow line member shut down the line. Hamper wrote, "within thirty seconds, every tie within a 300-yard radius was on the scene," and they wanted to know who turned the line off. The line was immediately turned back on and Hamper thought, "It was all so typical of General Motors.... It was perfectly fine for a foreman to the line and chew on your ass about some minor detail, but it was practically an act of treason for a worker to stop the line in order to extricate an unconscious old lady out of harm's way."[13] Hamper lamented about the relationship between production and safety. In the 1980s, Japanese competition began to take bites out of American automobile manufacturing hegemony. General Motors' answer, as exposed by Ben Hamper, was a mascot named Howie Makem. Howie was a life-sized cat who encouraged workers to build quality automobiles. Hamper wrote, "Howie was to become the messianic embodiment of the Company's new Quality drive. A livin' breathin' propaganda vessel assigned to spur on the troops."[14] The mascot became a company-wide joke. A few weeks later, Hamper was again laid off.[15]

Hamper was unemployed for nearly a year until GM landed a contract with the U.S. Army to build trucks, which Hamper referred to as "Ronnie's death wagons." Hamper managed to politic his way back to a position on the rivet line. Hamper then met a worker he called the "steering gear man," who worked a job at the end of the line. The steering gear man worked so hard that sweat poured from his chin. Hamper wondered at "the apportionment of duty in the plant so inconsistent that you would have half of the work force breaking their backs and chugging the work load while the other half were off playing cards."[16] Hamper observed his surroundings and found free time to write articles.[17] Meanwhile, the steering gear man found the bottle. He began to drink so much that he talked to himself, and other workers on the line had to compensate for his negligence. The macabre episode reached a climax when the steering gear man, Hamper's words, "turded in his skivvies," and was sent home. A few days later the steering gear man was back on the line, working next to Hamper. Hamper worked with a crew that invented games like Rivet Hockey and Dumpster Ball to pass time. The cadre included a Black man named Eddie who could match Hamper drink-for-drink. Also in the crew was Janice, a woman who conquered the rivet gun. Finally, there was Jerry, whom Ben nicknamed "the Polish Sex God" for his ability to court women. Alcohol played a central role in the lives of the workers. Hamper and his coworkers would drink before work, during breaks, at lunch, and after work. Hamper's account exposed the naïveté of General Motors. Management had placed a massive electronic message board directly across from Hamper and used it to transmit messages like QUALITY IS THE BACKBONE OF GOOD WORKMANSHIP, A WINNER NEVER QUITS & A QUITTER NEVER WINS, SAFETY IS SAFE, and SQUEEZING RIVETS IS FUN![18] To the last of which Hamper replied:

> I had several definitions of fun. Riveting was nowhere on the list. Taking in a Tigers game from the right field overhand was fun. Listening to Angry Samoans records while getting sloshed was fun. The episode of *Bewitched* where Endora hexed Dick York with elephant ears was fun. Dozing past noon with the phone off the hook was fun. Having sex in a Subaru was difficult — however, that was fun too. Squeezing rivets was not fun.[19]

Ben Hamper did not consider squeezing rivets fun, but he did consider it his specialty. When General Motors eliminated 30,000 jobs from factories in Flint, Hamper's job at the Truck and Bus Plant was moved to a new facility in Pontiac, Michigan. Hamper had two years to make the move, during which time he continued work on the assembly line. Then on July 12, 1986, Hamper thought he was having a stroke, but in actuality it was an intense episode of panic attack syndrome.[20] He ended up at a mental hospital.[21] He attempted to work at the new plant in Pontiac, but the attacks returned. The plant at Pontiac went beyond what Hamper had experienced in Flint. Hamper wrote, "Everything in this plant reeked of science gone too far."[22] After his second day at Pontiac East, Hamper had another panic attack on the way home. Finally, after one more try, the hospital nurse sent him home. He never returned to General Motors. Hamper described the work:

> The jobs were timed out to make sure workers wouldn't be allowed a moment's intermission. Anyone caught reading a newspaper or a paperback would be penalized. The union was nothing more than a powerless puppet show groveling in the muck.[23]

The Automobile and Contemporary Art

This second intense reaction to a shortage of oil and gasoline unleashed another wave of discontent related to the automobile and its place in American life. One amusing response was the work of California artist Dustin Shuler. On the night of October 23, 1980, at California State University Domingues Hills, a 1959 Cadillac was illuminated, elevated on four oil drums, and then pierced by a 20 foot "nail" that was dropped 100 feet from a boom crane.[24] The Cadillac was then pulled on to its side and left on display in an exhibit entitled "Death of an Era." Schuler saw this act as akin to a hunt for a wild animal, and later he took apart the Cadillac in a way that left it "skinned," like an animal pelt. Encouraged by this first work, Schuler subsequently skinned and created pelts of a VW Beetle, a Fiat Spider and a Porsche 356C! Schuler summarized his activities this way:

> All the cars I have skinned and, for that matter, all the cars on the road can be considered an endangered species. While I am not arguing for the preservation of this species, I notice the "evolution" that is going on right before my eyes [new cars coming off the docks and old cars being scrapped] and I want to collect a few good specimens before they are gone.[25]

Not all of the artists of the 1980s were this dark in their views concerning the automobile and its future, particularly after gasoline became more available and prices dropped precipitously. For example, at Meadowbrook Hall in Rochester, Michigan, a number of art exhibitions were held in conjunction with the Concours beginning in the mid–1980s. In reflecting on their interest in painting cars, several of the artists commented on impressions made during their youth. Argentinean Hector Luis Bergandi attributed his interest in cars to a racing mania that swept though his native county when he was a teenager. He wrote that his work on racing cars was similar to his technique when painting horses: "It's not only how they look, it's mostly what they do, how they smell, charge, pump, sweat...." Dennis Brown, from Covina, California, reflected on "spending countless hours with my best friend ... taking apart his '34 Ford coupe — polishing, cleaning and painting; watching the sun reflecting off that beautiful lacquer pint job or sparkling like a diamond in the chrome trim. The shadows were cool ... almost liquid pools of pure color reflecting the grass or trees or the neighbors' white fence." While the play of light and emotions were the focus of many artists of this era, some attempted to reconstruct the place of the automobile in American life. Finally, getting inside the machine — a popular genre of art often found in automobile magazines — was pursued by New York City artist Robert A. Pentelovitch, whose paintings of engines and transmissions were intended "to provide insight to a world of wonderful shapes and forms otherwise unacknowledged for their beauty by a society which takes machinery for granted."[26]

Lessons Not Learned

A far more serious response to the oil crisis as it related to the automobile in America than that of Dustin Schuler's art came from Lester Brown, of the Worldwatch Institute. In 1979 Brown, with Christopher Flavin and Colin Norman, coauthored *Running on Empty: The Future of the Automobile in an Oil-Short World.*[27] Brown's analysis, obviously rushed given the circumstances of the oil crisis, was based on common sense. He advised American manufacturers to market fuel-efficient automobiles while working on new technologies. Furthermore, Brown clearly pointed out that oil supplies would be depleted in the long run, yet in the years after the oil crisis subsided, few took Brown and others seriously. By 1985, large cars, mini-vans, trucks, and sport utility vehicles filled dealers' showrooms and lots. Manufacturers made huge profits on these larger vehicles, while claiming that consumers demanded these excessive forms of transformation. And thus lessons from Oil Shocks I and II were not learned, research projects in alternative fuels and power systems were abandoned, and large numbers of light trucks emerged on the American scene.

Trucks, Sport Utility Vehicles, and Crossovers

Within the past two decades, truck culture, and variants that include sport utility and crossover vehicles, emerged as a significant element of modern American life. This fundamental transition in the American automobile industry is most obvious in Texas, where a wide-body Ford pickup is better known as a "Texas limousine." The pervasiveness of the truck is also evident in American suburbia, where the station wagon in the driveway has been displaced by this simple utilitarian vehicle. And while the truck is generally advertised as a masculine object, it is remarkable how many women prize their pickups.[28]

The rapid rise of light trucks in the American marketplace after 1980 is only one episode in a new era in automobile history that is characterized by more Americans considering their cars as appliances, rather than machines to be loved and identified with. Additionally, the auto is now often leased rather than owned, and rented for vacation trips. Currently this "American Revolution," to coin the phrase used by Chevrolet in its advertising, has been extended into serious efforts to replace the internal combustion engine as the prime mover in personal transport technologies. Electrics, hybrids, diesels, and fuel cells are all competing for the prize of being the power plant of choice for the remainder of the twenty-first century.[29]

In 1981 light trucks represented just 19 percent of the American market. Some 22 years later, however, they totaled more than 54 percent of what was once thought of as "car makes." Table 9 illustrates the trend:

TABLE 9. SALES IN U.S.

Year	Passenger Cars	Commercial Vehicles	Total
1972	10,940,482	2,628,960	13,569,442
1977	11,183,412	3,675,439	14,858,851
1982	7,956,460	2,581,902	10,538,362
1987	10,191,877	5,001,069	15,192,946
1992	8,213,113	4,904,331	13,117,444
1997	8,272,074	7,225,786	15,497,860
2002	8,103,229	9,035,423	17,138,652

Source: *Ward's Motor Vehicle Data*, 2003.

Indeed, the market share of trucks increased each year from 1981 to the present, and this trend resulted in tremendous windfalls for American manufacturers.[30] Trucks were often sold at profits of $10,000 or more per unit, while small cars typically garnered minuscule profit numbers — at times only $1,000 was made on the sales of such vehicles. In 1999, annual sales of cars and light trucks in the U.S. reached a high of 16.9 million units, eclipsing by a million the previous high reached in 1986. Despite ending on this high point, the 1990s proved to be an extremely competitive and turbulent time for automakers.

It was recognized, however, that the expanding truck market had its limits. In what was perceived then to be a slow growth market increasing by no more than 1 percent per year, new products were called for. At first, product lines were revised to include sport utility vehicles. These vehicles, often featuring four-wheel drive, truck frames for rugged use, and plenty of room soon had their critics, however, as they were found to be prone to rollovers, encouraged drivers to exhibit risky behavior, decreased visibility for those in adjacent, lower-profile cars, and were excessive in terms of gasoline consumption and the release of pollutants. Descendents of the Chevrolet Suburban, Ford Bronco and Land Rover, SUVs included the Ford Explorer and Expedition, Jeep Cherokee and Grand Cherokee, and perhaps the ultimate example of excessive transportation, the Cadillac Escalade.

Subsequently, in an effort to find new market niches, a fresh type of vehicle, the crossover, appeared during 1997 and 1998. Crossovers were seen as "market segment busting" vehicles that mixed features previously unknown in the auto business — style, sturdiness, reliability, and luxury. Crossovers usually featured unibody construction, plush interiors, and better gas mileage than SUVs. After all, few of the SUVs of the 1980s and 1990s ever left the smooth roads of suburbia, and so crossovers were a better lifestyle fit for most Americans who wanted to drive something bigger and more imposing than a passenger car.

The Honda CRV, Mercedes M-Class, Subaru Forester, and Toyota RAV4 were built on car platforms but styled as sport utility vehicles. Another unique offering introduced at the end of the century was the "Mickey Mouse" looking DaimlerChrysler PT Cruiser. All manufacturers at the end of the decade were attempting to break through market segments by offering vehicles that uniquely mixed practicality with affordability, performance, and style. And just as product lines were revolutionized to include crossover vehicles, so too was the high end of the market.

These new vehicles were in part the consequence of a new generation of leaders in the industry, typically "motor heads" rather than the "bean counters" that had preceded them. As a result of making innovative vehicles that were of better quality, sales quantities and profits moved commensurately higher. After suffering staggering losses at the beginning of the 1990s, GM and Ford had a global net income of $52 billion on revenues of $1.3 trillion between 1994 and 1998. Given the flush times, the end of the twentieth century witnessed a flurry of merger activity involving U.S. auto companies and overseas manufacturers. The American auto industry was no longer just a cluster of enterprises centered for the most part in Detroit, but rather it was now profoundly global in scale and scope.[32]

Commensurate with the overall prosperity of the decade (or at least perceptions of prosperity, since in 2007 60 percent of luxury vehicles were leased rather than purchased), luxury product sales increased markedly with such products as the Lexus (1989), Infiniti (1989), Acura (1986), along with BMW 5 and 7 series vehicles. These high-end cars accounted for the decrease in the lucrative luxury sales on the part of American manufacturers (Lincoln and Cadillac) from 65 percent in 1996 to 52 percent in 1999. No longer was Cadillac the iconic symbol of status and wealth in America; rather it was the Lexus, built by Toyota to unprecedented standards of quality and comfort, or the BMW, with its advanced technology and panache.

The Car Hobby: Car Crazy

While the pickup truck is now commonplace in everyday life, and a widespread obsession with the car as status and fashion has somewhat waned, the late twentieth and early

twenty-first centuries also witnessed a remarkable upsurge in what may be called the celebration of car culture, quite different from car culture itself, the latter a phenomenon that reached
its apex in America during the 1950s and 1960s. This celebration was orchestrated largely by
Baby Boomers, although automobile collecting has a long history, particularly among the elite,
who beginning after World War II had assembled collections of Olympian vehicles. But the
hobby was now broadened to include many middle class collectors. Boomers reached middle
age by the 1980s, and their high levels of disposable income allowed for indulgence into a
rather expensive hobby, which created a demand for automobiles that were the object of a
generation's desire when they were too young to either drive them or own them. This demand
had parallels in Europe, although there the desire for mid-market marques was for the most
part quite different. The hobby, which has become a big business, is exemplified by the Barrett-Jackson auctions in Scottsdale, Arizona, and Palm Beach, Florida, among many others.
The demand for muscle cars, prototypes, customized roadsters and hot rods, and select foreign classics and exotics has been quite strong, with expected market volatility from time to
time. On a level above Barrett-Jackson are concours events that attract a generally higher-class
clientele; the most publicized of these events take place at Pebble Beach, California; Amelia
Island, Florida; and Meadowbrook, in Michigan. Since car culture includes both the moneyed elites and blue collar devotees, the lower end of this hobby can be found at the parts
swap meets, at places like Hershey, Pennsylvania, and Springfield, Ohio, where thousands flock
to find those rims, seats, or elusive 1955–57 Chevy parts that are missing from a work in progress.
Once restored, these vehicles are driven to the many cruise-ins held in mid–America, where
men and women unfolded garden chairs, met friends, and reminisced about times gone by.

     Concurrently, car museums have sprouted up in many communities during the past 25
years.[32] For example, in the author's hometown of Dayton, Ohio, we have two remarkable
museums, one centering on Packards and the other on Porsches. Perhaps the best auto museum
is the Petersen in Los Angeles, made possible by the support of Robert Petersen, founding
publisher of *Hot Rod Magazine*.[33] The cars at the Petersen are simply luscious. Past exhibits
have featured Ferraris; '32 Fords; Cars, Guitars, and Rock & Roll; Presidents, Popes and
Potentates; French Curves: The Automobile as Sculpture; Speed: The World's Fastest Cars;
Hot Wheels; Tuner Revolution; and the Art of the Flame. As a multi-purpose facility with
an educational program for children and families, as well as a facility for hosting social events,
the Petersen is perhaps the single best expression of the history of car culture in America.

     In addition to the classic car and classic street rod and hot rod hobbyists, a number of
whom we might want to label as "Rolex" car people, several other significant car subcultures
have emerged in recent times, each with its own distinctive ethnic and generational members. In the Latino communities of Southern California, "low-riders" have become so
significant that a special exhibit was dedicated to them at the Peterson Museum in 2005. Low-
rider culture was first institutionalized with *Low Rider Magazine* in 1978. The low-rider was
often a Chevrolet that had been tricked out with special hydraulically-operated shocks to shake
the car rhythmically. With powerful sound systems and brilliantly decorated and painted bodies, the low-rider reflects values associated with the Hispanic community, especially family
and community.[34]

     It is interesting to note, however, that a new automobile subculture emerged in the 1990s
despite the relative inability of owners to work on cars, and that is centered on tuners. The
tuners are a new generation of Americans obsessed with speed. The tuner drives a high revving,
four-cylinder automobile with front wheel drive and conspicuous exhaust outlet, referred to

by some a "fart can." In these cars, nitrous oxide (NOS) is used as an auxiliary oxidant when called on for an extra burst of speed. To give an imperfect definition, a tuner is an automotive enthusiast who enjoys modifying a modern compact vehicle both cosmetically and mechanically. It is an effort to display creativity, innovation, and individualism. The cars of choice have been Japanese models, especially Acuras, Hondas, Nissans and Mazdas, although some Fords and Chevrolets have also been modified. Typically, tuners are young—87 percent are under the age of 30—and are about 4 to 1 male to female. Further, they are ethnically diverse according to a 2003 study, as some 42 percent are White, 29 percent Asian, 16 percent Hispanic, and 8 percent African American. The tuner car world is diverse, but can generally be divided into five primary groups—street, strip, sport, show, and sound—according to type of customization and activities.

Tuner culture was well portrayed in *The Fast and the Furious*, a 2001 film loosely based on a magazine article about street clubs that race Japanese cars late at night. It is a depiction of the world of street racing. The film stars Vin Diesel as Dominic Toretto, the leader of a street gang who is under suspicion of stealing expensive electronic equipment. Paul Walker plays an undercover FBI officer, Brian O'Conner, who attempts to find out who exactly is stealing the equipment, while falling for Dominic's younger sister played by Jordana Brewster. In a 2003 sequel, *2 Fast 2 Furious*, set in Miami, Officer O'Conner, stripped of his badge, is recruited to infiltrate the Miami street racing circuit in an effort to redeem himself. It was a bad movie with well-worn plot lines and semi-plausible scenarios. But the movie is all about the cars, and the cars deliver with literal flying colors. They look cool. The film featured fast-

"Twin H-Power." The early 1950s Hudson Hornet was the car of choice in the early NASCAR events (author photograph).

paced scenes with quick-cutting standard shots and a frenetic tempo. Hip-hop music was played throughout.

Cars and Crime: The Drive-By

Tuners are but one reflection of the fluid nature of car culture in America since 1980. For another group of young people, the car made possible new forms of urban violence, or at least violence on a scale previously not experienced. Often associated with Southern California and youth gang behavior, the drive-by shooting became commonplace during the 1990s across America.[35]

While usually associated with adolescent crime, in the broadest sense the drive-by shooting has a long history going back to horses and muskets. It was from such a tactic that the Dutch prince William the Silent became the first national leader to be assassinated during the sixteenth century. With the coming of the automobile, the first documented drive-by shooting as we define it today took place during the 1919 Chicago race riots. Later in Chicago, during the Prohibition era, Thompson or "Tommy" machine guns were employed in drive-bys during mob turf wars. After World War II, street gangs began to use the drive-by, although it was referred to during the late 1940s as *japping*, the term taken from Japanese behind-the-line tactics practiced in the Pacific theater. *Japping* was basically a foray, a confrontation quite different than a rumble, where gangs met at an appointed time and place and fought it out.

It was on the West Coast beginning in the 1980s, however, that the drive-by became a commonplace tactic used by gangs. Unlike Eastern cities where population density is high, adjacent territories close, and safe areas to retreat to easily accessible, West Coast cities featured neighborhoods farther apart, numerous connecting roadways, and easy expressway accessibility.

The drive-by is usually characterized by the use of relatively massive firepower aimed at a stationary target with little concern for accuracy. From careful case studies of these incidents, it appears that there are several common factors. First, participants had previous criminal records and were members of gangs. Secondly, these acts were spontaneous rather than planned, and typically a response to an affront from a rival gang, although drugs were also often at the root of the conflict. Gang members, with a warrior mentality and eager for excitement, sought added prestige within their subculture.

Hip-hop music during the 1990s was intimately connected with drive-by shootings. Two of its most popular artists, Tupac Shakur and his rival Notorious B.I.G., were killed in drive-bys in 1996 and 1997. These two visible figures brought to the spotlight a crime that reflects the deterioration of order and the problems of widespread gun violence.

Ironically perhaps, while the drive-by remains a problem in American cities, it has become a favorite tactic used by the insurgency in Iraq.[36] The drive-by is difficult to defend against as it expands the number of targets of opportunity in Baghdad and elsewhere, as numerous American troops, Iraqi citizens, missionaries, CNN employees, and contractors were attacked after 2003.

NASCAR Nation

Cars create excitement for many Americans, and that can be the result of illegal or legal activity, as in the case of automobile racing. As a consequence of new sponsors, personalities, race tracks, and television exposure, automobile racing — and in particular NASCAR — reached unprecedented heights of popularity during the 1990s. Indeed, NASCAR, with its cafes and memorabilia, became a "way of life" for many Americans.[37]

While automobile racing has its origins at the turn of the twentieth century with the beginnings of the industry, at certain levels the sport was radically transformed during the 1990s. First, and particularly as a result of the spectacular success of NASCAR (National Association for Stock Car Auto Racing), automobile racing brought in enormous amounts of money. Secondly, it was no longer the automobile manufacturers that made the key decisions related to auto racing, but rather those controlling business aspects and the organization of the sport.

The influx of money was not true across the board, however. At the second level, beneath NASCAR and Formula 1 (primarily a European-based activity), stood races organized by CART (Championship Auto Racing Teams) and the IRL (Indy Racing League). Conflicts between these two organizations diluted fan interest and profits.

At a third level were those engaged in sports car road racing, governed by the SCCA (Sports Car Club of America) and IMSA (International Motor Sports Association). Finally, grass-roots level racing thrived, either at the club level or at oval dirt and asphalt tracks located in rural America, but more as a labor of love than a way to make money for those involved.

During the 1990s, NASCAR exploded on the American scene. Once confined to the Southeastern United States, NASCAR became a national sport, with highly paid drivers, a large and increasingly diverse fan base, extravagant sponsors, and broad media coverage. And money was everywhere.

For example, during the 1990s, sponsorship contributions rose 7 percent annually. By 1998 more than 50 companies invested more than $10 million each year. Top sponsors included Philip Morris, Anheuser-Busch, Coca-Cola, General Motors, PepsiCo, AT&T, RJR Nabisco, and McDonalds. New sponsors in sectors with little direct connection to the automobile business — fast food, home supplies, detergents — became commonplace.

Consequently, top drivers like Dale Earnhart and Jeff Gordon earned more than $10 million a year, and successful crew chiefs $300,000 to $500,000. Ultimately, the money was due to the fact that NASCAR was highly adaptable to television, and thus it was media executives rather than the auto industry that were now calling the shots in this business.

The 1990s also witnessed the rise of a new generation of NASCAR drivers. Heroes from the 1960s and 1970s, including Richard Petty, Bobby Allison, Cale Yarborough, David Pearson, and Buddy Baker, gave way to Jeff Gordon, Dale Jarrett, Ernie Ervin, Mark Martin, Bobby Labonte, Jeff and Ward Burton, Ricky Craven, Johnny Benson, and Jeremy Mayfield. Symbolically, Richard Petty's 1992 "Fan Appreciation Tour" ended winless. Petty's last race in Atlanta found him running his final laps at half speed, the consequence of an earlier crash.

New owners were also a part of the NASCAR scene during the 1990s. Included were stars from other sports, including NFL coach Joe Gibbs and the NBA's Julius Erving and Brad Daugherty. With new tracks located near Fort Worth, Texas, and Fontana, California, NASCAR was seemingly being transformed in virtually every possible way.

Perhaps the most dramatic event of the 1990s was NASCAR's coming to the legendary Indianapolis Motor Speedway for the inaugural Brickyard 400 in 1995. With NASCAR founder Bill France and long-time Indy track owner Tony Hulman now dead, their successors could bury long-term differences and realize the potential of such an event in terms of

1984 Plymouth Voyager Minivan. One of the reasons for the resurgence of the Chrysler Corporation under the leadership of Lee Iacocca, the minivan reflected mid–American values of home, children, and more work for mother in carting kids to soccer practices and other activities.

media coverage and fan enthusiasm. Thus, on August 6, 1995, Jeff Gordon won the inaugural 160-lap event in front of 300,000 fans.

Despite the great success of the Brickyard 400, during the 1990s controversy swirled around the Indianapolis Motor Speedway and its owner, Tony George. During the 1980s, CART and USAC were the two sanctioning bodies that governed racing at Indianapolis, and these two groups had an uneasy relationship. In 1994, George announced that the Indianapolis 500 would leave the CART series and become the centerpiece for George's own IRL series. Whether the decision was motivated by ego, a concern over the increased presence of foreign drivers, or a perception that Indy was dropping in status as a race is unclear. The upshot of all of this, however, was that in 1996 a group of unknown drivers raced at Indianapolis, while CART organized its own race, the U.S. 500, held in Michigan on the same day. The split greatly affected this level of racing, as it led to decreased television revenues and waning fan interest. In the end, the Indianapolis 500 prevailed, and after shifting the race date of the U.S. 500 to July, in 1999 CART cancelled the race altogether.

Since the early 1970s, tobacco companies have played a critical role in automobile racing through their sponsorship of teams and events. No longer able to advertise on radio or television, they could advertise on the side of cars, and did so freely in addition to sponsoring NASCAR's championship, the Winston Cup, through the 2003 season. After 31 years the series sponsorship ended, to be replaced by the NEXTEL Cup Series and subsequently the Sprint Cup Series.

Despite America's wavering love affair with the automobile, auto racing remains one of the nation's most popular sports, on the level of football, baseball and basketball. A huge and vibrant business, its fan base draws from virtually every class segment in society.

Saturn, Chrysler, and Germans in the New South

Most notable in reorganizing the American industry during the post–1980 era was the opening of the Saturn facility in 1990 in Spring Hill, Tennessee.[38] At the time, Saturn was the largest one-time investment in the history of U.S. free enterprise. GM's desire was to create a brand that could go toe-to-toe with the Japanese competition. The Saturn project involved a new deal with the UAW, along with the notion that workers were to be associates rather than adversarial employees. Just-in-time production techniques were to be followed, and Saturn initially worked closely with suppliers. In showrooms, the Saturn was to be sold differently than other American makes. Dealerships were limited in terms of geographical region, and one-price deals were offered. Additionally, women were treated specially. Upon purchase cars were "presented," and for a time there were annual "Homecomings" in Spring Hill. Despite the optimism prevalent as late as 2000, when a company public relations brochure proclaimed "Saturn's share of the compact market has nowhere to go but upward," in 2005 GM executives considered the closing the Spring Hill facility due to financial cutbacks. As of now, however, Saturn has gained a second life with new products and a new image.

An earlier notable event was the near bankruptcy and government bailout of the Chrysler Corporation in 1979, followed by its success in creating the minivan market. By the late 1970s, the Chrysler Corporation bore little resemblance to the once mighty firm forged by Walter Chrysler and made possible by the engineering expertise of the three musketeers Zeder, Skelton, and Breer. Put bluntly, their products after Oil Shock I were simply terrible. Bodies rusted, and perhaps well they should, given the styling of that time. Overall quality was poor, as exemplified by the intermediate-size Dodge Aspen and Plymouth Volaré introduced in the 1976 model year. The firm consisted of numerous fiefdoms with little communication between units and poor management and accounting controls. With the Iranian hostage crisis of 1979 and Oil Shock II, Chrysler was on the ropes, and it took the brilliance of Lee Iacocca, recently fired from Ford after an ongoing dispute with Henry Ford II, to bring the company back to profitability.

Iacocca was at his best in following a policy of "equality of sacrifice" to extract concessions for the UAW, and a $1.2 billion loan from the Carter administration. These temporary measures were followed by two product home runs: the 1981 K-car front-wheel-drive compacts and the minivan of 1984. Iacocca sold these vehicles personally in television ads, and what could have been an economic disaster was at least averted until a second major American manufacturing decline after 2000. In part, Iacocca blamed Detroit's problems in the early 1980s on Japanese imports and preferential tariffs in Japan, and to that criticism the Japanese cleverly responded.[39]

In May 1980, the Japanese government signed the Askew/Yasukawa Agreement to encourage Japanese automakers to invest in the United States and to purchase American-made parts. Until that time, Japanese cars sold in America were imported and made entirely of Japanese parts.[40] In the 25 years that followed, Japanese automakers invested $28 billion in the United States, and in the process established some 12 assembly plants and 13 parts plants. These facilities included Honda plants in Ohio, Georgia and Alabama; Subaru operations in Indiana; Mazda in Michigan; Mitsubishi manufacturing in Illinois; Nissan in Tennessee and Mississippi; and Toyota in Kentucky, Indiana, West Virginia, Alabama, and Texas.[41]

The Germans were also active in establishing new plants in the U.S. In Greer, South Carolina, BMW established a plant in the 1990s that ultimately made Z4 roadsters and X5

SUVs.[42] Former textile workers now worked the assembly line at BMW, and the presence of the company in the local community was felt in terms of connections with Clemson University to establish an automobile research center and in the employment of numerous Carolina college graduates in management positions.

The Germans were also active in Alabama, where in 1997 Mercedes established a plant to manufacture M-class and later R-class vehicles. Employing just-in-time techniques so that just two hours' worth of inventory is stocked, Mercedes' presence in Alabama resulted in a capital investment of nearly $680 million and the creation of 10,000 jobs.

The biggest news related to the German industry centered on the 1998 surprise acquisition and merger of the Chrysler Corporation with Daimler-Benz. At the time, it was the largest merger ever accomplished, and consequently DaimlerChrysler AG became the fifth largest manufacturer in the world.[43]

The 1998 merger of the Chrysler Corporation with Daimler-Benz was remarkable in terms of scale and scope. It brought together the "Big Three" auto firm established by Walter Chrysler during the 1920s with a venerable German organization with nineteenth century origins that consisted of far more than Mercedes-Benz automobiles.[44] Daimler-Benz also had aerospace and electronics operations under its umbrella. The Chrysler Corporation had been known for engineering excellence and innovation from its earliest days, while Mercedes-Benz was a legendary brand in terms of performance and quality. Chrysler had a significant influence in the American market, especially in terms of less expensive cars, while Mercedes-Benz was actively involved in markets in Europe, South America, and Asia. And while the main architects of this merger were Robert Eaton of Chrysler and Jürgen Schrempp of Daimler-Benz, numerous other executives from both firms played critical roles in the negotiations that led to this supposed union of equals. Nevertheless, within a few short months after signing the agreement, the notion of equality was supplanted by German managerial dominance.

The 1998 merger can only be understood within the historical context of both firms' individual histories, along with that of the global automobile industry. As historian Charles K. Hyde has correctly observed, the Chrysler Corporation's history was characterized by a roller coaster journey that had both stunning highs and dark lows. For example, in the mid–1920s, Chrysler autos contained refinements that were unmatched for the day; a decade later, the Chrysler Airflow pioneered mass-production streamlining but flopped in the marketplace. In the post–World War II era, Chrysler experienced success in terms of styling and engineering innovation during the 1950s. This golden era made possible by the designs of Virgil Exner was followed by poor market planning and quality issues that ultimately led to bankruptcy by the late 1970s. After being unceremoniously fired by Henry Ford II, Lee Iacocca came to Chrysler in 1979, negotiated a government bailout, and then turned around the company with innovative products. As with the Mustang during the 1960s, Iacocca had an uncanny knack for reading the market. However, by the early 1990s Chrysler was in financial trouble a second time, in part due to the penetration of Japanese automakers in the U.S. market, along with unfair measures that protected the Japanese home market. The decline in market share, coupled with ferocious price competition and perceived quality advantage of the Japanese imports, led to Iacocca's departure.

Chrysler, now led by Robert Eaton and Robert Lutz, was totally revitalized a second time in less than two decades, the result of new organizational and manufacturing practices that included the formation of platform teams and fresh products. One major investor in Chrysler, however, was not satisfied with either its stock price or dividends. In 1995, Kirk Kerkorian, owner of 36 million shares of Chrysler stock, with the assistance of Lee Iacocca, attempted to purchase Chrysler for nearly $23 billion. This takeover attempt was resisted by Chrysler CEO Robert Eaton, who contacted New York financial institutions and threatened to pull accounts if they did business with Kerkorian. It was during this tense time that Eaton had brief talks with then Mercedes-Benz CEO Helmut Werner, although nothing of substance materialized as the Kerkorian threat fizzled.

At Daimler-Benz, a new CEO was appointed in 1994, Jürgen Schrempp. Schrempp had previously served the firm in South Africa and then as chief executive of Daimler-Benz Aerospace (DASA). Schrempp had a reputation as a cost-cutter and organizational "change agent." In short order, Schrempp forced out Werner as head of Mercedes, and then set his sights on expanding into the American market. First making contact with Robert Lutz, Schrempp began a series of negotiations with Chrysler that found a willing ally in Robert Eaton. While basking in the glow of success between 1996 and 1998, Eaton did not want to play it safe. He had been concerned for some time with Chrysler's future, in particular its lack of presence in foreign markets, especially Asia and South America.

Beginning in February 1998, with an ever-increasing involvement by lawyers, bankers and second-level executives, negotiations proceeded to a point that ultimately led to the signing of a merger agreement in early May. Numerous obstacles had to be overcome, from the most formidable, like different organizational structures, to patterns of acceptable cultural behavior, language, and the more trivial, like headquarter time zone differences. Would the company be called ChryslerDaimler or DaimlerChrysler? In the end, the Germans got their way in terms of the new firm's name, and indeed that decision foreshadowed the ascendancy of the Germans within the organization in the years that followed. But it was a marriage that did not last. In 2006, Chrysler holdings were sold to a financial group, and at the time of this writing (late 2008) there are serious questions as to whether Chrysler will survive, or be "parted out." High gas prices coupled with an outdated product line top-heavy with trucks and gas-guzzling vehicles may do in what was once a mighty American corporation.

New Technologies

Since the oil crises of the 1970s, the mass-produced automobile has undergone a number of revolutionary technological changes. First, the quality of cars, including those made in America, increasingly improved over time, perhaps due to Japanese competition, highly influenced by quality control methods of W. Edwards Deming. As a result of a new emphasis on quality forced upon American manufacturers by the Japanese, warranties were lengthened. In terms of configuration, front-wheel drive displaced the rear-wheel drive as the most used arrangement in the typical car. Employed before World War II by Errett Lobban Cord in luxury vehicles and then after the war in mass-produced cars through the design efforts of Alec Issigonis with the 1959 Mini in Great Britain, front-wheel-drive architecture offered advantages in space efficiency and enhanced traction in bad weather. Further, with few exceptions, the unibody structure replaced the traditional separate steel box girder frame. Less expensive to manufacture and less prone to rattles, the unibody and attached components derived strength from curvature of thin sheet steel rather than thickness and weight. Crumple zones, along with reinforcement in doors, enhanced passenger and driver safety over previous designs.

Safety issues, driven by federal government standards and consumer demand, emerged as an important theme by the late 1970s. The development of the airbag, first introduced in select models during the mid–1970s, but employed almost universally by the 1990s, was an effective deterrent to fatal crashes, yet was highly controversial. The design is conceptually simple — accelerometers trigger the ignition of a gas generator propellant to very rapidly inflate a nylon fabric bag, which reduces the deceleration experienced by the driver and passenger as they come to stop in the crash situation.

Airbag-like devices have existed for airplanes since the 1940s. The first actual example in a production car was in the 1973 Oldsmobile Toronado, and dual airbags were an option the next year on several full-sized Cadillacs, Oldsmobiles, and Buicks. Infant deaths resulting from deployment of the airbag while the child was unrestrained occurred as early as 1973 in an Oldsmobile Toronado. In a 1974 test simulating infants that took place in Sweden, Volvo researchers found that 8 of 24 pigs died by the force of the airbag, and indeed all but three of the pigs were injured. Despite these and other warnings, the federal government through the National Highway Traffic Safety Administration (NHTSA) pushed for airbags through the 1970s and early 1980s. Joan Claybrook, NHTSA head, stated in 1979 that "the trade-off in terms of saving thousands of lives clearly outweighs these extraordinary and infrequent risks."[45] In 1984 the U.S. government required cars to have driver's side airbags or automatic seat belts by 1989. That same year, Lee Iacocca stated that airbags were a solution "worse than the problem."[46] In a dramatic reversal, however, in 1988 Chrysler became the first U.S. automaker to install driver airbags as standard equipment in all domestically made cars. In 1990 came the first report of a driver being killed by an airbag, as a 64-year-old woman suffered fatal chest injuries. In 1993, the first of 23 deaths over a three-year period from a passenger side airbag deployment was reported: Diana Zhang, age six, of Canton, Ohio. Yet despite the deaths, it can be concluded that 15,000 lives have been saved by airbags in the last 20 years.

Better braking systems, including the use of disc brakes on all four wheels and anti-lock braking systems (ABS) to equalize the braking system and prevent lockup, enhancing stability and shortening braking distances, became prevalent in the industry by the late 1990s. Antilock braking was a European development that originally came to America through imported German vehicles, namely the 1978 S-Class Mercedes and the 7-Series BMW. Bosch had patented elements of the system as early as 1936, and a number of innovations followed during the 1980s and 1990s.

Above all, the car became computerized. A central computer monitored ignition and combustion functions, thereby decreasing emissions to unprecedented low levels. The computer, coupled in a closed loop with electronic fuel injection and an oxygen sensor, enabled engines to burn fuel extremely efficiently, and with various sensors feeding information back to the computer, optimal efficiency became the rule by the early 1990s for even the least expensive vehicles.

What all of this technology did, however, was take automobile repair outside the skills of the shade tree mechanic and car owner. Automobiles were now technological "black boxes," so to speak, and any notion of the car as an autonomous technology accessible to the public was now history. Here again it was in Europe that Bosch pioneered production fuel injection, with the D-Jetronic system appearing in the Volkswagen 411 in 1967, L-Jetronic in the 1974 Porsche 914, and the Bosch Motronic system with all engine systems under the control of a single computer.

Automobiles, Women, Eros, and Film

The automobile remained central to the arts in the modern era, and in particular became a platform from which the previously marginalized spoke. Despite its use of exaggerated character stereotypes, the release and subsequent popularity of *Thelma and Louise* resulted in serious debates over gender and women's desires.[47]

Thelma and Louise, starring Susan Sarandon and Geena Davis, was far more than a simple road adventure. It was a commentary about life's relationships gone sour, betrayal, weakness and strength, and self-discovery during a journey that ends with a kiss and then death. Two bored women living in Arkansas, one a housewife and the other a waitress, pack their things, take a photo before departure, and then set out on what is intended to be a three-day getaway from routine (Louise) and spousal neglect and abuse (Thelma). Before long the trip snowballs into an adventure far beyond what was initially envisioned, as an attempted parking lot rape ends in a killing, the trigger pulled not so much because of the intended violence as the words uttered by the world-be perpetrator.

It is a 1966 Thunderbird convertible that brings the two temporary freedom. It is also in the automobile that the pair forms a bond of intimate friendship so tight that at the end of the film the two would rather die together holding hands than live in confinement. The elegant, beautifully restored Thunderbird was an unlikely automobile for a waitress to own. It is as gorgeous as the film's two heroines, with its luscious color, long sweeping lines, tasteful chrome, and pristine white interior. Even when covered with dust as it is driven to its final end, it exudes a feeling that life is to be lived on the edge.

The men in this film are portrayed in an over-simplistic manner, but there is a kernel of truth in the characterization of each of the types portrayed. Jimmy, Louise's boyfriend, can be both sensitive and loyal, but also violent when the least bit confused. Thelma's husband is the typical self-centered insensitive spouse, certainly reflective of a large group of men within American society. Male authority, as reflected in a traffic cop, is bold when he has access to his gun, but cowering when one is pointed at him. The cowboy lover (Brad Pitt) has the appearance of being sensitive and understanding, but behind the veneer he is deceitful and egotistical. Only detective Slocum (Harvey Keitel) shows an understanding of the pair's true situation and motives, and he turns out to be powerless.

Thelma and Louise legitimized the notion that women could be at the center of a first rank outlaw road film, in a way no different than *Midnight Run* or *Rain Man*. Autonomous women were now behind the wheel and not simply in the passenger's seat.

The backdrop of this rather unlikely story-road houses, gin mills, gas stations, motels, oil fields, and wild horses — provided the viewer with enough of a realistic context to raise serious questions concerning the dilemmas of life and roads taken, the consequence of both our personal choices and chance that inevitably confronts us along the way.

While *Thelma and Louise* was superficial in terms of plot and character development, it remains one of the most important films of the 1990s. In contrast, David Cronenberg's *Crash*, released in 1996, while far more complex and haunting, has been curiously marginalized.[48] Based on the 1973 novel by James Ballard, *Crash* brought together technology and sexuality on very deep psychological levels, as the violent intensity of a fatal accident was equated with sexual consummation. *Crash* is a tale reflective of the late 1990s, a time during which technology was moving at a pace that was outstripping humanity's ability to maintain an emotional equilibrium. Furthermore, the sexuality of the era — obviously connected in complex unconscious as well as conscious ways to a technological society — had failed in its promise to bring with it spiritual or psychic fulfillment.

This was not a movie for the fainthearted. *Crash* had numerous critics, including Ted Turner, who for a time attempted to keep the film from being shown in the United States. Starring James Spader (James Ballard), Holly Hunter (Dr. Helen Remington), Elias Koteas (Vaughan), Deborah Kara Unger (Ballard's wife Catherine) and Rosanna Arquette (Gabrielle), *Crash* centers on a sexually unfulfilled young couple (Ballard and Catherine) who ultimately find themselves united after an erotic journey into an underworld that was centered on violent automobile accidents, bizarre personalities, heterosexual and homosexual liaisons, and frequent sexual encounters in cars. And while there are many cars in this film — a Porsche 550 Spyder, a 1955 Ford, a new Mercedes, and nondescript sedans with unusual hood ornaments — it is neurotic Vaughan's mid–1960s Lincoln Continental convertible that takes center stage in perhaps the most steamy scene in the film.

As the Continental, with its top up, moves through a car wash and is drenched with soapy water and slapped by leather straps, Catherine and Vaughan engage in rough sex while husband James, sitting in the driver's seat, peers in the rear view mirror.[49] The scene ends as Catherine's semen-covered hand slides down the leather-covered front seat. Catherine, previously unable to achieve an orgasm with her husband, experienced an extreme moment differing from death only by degrees. In the scene that follows, as Ballard views the bruises on Catherine's body as she lies naked on their bed, it seems obvious that his wife will never be the same, no different than someone involved in a violent automobile accident.

The battered and bruised black 1964 Lincoln convertible, with its slab sides and suicide doors, certainly has a large enough backseat for the humping, twisting and turning that occurs on several occasions. When Vaughan engages a prostitute for backseat sex while James drives, its top is down and all the world can see what happens. Indeed, Vaughan's backseat encounter with a prostitute is visible to all who share one Toronto thoroughfare with the big Lincoln. *Crash* is unique in its presentation of sex in cars, a dominant mating ritual for several generations of Americans.

Poetry, Women, and Passion

The automobile's role in matters of sexuality, gender, and relationships can be seen in a body of poetry on the topic. It is the poets who have had something to say about what has been rarely said about human activities in cars. Their responses, particularly in writings after 1980, have resulted in a spontaneous overflow of powerful feelings, and a reconstruction of past events markedly distinct from that by historians employing textual sources.

Literary approaches to the understanding of technology and culture have had several strong advocates. Leo Marx has consistently argued that there is an inherent power to using literature to probe into intimate human relations. He stated in a 1988 essay that "The great writer is a sensitive observer, and needless to say, he does not merely project his culture. On the contrary, often he consciously reveals covert elements that less perceptive artists ignore; moreover, he sometimes reveals them precisely by turning stereotypes inside out."[50] Cynthia Golob Dettlebach, a pioneer in the realm of the automobile and culture, concurred with Marx, remarking in her 1976 monograph *The Driver's Seat: The Automobile in American Literature and Popular Culture* that "As the most favored — and problematic — offspring of that particularly American union of space, romance, and technology, the automobile occupies a central place in our fantasies as well as our daily lives. It is therefore not surprising that in a wide variety of American art forms, the car is the metaphor or microcosm of our ambivalent, dream/nightmare experiences."[51]

It is astonishing to note that so little has been written on either sex or poetry when it comes to the automobile. Perhaps the absence of work in poetry is understandable, but not sex. When I mention to colleagues and friends the topic of sex and the automobile, it is almost universally acknowledged that nearly all Baby Boomers or their parents have had some type of experience in a car that brings back a vivid memory. And while the automobile is no longer as popular a place for amorous activities as it was a generation or two ago in the United States, a recent survey of 4,000 respondents in Great Britain conduced by the car insurer *yesinsurance.co.uk* and published in the *Daily Mail* claimed that "a staggering 68 percent of folk have had nookie in a car. An overwhelming 81 percent of couples have got frisky in the car, but restrained themselves ... [and] More worryingly ... one in 10 thrill seekers have actually engaged in sex WHILST DRIVING."[52]

This information flies in the face of studies done in the United States during the 1970s in which it was claimed that the back seat had been displaced by the bedroom for many teenagers. According to Beth L. Bailey, during the twentieth century courtship moved from parlor to automobile and then to the bedroom, or from private to public and finally back to private spaces.[53] It was in the mid–1970s that the subject began to be openly discussed in newspapers, *The Chronicle of Higher Education, Car and Driver,* and *Motor Trend.*[54] Yet the only piece of serious historical scholarship devoted to the subject is David Lewis's essay "Sex and the Automobile: From Rumble Seats to Rockin' Vans," first published in 1980.[55] One approach to follow up on Lewis's work might possibly flesh out the topic by examining traffic or police records. A second tack might be to read impressionistic personal accounts, either on the Internet or in material like the *Penthouse* Forum.

I am taking a different angle, however, and that is to look at how female American poets have depicted sexuality and relationships associated with cars and driving, assuming that their sensibilities, and their power to flesh out latent meanings, will elucidate the topic in a fresh way. Without doubt, the automobile as an isolated artifact, quite divorced from those who ride in it, brings with it very different psychological sexual undertones and overtones for men and women, a notion that S. I. Hayakawa clearly articulated in 1957.[56] While it is commonly thought that the automobile is associated with masculinity in America, female poets writing on sex and the automobile have written the most revealing material on the subject. Indeed, with the rise of feminism as a mass movement by the late 1970s, they claimed possession of an object often thought masculine in nature, but one that has done more to transform the everyday lives of females than males.

Just as sex and the automobile has been neglected by scholars, so has the topic of poetry and the automobile. In 1980, Laurence Goldstein authored the one scholarly exploration in the area, and it is a valuable introduction to what is a most difficult body of knowledge for a disciplinary outsider to interpret.[57] Goldstein's analysis was limited in utility, however, both in terms of what poems he chose to use in his essay and by the fact that his work is now dated. Much poetry involving cars and relationships has been written since his essay was published. It was precisely after 1980 when, according to David Lewis and other observers, sexual activity was no longer common in the automobile (although the British insurance survey seems to suggest otherwise!), that poets began to write explicitly on the topic. Perhaps it was the end of backseat sex, or perhaps it was the sexual revolution, or perhaps backseat sex has been replaced by sex in the front reclining seat, now that the recliner has become for the most part standard equipment. While jogging in quiet, residential neighborhoods I occasionally find used condoms on the side of the road, a testimony that sex in cars is not totally dead. Whatever the case, contemporary poetry has by no means neglected love, the automobile, and the road.

To keep things manageable, I have chosen to discuss only female poets, although men also made important contributions to this genre.[58] Initially, my decision was based in large part on trying to limit the scope of this study, and to manage the length of this presentation. Yet, I was also drawn to women poets because of the remarkable sensitivity that they had for the subject. Serving as source material for this recent wave of poetry were two particular anthologies: Kurt Brown's *Drive, They Said: Poems about Americans and Their Cars* (1996), and Elinor Nauen's *Ladies, Start Your Engines: Women Writers on Cars and the Road* (1996).[59]

The female poets that follow are all considered important by the literary community; their work has appeared either in anthologies or published collections. Many of the following have won regional or national awards, and almost all have held teaching positions at colleges or universities. After reviewing a wide range of writings, my selection process reflected personal taste and a historical sense of what constitutes the most significant poetry conveying spontaneous emotions related to the automobile, relationships and sexuality. However, the very breadth and complexity of the topic and the vast number of writings precludes any thoughts that it is a definitive study. Indeed, I consider it far more as an exploration.

To bring order into what seemed to me as chaos, I have categorized my selections into a number of discrete areas to facilitate analysis and discussion:

- Driving, and thinking about you;
- When things don't go quite as planned;
- The person as an automobile;
- Similar rhythms — making love and making time;
- Sex, adventure, and the road.

As an enclosed personal space, made quiet by enhanced technologies especially during the past 20 years, the automobile not only brings people together for an extended period of time during a road trip, but also enables the driver and passengers to think without distraction. One enters a near hypnotic state when on long drives, and with it the subconscious and conscious flow together. We think of those we love or hate and we fantasize about those whom we would like to love. Thus, in "Angel Fire," Joyce Carol Oates describes the car, the world, the heat, the windshield, and the person sitting next to her.

A road trip like that described by Oates can bring two bodies and minds together, but a solitary road trip, as in the case of Linda Gregg in her "Driving to Houston," allows one to think about ending a relationship.[60] It is on such a drive that Gregg thinks hard about her relationship with a married man.

Oates and Gregg are mature women discussing the intricacies of relationships, and the car is the place where these thoughts flow. However, when we think of sex and automobiles, it is usually about youth. Lynne Knight fleshes out the reality of such a youthful experience in her "There, in My Grandfather's Old Green Buick." In the poem, Knight tells us much about parking: surprisingly, perhaps, male rather than female restraint; distracting thoughts about somehow damaging the car; memories of Catholic religious instruction; exploration and self-control; and a new sense of a more mature self. Knight later stated that the poem "Pretty much encapsulates my sexual experiences as a teenager although it probably makes me sound a little more sexually aware than I actually was. There was a fierce desire, yes, but also lots of blind fumbling."[61]

Knight recently recalled some of the circumstances surrounding the writing of the poem: "When I wrote the poem, I had returned to poetry after a 20-year hiatus.... When I finally got back to where I could tell the truth about my life, I was able to write poetry again. I think of this poem as one of my breakthrough poems — it showed me I could take memory and make of it something new, something that would speak to others."[62]

Knight's poetry subtly places us with her and her lover in the car; its power is in its ability to probe the inner recesses of our own memories concerning similar circumstances. One feels the electricity present in the old Buick and its absence in our lives as adults. Sensations of sex are also expressed as electric by Linda Pastan in her poem "Cable Jumping."

Analogies and imagery involving car parts and human parts have been drawn in art and music in the past, whether it be the words in Robert Johnson's "Terraplane Blues," Mel Ramos' canvas "Kar Kween," or the "Dagmars" on early 1950s Cadillacs.[63] Pastan spoke in terms of organs analogous to car parts, and connections no different than the flow of electricity under a hood. The end result of coming together or jump starting is the achievement of synchronicity, of reaching similar voltages.

In a similar fashion, achieving synchronicity between the tactile and sensory experiences of driving and the rhythm of a wholesome sexual relationship, imagined or real, was the achievement of California poet Eloise Klein Healy. In her flowing, elegant, and sensitive "This Darknight Speed" (1979), Healy connected driving with an imagined love. It takes place first in a dance between cars merging from a ramp, and subsequently results in an animal joy, little different than two bodies joined together. In one's subconscious and conscious mind, despite being alone in a car, one is for a time not alone on the highway.[64]

Healy's exhilaration for the car, the road, and the mysterious other vehicle is most fanciful and remarkable. The two disconnected hearts, however, are more than likely destined never to meet. The connection and flow is transitory at best. With a turn off an exit ramp, the fantasy and adventure ends.

Adventure can be very real, however. Real and in the car, that is the case in the verse of Louisiana poet Martha McFerren. McFerren begins her "Women in Cars" with a sexually provocative statement, and she goes on to recount a long, boring, trip across Texas, but her account dispels that notion. Certainly, riding with Martha had to be an adventure and more. To be young and crazy again! And so too with another female Louisiana poet, Sheryl St. Germain, who takes the adventures to the side of the road in her "Wanting to be in Death Valley."

St. Germain's erotic poetry is stunning: she takes us to the side of a road only accessible by car, and one where raw nature prevails. There is the possibility of death, a death very different than the outcome of a sexual encounter. St. Germain considered this poem as "unsuccessful," but in my opinion it is a powerful expression of creative thoughts flowing during a road trip:

> I was thinking about the sensuous quality of Death Valley and of the desert in general, and also of the extremity of DV and of deserts, and thinking about desire and how it goes away although you wish that it wouldn't. I was nearly at the end of a long and mostly satisfying relationship, and I suppose I was thinking that I wanted to be marked by this man in the way

that I felt marked by the desert. I was thinking about my own restlessness and desire to move from relationship to relationship and admiring the mesquite, and the other desert plants that set roots down so firmly, so deeply, and wishing I could be like that, somehow knowing that I couldn't. Thinking about how closing death and sex are linked as well.[65]

The automobile is perhaps the most sexual object ordinary people deal with. It is a place of refuge for quiet thought; an isolated space for us to be together; a public place for romance beyond the control of others; an object for imagination and imagery; and a vehicle to take us to places on the side of the road that stimulates the innermost recesses of our mind and heart, thereby revealing our souls. The women poets discussed in this chapter have come to intimate terms with the automobile and American life, and indeed reclaimed the car from its previous-masculine identity.

Where Does the Automobile in American Life Go from Here?

Be wary of historians who claim that they can look into their crystal balls and see the future. For if history teaches us anything, it is that life is complex and unpredictable, and turning points take place when one least expects it. Yet, it is safe to say that times will be anything but easy for American automobile manufacturers in the years ahead. It is also safe to say that for many Americans the automobile — in whatever technological form — will continue to shape everyday life and popular culture.

First, "peak oil" and other energy constraints will challenge the industry for the foreseeable future, whether the automobile prime mover continues to be the internal combustion engine, an ICE/electric hybrid, or perhaps fuel cell/hydrogen powered. Energy, and where to get it, along with pure water, stand with climate change and the fate of the Middle East as the central issues of the twenty-first century. How personal transportation fits into this matrix remains unanswered.

Secondly, there will be ongoing and continuing pressures to reduce costs and improve manufacturing efficiencies. More efforts will certainly be exerted to expand into emerging markets, particularly China, where one analyst has predicted that 50 percent of the global market will reside by the year 2050. The future of the automobile in Latin America and particularly Africa remains an open question.

In the immediate future, and as the United States fights to keep its significant place in the global automobile market as well as at home, supply chain efficiencies will be intensified, as will a reduction in costs due to excess labor production capacities and inventories. Legacy costs will need to be managed, and retail and distribution efforts will need to be incrementally improved, even beyond what computers and the Internet have achieved to date.

Given the history of the industry over the past 30 years, the federal government will continue to play a major role in shaping the industry, especially with regards to CO_2 regulations and CAFE standards. Perhaps it will remain for government to take on the role of active agent for positive change, as it did during the New Deal era, if the automobile in its present form is to survive as a central feature of our economy and culture. As of this writing, however, it appears that government is operating on a ragged edge, and if that is the case, both the American automobile industry and the nation are in great peril.

Whatever happens, the past century's story of the automobile and American life has resulted in Americans gaining substantial economic and social freedom, although some of it clearly was illusory. That freedom has become so ingrained that it is doubtful that any technology or institutional system that attempts to restrain any of our degrees of freedom will succeed. Americans are wedded to the road, and their freedom to move is one of the most important characteristics of what they have been and who they now are.

EPILOGUE: THE AUTOMOBILE AND ONE AMERICAN LIFE

I'm sitting on the porch of the home where I grew up, thinking of the years gone by and folks who are no longer around. Those memories of early childhood and cars stick with me in ways that many other thoughts of the past do not. I can remember making model cars out of cardboard boxes, using wheels taken from the paper tops of glass milk jugs. As I look back, I recollect my most treasured book at age 5 — a Golden Book of automobiles in which I stuck a series of "stamps" of various cars. At age 5 (an important year, if for no other reason than because at Christmas I received a Lionel train), I went over those stamp images time after time, thinking of Stutzes and Pierce-Arrows when in fact my father had just purchased a used 1948 Chevrolet Fleetline, painted black with a gray interior.

My parents were World War II refugees, a story too complex to detail here, but now living in the United States and trying to get back on their feet economically during the early 1950s. In fact, before we bought that car, my father would ride his bike some seven miles each way to work in the rain and snow. And it was so cold in the winter that I can recall him taking the spark plugs out of the car before he went to work, heating them on the stove, and then trying to start the car so that he could get to Niagara Falls before 7 a.m. Clearly, automobility came late to the Heitmann family.

I remember the interior of that '48 Chevy like it was yesterday, especially the place on the dash where the radio was *supposed* to be, but was not, covered by a dash plate. Oh, how I longed for a radio, like the one in my much older cousin George's '49 Chevy. It was George who took me on one of my first thrilling rides, going 50 over a hill, a daring deed that I reported to my mother as soon as I got back to the house, hoping to get George in trouble. The other great car of my early childhood a 1950 Oldsmobile Rocket 88 owned by another cousin of mine, Fred. It was light blue and very fast, but what distinguished it was a vacuum-operated bird on the top of the dash that "popped up" whenever the engine vacuum was steady and collapsed when the driver was hard on the accelerator. It was like magic, and at the same time brought rare humor into my life. I wonder where that bird is today.

Fred later owned other cool cars, including a 1957 Ford with a Thunderbird engine, a 1961 Dodge with a 383 cubic inch engine that never could stay in tune, and, most unforgettable, a 1964 Pontiac GTO convertible that he bought new off the showroom floor. I learned a lot from Fred during those years, the consequence of reading his *Hot Rod* and *Motor Trend* magazines and of hands-on assistance in setting spark-plug and point gaps.

My first car was a 1959 MGA that I bought in high school, a car filled with bondo and needing a ring-job. It was fun at the time, and took me where I wanted to go without exception (despite reports of the unreliability of Lucas electrics, it never failed me). With college that car had to go, and as an upperclassman I graduated to a 1966 Ford Mustang, one of the best cars I ever owned. It was also the car in which I took my wife on our first date, and in which she pulled off the knob on the radio, much to my irritation. Since then we have ridden many places together in a number of cars, and we still irritate each other at times.

I won't bore you with the list of cars that followed college and have taken me far and wide to this day. The point is that for me, and for many other Americans, automobiles have

The author on the hood of an Oldsmobile "Rocket 88," 1955, with his mother (left) and aunt. Family photographs were often taken with the car as an integral part of the picture (author's collection).

been indelibly linked to our lives, past, present, and future. They are a part of our first memories, our triumphs and tragedies, and a reflection of our good times and bad. They have been the spaces in which some of our most important words have been spoken to those we hold dear, and to those we would like to forget. For some, cars are more important than a home, and unfortunately, for a number of the down and out, they are a home.

The automobile is the quintessential reflection of American individuality, a virtue, perhaps, but one often followed to the extreme at the expense of concern for others and human obligations. Yes, cars are fun to drive and look at, they reflect who we are and our status, but they are no substitute for people and relationships. It is human ingenuity and the spirit that led to the design and mass production of the car, and not the car itself that is to be cultivated and celebrated. Yes, cars can be beautiful objects, but it is the people who created them and used them that are the focal point for further study.

CHAPTER NOTES

Introduction

1. G. K Chesterton, "The Hollow Horn," *G. K.'s Weekly*, 24 (October 1, 1936): 57.

2. A number of recent essays and books have taught me to think differently about the history of the automobile. They include Bernhard Rieger, "'Fast Couples': Technology, Gender, and Modernity in Britain and Germany During the Nineteen-Thirties," *Historical Research*, 76 (August 2003): 364–88; Rudy Kosher, "Cars and Nations: Anglo-German Perspectives on Automobility Between the World Wars," *Theory, Culture, & Society*, 21 (2004): 121–144; Wolfgang Sachs, *For Love of the Automobile: Looking Back into the History of Our Desires* (Berkeley, CA: University of California Press, 1992); Sean O'Connell, *The Car and British Society: Class, Gender and Motoring 1896–1939* (Manchester: Manchester University Press, 1998).

3. James J. Flink, *The Automobile Age* (Cambridge, MA: MIT Press, 1988).

4. On the importance of culture in understanding technology, the social construction of technology, and flaws in interpretations which take a determinist approach, see David E. Nye, *Consuming Power: A Social History of American Energies* (Cambridge, MA: MIT Press, 1998), 1–12.

5. David Gartman, *Auto Slavery: The Labor Process in the American Automobile Industry, 1897–1950* (New Brunswick, NJ: Rutgers University Press, 1986).

6. Much of this psychological analysis comes from Peter Marsh and Peter Collett, *Driving Passion: The Psychology of the Car* (Boston and London: Faber and Faber, 1987).

7. On the trend to increase the number of varieties of models and accessorize, see Alfred P. Sloan, *My Years with General Motors* (Garden City, NJ: Doubleday, 1964), 439–442.

8. In Stephan Wilkinson's humorous *The Gold-Plated Porsche: How I Sank a Small Fortune into a Used Car, and Other Misadventures (*Guilford, CT: Lyons, 2004*)*, 6, the author tells the joke, "What's the difference between a Porsche and a porcupine? In the case of the porcupine, the prick is on the outside."

9. http://undersire.msn.com/underwire/realife/Lu/103lucilleA.asp.

10. http://autotags4u.com/business-custom-personalized-license-plates-1.html.

11. An interesting film that explores Native American attitudes towards the natural world and the automobile (a 1964 Buick Wildcat) is *Pow Wow Highway*, VHS, Paragon Entertainment, 1997.

12. Marsh and Collett, *Driving Passion*, 15; www.trivia-library.com/b/buried-treasure-11-people-buried-with-objects-part-2.htm (accessed July 17, 2008).

13. http://www.youtube.com/watch?v=I2cPBl6scJk (accessed July 17, 2008).

14. Harrod Blank, *Wild Wheels* (San Francisco: Pomegranate Artbooks, 1993).

Chapter 1

1. Lester S. Levy, *Give Me Yesterday: American History in Song, 1890–1920* (Norman, OK: University of Oklahoma Press, 1975), 65. Frank P. Banta, *Kareless Koon, an Ethiopian Two Step* (New York: Spaulding, 1899).

2. James J. Flink, *The Automobile Age* (Cambridge, MA: MIT Press, 1988), 1.

3. L. J. K. Setright, *Drive On! A Social History of the Motor Car* (London: Granta Books, 2003), 14.

4. Michael Sedgwick, *Early Cars* (London: Octopus Books, 1962), 8–32.

5. Patricia W. Lipski, "The Introduction of 'Automobile' into American English," *American Speech*, 38 (October 1964): 176–187.

6. James J. Flink, *America Adopts the Automobile, 1895–1910* (Cambridge, MA: MIT Press, 1970); James Laux, *In First Gear: The French Automobile Industry* (Montreal: McGill-Queen's University Press, 1976); Brian Laban, *Cars: The Early Years* (Köln: Könemann, 2000).

7. Richard Shelton Kirby, et al., *Engineering in History* (New York: McGraw-Hill, 1956), 267–273.

8. David Beasley, *The Suppression of the Automobile: Skullduggery at the Crossroads* (New York and Westport, CT: Greenwood Press, 1988).

9. David V. Herlihy, "The Bicycle Story," *American Heritage Invention & Technology*, 7 (Spring 1992): 48–59; David V. Herlihy, *Bicycle: The History* (New Haven, CT: Yale University Press, 2004).

10. Stephen B. Goddard, *Colonel Albert Pope and His American Dream Machines: The Life and Times of a Bicycle Tycoon Turned Automotive Pioneer* (Jefferson, NC: McFarland, 2000).

11. Sidney H. Aronson, "The Sociology of the Bicycle," *Social Forces*, 30 (March, 1952): 308.

12. http://kids.niehs.nih.gov/lyrics/daisy.htm

13. Walter Burton, *The Story of Tire Beads and Tires* (New York: McGraw-Hill, 1954).

14. Aronson, "Sociology of the Bicycle," 312.

15. Timothy Beatley, *Green Urbanism: Learning from European Cities* (Washington, DC: Island Press, 2000), 166–193.

16. "A New Caloric Engine," *Scientific American*, 3 (September 22, 1860): 193.

17. Pál Garamvári, "100 Years of the Carburetor," *Technikat Ort Enetio Szemle*, 20 (1993): 11–15.

18. James M. Laux, *In First Gear: The French Automobile Industry to 1914* (Montreal: McGill-Queen's University Press, 1976); Jan P. Norbye, "Panhard et Levassor: Limelight to Twilight," *Automobile Quarterly*, 6 (Fall 1967): 127–143.

19. Flink, *The Automobile Age*, 15.

20. "Motor Vehicles," *Encyclopædia Britannica* (13th ed), vol. 18, 920.

21. Tom McCarthy, "The Coming Wonder? Foresight and Early Concerns about the Automobile," *Environmental History*, 6 (January 2001): 46–74.

22. Kit Foster, *The Stanley Steamer: America's Legendary Steam Car* (Kingfield, ME: Stanley Museum, 2004); John F. Katz, "The Challenge from Steam," *Automobile Quarterly* (First Quarter 1987): 15–29; Susan S. Davis, *The Stanleys: Renaissance Yankees: Innovation in Industry and the Arts* (New York: Newcomen Society of the United States, 1997); Floyd Clymer, *Floyd Clymer's Steam Car Scrapbook* (New York: Bonanza Books, 1945).

23. Gijs Mom, *The Electric Vehicle: Technology and Expectations in the Automobile Age* (Baltimore: Johns Hopkins University Press, 2004); David Kirsch, *The Electric Vehicle and the Burden of History* (New Brunswick, NJ: Rutgers University Press, 2000); Adam Gowns Whyte, *Electricity in Locomotion: An Account of Its Mechanism, Its Achievements, and Its Prospects* (Cambridge: Cambridge University Press, 1911).

24. Hiram Percy Maxim's *Horseless Carriage Days* (New York: Dover, 1962) is a fascinating account of developments in both electric and ICE vehicle technologies at the end of the nineteenth century.

25. Maurice D. Hendry, "Thomas!," *Automobile Quarterly*, 8 (Summer 1970): 418–30.

26. George W. May, *Charles E. Duryea Automaker* (Chillicothe, IL: River Beach Publishing, 1996). Frank Duryea's claim to be first is asserted in J. Frank Duryea, *America's First Automobile* (Springfield MA: MacAulay, 1942).

27. On Maxim, see Iain McCallum, *Blood Brothers: Hiram and Hudson Maxim; Pioneers of Modern Warfare* (London: Chatham, 1999); on the Appersons, see W. C. Madden, *Haynes-Apperson and America's First Practical Automobile: A History* (Jefferson, NC: McFarland, 2003); on Winton, see Thomas F. Saal, *Famous but Forgotten: The Story of Alexander Winton, Automotive Pioneer and Industrialist* (Twinsburg, OH: Golias Publishing, 1997).

28. John B. Rae, *The American Automobile Industry* (Boston: G.K. Hall, 1984), 28.

29. Maurice D. Hendry, "Henry M. Leland," in Ronald Barker and Anthony Harding, eds., *Automobile Design: Twelve Great Designers and Their Work*, 2nd ed. (Warrendale, PA: Society of Automotive Engineers, 1992).

30. "Motor Vehicles," *Encyclopædia Britannica* (13th ed), vol. 18, 920.

31. Richard Wager, *Golden Wheels: The Story of the Automobiles Made in Cleveland and Northeastern Ohio 1892–1932*, 2nd ed. (Cleveland: John T. Zubal, 1986), xiii.

32. Letter to the editor of the *Horseless Age*, from Charles B. King, October 8, 1895, *The Horseless Age* 1:1 (1895): 8.

33. See Volume 1 of *The Horseless Age*, no. 2: 27; no. 3: 15; no. 4: 3; no. 6: 14; no. 10: 22.

34. See Flink, *The Automobile Age*, 51–55; *William Greenleaf, Monopoly on Wheels: Henry Ford and the Selden Patent Suit* (Detroit: Wayne State University Press, 1961).

35. On early clubs, see Flink, *America Adopts the Automobile*, 143–63.

36. *The Automobile Club of America* (New York, 1903), 9.

37. Bellamy Partridge, *Fill'er Up! The Story of Fifty Years of Motoring* (New York: McGraw-Hill, 1952), 78–85.

38. "Effect on Land Values and the Distribution of Population," *The Horseless Age*, 1 (March, 1896): 1.

39. Lowell Julliard Carr, "How the Devil-Wagon Came to Dexter: A Study of Diffusional Change in an American Community," *Social Forces*, 11 (October 1932): 64–70.

40. "The Lesson of a Runaway," *The Horseless Age*, 1 (December 1895): 27.

41. See "Dr. Booth's Motor Carriage," *The Horseless Age*, 1 (January 1896): 17 and "Dr. Booth's Motor Cab in Completed Form," *The Horseless Age*, 1 (July 1896): 21.

42. Booth Tarkington, *The Magnificent Ambersons* (Garden City, NY: Doubleday, Page, 1918).

43. The benchmark study on the early social history of the automobile in rural America is Michael L. Berger's *The Devil Wagon in God's Country: The Automobile and Social Change in Rural America, 1893–1929* (Hamden, CT: Archon Books, 1979).

44. See Christy Borth, "The Automobile in Popular Song," typescript, Forty-third National Automobile Show, Automobile Manufacturers Association, Detroit, Michigan 15–23 October 1960.

45. Floyd Clymer, *Those Wonderful Old Automobiles* (New York: Bonanza, 1953), 53.

46. Julian Smith, "Transports of Delight: The Image of the Automobile in Early Films," *Film & History*, 11, no. 3 (1981): 59–67.

47. To view the film *Automobile Parade* on the Internet, see http://memory.lc.gov. Digital ID lcmp002 m2b 46029. http://hdl.loc.gov/loc.mbrsmi/lcmp002.m2b460 29

48. http:memory.lc.gov/ digital ID awal 1952 http://hdl.loc.gov/loc.mbrsmi/awal.1952

49. Donald W. McCaffrey, "The Evolution of the Chase in the Silent Screen Comedy," *The Journal of the Society of Cinematologists* 4 (1964–5): 1–8.

50. *Gussle's Day of Rest*, March 1915. *The Original Keystone Comedies*, Vol. 8, VHS, Kartes Video Communications, Indianapolis, IN.

51. Cord Scott, "The Race of the Century," *Journal of the Illinois State Historical Society* 96:1 (2003): 37–48.

52. Beverly Rae Kimes, "The Dawn of Speed," *American Heritage*, 38:7 (1987): 92–101; Robert Casey, "The Vanderbilt Cup, 1908," *Technology and Culture*, 40 (1999): 358–62.

53. Timothy Messer-Kruse, "You Know Me: Barney Oldfield," *Timeline*, 19:3 (2002): 219.

54. Robert B. Jackson, *Road Race Round the World: New York to Paris, 1908* (New York: Scholastic, 1965).

55. Michael Gianturco, "The Infinite Straightaway," *American Heritage of Invention & Technology*, 8:2 (1992): 34–41. Gianturco argues that with the oval board track, race cars could be driven as if they were on an infinite straightaway, and thus engine performance was continu-

ally improved at the expense of chassis and suspension improvements during the 1920s and 1930s.

Chapter 2

1. See George David Smith, *Wisdom from the Robber Barons: Enduring Business Lessons from Rockefeller, Morgan, and the First Industrialists* (N.P.: Perseus, 2000).

2. John B. Rae, ed., *Henry Ford* (Englewood Cliffs, NJ: Prentice-Hall, 1969), 3.

3. Robert Weibe, *The Search for Order, 1877–1920* (New York: Hill and Wang, 1967).

4. Definitive histories include Allan Nevins, *Ford*, 3 vols. (New York: Scribner's, 1954–1963); Robert Lacey, *Ford, the Men and the Machine* (New York: Little, Brown, 1986); John Bell Rae, *Henry Ford* (New York: Prentice-Hall, 1969); Douglas Brinkley, *Wheels for the World: Henry Ford, His Company, and a Century of Progress, 1903–2003* (New York: Viking, 2003); Steven Watts, *The People's Tycoon: Henry Ford and the American Century* (New York: Knopf, 2005); Anne Jardim, *The First Henry Ford: A Study in Personality and Leadership* (Cambridge, MA: MIT Press, 1970). On his early years, see Sidney Olson, *Young Henry Ford: A Picture History of the First Forty Years* (Detroit: Wayne State University Press, 1963).

5. Quoted in Harold Livesay, *American Made* (Boston: Little, Brown, 1977), 166.

6. *The Automobile*, 14 (January 11, 1906): 107–19, quoted in Rae, *Henry Ford*, 18–19.

7. Quoted in Livesay, *American Made*, 168.

8. See Leo Levine, *Ford: The Dust and the Glory: A Racing History* (SAE, 2001).

9. Livesay, *American Made*, 166.

10. The definitive monograph on mass production is David A. Hounshell, *From the American System to Mass Production 1800–1932: The Development of Manufacturing Technology in the United States* (Baltimore: Johns Hopkins, 1984). See also Ray Batchelor, *Henry Ford: Mass Production, Modernism and Design* (Manchester: Manchester University Press, 1994). For a first-hand account from a key figure at Ford, see Charles E. Sorenson, *My Forty Years with Ford* (New York: Norton, 1956).

11. Stephen Meyer, "The Persistence of Fordism: Workers and Technology in the American Automobile Industry, 1900–1960," in *On the Line: Essays in the History of Autowork*. eds. Nelson Lichtenstein and Stephen Meyer (Urbana and Chicago: University of Illinois Press, 1989), 74.

12. Stephen Meyer, "The Degradation of Work Revisited," in Thomas J. Sugrue, *Automobile in American Life and Society* (online database, University of Michigan, accessed 10 June 2008) available from http://www.autolife.umd.umich.edu/Labor/L_ Overview/L_Overview1.htm.

13. James J. Flink, *The Automobile Age* (Cambridge: MIT Press, 1989), 27.

14. "The Degradation of Work Revisited," in Thomas J. Sugrue, *Automobile in American Life and Society* [Database Online].

15. Meyer, "The Persistence of Fordism," 77.

16. On Taylor, see Gail Cooper, "Frederick Winslow Taylor and Scientific Management," in Carroll W. Pursell, Jr., ed. *Technology in America*, 2nd ed. (Cambridge, MA: MIT Press, 1990) 163–176; Robert Kanigel, *The One Best Way: Frederick Winslow Taylor and the Enigma of Efficiency* (New York: Viking, 1997).

17. Henry Ford, "Mass Production," *Encyclopædia Britannica* (13th edition, 1926), XXIX, 821.

18. Flink, *Automobile Age*, 50.

19. Hounshell, *From the American System to Mass Production*, 217–261.

20. The best description of mass production at Ford is Horace Lucien Arnold and Fay Leone Faurote, *Ford Methods and Ford Shops* (New York: The Engineering Magazine Company, 1915). This treatise describes unit-by-unit the manufacturing process, with a related discussion of labor as well. Its photographs are invaluable in understanding how the Ford Model T was made.

21. Joyce Shaw Peterson, "Autoworkers and Their Work, 1900–1933" *Labor History* 22 (1981): 213–236.

22. Flink, *The Automobile Age*, 117.

23. *Ibid.*, 120.

24. Arnold and Faroute, *Ford Methods and the Ford Shops*, 112.

25. *Ibid.*, 193.

26. Harry Braverman, *Labor and Monopoly Capital: The Degradation of Work in the Twentieth Century* (New York: Monthly Review Press), 1974.

27. David Gartman, *Auto Slavery: The Labor Process in the American Automobile Industry, 1897–1950* (New Brunswick, NJ: Rutgers University Press, 1986).

28. Joyce Shaw Peterson, *American Automobile Workers, 1900–1933* (Albany: State University of New York Press, 1987) 40.

29. Joyce Shaw Peterson, "Autoworkers and Their Work, 1900–1933," 227.

30. See August Meier, *Black Detroit* (New York: Oxford University Press, 1979). See also Zaragosa Vargas, *Proletarians of the North: A History of Mexican Industrial Workers in Detroit and the Midwest, 1917–1933* (Berkeley: University of California Press, 1993).

31. Flink, *The Automobile Age*, 117.

32. *Ibid.*, 118.

33. *Ibid.*

34. Stephen Meyer, *The Five Dollar Day* (Albany, NY: State University of New York Press, 1981), 71.

35. *Ibid.*, 65.

36. Meyer, "The Degradation of Work Revisited," in Sugrue, database online.

37. Meyer, *The Five Dollar Day*, 77.

38. Allan Nevins and Frank Hill, *Ford: Expansion and Challenge, 1915–1933* (New York: Scribner's, 1957), 514.

39. Joyce Shaw Peterson, "Black Automobile Workers in Detroit, 1900–1933," *The Journal of Negro History* 64 (Summer 1979): 183.

40. See August Meier, *Black Detroit*, and Flink, *The Automobile Age*, 126–8.

41. *Ibid.*, 4.

42. Joyce Shaw Peterson, "Black Automobile Workers in Detroit, 1900–1933," 183.

43. *Ibid.*, 183.

44. *Ibid.*, 186.

45. *Ibid.*, 187.

46. Meier and Rudwick, *Black Detroit*, 17.

47. *Ibid.*, 8.

48. *Ibid.*, 9.

49. *Ibid.*

50. *Ibid.*

51. Flink, *The Automobile Age*, 127.

52. *Ibid.*

53. *Encylopædia Britannica*, 13th edition (1926), XXIX, 823.

54. But it was far from a sweeping success. See Stephen L. McIntyre, "The Failure of Fordism: Reform of the Automobile Repair Industry, 1913–1940," *Technology and Culture*, 41 (2000): 269–299.

55. Bruce W. McCalley, *Model T Ford: The Car That Changed the World* (Iola, WI: Krause Publications, 1994), 462. Data taken from Ford Archives, accession 231.

56. Anthony Patrick O'Brien, "The Importance of Adjusting Production to Sales in the Early Automobile Industry," *Explorations in Economic History* 34 (1997): 195–219.

57. McCalley, *Model T Ford*, 463–73.

58. Upton Sinclair, *The Flivver King* (Emmaus, PA; Rodale Press, 1937), 33. For a more objective assessment of assembly line work based on a real-life story, see "Success Story: The Life and Circumstances of Mr. Gerald Corkum — paint sprayman in the Plymouth plant," *Fortune*, 12 (1935): 115–22, 124, 126.

59. Sinclair, *Flivver King*, 35.

60. *Ibid.*, 58.

61. *Ibid.*, 66.

62. *Ibid.*, 67.

63. *Ibid.*, 94.

64. *Ibid.*

65. *Ibid.*, 117.

66. *Ibid.*, 146.

67. *Ibid.*, 170.

68. *Ibid.*, 20.

69. Floyd Clymer, *Henry's Wonderful Model T 1908–1927* (New York: McGraw-Hill, 1955). For travel experiences with the Model T, see E. B. White, *Farewell to Model T: From Sea to Shining Sea* (The Little Bookroom, 2003); Rose Wilder Lane, *Travels with Zenobia: Paris to Albania by Model T Ford* (University of Missouri Press, 1983).

70. Reynold M. Wik, *Henry Ford and Grass-Roots America* (Ann Arbor, MI: University of Michigan Press, 1972).

71. John Steinbeck, "A Model T Named 'It,'" in *High Gear*, ed. Evan Jones (New York: Bantam, 1963), 163.

72. Ford Motor Company, *Instruction Book for Ford Model T Cars* (Detroit: n.p., 1913, rpr. March 1954).

73. Ford Motor Company, *Model "A" Instruction Book* (Detroit, n.p., 1931 rpr. April 1992).

74. *Funny Stories About the Ford* (Hamilton, OH, 1915), quoted in "Funny Stories About the Ford, Volume 1," *Automotive History Review*, 47 (Spring 2007): 38.

75. On Ford's own take on his life, see Henry Ford, *My Life and Work* (Garden City, NY: Doubleday, Page & Company, 1922); Henry Ford, *Today and Tomorrow* (Cambridge, MA: Productivity Press, 1988).

76. Samuel S. Marquis, *Henry Ford: An Interpretation* (Boston: Little, Brown, 1923), quoted in Rae, *Henry Ford*, 83.

77. Jacqueline Fellague Ariout, "The Dearborn Independent, A Mirror of the 1920s," *Michigan History Magazine* 80 (1996): 41–47. Ariout's article is just a cursory survey of the newspaper's contents. A close read and analysis might lead to a most interesting study.

78. On Ford, Germany and anti–Semitism, see Neil Baldwin, *Henry Ford and the Jews: The Mass Production of Hate* (Public Affairs, 2001); Max Wallace, *The American Axis: Henry Ford, Charles Lindbergh, and the Rise of the Third Reich* (New York: St. Martin's, 2003). On the German response to Ford's ideas, see Wolfgang Konig, "Adolf Hitler VS. Henry Ford: The Volkswagen, the Role of America as Model, and the Failure of a Nazi Consumer Society," *German Studies Review*, 27 (2004): 249–268.

79. Floyd Clymer, *Henry's Wonderful Model T*, 109.

80. See Walter Langford, "What the Motor Vehicle Is Doing for the Farmer," *Scientific American* (January 15, 1910): 50, and Franklin M. Reck, "The Automobile Between the Wars," in "How the Automobile Has Changed the Lives of People," typescript, August 4, 1944, Automobile Manufacturers Association, Vertical File, Social Effects #2, National Automotive History Collection, Detroit Public Library.

81. Upton Sinclair, *The Flivver King*.

82. William Holtz, ed., *Travels with Zenobia: Paris to Albania by Model T Ford*, a journal by Rose Wilder Lane and Helen Dore Boylston (Columbia, MO: University of Missouri Press, 1983), 50.

83. See Harry Wilkin Perry, "Anti Joy Ride Devices," *Scientific American* (January 15, 1910): 51.

84. For an excellent discussion on the history of car keys, see Michael Lamm, "Are Car Keys Obsolete," *American Heritage Invention & Technology* 23 (Summer 2008): 7.

85. Alexander Johnson, "Stop Thief!" *Country Life* (June 1919): 72.

86. Roy Lewis, "Watch Your Car," *Outing* (May 1917): 170.

87. Roy Lewis, "Watch Your Car," 168.

88. "The All-Conquering Auto Thief and a Proposed Quietus for Him," *Literary Digest* (February 7, 1920): 111–15. The author referred to Alexander C. Johnston's article in *Munsey's Magazine*, New York, 1920.

89. "More Than a Quarter of a Million Cars Stolen Each Year," *Travel* (October 1929): 46. See also William G. Shepard, "I wonder who's driving her now?" *Colliers* (July 23, 1927): 14.

90. *Automotive Industries* 56 (February 19, 1927): 283.

91. William J. Davis, "Stolen Automobile Investigations." *Journal of Automobile Investigations* 28 (Jan.-Feb. 1938): 721.

92. Federal Bureau of Investigation, "Lawless Years: 1921–1933," (online database, accessed 17 May 2008), available from http://www.fbi.gvov/libref/ historic/history/lawless.htm.

93. James M. Hepbron, "The Baltimore Criminal Justice Commission," *Annals of the American Academy of Political and Social Science*, Vol. 125, *Modern Crime: Its Prevention and Punishment* (May 1926): 103.

94. Arch Mandel, "The Automobile and the Police," *Annals of the American Academy of Political and Social Science*, Vol. 116, *The Automobile: Its Provinces and Its Problems* (Nov. 1924): 193.

95. Arch Mandel, "The Automobile and the Police," 193.

96. Bennett Mead, "Police Statistics," *Annals of the American Academy of Political and Social Science*, Vol. 146, *The Police and the Crime Problem* (Nov. 1929): 91.

97. Ellen C. Potter, "Spectacular Aspects of Crime in Relation to the Crime Wave." *Annals of the American Academy of Political and Social Science*, Vol. 125 (May 1926): 12. Potter noted, "the automobile has added its spectacular element to causes for arrest in Philadelphia by approximately 10 percent. Assault and battery by the good old-fashioned human fist lacks some of the elements which make the same offense by automobile a new story

and more than 8,800 arrests were made in 1925 out of a total of 137,263."

98. Henry Barrett Chamberlain, "The Proposed Illinois Bureau of Criminal Records and Statistics," *Journal of the American Institute of Criminal Law and Criminology* 13 (Feb. 1922), 522. Allegedly, the police moved one-third as fast as the criminals they chased.

99. Alexander Johnson, "Stop Thief!" 72.

100. Bennett Mead, "Police Statistics," 94.

101. *Ibid.*

102. Scott Bottles, *Los Angeles and the Automobile: The Making of a Modern City.* (Berkeley and Los Angeles, 1987), 92.

103. Alexander Johnson, "Stop Thief!" 72.

104. Bennett Mead, "Police Statistics," 93.

105. E. Austin Baughman, "Protective Measures for the Automobile and Its Owner," *Annals of the American Academy of Political and Social Science,* Vol. 116, *The Automobile: Its Provinces and Its Problems* (Nov. 1924), 197.

106. By 1919, Michigan, Indiana, Virginia, Delaware, Missouri, North Carolina, Florida, Pennsylvania and Maryland had adopted titles laws.

107. Baughman, 198.

108. "Checking Automobile Thefts as Massachusetts Does It," *Literary Digest* (October 9, 1920): 84.

109. James E. Bulger, "Automobile Thefts," *Journal of Criminal Justice and Criminology,* 23 (January-February 1933): 808.

110. Arch Mandel, "The Automobile and the Police," 193.

111. Ernest M. Smith, "Services of the American Automobile Association," *Annals of the American Academy of Political and Social Science,* Vol. 116, *The Automobile: Its Provinces and Its Problems* (Nov. 1924), 273.

112. Edward Rubin, "A Statistical Study of Federal Criminal Prosecutions," *Law and Contemporary Problems,* Vol. 1, *Extending Federal Powers over Crime* (Oct. 1934), 501. These figures include the theft of freight cars, which were probably nominal.

113. In Dana Gatlin, "In Case of a Thief," *Colliers* (January 8, 1919): 94.

114. *Ibid.*

115. "Two Kinds of Motor Thefts — Real and Imagined," *Literary Review* (August 26, 1922): 50.

116. "How Safe Is Your Automobile?" *Popular Mechanics Magazine* 42 (October 1924): 529.

117. See John Brennan, "Automobile Thefts," *The American City* (December 1917): 565–7.

118. John Brennan, "Automobile Thefts," 565.

119. "How Safe Is Your Automobile?" 532.

120. "Preventing Auto Theft," *Popular Mechanics Magazine* 45 (March 1926): 503.

121. "Tricks of the Auto Thief," *Popular Mechanics Magazine* (May 1929): 775.

122. William J. Davis, "Stolen Automobile Investigations," *Journal of Automobile Investigations* 28 (Jan-Feb 1938): 731–2.

123. "More About the Smooth Wiles of the Auto Thief," *The Literary Digest,* 66 (July 17, 1920): 77–8.

124. "Two Kinds of Motor Thefts — Real and Imagined," 50.

125. Brennan, "Automobile Thefts," 565–7.

126. Roy Lewis, "Watch Your Car," 169. W. S. Rowe, Chief of Police of Cleveland, also estimated that in 1916 a majority or autos were stolen by joy-riders.

127. "The All-Conquering Auto Thief and a Proposed Quietus for Him," *Literary Digest,* 64 (February 7, 1919): 112.

128. "Two Kinds of Motor Thefts — Real and Imagined," 50.

129. David Wolcott, "'The Cop Will Get You': The Police and Discretionary Juvenile Justice, 1890–1940," *Journal of Social History* 35 (Winter 2001): 358. Wolcott stated that, "Auto theft represented a [sic] especially serious problem in South California, where automobile ownership was much more common than in the rest of the country."

130. The official distinction was drawn in *Impson v. State,* 47 Ariz., 573, 1930. See also William R. Outerbridge et al., "The Dyer Act Violators: A Typology of Car Thieves," School of Criminology, University of California (January 1967): iv-v.

131. Quoted in Jerome Hall, "Federal Anti-Theft Legislation," *Law and Contemporary Problems,* Vol. 1, *Extending Federal Powers over Crime* (Oct. 1934), 428. See also "Undoing Dyer," *Time Magazine* (March 24, 1930): 13.

132. "The All-Conquering Auto Thief," 112.

133. Edward C. Crossman, "How Your Automobile May Be Stolen," *Illustrated World* (March 1917): 34.

134. *Ibid.,* 37.

135. *Ibid.,* 38.

136. "Tricks of the Automobile Thief," *Popular Mechanics Magazine* (May 1929): 772–3.

137. *Ibid.,* 774.

138. *Ibid.,* 773.

139. W.M. Weishaar, "Joe Newell Recovered 630 Stolen Automobiles Last Year," *American Magazine* (February 1925): 67.

140. William J. Davis, "Stolen Automobile Investigations," *Journal of Automobile Investigations* (Jan-Feb 1938): 732.

141. Edwin Teale, "Auto Stealing Racket Now $50,000,000-a-Year Racket." *Popular Science Monthly,* January 1933, 13.

142. See Thomas J. Courtney, "Hot Shorts," *Saturday Evening Post,* Nov. 30, 1935, 12. See also William G. Shepard, "I wonder who's driving her now?" *Colliers,* July 23, 1927, 14.

143. Edwin Teale, "Auto Stealing Racket," 96.

144. Weishaar, "Joe Newell Recovered," 67.

145. J. Edgar Hoover, "Bla-Bla Black Man," *American Magazine* (September 1936): 32.

146. *Mexico — providing for the recovery and return of stolen or embezzled motor vehicles, trailers, airplanes, or the component parts of any of them: message from the President of the United States transmitting a convention between the United States of America and the United Mexican States for the recovery and return of stolen or embezzled motor vehicles, trailers, airplanes, or the component parts of any of them, signed at Mexico City on October 6, 1936.* Washington: U.S. GPO. 1937. The Bush Administration made similar treaties with Panama (2000), Honduras (2001), and Guatemala (2002).

147. United States, 1937, *Convention with Mexico providing for the recovery and return of stolen or embezzled motor vehicles, trailers, airplanes, or the component parts of any of them: report (to accompany Executive A, 75th Cong., 1st session.).* Washington: U.S. GPO.

148. "Let the Auto Thief Beware," *Illustrated World* (August 1919): 858.

149. "Catching Auto Thieves," *The American City* 51 (October 1936): 15.

150. Sterling Gleason, "Auto-Stealing Racket Smashed by New Methods," *Popular Science Monthly* 125 (August 1934): 13.

151. *Ibid.*, 12.

152. *Ibid.*

153. *Ibid.*, 13.

154. "Science Fights Crime with New Inventions," *Science News Letter* (March 16, 1935): 164.

155. Sterling Gleason, "Auto-Stealing Racket Smashed," 13.

Chapter 3

1. Surprisingly, perhaps, little critical material has been written on the history of General Motors. See William Pelfrey, *Billy, Alfred, and General Motors: The Story of Two Unique Men, a Legendary Company, and a Remarkable Time* (New York: AMACOM American Management Association, 2006); Alan K. Binder and Deebe Ferris, eds., *General Motors in the 20th Century* (Southfield, MI: Wards Communications, 2000); Timothy Jacobs, *A History of General Motors* (New York: Smithmark, 1992); Richard M. Langworth and Jan P. Norbye, *The Complete History of General Motors, 1908–1986* (Skokie, IL: Publications International, 1986); *General Motors: The First 75 Years of Transportation Products* (Detroit: General Motors Photographic, 1983); Ed Cray, *Chrome Colossus: General Motors and Its Times* (New York: McGraw-Hill, 1980).

2. For an insight into the most dynamic automobile industry leader since Lee Iacocca, see Robert A. Lutz, *Guts: The Seven Laws of Business That Made Chrysler the World's Hottest Car Company* (New York: John Wiley, 1998).

3. Alfred D. Chandler, *Strategy and Structure: Chapters in the History of Industrial Enterprise* (Cambridge, MA: MIT Press, 1962).

4. On Durant, see Axel Madsen, *The Deal Maker: How William C. Durant Made General Motors* (New York: Wiley, 1999); Lawrence R. Gustin, *Billy Durant: Creator of General Motors* (Grand Rapids, MI: Eerdmans, 1973).

5. "General Motors," *Fortune* 18 (December 1938): 161.

6. On Sloan, see David R. Farber, *Sloan Rules: Alfred P. Sloan and the Triumph of General Motors* (Chicago: University of Chicago Press, 2002). Among Sloan's writings are *Adventures of a White Collar-Man* (New York: Doubleday, Doran, 1941); *My Years with General Motors* (Garden City, NY: Doubleday, 1964). For a contemporary look at Sloan, see "Alfred P. Sloan, Jr., Chairman," *Fortune* 17 (April 1938): 72–7.

7. Stewart W. Leslie, *Boss Kettering* (New York: Columbia University Press, 1983).

8. "General Motors IV: A Unit in Society," *Fortune* 14 (March 1939): 49.

9. In addition to Leslie's fine biography, see Sigmund A. Lavine, *Kettering: Master Inventor* (New York: Dodd, Mead, 1960); Rosamond McPherson Young, *Boss Ket: A Life of Charles F. Kettering* (New York: Longmans, Green, 1961). "General Motors: Boss Ket, Vice President and Distinguished Head of the Research Laboratories Division," *Fortune* 19 (March 1939): 44–52.

10. Leslie, *Boss Kettering*, 39.

11. For a clear description of how the system worked, see Dayton Engineering Laboratories Company, *The Delco Electric Self Cranking Lighting and Ignition System* (N.P. [Dayton?]: n.p., n.d. [January, 1913?]).

12. David Rosner and Gerald Markowitz, "A 'Gift of God?': The Public Health Controversy Over Leaded Gasoline During the 1920s," *American Journal of Public Health*, 75 (1985): 344–52; William Graebner, "Ethyl in Manhattan: A Note on the Science and Politics of Leaded Gasoline," *New York History*, 57 (1986): 436–443; Alan P. Loeb, "Birth of the Kettering Doctrine: Fordism, Sloanism and the Discovery of Tetraethyl Lead," *Business and Economic History*, 24 (1995): 72–87.

13. "G.M. III: How to Sell Automobiles," *Fortune* 19 (February 1939): 70–8, 105–110.

14. "General Motors IV: A Unit in Society," *Fortune* 14 (March 1939): 44–52, 136–152.

15. "What the Public Wants," *Business Week* (August 19, 1933): 14.

16. Ronald Edsforth and Robert Asher, "The Speedup: The Focal Point of Worker's Grievances, 1919–1941," in *Autowork*, eds. Robert Asher and Ronald Edsforth (Albany: State University of New York Press, 1995), 67.

17. *Ibid.*

18. Apparently GM, like Ford, considered the private lives of its workers to be company property. Like the Black legion in Dearborn, GM workers in Pontiac were fearful of "the Bullet Club," a secret political organization that had a role in hiring and firing. See Samuel Romer, "Profile of General Motors," *The Nation* 144 (January 23, 1937): 98.

19. Stephen Meyer, "The Persistence of Fordism: Workers and Technology in the American Automobile Industry, 1900–1960," in *On the Line: Essays in the History of Autowork*. eds. Nelson Lichtenstein and Stephen Meyer (Urbana and Chicago: University of Illinois Press, 1989), 77.

20. Stephen Meyer, "The Degradation of Work Revisited" in Thomas J. Sugrue, *Automobile in American Life and Society* (online database, University of Michigan, accessed 10 June 2008), available from http://www.autolife.umd.umich.edu/Labor/L_Overview/L_Overview1.htm.

21. Joyce Shaw Peterson, "Auto Workers and Their Work, 1900–1933," *Labor History* 22 (1981): 228.

22. James J. Flink, *The Automobile Age* (Cambridge: MIT Press), 244.

23. *Ibid.*

24. "General Motors," *Fortune* 18 (December 1938): 41.

25. "General Motors II: Chevrolet," *Fortune* 19 (January 1939): 37–46, 103–4, 107–9.

26. G. N. Georgano, *Art of the American Automobile: The Greatest Stylists and their Work* (New York: Smithmark, 1995).

27. See Stephen Bayley, *Harley Earl and the Dream Machine* (New York: Knopf, 1983); Stephen Bayley, *Harley Earl* (New York: Taplinger, 1990); Anthony J. Yanik, "Harley Earl and the Birth of Modern Automotive Styling," *Chronicle: The Quarterly Magazine of the Historical Society of Michigan*, 21 (1985): 18–22; Sally Clarke, "Managing Design: the Art and Colour Section at General Motors, 1927–1941," *Journal of Design History* 12 (1999): 65–79.

28. Quoted in Sally Clarke, "Managing Design," 65.

29. Regina Lee Blaszczyk, DuPont and the Color Revolution," *Chemical Heritage* (Fall 2007): 20–5. See also Leslie, *Boss Kettering*, 191–4 and Jan Todd, "Cars, Paint,

and Chemicals: Industry Linkages and the Capture of Overseas Technology Between the Wars," *Australian Economic History Review* 38 (July 1998): 176–93.

30. Natalie Sumner Lincoln, *The Blue Car Mystery* (New York: D. Appleton, 1926).

31. Carolyn Keene, *The Secret of the Old Clock* (New York: Grosset & Dunlap, 1930). During World War II, Nancy's car is referred to a coupe, but after 1945 titles again feature blue cars and convertibles. My thanks to colleague Marybeth Carlson for this insight.

32. "News Release," n.d., in Vertical File GM Futurama, National Automotive History Collection, Detroit Public Library. Norman Bel Geddes, *Magic Motorways* (New York: Random House, 1940). Bel Geddes' autobiography, edited by William Kelley, is *Miracle in the Evening* (Garden City, NY: Doubleday, 1960). See also C. D. Innes, *Designing Modern America: Broadway to Main Street* (New Haven: Yale University Press, 2005) and J. Mabie, "Seeking Forms that Function," *Christian Science Monitor Magazine* (July 8, 1939): 6.

33. "General Motors," *Fortune* 18 (December 1938): 40–7, 146.

34. Dennis Adler, *Chrysler* (Osceola, WI: MBI, 2000); Carl Breer, *The Birth of Chrysler Corporation and Its Engineering Legacy* (Warrendale, PA: Society of Automotive Engineers, 1995); Richard M. Langworth and Jan P. Norbye, *The Complete History of Chrysler Corporation, 1924–1985* (New York: Beekman House, 1985); George H. Dammann, *Seventy Years of Chrysler* (Glen Ellyn, IL: Crestline, 1974); Chrysler Corporation, *The Story of an American Company* (Detroit, MI: Chrysler, 1955).

35. Vincent Curcio, *Chrysler: The Life and Times of an Automotive Genius* (New York: Oxford University Press, 2000); Fred Morrell Zeder, *Leadership: A Message to America* (New York: Newcomen Society, 1947).

36. Curcio, *Chrysler: The Life and Times*, 310.

37. *Ibid.*, 319–20.

38. Charles K. Dodge, "The Dodge Brothers, the Automobile Industry, and Detroit Society in the Early Twentieth Century," *The Michigan Historical Review* 22 (1996): 48–82.

39. Curcio, *Chrysler: The Life and Times*, 370.

40. Beverly Rae Kimes, "Plymouth: Walter Chrysler's Trump Car," *Automobile Quarterly* 5 (Summer 1966): 74.

41. *Automotive Industries*, 56 (February 19, 1927): 240–2.

42. See Stephen G. Ostrander, "A Car Worthy of Its Name," *Michigan History Magazine* 76 (January/February 1992); Ken Gross, "The Car Worthy of Its Name: 1925 Rickenbacker Series D," *Special Interest Autos*, 28 (May/June 1975); Edward V. Rickenbacker, *Rickenbacker* (Englewood Cliffs, N.J.: Prentice Hall, 1967); W. David Lewis, *Eddie Rickenbacker: An American Hero in the Twentieth Century* (Baltimore: Johns Hopkins University Press, 2005); Special Catalog File F2, Rickenbacker, National Automotive History Collection, Detroit Public Library.

43. Leo Wood, "In My Rickenbacker Car," 1923, Sheet Music Collection, National Automotive History Collection, Detroit Public Library.

44. James H. Lackey, *The Jordan Automobile: A History* (Jefferson, NC: McFarland, 2005), 24.

45. My understanding of advertising and history was shaped by the following sources: Pamela Walker Laird, "'The Car Without a Single Weakness': Early Automobile Advertising," *Technology and Culture* (1996): 796–

812; Peter Roberts, *Any Color So Long as It's Black ... the First Fifty Years of Automobile Advertising* (New York: Morrow, 1976); Yasutoshi Ikuta, *The American Automobile: Advertising from the Antique and Classic Eras* (San Francisco: Chronicle, 1988); Helen Damon-Moore, *Magazines for the Millions: Gender and Commerce in the* Ladies' Home Journal *and the* Saturday Evening Post (Albany: State University of New York Press, 1994); T.J. Jackson Lears, *Fables of Abundance: A Cultural History of Advertising in America* (New York: Basic, 1994); William M. O'Barr, *Culture and the Ad: Exploring Otherness in the World of Advertising* (Boulder: Westview, 1994); Daniel Pope, *The Making of Modern Advertising* (New York: Basic, 1984); Judith Williamson, *Decoding Advertisements: Ideology and Meaning in Advertising* (London: Boyars, 1978); Claude C. Hopkins, *My Life in Advertising* (New York: Harper and Brothers, 1917); Richard Tedlow, *New and Improved: The Story of Mass Marketing in America* (New York: Basic, 1990), ch. 3; Julian L. Watkins, *The 100 Greatest Advertisements: Who Wrote Them and What They Did* (New York: Dover, 1959).

46. On the Jordan Motor Car Company, see James H. Lackey, *The Jordan Automobile: A History* (Jefferson, NC: McFarland, 2005).

47. *Literary Digest* (November 13, 1920): 94–5.

48. "Automobiles II: The Dealer," *Fortune* (December 1931): 43.

Chapter 4

1. Quoted in William Least Heat Moon, *Blue Highways: A Journey Into America* (New York: Fawcett Crest, 1982), 39.

2. John B. Rae, *The Road and the Car in American Life* (Cambridge, MA: MIT Press, 1971), 56. See also John C. Burnham, "The Gasoline Tax and the Automobile Revolution," *Mississippi Valley Historical Review* 48 (December 1961): 435–459; James J. Flink, *The Automobile Age* (Cambridge, MA: MIT Press, 1988), 169.

3. Eric H. Monkkonen, *America Becomes Urban: The Development of U.S. Cities and Towns 1780–1980* (Berkeley, CA: University of California Press, 1988), 167.

4. Clay McShane, *Down the Asphalt Path: The Automobile and the American City* (New York: Columbia University Press, 1994), xii.

5. See Corey T. Lesseig, *Automobility: Social Changes in the American South 1909–1939* (New York and London: Routledge, 2001).

6. On Horatio Nelson Jackson's 1903 transcontinental trip see Dayton Duncan, *Horatio's Drive: America's First Road Trip* (New York: Knopf, 2003). For a complete bibliography of transcontinental trips in America prior to World War II, see Carey S. Bliss, *Autos Across America: A Bibliography of Transcontinental Automobile Travel: 1903–1940* (Austin and New Haven: Jenkins & Reese, 1982).

7. For example, see Jim Donnelly, "Franklin August Seiberling," *Hemmings Classic Car* (August 2005): 82.

8. U.S. Department of Agriculture, Office of Road Inquiry, *Proceedings of the Virginia Good Roads Convention ... October 18, 1894* (Washington, GPO, 1895), 14.; *Proceedings of the National Good Roads Convention Held at St. Louis MO, April 27 to 29, 1903* (Washington, DC: GPO, 1903). See also "Good Roads and Convict Labor," in *Proceedings of the Academy of Political Science in the*

City of New York (New York: Academy, 1914), 241–308; Alex Lichtenstein, "Good Roads and Chain Gangs in the Progressive South: 'The Negro Convict as a Slave,'" *Journal of Southern History*, 59 (1993): 85–110.

9. Thomas H. MacDonald, "The History and Development of Road Building in the United States," *Transactions, American Society of Civil Engineers*, 92 (1928): 1197.

10. See Wayne E. Fuller, "Farmers, Postmen, and the Good Roads Movement," in Ralph D. Gray, ed., *Indiana History: A Book of Readings* (Bloomington, IN: Indiana University Press, 1994), 221–7; Christopher W. Wells, "The Changing Nature of Country Roads: Farmers, Reformers, and the Shifting Use of Rural Space, 1880–1905," *Agricultural History* 80 (2006): 143–66.

11. *Arizona Good Roads Association Illustrated Road Maps and Tour Book* (Phoenix, AZ: *Arizona Highways Magazine*, 1913, repr. 1987).

12. Effie Price Gladding, *Across the Continent by the Lincoln Highway* (New York: Brentano's, 1915), ix.

13. Beatrice Larned Massey, *It Might Have Been Worse: A Motor Trip from Coast to Coast* (San Francisco: Harr Wagner, 1920), 146.

14. The Lincoln Highway Association, *A Picture of Progress on the Lincoln Way* (Detroit: n.p., 1920). For a current photographic view of the highway with an excellent narrative, see Michael Wallis and Michael S. Williamson, *The Lincoln Highway: The Great American Road Trip* (New York: Norton, 2007). For its impact on the Western states, see Richard H. Jackson and Mark W. Jackson, "The Lincoln Highway: The First Transcontinental Highway and the American West," *Journal of the West* 42 (2003): 56–64.

15. For a general discussion of the Good Roads Movement and the place of the automobile in the story, see Peter J. Hugill, "Good Roads and the Automobile in the United States, 1880–1929," *Geographical Review* 72 (July 1982): 327–49.

16. See "Harding's Road Issue," *New York Times*, April 17, 1921, 87; "$75,000,000 for Roads," *New York Times*, November 20, 1921, 34.

17. On macadam road building, see Harwood Frost, *The Art of Roadmaking* (New York: The Author, 1910), 154–88.

18. For example, see *Good Roads for Farmers* (Columbus, Ohio: Interstate Stone Manufacturers Association, n.d. [1914?]).

19. Charles W. Wixom, *A Pictorial History of Road Building* (Washington, DC: American Road Builders' Association, 1975), 88–105.

20. John C. Burnham, "The Gasoline Tax and the Automobile Revolution," *Mississippi Valley Historical Review* 48 (December 1961): 435–59.

21. Drake Hokanson, *The Lincoln Highway: Main Street Across America* (Iowa City: University of Iowa Press, 1988), 37.

22. Several of these named highways are described in detail in John T. Faris, *Roaming American Highways* (New York: Farrar & Rinehart, 1931). For an excellent discussion of the impact of road construction in the South, see Howard Lawrence Preston, *Dirt Roads to Dixie: Accessibility and Modernization in the South, 1885–1935* (Knoxville: University of Tennessee Press, 1979), 128–170.

23. On Huey Long and highway building, see Phil Patton, *Open Road: A Celebration of the American Highway* (New York: Simon and Schuster, 1986), 49–54; T.

Harry Williams, *Huey Long* (New York: Knopf, 1970), 303–7, 332–3, 486–9; William Ivy Hair, *The Kingfish and His Realm* (Baton Rouge: Louisiana State University Press, 1991), 112, 120–3, 227.

24. C. Clem LaFleur, "Law Enforcement and Collection of Fees," *The Louisiana Highway Magazine* 1 (March 1925): 11.

25. *Statement of Facts Issued by Louisiana Highway Commission Baton Rouge Showing Activities During Twelve Months Under Present Administration* (Baton Rouge, LA, 1929), 34.

26. "Louisiana Goes Airline," *Concrete Highways and Public Improvements*, 20 (July–August 1939): 3–5.

27. Frank Milton Masters, *Mississippi River Bridge at New Orleans, Louisiana, final report...* (Harrisburg, PA: n.p., 1941).

28. There exists a massive industry focusing on Route 66. Perhaps the best work on the Mother Road has been authored by Michael Wallis, in his *Route 66: The Mother Road* (New York: St. Martin's, 2001). Other sources include Michael Karl Witzel, *Route 66 Remembered* (Osceola, WI: Motorbooks, 1996) and William Kaszynski, *Route 66: Images of America's Main Street* (Jefferson, NC: McFarland, 2003).

29. William Kaszynski, *Route 66: Images of America's Main Street* (Jefferson, NC: McFarland, 2003).

30. John Steinbeck, *The Grapes of Wrath* (New York: Viking, 1939), 161–2.

31. The definitive work on this topic is Warren James Belasco, *Americans on the Road: From Autocamp to Motel, 1910–1945* (Baltimore: Johns Hopkins University Press, 1979).

32. For example, see *The Complete Camp Site Guide and Latest Highway Map of U.S.A., Together with Official Directory of Aeroplane Landing Fields* (Waterloo, IA: United States Touring Information Bureau, 1923).

33. James Agee, "The Great American Roadside," *Fortune* (September, 1934): 54.

34. Agee, 61–62.

35. Hilaire Belloc, *The Road* (New York: Harper & Brothers, 1925), 196.

36. Virtually nothing in English has been written on Mussolini's highways. On the Autostrade, see Massimo Moraglio, "Per Una Storia Della Autostrade Italiane," *Storia Urbana* 26 (2002): 11–25. On the Reichsautobahn, see *Vier Jahre Arbeit an den Strassen Adolf Hitlers* (Berlin: Volk und Reich Verlag) 1937; James D. Shand, "The Reichsautobahn: Symbol for the Third Reich," *Journal of Contemporary History*, 19 (1984): 189–200, William H. Rollins, "Whose Landscape? Technology, Fascism, and Environmentalism on the National Socialist Autobahn," *Annals of the Association of American Geographers*, 85 (September 1995), 494–520.

Chapter 5

1. On religion, the automobile, and changes in rural America to 1929, see Michael Berger, *The Devil Wagon in God's Country* (Hamden, CT: Archon Books, 1979), 127–45.

2. Quoted in F. Eugene Melder, "The 'Tin Lizzie's' Golden Anniversary," *American Quarterly* 12 (Winter 1960): 477–8. See also H. E. Barnes, *Society in Transition* (New York: Prentice Hall, 1939), 597–8; "Good Roads

and Better Churches," *Literary Digest* 67 (November 6, 1920): 35.

3. The following table summarizes a brief survey that was done of the *Catholic Literature and Periodical Index* for the years 1930 to 1960. A review of automobile topic headings was performed in which articles on key subjects were totaled. Heading titles reflect the categories listed in the *Index*, and while not every article is included — popular "folksy" essays were ignored as were those appearing in foreign journals — the bulk of the literature falls into one of the four subheadings chosen.

NUMBERS OF ARTICLES ON SELECT AUTOMOBILE
TOPICS AND PERCENTAGE, BY DECADE

Decade	Accidents	Driving	Industry	Safety
1930–1938	7 (27%)	10 (37%)	8 (31%)	1 (4%)
1939–1950	6 (15%)	12 (30%)	22 (55%)	0
1950–1960	28 (20%)	67 (48%)	39 (28%)	5 (4%)

One pattern that emerges is that articles on accidents — their causes, the number, and accidents as a social problem — comprised roughly one-fifth to one-fourth of all published works on automobiles. The topic of driving was the focus of even more writing in the Catholic press, as diverse subjects that included psychology, technique, alcohol, and education were covered. While industry (and trade) comprised a broad field of potential articles, the bulk of material in this group consisted of essays and comment dealing with labor relations and managerial practices. Given the interest in accidents, one might think that the issue of safety would be emphasized in the literature. However, it appears that the Catholic press was no more or less engaged in articulating on this matter than was the secular sphere.

4. Robert S. and Helen Merrell Lynd, *Middletown, A Study in Contemporary Culture* (New York: Harcourt, Brace, 1929), 251–258.

5. See these articles in *The Christian Century*: "Automobile Deaths at a New High," 52 (March 20, 1935): 357; "The Massacre of Automobile Victims Continues," 52 (August 28, 1935): 1076; "Motor Speed and Sudden Death," 52 (November 6, 1935): 1397; "3640 Dead!," 52 (December 11, 1935): 1584–5; "Is Medicine About to Rebel?," 53 (November 25, 1936): 1547; "Even the Distillers Are Getting Scared," 54 (July 14, 1937): 893; "A Massachusetts Daniel," 54 (December 1, 1937): 1475; Mathieson Smith, "The Car and the Bottle," 55 (August 3, 1938): 936–8; "'If You Drink, Don't Drive; If You Drive, Don't Drink,'" 54 (August 24, 1938): 1005–6.

6. "Finds Liquor Cause of Motor Death Toll," *The Christian Century*, 55 (April 20, 1938): 483.

7. "Drunken Drivers," *The Ave Maria* (1942): 772.

8. Theodore Maynard, "On Driving a Car," *The Commonweal* 14 (May 13, 1931): 43–4.

9. Dana Doten, "America's Car of Juggernaut," *The Christian Century*, 51 (November 21, 1934): 1485–7; T. F. Gullixson, "Victims of Speed Mania, Unite," *The Christian Century*, 52 (March 27, 1935): 397–8; "Murder by Automobile Still Uncurbed," *The Christian Century*, 53 (July 15, 1936): 980–1; "Automobile Makers Will Not Advertise Speed," *The Christian Century*, 53 (September 16, 1936): 1212.

10. "The Great Current Story," *The Commonweal* 13 (February 11, 1931): 398.

11. Victor W. Page, *Prevention of Automobile Accidents* (New York, 1932), 9. See also National Safety Council, *The New War on Accidents* (Chicago: n.d.[1936?]); The Travelers Insurance Company, *Worse Than War: Impressive Statistics and Facts on 1930's Loss of Life and Limb in Automobile Accidents* (Hartford, CT: n.d. [1931?]).

12. "The Great Current Story," 397–8.

13. "Herod and the Innocents," *The Commonweal* 14 (August 19, 1931): 375.

14. G. K. Chesterton, "Murder on the Way," *G. K.'s Weekly* 18 (November 2, 1933): 135.

15. "Road Building," *The Commonweal* 15 (March 16, 1932): 536; "Those Who Should Not Drive," *The Commonweal* 16 (October 5, 1932): 520–1. For examples of secular literature, see John J. Maher, *Mind Over Motor* (N.P., 1937); *Psychology and the Motorist* (Columbus, OH: 1938); Robbins Battell Stoeckel, Mark Arthur May, and Richard Shelton Kirby, *Sense and Safety on the Road* (New York, 1936); Albert Whitney, *Man and the Motor Car* (New York: n.p., 1936).

16. Robert S. and Helen Merrell Lynd, *Middletown in Transition: A Study in Cultural Conflicts* (New York, 1937), 265.

17. Curtis Billings, "The Nut that Holds the Wheel," *Atlantic Monthly*, 150 (1932), 439–45.

18. *Ibid.*, 445.

19. Paul L. Blakely, S.J., "The Automobile Slave Trade," *America* 52 (February 23, 1935): 473.

20. *Ibid.*, 474.

21. Paul L. Blakely, S.J., "Satan Proposes to Embrace Religion," *America* 58 (January 8, 1938): 316–7. See also "Workers Tell of Speed-Up System at Ford Plant," *The Catholic Worker* 8 (December 1940).

22. See "Reuther Proposals," *Commonweal* 67 (January 31, 1958): 443–4; "Auto Workers' Program," *Commonweal* 80 (June 19, 1964): 30; S. Lens, "Decline of Labor," *Commonweal* 80 (June 19, 1964): 391–4; W. V. Shannon "Split in Labor," *Commonweal* 85 (February 24, 1967): 584–5; B. L. Masse, "Dividends, Profits, and Wages," *America* 116 (June 17, 1967): 849; S. Lens, "Public Interest and the Ford Strike," *Commonweal*, 86 (September 29, 1967): 598–9; "Mr. Reuther's Ploy," *America* 117 (October 28, 1967): 462.

23. For example, see "After the Motors Strike," *The Christian Century* 54 (February 24, 1937): 239–40. Postwar articles on labor-management conflict in *The Christian Century* include: "If Watchdogs be Good Ones," 74 (May 1, 1957): 549–50; M. L. Scott, "The Kohler Strike," 74 (November 20, 1957): 1378–80; "Share Whose Profits?," 75 (February 5, 1958): 157; C. M. Cook, "Import of the Auto Contracts," 79 (February 14, 1962): 195–7.

24. Harold P. Morley, "Homer Martin Changes Pulpits," *The Christian Century* 54 (April 7, 1937): 454–6.

25. Christy Borth, "The Automobile in Popular Song," typescript, Forty-Third National Automobile Show, 15–23 October, 1960, Cobo Hall, Detroit, Automobile Manufacturers Association.

26. http://johnnohammond.net/songs/oldsmobile.htm (accessed August 7, 2008).

27. Borth, "The Automobile in Popular Song," n.p.

28. David L. Lewis, "Sex and the Automobile: From Rumble Seats to Rockin' Vans," in Lewis and Laurence Goldstein, eds., *The Automobile and American Culture* (Ann Arbor, MI: University of Michigan Press, 1983) 123–33.

29. Frederick Lewis Allen, *Only Yesterday* (New York: Harper and Row, 1931), 73–101.

30. Alfred Kinsey, et al., *Sexual Behavior in the Human Female* (Philadelphia: W. B. Saunders, 1953), 336.

31. *Ibid.*, 310.

32. James J. Flink, *The Automobile Age* (Cambridge, MA: MIT Press, 1988), 162.

33. Virginia Scharff, *Taking the Wheel: Women and the Coming of the Motor Age* (Albuquerque, NM: University of New Mexico Press, 1992).

34. *Ibid.*, 101.

35. *Ibid.*

36. Laura L. Behling, "'The Woman at the Wheel': Marketing Ideal Womanhood, 1915–1934," *Journal of American Culture* 20 (Fall 1997): 13. See also Nancy Artz, Jeanne Munger, and Warren Purdy, "Gender Issues in Advertising Language," *Women and Language* 22 (Fall 1999): 20–6; Linda J. Busby and Greg Leichty, "Feminism and Advertising in Traditional and Non-Traditional Women's Magazines," *Journalism Quarterly* 70 (Summer 1993): 247–64.

37. For example, see Chase Drednaut Motor Topping ad, *Atlantic Monthly* 126 (September 1920): 56; Lincoln Motor Car company ad, *Time* 4 (July 14, 1924); Rolls Royce ad, *Time* 4 (November 24, 1924); Edward G. Budd Manufacturing Company ad, *Time* 7 (February 1, 1926): 19; Studebaker ad for the Big Six Custom Brougham, *Saturday Evening Post* 199 (December 11, 1926): 152; Desoto ad for the Desoto Six, *Saturday Evening Post* 201 (November 24, 1928): 43.

38. Ruth Schwartz Cowan, *More Work for Mother* (New York: Basic Books, 1983), 85.

39. For example, see "Your Room on Wheels," *Good Housekeeping*, 106 (January 1938): 589; "All the Comforts of Home," *House Beautiful* 82 (November 1940): 56–7.

40. Mihaly Csikszentmihalyi and Eurgen Rochberg-Halton, *The Meaning of Things: Domestic Symbols and Self* (Cambridge: Cambridge University Press, 1981), p. 121 and chapter 5.

41. James J. Flink, *The Automobile Age*, 213.

42. *Saturday Evening Post* 199 (June 26, 1926). My understanding of advertising and history was shaped by the following sources: Pamela Walker Laird, "'The Car Without a Single Weakness': Early Automobile Advertising," *Technology and Culture* (1996): 796–812; Peter Roberts, *Any Color So Long as It's Black.... The First Fifty Years of Automobile Advertising* (New York: Morrow, 1976); Yasutoshi Ikuta, *The American Automobile: Advertising from the Antique and Classic Eras* (San Francisco: Chronicle, 1988); Helen Damon-Moore, *Magazines for the Millions: Gender and Commerce in the Ladies' Home Journal and the Saturday Evening Post* (Albany: State University of New York Press, 1994); T. J. Jackson Lears, *Fables of Abundance: A Cultural History of Advertising in America* (New York: Basic, 1994); William M. O'Barr, *Culture and the Ad: Exploring Otherness in the World of Advertising* (Boulder: Westview, 1994); Daniel Pope, *The Making of Modern Advertising* (New York: Basic, 1984); Judith Williamson, *Decoding Advertisements: Ideology and Meaning in Advertising* (London: Boyars, 1978); Claude C. Hopkins, *My Life in Advertising* (New York: Harper and Brothers, 1927); Richard Tedlow, *New and Improved: The Story of Mass Marketing in America* (New York: Basic, 1990): ch. 3; Julian L. Watkins, *The 100 Greatest Advertisements: Who Wrote Them and What They Did* (New York: Dover, 1959).

43. *Saturday Evening Post* 199 (August 14, 1926): 43.

44. *Saturday Evening Post* 208 (July 6, 1935): 29.

45. This emphasis on the convertible in advertising during the early 1930s was due to the influence of Ned Jordan of Jordan Playboy fame. Jordan is recognized as producing perhaps the one most significant automobile ad in history with his "Somewhere West of Laramie" pitch in 1923. After his company went bankrupt in 1930, Jordan worked for other firms. See Jordan ad, *Saturday Evening Post* 199 (August 21, 1926): 82, and compare with Dodge ad, *Saturday Evening Post* 205 (August 27, 1932): 35.

46. For example, see Sherwin-Williams advertising in *Providence Journal* (March 23, 1941).

47. *Saturday Evening Post* 213 (September 7, 1940): 42–3.

48. Flink, *Automobile Age*, 291.

49. "Automobile Ride, Handling, and Suspension Design," http://www.rqriley.com/ suspensn.html, 12/6/04.

50. "Early Suspension Systems," http://www.AutomobileIndia.com, 12/6/04.

51. On suspension systems see "Taking the Jolt Out of Motoring," *Literary Digest* 74 (September 9, 1922): 23–4; "Suspending the Motor Car Body on Air," *Scientific American* 130 (February 1924): 93; "Knee Action," *Living Age* 346 (May 1934): 273; "Leaf Action Springs," *Business Week* (May 19, 1934):10; "Wheel Knees," *Business Week* (September 15, 1934): 9–10; "Variable-Rate Spring for Cars," *Scientific American* 160 (April 1939): 241.

52. Mohinder S. Bhatti, Riding in Comfort: Part I, *ASHRAE Journal* (August 1999): 51–7; "Automobile Heaters Hot Water Type," *Consumers' Digest* 9 (February 1941): 19–25.

53. "First Air Conditioned Auto," *Popular Science* 123 (November 1933): 30; "Auto Air-Conditioned for Summer and Winter," *Popular Mechanics* 73 (March 1940): 391; Mohinder S. Bhatti, "Riding in Comfort: Part II," *ASHRAE Journal* (September 1999): 44–50.

54. *Saturday Evening Post* 213 (August 24, 1940): 46.

55. Sources include: http://www.the-directsource.com/info.php/Car-Radio-History.php; "Radio Car," *Literary Digest* 74 (September 2, 1922): 31; "Radio as you Ride," *Literary Digest* 75 (November 11, 1922): 28; "Radio on the Auto," *Literary Digest* 114 (July 9, 1932): 14; "Winter Drivers Want Radios in their Cars," *Business Week* (November 9, 1932): 23; "Music at Sixty Miles an Hour," *Etude* 51 (November 1933): 730; "FM Reception on Wheels," *Electronics World* 64 (September 1960): 64–5.

56. "Tuning In on Your Tour," *Literary Digest* 110 (July 4, 1931): 42.

57. *Saturday Evening Post* 206 (May 5, 1934): 3.

58. Edward Suchman, "Radio Listening and Automobiles," *Journal of Applied Psychology* 23 (February 1939): 148–57.

Chapter 6

1. James J. Flink, *The Automobile Age* (Cambridge: MIT Press, 1988), 189.

2. "Automobiles III Competitors," *Fortune* 4 (December 1931): 136, 143–4.

3. Flink, *The Automobile Age*, 212.

4. James J. Flink, "The Olympian Age of the Automobile," *American Heritage of Invention & Technology* 7

(Winter 1992): 54–63. The V-16 Cadillac, introduced in 1930, set the standard for engineering excellence in that era. It was the first V-16 put in production, its engine was smooth and quiet, and its valves were self-adjusting. On Pierce-Arrow, see Marc Ralston, *Pierce-Arrow* (San Diego: A.S. Barnes, 1980); Maurice D. Hendry, "Pierce-Arrow: An American Aristocrat," *Automobile Quarterly* 6 (Winter 1968): 240–65; Brock Yates, "Duesenberg," *American Heritage* 45, no. 4 (1994): 88–99. See also Louis William Steinwedel and J. Herbert Newport, *The Duesenberg* (New York: Norton, 1982); Dennis Adler, *Duesenberg* (N.P.: Krause Publications, 2004); J.L Elbert, *Duesenberg: the Mightiest American Motor Car* (Arcadia, CA: Post-Era Books, 1975).

5. Clipping, John Bond, "1933 Cadillac V-16 Fleetwood Victoria," n.d. {1963?], G. Risley Collection, National Automotive Historic Collection.

6. Timothy Gerber, "Built for Speed: the Checkered Career of Race Car Designer Harry A. Miller," *Wisconsin Magazine of History* 85, no. 3 (2002): 32–41. See also Griffith Borgeson's wonderfully illustrated *Miller* (Osceola, WI: Motorbooks, 1993).

7. According to the *Oxford English Dictionary, doozy* as an adjective was in use as early as 1903. In 1911 was used to mean sporty or flossy. As a noun, *dozy* was used in 1916 with a similar meaning.

8. For the story of a discovery of a 1933 Duesenberg packed away in an old garage, see Jay Leno, "Barnyard Dreams," *Popular Mechanics* 181 (November 2004): 44–6.

9. See Beverly Rae Kimes, "His Cord and His Empire," *Automobile Quarterly* 18 (Second Quarter 1980): 193–201.

10. Don Butler, *Auburn Cord Duesenberg* (Osceola, WI: Motorbooks, 1992).

11. E. L. Cord, *Why We Introduce a Front Drive Automobile* (Auburn, IN: Auburn Automobile Company, 1929), reprinted in Dan Post, *Cord: Without Tribute to Tradition* (Arcadia, CA: Post-Era Books, 1974), 19–21.

12. Eugene Jaderquist, "The Model 810" (clipping), *Motor Trend*, n.d. [1952?], G. Risley Collection, National Automotive History Collection. Roger Huntington, *The Cord Front-Drive* (Minneapolis, MN: Motorbooks, 1975). For a broader view of how the Cord fit in automobile design trends of the 1930s, see Sally Clarke, "The Art and Colour Section at General Motors, 1927–1941," *Journal of Design History* 12 (1999): 65–79.

13. On Gordon M. Buehrig, see clipping, "Buehrig," *Road & Track* (February 1966), and Alfred W. Loman, "Cord's Designer's Retirement Recalls That Car's Brief Life," *Detroit News*, May 3, 1965, both in Biography File, National Automotive Historic Collection.

14. Gordon M. Buehrig, *Auburn. The Year 1936 Is Viewed 50 Years Later* (N.P.: n.p., 1986).

15. James Newcomb, "Depression Auto Styling," *Winterthur Portfolio*, 35 (Spring 2000): 81.

16. Hugo Pfau, "Dr. Rumpler's 'Volkswagen,'" *Cars & Parts* 20 (August 1977): 28–32.

17. Lowell L. Brown and Herbert Chase, "Half of Streamlined Body Revolution Called Ideal Aerodynamic Form for Cars," *Automotive Industries* (June 23, 1934).

18. David P. Billington and David P. Billington, Jr., *Power, Speed, and Form: Engineers and the Making of he Twentieth Century* (Princeton, NJ: Princeton University Press, 2006), 199–205.

19. George L. McCain, "How the Airflows Were Designed," *Automotive Industries* (June 23, 1934); "Engineers Argue Streamlining at S.A.E. Summer Convention," *Automotive Industries* (June 30, 1934).

20. On Fuller, see Amy Edmondson, "Who was Buckminster Fuller Anyway?" *American History of Invention & Technology* 3 (1988): 18–25. On the Dymaxion Car, see Michael John Gorman, "Dymaxion Passengers," shl.stanford.edu/Bucky/dymaxion/index.htm (accessed July 21, 2008).

21. For an excellent discussion of both the history of automobile aerodynamics to World War II and the Airflow, see Curcio, *Chrysler*, 518–57.

22. See Howard Irwin, "The History of the Airflow Car," *Scientific American*, 237 (August, 1977): 98–104.

23. James J. Flink, "The Path of Least Resistance," *American Heritage of Invention & Technology* 5 (Fall 1989): 34–44.

24. Flink, *The Automobile Age*, 226.

25. Meyer, "The Degradation of Work Revisited," in Thomas J. Sugrue, *Automobile in American Life and Society* (online database, University of Michigan, accessed June 10, 2008), available from http: www.autolife. umd.umich.edu/Labor/L_Overview/L_Overview1.htm.

26. *Ibid.*

27. See Sidney Fine, "The Origins of the United Automobile Workers, 1933–1935," *The Journal of Economic History* 18 (September 1958): 260. See also Irving Bernstein, *The Turbulent Years: A History of The American Worker, 1933–1941* (Los Angeles: University of California Press, 1969), 502–3.

28. Richard Oestreicher, "The Rules of the Game: Class Politics in Twentieth-Century America," in *Organized Labor and American Politics, 1894–1994*, ed. Kevin Boyle (Albany: State University of New York Press, 1998), 122.

29. Steven Jeffreys, *Management and the Managed: 50 Years of Crisis at Chrysler* (Cambridge: Cambridge University Press, 1986), 6.

30. *Ibid.*, 3.

31. Ronald Edsforth and Robert Asher, "The Speedup: The Focal Point of Workers' Grievances, 1919–1941," in *Autowork*, ed. Robert Asher and Ronald Edsforth (Albany: State University of New York Press, 1995), 70.

32. See Henry Kraus, *Heroes of Unwritten Story: The UAW 1934–1939* (Urbana and Chicago: University of Illinois Press, 1993).

33. Bernstein, *Turbulent Years*, 509.

34. *Ibid.*, 500–1.

35. Stephen Meyer, "The Degradation of Work Revisited."

36. Bruce Nelson, "Autoworkers, Electoral Politics,. and the Convergence of Class and Race, Detroit, 1937–1945," in *Organized Labor and American Politics, 1894–1994*, ed. Kevin Boyle (Albany: State University of New York Press, 1998), 135.

37. Bernstein, *Turbulent Years*, 571.

38. Meyer, "The Degradation of Work Revisited."

39. See, for example, Cornelia Walter McCleary, "The Little Old Man in the Automobile," *St. Nicholas* 35 (August 1908): 883; James Ball Naylor, "The Song of the Motor Car," *Collier's* 42 (January 16, 1909): 22; Grace Duffield Goodwin, "To an Automobile," *Good Housekeeping* 49 (November 1909): 52; Percy MacKaye, "From an Automobile," *Scribner's Magazine* 47 (January 1910): 114; D. B. Bary, "The Motor Road," *Sunset* 28 (June 1912): 721; Wallace Irwin, "The Autopilgrim's Progress," *Harper's Weekly* 58 (August 6, 1913): 26; Henry Knott,

"The Race," *Collier's* 52 (January 10, 1914): 7; Minna Irving, "A Song of the Automobile," *The House Beautiful* 34 (October 1913): 44.

40. For example, there are two curious lines in the 1906 poem by Carrie Foote Weeks entitled "The ABC of the Automobile" in which the author goes through the alphabet and at U states, "U is Unruly and also Uncertain./ On the manners of autos and Maids drop the curtain." *The Outing Magazine* 47 (March 1906): 687. In his essay, Goldstein discusses two poems of relevance: Carl Sandberg's 1918 "Portrait of a Motorcar" and Karl Shapiro's 1942 "Buick." In the former, Goldstein argues that for Sandberg, the automobile is a totem for the male conquest of speed; in the latter, Goldstein convincingly argues that Shapiro wrote a love poem to an automobile, bringing together a girl and a car.

41. E. L. Widmer, "Crossroads: The Automobile, Rock and Roll and Democracy," in Peter Wollen and Joe Kerr, *Autopia: Cars and Culture* (London: Reaktion, 2002), 65–74.

42. In 1993, Detroit blues musician Richard Wright listed the top 10 blues titles featuring automobiles as "Thunderbird Blues," Booker T. Washington White; "Terraplane Blues," Robert Johnson; "Dynaflow Blues," Johnny Shines; "Poor Man's Friend," Sleepy John Estes; "My Black Cadillac," Sam Lightnin' Hopkins; "Been Burning Bad Gasoline," Lightnin' Hopkins; "Cadillac Daddy," Chester Burnett (Howlin' Wolf); "No Money Down," Chuck Berry; "Too Many Drivers," Big Bill Broonzy; "Cadillac Assembly Line," Albert King. Clipping, "Motor Melodies," *Detroit News*, August 18, 1993, in Vertical File, Songs, National Automotive History Collection.

43. *The Crowd Roars* (1932), http://www.imdb.com/title/tt0022792/ (accessed July 30, 2008). The theme of a driver turned yellow was echoed in *High Gear* (1935), starring James Murray and Joan Marsh. The featured Red Lion race car (a Gilmore Oil racer) is the best part of a film that contained a weak plot and even weaker acting skills.

44. DVD, *Burn 'Em Up Barnes* (1934), Alpha Video, Narbeth PA, 2004.

45. http://www.archive.org/details/MasterHa1936 (accessed July 30, 2008).

Chapter 7

1. For an excellent photographic essay on this arsenal of democracy, see Michael W. R. Davis, *Detroit's Wartime Industry, Arsenal of Democracy* (Charleston, SC: Arcadia, 2007).

2. John Barnard, *American Vanguard: The United Autoworkers During the Reuther Years, 1935–1970* (Detroit: Wayne State University Press, 2004), 165.

3. Barton J. Bernstein, "The Automobile Industry and the Coming of World War II," *The Southwestern Social Science Quarterly* 47 (1966): 22–33.

4. *Ibid.*, 23.

5. John B. Rae, *The American Automobile* (Chicago: University of Chicago Press, 1965), 144.

6. Bernstein, "The Automobile Industry and the Coming of World War II," 30.

7. *Ibid.*, 30.

8. John B. Rae, *The Automobile Industry* (Boston: Twayne Publishers, 1984), 87.

9. For a comprehensive list of war goods produced by the automobile industry see John B. Rae, *The American Automobile,* 156–8.

10. Larry Lankton, "Autos to Armaments: Detroit Becomes the Arsenal of Democracy," *Michigan History* 75 (1991): 45.

11. *Ibid.*, 46.

12. Rae, *The Automobile Industry,* 91.

13. *Ibid.*, 92.

14. Ed Cray, *Chrome Colossus: General Motors and Its Times* (New York: McGraw-Hill, 1980), 317.

15. James J. Flink, *The Automobile Age* (Cambridge, MIT Press, 1988), 275.

16. Automobile Manufacturers Association, *Freedom's Arsenal: The Story of the Automotive Council for War Production* (Detroit, AMA, 1950), 105.

17. Flink, *The Automobile Age,* 276.

18. Rae, *The Automobile Industry,* 88.

19. Rae, *The American Automobile,* 149.

20. *Ibid.*

21. *Ibid.*, 151.

22. Doug Stewart, "Hail to the Jeep! Could We Have Won Without it?" *Smithsonian* 23 (1992): 62.

23. A. Wade Wells, *Hail to the Jeep* (New York: Harper and Brothers, 1946), 20.

24. See Flink, *The Automobile Age,* 266. See also Rae, *The Automobile Industry,* 91. See also John B. Rae, *The American Automobile,* 146.

25. Herbert R. Rifkin, *The Jeep: Its Development, and Procurement Under the Quartermaster Corps, 1940–1942* (Washington DC: Quartermaster Corp, 1943), 3.

26. *Ibid.*

27. Wells, *Hail to the Jeep,* 2.

28. "Jeep Salvages Oil Crop in Sicily," *The Science News-Letter* 45 (April 29, 1944): 277.

29. Robert Sonkin, "Bleeding Betty's Brakes: Or, the Army Names a Jeep," *American Speech* 29 (December 1954): 257.

30. *Ibid.*, 258–62. A full list of names can be found in the article.

31. Henderson Le Grand, *Augustus Drives a Jeep* (Indianapolis: Bobbs-Merrill, 1946), 37.

32. Carole Landis, *Four Jills in a Jeep* (New York: Random House, 1944).

33. Fairfax Downey, *Jezebel the Jeep* (New York: Dodd, Mead, 1944), 4.

34. Stewart, "Hail to the Jeep!," 70.

35. Barnard, *American Vanguard,* 165–6.

36. Historian Wayne A. Lewchuck estimated that "throughout the interwar period, the level of female employment in production departments hovered around 1 percent at the Ford Motor Company." See Wayne A. Lewchuck, "Men and Monotony: Fraternalism as a Managerial Strategy at the Ford Motor Company," *The Journal of Economic History* 4 (December 1993): 824.

37. Ruth Milkman, "Rosie the Riveter Revisited: Management's Postwar Purge of Women Automobile Workers," in *On the Line: Essays in the History of Autowork,* eds. Nelson Lichtenstein and Stephen Meyer (Urbana and Chicago: University of Illinois Press, 1989), 131.

38. Barnard, *American Vanguard,* 191.

39. Nelson Lichtenstein, "Auto Worker Militancy and the Structure of Factory Life, 1937–1955," *The Journal of American History* 67 (September 1980): 342.

40. Barnard, *American Vanguard,* 187.

41. *Ibid.*, 174–176.

42. *Ibid.*, 175.

43. John Morton Blum, *V Was for Victory: Politics and American Culture During World War II* (New York: First Harvest, 1976), 92.

44. *Ibid.*, 93.

45. Harold F. Williamson, et al., *The American Petroleum Industry, 1899–1959: The Age of Energy* (Evanston: Northwestern University Press, 1963), 766.

46. James A. Maxwell and Margaret N. Blacom, "Gasoline Rationing in the United States, I," *The Quarterly Journal of Economics* 60 (August 1946): 564.

47. Bradley Flamm, "Putting the Brakes on 'Non-essential' Travel: 1940s Wartime Mobility, Prosperity, and the US Office of Defense," *Journal of Transport History*, 27 (March 2006): 71.

48. Williamson, et al., *The American Petroleum Industry,* 766.

49. District 1 included New York, Pennsylvania, Maryland, Virginia, North and South Carolina, Georgia, Florida, Maine, Vermont, New Hampshire, the District of Columbia, Rhode Island, Massachusetts, New Jersey, Connecticut.

50. John W. Frey, ed. *A History of the Petroleum Administration for War, 1941–1945* (U.S. Government Printing Office: Washington, DC, 1946), 119.

51. Flamm, "Putting the Brakes on 'Non-essential' Travel," 76.

52. "The Taxi Driver's Golden Age," *New York Times Magazine* (April 11, 1943).

53. *Ibid.*

54. Flamm, "Putting the Brakes on 'Non-essential' Travel," 77.

55. *Ibid.*

56. James A. Maxwell and Margaret N. Blacom, "Gasoline Rationing in the United States, II," *The Quarterly Journal of Economics* 61 (November 1946): 146.

57. In May of 1942 the OPA issued the "Emergency Plan for Gasoline Rationing: Instructions for dealers, dealer outlets, and suppliers" which outlined the rationing process of District I, using cards.

58. Milton Derber, "Gasoline Rationing Policy and Practice in Canada and the United States," *Journal of Marketing* 8 (October 1943): 143.

59. Maxwell and Balcom wrote, "to qualify for the B book an applicant had only to show that he regularly drove to and from, or in the course of, his work, that alternate means of transportation were unavailable or inadequate, or that he shared his car. This could total 470 miles a month." The C Book was provided to government, education, public health and welfare, religion, and public information. The mileage for a C coupon was tailored to the individual.

60. A hardship ration would be provided to an applicant who, for example, would ask for gasoline to visit a sick member of the family. Furlough rations were provided to members of the military on leave in the United States. The fleet ration was provided to businesses with three or four vehicles of the same type. The transport ration was provided to public transportation — trucks, busses, taxis — up to as much as an applicant required.

61. Derber, "Gasoline Rationing Policy," 141.

62. Joe M. Dawson, "Life on a Ration Board," *Saturday Evening Post* 215 (April 24, 1943): 19.

63. *Ibid.*, 20.

64. Flamm, "Putting the Brakes on 'Non-essential' Travel," 76.

65. *Ibid.*

66. *Ibid.*, 85.

67. "Do Americans Support Gasoline Rationing? Trend Report Based on Eight Nation-Wide Surveys (11,144 Interviews)," *National Opinion Research Center* (University of Denver, Report No. 15, October 1943).

68. See Maxwell and Blacom, "Gasoline Rationing in the United States, II," 150–3, see also Williamson et al., *The American Petroleum Industry,* 770–1.

69. John W. Frey, ed. *A History of the Petroleum Administration for War, 1941–1945* (U.S. Government Printing Office: Washington, DC, 1946), 23.

70. Flamm, "Putting the Brakes on 'Non-essential' Travel," 78.

71. Maxwell and Blacom called this "shocking," and wrote, "A great excess of unspent coupons existed which hung over the market and which represented potential consumption." See "Gasoline Rationing in the United States, II," 150.

72. "Theft by Counterfeit," *Newsweek* (March 27, 1944): 46.

73. *Jitterbugs*, 1944, DVD, 2006, 20th Century–Fox.

74. Mark Miller, "Border to Border on Bootleg Gas," *Colliers* (October 2, 1943): 614.

75. "Smash the Black Market Menace!" *Senior Scholastic* (May 1944): 4.

76. "Gas Pinch Ahead," *Business Week* (September 25, 1943): 19.

77. Chester Bowles, "The Deadly Menace of Black Gasoline," *The New York Times Magazine* (July 30, 1944).

78. *Ibid.*

79. *Ibid.*

80. V. Dennis Wrynn, *Detroit Goes to War: The American Automobile Industry in World War II* (Osceola, WI: Motorbooks International: 1993), 115.

81. U.S. Congress. "Petroleum Investigation (Black Market in Gasoline), Hearings Before a Subcommittee of the Committee on Interstate and Foreign Commerce, House of Representatives. Resolutions Relating to Petroleum Investigation in Connection with National Defense Including Petroleum Pipe-Line Transportation to the Atlantic Seabo and in the South Eastern United States" (April and May 1944).

82. "Gas Pinch Ahead," 19

83. *Ibid.*

84. "Lots of Gas, But —," *Business Week* (June 5, 1943): 26.

85. *Ibid.*

86. "Less Gas for All," *Business Week* (May 29, 1943): 30.

87. Flamm, "Putting the Brakes on 'Non-essential' Travel," 88–9.

88. Michael J. French, *The United States Tire Industry* (Boston: Twayne, 1991), 75.

89. Paul Wendt, "The Control of Rubber in World War II," *Southern Economic Journal* 13 (January 1947): 204.

90. For a list of rubber in American armaments and photographs, see *The Rubber Industry and the War* (New York: Rubber Manufacturers Association, 1944).

91. French, *The United States Tire Industry,* p. 73.

92. Quoted in Charles Morrow Wilson, *Trees and Test Tubes* (New York: Henry Holt, 1943), 231.

93. See Joseph A. Russell, "Alternative Sources of Rubber," *Economic Geography* 17 (October 1941).

94. Alex Schulman, *The Story of Scrap Rubber* (Cleveland: Corday and Gross, 1943), 55.

95. Michael G. Blackford and K. Austin Kerr, *B. F. Goodrich: Tradition and Transformation, 1870–1995* (Columbus: Ohio State University Press, 1996), 177.

96. William M. Tuttle Jr., "The Birth of an Industry: The Synthetic Rubber 'Mess' in World War II," *Technology and Culture* 22 (January 1981): 46.

97. Wendt, "The Control of Rubber in World War II," p. 218.

98. Tuttle, "The Birth of an Industry: The Synthetic Rubber 'Mess' in World War II," 38.

99. Glenn D. Babcock, *A History of the United States Rubber Company* (Bloomington: Indiana School of Business, 1966), 387.

100. Small firms also expanded. See Michael J. French, "Structure, Personality, and Business Strategy in the U.S. Tire Industry: The Seiberling Rubber Company, 1922–1964," *The Business History Review* 67 (Summer 1993), 254.

101. Babcock, *A History of the United States Rubber Company*, p. 396.

102. Tuttle, "The Birth of an Industry: The Synthetic Rubber 'Mess' in World War II," 64.

103. On the reconversion economy, see Paul A.C. Koistinen, *Arsenal of World War II: The Political Economy of American Warfare, 1940–1945* (Lawrence, KS: University Press of Kansas, 1994), 445–498.

104. On the independents of the postwar era, see Stan Grayson, "Crosley of Cincinnati," *Automobile Quarterly* 16:1 (First Quarter 1978): 6–20, and Richard M. Langworth, "The Glorious Madness of Kaiser Frazer," *Automobile Quarterly* 9:3 (Spring 1971): 266–283.

105. Lisa E. Cowan, "The Making of Tucker," *1989 International Auto Show, Special Tucker Edition* (N.P.: n.p., n.d. [1989?]).

106. Mike Mueller, "Tucker: A Man and His Car," *American History Illustrated*, 23, no. 9 (1989): 36–41.

107. Preston Tucker, "An Open Letter to the Automobile Industry in the Interests of the American Motorist," June 15, 1948, www.tuckerclub.org/tuckopen.html (accessed February 24, 2004).

Chapter 8

1. Martin E. Marty, "The Altar of Automobility," *The Christian Century* 75 (January 22, 1958): 95.

2. A starting point to my work on the 1950s is the indispensable monograph by James Flink, *The Automobile Age* (Cambridge, MA: MIT Press, 1988), 277–293. See also Rudi Volti, *Cars & Culture: The Life Story of a Technology* (Baltimore: Johns Hopkins University Press, 2004), 87–114. An older account but still valuable is John B. Rae, *The American Automobile Industry* (Boston: Twayne, 1984), 99–115. Popular literature on the subject is voluminous, particularly in terms of histories of particular marques. For a more comprehensive popular treatment, see Dan Lyons, *Cars of the Fantastic '50s* (KP Books, 2005).

3. Examining automobiles through the lens of television during the 1950s is a major theme in Karal Ann Marling's *As Seen on TV: The Visual Culture of Everyday Life in the 1950s* (Cambridge, MA: Harvard University Press, 1994), 129–162.

4. On the uncertainty of the era, see Paul S. Boyer, *By Bomb's Early Light: American Thought and Culture at the Dawn of the Atomic Age* (New York: Pantheon, 1985). Chilling, perhaps, is an article on the automobile of the early 1950s and survival after a nuclear detonation. See A. L. Haynes, "The Post War Car and the A-Blast.... What Are the Odds?" Report of the SAE–Federal Civil Defense Administration Advisory Committee, *SAE Transactions*, 62 (1954): 13–23.

5. On the memory that can be deceiving, see Norman H. Finkelstein, *The Way Things Never Were: The Truth About the "Good Old Days"* (New York: Atheneum, 1999). Also see Gary Donaldson, *Abundance and Anxiety: America, 1945–1960* (Westport, CT: Praeger, 1997); William L. O'Neill, *American High: The Years of Confidence, 1945–1960* (New York: Free Press, 1986).

6. Henry Gregor Felsen, *Hot Rod* (New York: E. P. Dutton, 1950), 17.

7. "A Boy's Big Deal: His First Car," *Life* 44 (June 1958): 124–127.

8. John Keats, *The Insolent Chariots* (Greenwich, CT: Fawcett, 1959), 26.

9. Gartman's studies include *Auto Opium: A Social History of American Automobile Design* (London: Routledge, 1994). More recently, he has divided the history of the automobile in America into three distinct periods, with change taking place in dialectical fashion. See David Gartman, "Three Ages of the Automobile: The Cultural Logistics of the Car," *Theory, Culture & Society* 21, 4/5 (2004): 169 ff.

10. http://www.autolife.umd.umich.edu/Race/R_Casestudy/R_Casestudy.htm (December 9, 2005).

11. Warren Brown, "Automobile Played Role on Long Ride to Freedom," *Washington Post* (September 5, 2004): G-2, 61.

12. For example, see segments contained in the documentary film *Atomic Café* (1983). For an excellent compilation of automobile advertising during the 1950s, see Yatutoshi Ikuta, *Cruise O Matic: Automobile Advertising of the 1950s* (San Francisco: Chronicle Books, 2000).

13. Avner Offer, "The American Automobile Frenzy of the 1950s," in K. Bruland and P. K. O'Brien, eds., *From Family Firms to Corporate Capitalism: Essays in Business and Industrial History in Honour of Peter Mathias* (Oxford: Oxford University Press, 1998), 315–353. See also Harold G. Vatter, *The U.S. Economy in the 1950s* (Chicago: University of Chicago Press, 1963), 158–163.

14. Eric Larrabee, "Detroit's Great Debate: 'Where Did We Go Wrong?,'" *Reporter*, 18 (April 17, 1958): 19.

15. Ken Steacy, *Brightwork: Classic American Car Ornamentation* (San Francisco: Chronicle Books, 1999); Nick Georgano, *Art of the American Automobile: The Greatest Stylists and Their Work* (Smithmark, 1995). On tailfins, see Grady Grammage, Jr., and Stephen L. Jones, "Orgasm in Chrome: The Rise and Fall of the Automobile Tailfin," *Journal of Popular Culture* 8 (1974): 132–47.

16. "Hot Rod History," *Hot Rod Magazine* 1 (March 1948): 7. In *Hot Rod Magazine: The First Twelve Issues* (Osceola, WI: MBI, 1998). Especially important on this topic and more is Robert C. Post, *High Performance: The Culture and Technology of Drag Racing, 1950–2000* (Baltimore: Johns Hopkins University Press, 2001). For a British sociologist's history of the hot rod, see H. F. Moorehouse, *Driving Ambitions: An Analysis of the American Hot Rod Enthusiasm* (Manchester: Manchester University Press, 1991). See also Dean Batchelor, *Dry Lakes and Drag Strips: The American Hot Rod* (St. Paul, MN:

MBI, 2002), and Tom Medley, *Tex Smith's Hot Rod History* (Osceloa, WI: Motorbooks International, 1990).

17. Anthony (Andy) Granatelli, *They Call Me Mister 500* (Chicago: Henry Regency, 1969), 46–63.

18. The definitive work on the history of drag racing and its technologies is Robert C. Post, *High Performance: The Culture and Technology of Drag Racing, 1950–1990* (Baltimore: Johns Hopkins University Press, 1994; rev. ed. 2001). See also Stephan Wilkinson, "Tanks, Hot Rods, and Salt," *Air & Space Smithsonian* 12 (1997): 60–63.

19. Felsen, *Hot Rod*, 183.

20. Henry Gregor Felsen, "First Skirmish," in Evan Jones, ed., *High Gear* (New York: Bantam, 1963), 10–11.

21. Joe Wajgel, "A Short History & Evolution of 'Hot Rod Lincoln,'" http://www.rockabillyhall.com/HotRod Lncln.html (February 26, 2004).

22. *Hot Rod Girl*, Alpha Video (1956), 203.

23. For an interesting interview with Hilborn that discusses the various steps that led to his development of fuel injection, see http://www.cruzinmag.com/feature3.html (July 2, 2007).

24. See ad for Ditzler custom colors for custom cars, *Hot Rod Magazine* 1 (October 1948): 28. See Andy Southard, Jr., and Tony Thacker, *Custom Cars of the 1950s* (Osceola, WI: MBI, 1993), and Nora Donnelly, ed., *Customized: Art Inspired by Hot Rods, Low Riders and American Car Culture* (New York: Harry N. Abrams, 2000).

25. Tom McCahill, *The Modern Sports Car* (New York: Prentice-Hall, 1954), 2–3.

26. http://www.motortrend.com/classic/features/c12_0603_icons_uncle_tom_mccahill (July 3, 2007); B. Beason, "Tom McCahill 25 Years Later," *Mechanix Illustrated* 67 (February 1971): 53–56; Richard M. Langworth, "The True Tale of Uncle Tom McCahill," *Automobile Quarterly* 14 (First Quarter 1976): 68–73.

27. "Road Racing's Toughest Test," *Popular Science* 161 (November 1952): 156–7; "Mercedes Shatters Road-Race Record," *Popular Science* 162 (January 1953): 172–3; "Death and Daring Win Mexico's Killer Race," *Popular Science* 164 (January 1954): 108–10. On one successful driver's experiences in Mexico, see Mickey Thompson with Griffith Borgeson, *Challenger* (Englewood Cliffs, NJ: Prentice-Hall, 1965), 54–86.

28. Don Stanford, *The Red Car* (Cutchogue, NY: Buccaneer Books, 1954), 8.

29. *Ibid.*, 250.

30. *The Fast and the Furious*, DVD, Digiview Productions, 2004.

31. Tom Burnside and Denise McCluggage, *American Racing: Road Racing in the 50s and 60s* (Cologne: KŒnemann, 1996).

32. E. J. Premo, "The Corvette Plastic Body," *SAE Transactions* 62 (1954): 449–85.

33. Michael Antonick, *California Screamin': The Glory Days of Corvette Road Racing* (Osceola, WI: MBI, 1990).

34. For an important history written by one of the early designers of the Thunderbird, see William P. Boyer, *Thunderbird: An Odyssey in Automotive Design* (Dallas, TX: Taylor Publishing, 1986). John Gunnell, ed., *T-Bird: 40 Years of Thunder* (Iola, WI: Krause Publications, 1995) is a "buff" history containing plenty of useful detailed information.

35. Gene Vincent & His Blue Caps, "Pink Thunderbird," from the album *Gene Vincent and His Blue Caps*, Capital, #811, 1957.

36. The Delicates, "Black & White Thunderbird," Unart single, #2017, 1959.

37. Flink, *Automobile Age*, 281–3. For a survey summarizing critics on styling and design, see David Gartman, "A History of Scholarship on American Automobile Design," http://www.autolife.umd.umich.edu/Design/Gartman/D_Overview/D_Overview.htm (July 5, 2007).

38. For example, see the scathing review of the 1958 Edsel—"The New Edsel," *Consumer Reports* 23 (January 1958): 30–3; "Safety," *Consumer Reports* 23 (April 1958): 194–5; Henry Dreyfuss, "It's Time the U.S. Auto Industry Adopted New Standards in Planning New Models, *Consumer Reports* 23 (July 1958): 351–5.

39. Ken W. Purdy, "The Unbelieving Auto Inventor," *Catholic Digest* 16 (September 1952): 72–4. Purdy took the issue of safe driving seriously, so much so that he authored a book entitled *Young People and Driving: The Use and Abuse of the Automobile* (New York: John Day, 1967).

40. Robert Switzer, "Head-On," in Evan Jones, ed., *High Gear* (New York: Bantam, 1963). First published in 1953 in *Esquire*.

41. See Elizabeth Brenner Drew, "The Politics of Auto Safety," *Atlantic Monthly* 218 (October 1966): 95–105; Joel W. Eastman, *Styling vs. Safety: The American Automobile Industry and the Development of Automotive Safety, 1900–1966* (Lanham, MD: University Press of America), 1984.

42. Lawrence J. White, *The Automobile Industry Since 1945* (Cambridge, MA: Harvard University Press, 1971), 238–9. See also Flink, *The Automobile Age*, 386–7.

43. Dale H. Hutchinson and Francis R. Holden, "An Inventory of Automobile Gases," *SAE Transactions*, 63 (1955): 585. See also A. J. Haagen-Smit, "Chemistry and Physiology of Los Angeles Smog," *Industrial & Engineering Chemistry* 44 (June 1952): 1342–46. The first instance of the federal government addressing this issue appears to be in 1958. See United States Congress, House Committee on Interstate and Foreign Commerce, Special Committee on Traffic Safety, *Unburned Hydrocarbons* (Washington, GPO, 1958).

44. *Unburned Hydrocarbons*, 111–18.

45. Robert Genat, *The American Car Dealership* (Osceola, WI: MBI, 1999).

46. *Slasher,* DVD, New Video Group, 2003.

47. Flink, *The Automobile Age*, pp. 281–283. This summary analysis is based on testimony recorded in United States Senate, Committee on Interstate and Foreign Commerce, *Automobile Marketing Practices* (Washington: GPO, 1956).

48. My thanks to colleague Edward Garten for this information and accompanying photographs.

49. Douglas Brinkley, *Wheels for the World* (New York: Viking, 2003), 503.

50. Personal interview, Edward Garten with Magee Garten, October 21, 2006.

51. Robert Asher and Ronald Edsforth, "A Half Century of Struggle: Auto Workers Fighting for Justice," in *Autowork*, eds. Robert Asher and Ronald Edsforth (Albany: State University of New York Press, 1995), 19.

52. Barnard, *American Vanguard*, p. 260.

53. Nelson Lichtenstein, *The Most Dangerous Man in Detroit* (New York: Basic Books, 1995), 300.

54. Barnard, *American Vanguard,* p. 264.

55. Eli Chinoy, *Automobile Workers and the American Dream* (Garden City, NY: 1955).

56. Stephen Meyer, "An Economic 'Frankenstein'":

UAW Workers' Response to Automation at the Ford Brook Park Plant in the 1950s," found online at *Automobile in American Life and Society* (online database, University of Michigan), accessed 7 June 2008) available from http://www.autolife.umd.umich.edu/Labor/L_Casestudy/L_casestudy1.htm

57. Flink, *The Automobile Age*, 244.

58. *Ibid.*

59. Meyer, "An Economic 'Frankenstein.'"

60. An important article on this subject is Maurice Olley, "European Postwar Cars," *SAE Transactions* 61 (1953): 503–28.

61. Interestingly, V-8 engines at the beginning of the decade were shorter in stroke and with more main bearings than the engines they replaced, and thus were efficient, reliable, and relatively economical. See Robert Stevenson, "The New Ford V-8 Engine," *SAE Transactions* 62 (1954): 595–605; R. F. Sanders, "The New Chevrolet V-8 Engine," *SAE Transactions* 63 (1955): 401–19.

62. "How to Buy a Used Car," *Consumer Reports* 20 (January 1955): 4–14.

63. Conversation with former Dayton, Ohio, Studebaker dealer Bob Pool.

64. On Packard, see James A. Ward, *The Fall of the Packard Motor Car Company* (Stanford, CA: Stanford University Press, 1995). For a Studebaker history, see Donald T. Critchlow, *Studebaker: The Life and Death of an American Corporation* (Bloomington, IN: Indiana University Press, 1996).

65. Quoted in Stan Grayson, "Crosley of Cincinnati," *Automobile Quarterly* 16:1 (1978): 10.

66. Robert F. Andrews, "On Designing the 'Step-down' Hudson" *Automobile Quarterly* 9:4 (Summer 1971): 393–7.

67. Richard M. Langworth, "The Glorious Madness of Kaiser Frazer," *Automobile Quarterly* 9:3 (Spring 1971): 266–83.

68. Quoted in Timothy Jacobs, *Lemons: The World's Worst Cars* (Greenwich, CT: Dorsey, 1991), 88. See Sam Medway, "Nash-Kelvinator to American Motors," *Automobile Quarterly* 16:2 (1977): 140–59.

69. On styling, see Gartman, *Auto Opium*; Stephen Bayley, *Design Heroes: Harley Earl* (London: Grafton, 1992).

70. Walter Henry Nelson, *Small Wonder: The Amazing Story of the Volkswagen* (Boston: Little, Brown, 1967), ix. In addition to Nelson, there are numerous other works on the history of VW. The most carefully researched volume on VW's early years is Karl Ludvigsen's *Battle for the Beetle* (Cambridge, MA: Bentley, 2000). See also Phil Patton's well-written *Bug: The Strange Mutations of the World's Most Famous Automobile* (New York: Simon and Schuster, 2002). For a discussion of VW's advertising campaign, see Alfred Marcantonio, David Abbot, and John O'Driscoll, *Is the Bug Dead? The Great Beetle Ad Campaign* (New York: Stewart, 1983).

71. Timothy Jacobs, *Lemons: The World's Worst Cars* (Greenwich, CT: Brompton, 1991), 88.

72. Paul Gruskin's *Rock'n Down the Highway: The Cars That Made Rock Roll* (St. Paul, MN: Voyageur Press, 2006) is a remarkable pictorial work that traces the linkage between cars and rock in a visual manner. The author's use of ephemeral materials to depict this history is outstanding.

73. For a comment on the lack of scholarship on the topic of popular music and the automobile, see Michael Berger, "President's Perspective, Humming Along," Auto History Online, Society of Automotive Historians, http://www.autohistory.org/president_26.html (July 20, 2006).

74. Sean Cubitt, "'Maybellene': Meaning and Listening Subject," *Popular Music* 4 (1984): 207–24.

75. Richard A. Peterson, "Why 1955? Explaining the Advent of Rock Music," *Popular Music* 9 (January 1990): 97–116.

76. Remarkably, little has been written on the history of automobile radios. The exception is Donald W. Matteson, *The Auto Radio: A Romantic Genealogy* (Jackson, MI: Thornridge, 1987). Matteson's story stops in 1940, however. See also "New Car Radio Finds Stations for You," *Popular Science* 156 (June 1950): 130–1; "Auto Radios," *Consumer Reports* (September 1955): 396–400; "Automobile Radios," *Consumer Bulletin* (August 1957): 15–7; "Delco's All-Transistor Radio," *Radio & Television News* 58 (August 1957): 60–1; "Rear Deck Speakers," *Consumer Reports* (January 1958): 11.

77. www.brightlemon.com/ma/what_use/MathematicalModellingInTrafficFlows.doc

78. "The History of the Stratocaster," http://www.fender-strat.com/fender-guitar-history.html (July 9, 2007).

79. E.L Widmer, "Crossroads: The Automobile, Rock and Roll, and Democracy," in Peter Wollen and Joe Kerr, eds., *Autopia: Cars and Culture* (London: Reaktion, 2002), 65–74. See also Roy Clifton Ames, "Cars in Song," *Special-Interest Autos* (January-February 1977): 45; John L. Wright, "Croonin' About Cruisin'," in *The Popular Culture Reader*, Jack Nachbar, Deborah Weiser, and John L. Wright, eds. (Bowling Green, OH: Bowling Green University Press), 109–17.

80. Warren Belasco, "Motivatin' with Chick Berry and Frederick Jackson Turner," in David L. Lewis and Laurence Goldstein, eds., *The Automobile and American Culture* (Ann Arbor: University of Michigan Press, 1980), 262–279.

81. Katie Mills, *The Road Story and the Rebel: Moving Through Film, Fiction, and Television* (Carbondale, IL: Southern Illinois University Press, 2006)

82. Richard Wedekind, "Automobile Theft, the Thirteen Million Dollar Parasite," *The Journal of Criminal Law, Criminology, and Police Science* 48 (November-December 1957): 443–46.

83. Stephen Bayley, *Sex, Drink and Fast Cars* (New York: Pantheon, 1986): 52–7.

84. *Thunder Road*, 1958, Sony Pictures, 2006.

85. Clipping, New Center News, August 23, 1993, Vertical File, Drive-In Movies, National Automotive History Collection, Detroit Public Library.

86. Jack Kerouac, *On the Road* (New York: Viking, 2007). For an excellent interpretation of *On the Road* and its broader context, see Katie Mills, *The Road Story and the Rebel: Moving through Film, Fiction and Television* (Carbondale, IL: Southern Illinois University Press, 2006), 35–63.

87. *Detour* (1945), starring Tom Neal and Ann Savage, DVD, Alpha Video, 2002. Henry Miller, *The Air-Conditioned Nightmare* (New York: New Directions, 1945); John Steinbeck, *The Wayward Bus* (New York: Penguin, 1986 [c. 1947]).

88. Kerouac, *On the Road*, 307.

89. William Least Heat Moon, *Blue Highways: A Jour-*

ney into America (Boston: Little, Brown, 1982); Michael Wallis, *Route 66: The Mother Road* (New York: St. Martin's, 1990).

90. On the history of the interstates, see Bruce E. Seely, *Building the American Highway System: Engineers as Policy Makers* (Philadelphia: Temple University Press, 1987); Tom Lewis, *Divided Highways: Building the Interstate Highways, Transforming American Life* (New York: Viking, 1997); Dan McNichol, *The Roads That Built America: The Incredible Story of the U.S. Interstate System* (New York: Sterling, 2006); Owen D. Gutfreud, *Twentieth-Century Sprawl: Highways and the Reshaping of the American Landscape* (New York: Oxford University Press, 2004).

Chapter 9

1. The extreme contrast is best seen by comparing the analysis of Larry Schweikart and Michael Allen, *A Patriot's History of the United States* (New York: Sentinel, 2004), with Howard Zinn, *A People's History of the United States: 1492–Present* (New York: Perennial, 2001). On the 1960s, see the following: David Farber and Beth Bailey, eds., *The Columbia Guide to America in the 1960s* (New York: Columbia University Press, 2001); Maurice Isserman, *America Divided: The Civil War of the 1960s* (New York: Oxford University Press, 2000); Charles Kaiser, *1968 in America: Music, Politics, Chaos, Counterculture, and the Shaping of a Generation* (New York: Weidenfeld & Nicholson, 1988); John C. McWilliams, *The 1960s Cultural Revolution* (Westport, CT: Greenwood, 2000).

2. James Flink's *The Automobile Age* treats the 1960s as part of broader post–World War II discussions that also deal with the 1950s and 1970s on pp. 327–376.

3. Bill Davidson, "If We Can't Solve the Problems of the Ghetto *Here*, God Help our Country," *Saturday Evening Post* 241 (October 5, 1968): 29–44.

4. Danny Hakim, "California/Motor City: The Motor City and California: Is it Splitsville?" *New York Times*, October 22, 2003.

5. John Robert Howard, "The Flowering of the Hippie Movement," *Annals of the American Academy of Political and Social Science* 382 (March 1969): 43–55.

6. "Tripping Down Hippie Highway," *Newsweek* 76 (July 27, 1970): 22–4.

7. In Pixar's *Cars*, a Transporter is portrayed with the name "Fillmore," with George Carlin's voice.

8. http://mydrive.roadfly.com/blog/dwilsonc/334/ (accessed 11/15/2007).

9. Peter Jedick, *Hippies* (Berkeley, CA: Creative Arts Book, 1998), 52.

10. Burton H. Wolfe, *The Hippies* (New York: Signet, 1968), 30.

11. Tom Wolfe, *The Electric Kool-Aid Test* (New York: Farrar, Straus & Giroux, 1968), 68.

12. John Muir and Tosh Gregg, *How to Keep your Volkswagen Alive: A Manual of Step by Step Procedures for the Compleat Idiot*, 16th ed. (Santa Fe, NM: John Muir Publications, 1995): 3.

13. On the history of Cadillac, see Maurice D. Hendry, *Cadillac, Standard of the World: The Complete History* (Princeton, NJ: Automobile Quarterly Publications, 1977); Thomas E. Bonsall, *The Cadillac Story: The Postwar Years* (Stanford, CA: Stanford University Press, 2004).

14. Robert Sheehan, "A Cadillac is a Cadillac is A Cadil-

lac," *Fortune* 77 (April 1968): 117–19. See also "No Waiting In Line for a 1955 Cadillac," *Business Week* (August 13, 1955): 54; Geoffrey Hellman, "Some Cadillac Ruminations," *The New Yorker* 31(July 23, 1955): 20; "Cadillac Kicks Up Its Heels," *Business Week* (August 17, 1963): 98.

15. William H. Whyte, "Cadillac Phenomenon," *Fortune* 51 (February 1955): 107.

16. Richard W. Gable, "The Politics and Economics of the 1957–1958 Recession," *The Western Political Quarterly* 12 (June 1959): 557–9.

17. Critics that followed Keats included Helen Leavitt, *Superhighway—Superhoax* (New York: Ballantine, 1970); Kenneth Schneider, *Autokind vs. Mankind: An Analysis of Tyranny, a Proposal for Rebellion, A Plan for Reconstruction* (New York: Schocken Books, 1972); John Jerome, *The Death of the Automobile: The Fatal Effect of the Golden Era, 1955–1970* (New York: Norton, 1972); Ronald Buel, *Dead End: the Automobile in Mass Transportation* (Englewood Cliffs, NJ: Prentice-Hall, 1972); and Emma Rothschild, *Paradise Lost: The Decline of the Auto-Industrial Age* (New York: Random House, 1973).

18. Lawrence J. White, *The Automobile Industry Since 1945* (Cambridge, MA: Harvard University Press, 1971).

19. James J. Flink, "Three Stages of American Automobile Consciousness," *American Quarterly* 24 (October 1972): 468.

20. Tom Wolfe, *The Kandy-Kolored Tangerine-Flake Streamline Baby* (New York: Vintage, 2005).

21. Harry Crews, *Car* (New York: William Morrow, 1972), 73–4.

22. Ralph Nader, *Unsafe at any Speed* (New York: Grossman, 1965). On Nader, see Justin Martin, *Nader: Crusader, Spoiler, Icon* (Cambridge, MA: Perseus, 2002). See also Mervyn Kaufman, "Ralph Nader: "Crusader for Safety," *Automobile Quarterly* 5 (Summer 1966), 4–7.

23. Maurice Olley, "European Postwar Cars," *SAE Transactions* 61 (1953): 503–28.

24. Corvair enthusiasts and apologists abound, despite the historical record concerning its safety in models manufactured between 1960 and 1963. See David E. Davis, "Why Ralph Nader Was Wrong," *Automobile* (January 2006): 87–90.

25. "Automobile Design Liability: Larsen v. General Motors and its Aftermath," *University of Pennsylvania Law Review* 118 (December 1969), 299–312; Ralph Nader and Joseph A. Page, "Automobile Design and the Judicial Process," *California Law Review* 55 (August 1967): 64577.

26. Alden H. Sypher, "Why Safety Laws Aren't Safe," *Nation's Business* 56 (March 1968), 29–30; Sam Peltzman, *Regulation and the Natural Progress of Opulence* (Washington, DC: AEI-Brookings, 2004): 4–9.

27. "After a Crackdown on Drinking Drivers —," *U.S. News & World Report* 64 (January 8, 1968): 9.

28. See Lawrence J. White, *The Regulation of Air Pollutant Emissions from Motor Vehicles* (Washington: American Enterprise Institute, 1982).

29. "Autos: The Mess in the Garage," *Time* 92 (December 13, 1968): 92, 94; "Autos: The Repair Jungle," *Newsweek* 72 (December 16, 1968): 78, 83; Kevin L. Borg, *Automechanics: Technology and Expertise in Twentieth-Century America* (Baltimore: Johns Hopkins University Press, 2007): 138–46.

30. "The Business with 103 Million Unsatisfied Customers," *Time* 91 (January 26, 1968): 201.

31. http://www.valiant.org/valiant/introduction/html (15 June 2007).

32. Lawrence J. White, *The Regulation of Air Pollutant Emissions,* 212–3. On page 214, White lists automobile manufacturer innovations that included the following: (1) GM — High compression V-8 engine (1949); simplified overhead cam engine (1966); front wheel drive (1967). (2) Ford — Ball joint front suspension (1952); safety equipment (1956); hardtop convertible (1957). (3) Chrysler — Power steering (1951); power brakes (1952); cruise control (1958); alternator (1960). (4) American Motors — Dual braking system (1962). (5) Studebaker-Packard — Self-adjusting brakes (1946); torsion bar suspension (1955); disc brakes (1962).

33. General Motors Corporation, *GM Progress of Power: A General Motors Report on Vehicular Power Systems,* Presented at the General Motors Technical Center, Warren, Michigan, May 7–8, 1969.

34. J. Patrick Wright, *On a Clear Day You Can See General Motors* (Grosse Pointe, MI: Wright Enterprises, 1979), 87–97.

35. Steve Statham, *Pontiac GTO* (Ann Arbor, MI: Lowe & B. Hould, 2003).

36. Lee Iacocca with William Novak, *Iacocca: An Autobiography* (New York: Bantam Books, 1984), 61–77.

37. "Stray Mustang," *Newsweek* 63 (March 16, 1964): 80; "CU's First Look at the Mustang, *Consumer Reports* 29 (July 1964): 320–1; "Runaway Success," *Newsweek* 65 (April 26, 1965): 76.

38. Jonathan Gould, *Can't Buy Me Love: The Beatles, Britain, and America* (New York: Harmony Books, 2007), 198–9.

39. The definitive history of the oil companies remains Daniel Yergin, *The Prize: The Epic Quest for Oil, Money and Power* (New York: Simon and Schuster, 1991), 606–666. See also Alvin Alm and Robert J. Weiner, *Oil Shock* (Cambridge: Ballinger, 1984); David Frum, *How We Got Here: The 70's* (New York: Basic Books, 2000); Leonardo Maugeri, *The Age of Oil: The Mythology, History, and the Future of the World's Most Controversial Resource* (Westport: Praeger, 2006); David E. Nye, *Consuming Power: A Social History of American Energies* (Cambridge, MA: MIT Press, 2001); T. M. Rybczynski, *The Economies of the Oil Crisis* (New York: Holmes and Meier, 1976).

40. Leonardo Maugeri, *The Age of Oil,* 113.

41. *Ibid.*

42. "Fix-It-Yourself Approach: Ford Pinto," *Time* 96 (August 17, 1970): 57–8; "Ford Goes to Trial," *Newsweek* 95 (January 7, 1980): 70; Matthew T. Lee, "The Ford Pinto Case and the Development of Auto Safety Regulations, 1893–1978," *Business and Economic History* 27 (1998): 390–401.

43. James J. Flink, *The Automobile Age,* 327–345.

44. David Halberstam, *The Reckoning* (New York: William Morrow, 1986).

45. W. Edwards Deming, *Out of the Crisis* (Cambridge, MA: MIT Press, 1982).

46. James P. Womack, Daniel T. Jones, and Daniel Roos, *The Machine That Changed the World* (New York: Rawson Associates, 1990).

47. While I partially disagree on the ranking of his films, see Jesse Crosse, *The Greatest Movie Car Chases of All Time* (St. Paul, MN: Motorbooks, 2006).

48. Tim Satchell, *McQueen* (London: Sidgwick and Jackson, 1981), 70–3; Casey St. Charnez, *The Films of Steve McQueen* (Secaucus, NJ: Citadel, 1984), 145–48.

49. See Marshall Terrill, *Steve McQueen: Portrait of an American Rebel* (New York: D. I. Fine, 1993); William F. Nolan, *McQueen* (New York: St. Martin's, 1984); Michael Keyser, *French Kiss with Death: Steve McQueen and the Making of Lemans: The man — the Race — the Cars — the Movie* (Cambridge, MA: Robert Bentley, 1999).

50. Darren Wright, Steve McQueen Online (November 2007), http://www.mcqueenonline.com/racer.

51. *Facts for Editorial Reference: Grand Prix* (New York: MGM Publicity, 1966).

Chapter 10

1. On Oil Shock II, see Daniel Yergin, *The Prize: The Epic Quest for Oil, Money and Power* (New York: Simon and Schuster, 1991), 674–714. For the perspective of the American automobile industry, see Lee Iacocca with William Novak, *Iacocca: An Autobiography* (New York: Bantam, 1984), 182–91.

2. Norman S. Fieleke, "The Automobile Industry," *Annals of the American Academy of Political and Social Science* 460 (March 1882): 83–91.

3. Quote taken from Rebecca Morales, *Flexible Production: Restructuring the International Automobile Industry* (Cambridge, MA: Polity Press, 1994), 57.

4. Robert F. Arnold, "Termination or Transformation? The 'Terminator' Films and Recent Changes in the U.S. Auto Industry," *Film Quarterly* 52 (Autumn 1998): 23.

5. Steven Jeffreys, *Management and the Managed* (Cambridge Press: London, 1986), 212.

6. Michael Moore, *Roger and Me,* 1989, DVD Warner Home Video, 2003.

7. Moore, *Roger and Me.*

8. Hamper's articles have been published in the *Flint Voice, Michigan Voice,* and *Mother Jones.* In 1991 Hamper published *Rivethead* and it became a national bestseller. Michael Moore wrote in the introduction to *Rivethead:* "Hamper's "Impressions of a Rivethead" became the most widely read page in the *Flint Voice,* and when the paper became the *Michigan Voice,* his popularity soared. *The Wall Street Journal* ran a front page story on him, *Harper's* magazine reprinted one of his pieces and some shoe company wanted him to endorse their industrial boots.... Meanwhile he would take off work in the middle of night shift at GM, come over to the *Voice* office, and try to get the staff to stop working and join him in his various vices. See Ben Hamper, *Rivethead* (New York: Warner Books, 1992), xii.

9. *Ibid.,* 2.

10. *Ibid.,* 35.

11. It was around this time that Hamper first sent his first writing to the *Flint Voice.* His initial piece was a review of a band called Shoes. A week later, Michael Moore requested to meet with Hamper.

12. Ben Hamper, *Rivethead,* 95.

13. *Ibid.,* 111.

14. *Ibid.,* 112.

15. Hamper wrote, "Meanwhile, I was becoming somewhat of a favorite read in the pages of the *Flint Voice.*"

16. Ben Hamper, *Rivethead,* 132.

17. When he was on the Rivet Line the *Flint Voice* went statewide and expanded to the *Michigan Voice.* Hamper wrote, "The timing of the *Voice* expansion jibed perfectly with my new gig on the Rivet Line."

18. Ben Hamper, *Rivethead,* 160.

19. *Ibid.,* 161.

20. *Ibid.,* 213.

21. Michael Moore interviewed Ben Hamper at the mental hospital in *Roger and Me*.

22. Ben Hamper, *Rivethead*, 225.

23. *Ibid.*, 225. Hamper, on page 227, again wrote, "The workers from Pontiac seemed cold, indifferent, resigned to the fact that union was nothing more than a charade and that management took full advantage of the fact."

24. Dustin Schuler, "Skinning Cars in the American West: Transforming Automobile Bodies into Relief Sculptures," *Leonardo* 17 (1984): 241–44.

25. *Ibid.*, 242.

26. See brochure "Automotive Art Exhibit," August 4, 1985, Concours d' Elegance, Meadow Brook Hall, Oakland University, Rochester, Michigan. In Vertical File Artists, National Automotive History Collection, Detroit Public Library.

27. Lester R. Brown, Christopher Flavin, and Colin Norman, *Running on Empty: The Future of the Automobile in an Oil-Short World* (New York: Norton, 1979).

28. There exists an abundance of buff literature on the pickup truck. See *Don Bunn, Classic Ford F-Series Pickup Trucks: 1948–1956* (Osceola, WI: MBI, 1998); Robert C. Ackerson, *Ford F100/F150 Pickup: America's Best-Selling Truck* (Dorchester, UK: Veloce, 1997); Peter C. Sessler, *Ford Pickup Red Book* (Osceola, WI: MBI, 1993); Mike Mueller, *The American Pickup Truck* (Osceola, WI: MBI, 1999); Henry Rasmussen, *The Great American Pickup Truck: Stylesetter, Workhorse, Sport Truck* (Osceola, WI: MBI, 1988).

29. See for example Norman Mayersohn, "Hydrogen Car Is Here, a Bit Ahead of Its Time," *New York Times*, December 9, 2007, and Lawrence Ulrich, "G.M.'s Fuel-Cell Test: 100 Cars, No Charge," *New York Times*, December 9, 2007.

30. For an exposé of safety issues connected with the SUV, see Keith Bradsher, *High and Mighty: SUVs—the World's Most Dangerous Vehicles and How They Got that Way* (New York: Public Affairs, 2002). See also United States, Congress, Senate, Committee on Commerce, Science and Transportation, *SUV Safety* (Washington: GPO, 2006). For a general discussion of the recent automobile industry, see Jay Exum Kaitlen and Lynn M. Messina, *The Car and Its Future* (New York: H. W. Wilson, 2004); Paul Ingrassia, *Comeback: the Fall and Rise of the American Automobile Industry* (New York: Simon and Schuster, 1995); Jonathan Mantle, *Car Wars: Fifty Years of Greed, Treachery, and Skulduggery in the Global Marketplace*. New York: Arcade, 1995; Mary Walton, *Car: A Drama of the American Workplace* (New York: Norton, 1997).

31. Peter Dicken, *Global Shift: Mapping the Changing Contours of the World Economy* (New York: Guilford Press, 2007); Joanne E. Oxley and Bernard Yeung, *Structural Change, Industrial Location and Competitiveness* (Cheltenham, UK: E. Elgar, 1998); James M. Rubenstein, *The Changing U.S Auto Industry: A Geographical Analysis* (New York: Routledge, 2002).

32. One website lists more than 125 automobile museums in the United States. Some, like the national Automobile Museum in Reno, Nevada, and the Auburn Cord Duesenberg Museum in Auburn, Indiana, have a long and distinguished history. Others are small but nevertheless significant in terms of local interest and tourism. See http://www.hubcapcafe.com/resources/classic_car_museums.htm.

33. http://www.petersen.org.

34. On low-riders and culture, see Denise Michelle Sandoval, "Cruising Through Low Rider Culture: Chicana/o Identity in the Marketing of *Low Rider* Magazine," in Alicia Gasper de Alba, ed., *Velvet Barrios: Popular Culture and Chicana/o Sexualities* (Basingstoke: Palgrave Macmillan, 2003), 179–98; Tracy Maurer, *Lowriders* (Vero Beach, FL: Rourke, 2004).

35. Roger H. Davis, "Cruising for Trouble: Gang-Related Drive-By Shootings." *FBI Law Enforcement Bulletin* 64:1 (January 1995): 16–23. William B. Sanders, *Gangbangs and Drive-Bys: Grounded Culture and Juvenile Gang Violence.* New York: Aldine De Gruyter, 1994.

36. See Mike Davis, *Buda's Wagon: A Brief History of the Car Bomb* (London: Verso, 2007).

37. For an account of the 1996 NASCAR racing season, see Shaun Assael, *Wide Open: Days and Nights on the NASCAR Tour* (New York: Ballantine Books, 1998). For a most useful compendium on NASCAR that contains many important facts about racing events and personalities during the 1990s, see Bill Fleischman and Al Pearce, *Inside Sports NASCAR Racing* (Detroit, MI: Visible Ink, 1998). For a business perspective on a $2 billion sport, see Robert G. Hagstrom, *The NASCAR Way: The Business That Drives the Sport (*New York: John Wiley, 1998). A very perceptive analysis of automobile racing as business sponsors, advertising, and the role of the media, especially TV, is discussed in Leo Levine, "The Business of Racing," *Road & Track* 51, no. 4 (April 1999): 146–149. David Poole and Jim McLaurin, *NASCAR Essential* (Chicago, IL: Triumph Books, 2007), is a fun read that contains many statistics as well as interesting stories.

38. See Joe Sherman, *In the Rings of Saturn* (New York: Oxford University Press, 1994); Jack O'Toole, *Forming the Future: Lessons from the Saturn Corporation* (Cambridge, MA: Blackwell, 1996).

39. Lee Iacocca with William Novak, *Iacocca: An Autobiography* (New York: Bantam, 1984).

40. Michael A. Cusumano, *The Japanese Automobile Industry: Technology and Management at Nissan and Toyota* (Cambridge, MA: Harvard University Press, 1985); Wanda James, *Driving from Japan: Japanese Cars in America* (Jefferson, NC: McFarland, 2005).

41. See James G. Hougland, Jr., "Public Perception of Toyota Motor Corporation," in P. P. Karan, ed., *Japan in the Bluegrass* (Lexington: University of Kentucky Press, 2001), 275–310.

42. Pu Gao, "Driving Force Behind the New Roadster in America," unpublished M.A. thesis, Miami University (Ohio), 1996.

43. Bill Vlasic and Bradley A. Stertz, *Taken for a Ride: How Daimler-Benz Drove Off with Chrysler* (New York: HarperCollins, 2000).

44. See Charles K. Hyde, *Riding the Roller Coaster: A History of the Chrysler Corporation* (Detroit: Wayne State University Press, 2003); Robert A. Lutz, *Guts: The Seven Laws of Business That Made Chrysler the World's Hottest Car Company* (New York: John Wiley, 1998).

45. Cited in "motorvista: History of Airbags," www.motorvista.com/airhist.htm.

46. *Ibid.*

47. Harvey R. Greenberg, Carol J. Clover, et al. "The Many Faces of 'Thelma and Louise.'" *Film Quarterly* 45:2 (Winter 1991–1992): 20–31. Cathy Griggers, "Thelma and Louise and the Cultural Generation of the New Butch-Femme," in Jim Collins, Hillary Rader and Ava Preacher Collins, *Film Theory Goes to the Movies* (New York: Routledge, 1993). Katie Mills, *The Road Story and the Rebel Mov-*

ing through Film, Fiction, and Television (Carbondale, IL: Southern Illinois University Press, 2006).

48. David Cronenberg, *Crash*, New Line Video, 1997.

49. For an excellent scene by scene analytical description of this film, see http://www.cronenbergcrash.com/

50. Leo Marx, "Literature, Technology, and Covert Culture," in Marx, *The Pilot and the Passenger* (1988), 132.

51. Cynthia Golob Dettelbach, *In the Driver's Seat: The Automobile in American Literature and Popular Culture* (Westport, CT: Greenwood Press, 1976), 2.

52. http://www.dailymail.co.uk/pages/text/print.html?in_article_id=408674&in_page_id+1770 (12/11/2006).

53. See Beth L. Bailey, *From Front Porch to Back Seat: Courtship in Twentieth-Century America* (Baltimore: Johns Hopkins University Pres, 1988), 3.

54. See a special issue of *Motor Trend*, published in February 1973, on the topic of "Love and the Automobile." Included were articles by David E. Davis, "50 Years of Back Seats"; Carol Troy, "Confessions of a Back-Seat Girl"; Steve Pence, "How to Score with Your Car"; and Allan Cartnel, "Love Vans." See also Charles Fox, "Autosex," *Car and Driver* 23 (June 1978): 25.

55. David L. Lewis, "Sex and the Automobile: From Rumble Seats to Rockin' Vans," in Lewis and Goldstein, eds., *The Automobile and American Culture* (Ann Arbor: University of Michigan Press, 1983), 123–36.

56. S. I. Hayakawa, "Sexual Fantasy and the 1957 Car," *Etc.: A Review of General Semantics* 14 (1957): 163–8.

57. Laurence Goldstein, "The Automobile and American Poetry," in Lewis and Goldstein, pp. 224–243.

58. Male poets whose work I had initially selected include: Richard Hugo, "Driving Montana," from his *Making Certain It Goes On: The Collected Poems of Richard Hugo* (New York: Norton, 1984); Tony Hoagland, "Perpetual Motion," from *Sweet Ruin* (Madison, WI: University of Wisconsin Press, 1992); David Clewell, "Traveller's Advisory," from his *Blessings in Disguise* (New York: Viking Penguin, 1991); Reg Saner, "Road Life," from (Ohio Review Books, 1984); Philip Booth, "Pickup;" from his *Selves* (New York: Viking Penguin, 1990); Russell Edson, "The Automobile," from *The Childhood of an Equestrian* (New York: Harper & Row, 1973); Stephen Dunn, "Truck Stop: Minnesota," from his *Full of Lust and Good Usage* (Pittsburgh, PA Carnegie-Mellon Press, 1992); and J. D. Reed, "Drive-In," in Reed, *Expressways* (New York: Simon and Schuster, 1969).

59. Kurt Brown, ed., *Drive, They Said: Poems about Americans and Their Cars* (Minneapolis, MN: Milkweed, 1994); Elinor Nauen, *Ladies, Start Your Engines: Women Writers on Cars and the Road* (Boston: Faber and Faber, 1996). Lisa M. Steinman's *Made in America: Science, Technology, and American Modernist Poets* (New Haven: Yale University Press, 1987) discusses modernist poets William Carlos Williams, Marianne Moore and Wallace Stevens and the place of science and technology in their thought; however, beyond the general notion of clean lines and the machine, automobile themes are not discussed or developed.

60. Linda Gregg is a lecturer in creative writing at Princeton University. Her publications and awards include: *In the Middle Distance* (2006); *Things and Flesh* (1999), finalist, Kingsley Tufts Award for Poetry; *Chosen by the Lion* (1994); *The Sacraments of Desire* (1991); *Alma* (1985); *Eight Poems* (1982); *Too Bright to See* (1981). Lannan Literary Fellowship (2003); Sara Teasdale Award (2003), Jerome J. Shestack Poetry Prize (1999), National Endowment for the Arts (1993), Pushcart Prize (1981, 1982, 1985, 1986, 1991–92), Whiting Writer's Award (1985), Guggenheim Fellowship (1983).

61. Personal communication, Lynne Knight to the author, March 16, 2007.

62. Personal communication, Lynne Knight to the author, March 16, 2007.

63. Johnson used the car-woman metaphor as follows: "I'm gonna hoist your hood mama, I'm going to check your oil. I'm gonna get down deep in this connection, keep on tangling with your wires/ And when I mash down on your little starter, then your spark plugs gonna give me fire." See E. L. Widmer, "Crossroads: The Automobile, Rock and Roll and Democracy," in *Autopia: Cars and Culture* (London, Reaktion, 2002), 65–74.

64. I can think of at least two instances in my own life similar to that expressed by Healy. One was on I-90 between Cleveland and Erie, when I was driving my Mustang convertible and a lady was driving a similar car. We kept pace for miles, only to smile at each other and wave when one of us left the interstate. A similar top-down episode took place while driving my Porsche 911 in pace with a woman car devotee driving a rare old Mopar convertible.

65. Personal communication, Sheryl St. Germain to the author, March 22, 2007.

Select Bibliography

Journal Articles

Alkalay-Gut, Karen. "Sex and the Single Engine: E. E. Cummings' Experiment in Metaphoric Equation." *Journal of Modern Literature* 20 (Winter 1996): 254–8.

Ames, Roy Clifton. "Cars in Song." *Special-Interest Autos* (January-February 1977): 40–45.

Andrews, Robert F. "On Designing the 'Step-down' Hudson." *Automobile Quarterly* 9:4 (Summer 1971): 393–7.

Ariout, Jacqueline Fellague. "The Dearborn Independent, A Mirror of the 1920s." *Michigan History Magazine* 80 (1996): 41–7.

Arnold, Robert F. "Termination or Transformation? The 'Terminator' Films and Recent Changes in the U.S. Auto Industry." *Film Quarterly* 52 (Autumn 1998): 20–30.

Aronson, Sidney H. "The Sociology of the Bicycle." *Social Forces.* 30 (March 1952): 305–12.

Artz, Nancy, Jeanne Munger, and Warren Purdy. "Gender Issues in Advertising Language." *Women and Language* 22 (Fall 1999): 20–6.

Behling, Laura L. "'The Woman at the Wheel': Marketing Ideal Womanhood, 1915–1934." *Journal of American Culture* 20 (Fall 1997): 13–31.

Bernstein, Barton J. "The Automobile Industry and the Coming of World War II." *The Southwestern Social Science Quarterly* 47 (1966): 22–33.

Blaszczyk, Regina Lee. "DuPont and the Color Revolution." *Chemical Heritage* (Fall 2007): 20–5.

Burnham, John C. "The Gasoline Tax and the Automobile Revolution." *Mississippi Valley Historical Review* 48 (December 1961): 435–59.

Busby, Linda J., and Greg Leichty. "Feminism and Advertising in Traditional and Non-Traditional Women's Magazines." *Journalism Quarterly* 70 (Summer 1993): 247–64.

Carr, Lowell Julliard. "How the Devil-Wagon Came to Dexter: A Study of Diffusional Change in an American Community." *Social Forces* 11 (October 1932): 64–70.

Casey, Robert. "The Vanderbilt Cup, 1908." *Technology and Culture* 40 (1999): 358–62.

Chesterton, G. K. "The Hollow Horn." *G. K.'s Weekly* 24 (October 1, 1936): 57.

Clarke, Sally. "Managing Design: the Art and Colour Section at General Motors, 1927–1941." *Journal of Design History* 12 (1999): 65–79.

Cooper, Gail. "Frederick Winslow Taylor and Scientific Management." In *Technology in America*, edited by Carroll W. Pursell, Jr., 163–176. Cambridge, MA: MIT Press, 1991.

Cubitt, Sean. "'Maybellene': Meaning and Listening Subject." *Popular Music.* 4 (1984): 207-24.

Edmondson, Amy. "Who Was Buckminster Fuller Anyway?" *American History of Invention & Technology* 3 (1988): 18–25.

Edsforth, Ronald, and Robert Asher. "The Speedup: The Focal Point of Workers' Grievances, 1919–1941." In Robert Asher and Ronald Edsforth, eds. *Autowork.* Albany, NY: State University of New York Press, 1995: 65–98.

Fine, Sidney. "The Origins of the United Automobile Workers, 1933–1935." *The Journal of Economic History* 18 (September 1958): 249–82.

Flamm, Bradley. "Putting the Brakes on 'Non-Essential' Travel: 1940s Wartime Mobility, Prosperity, and the U.S. Office of Defense." *Journal of Transport History* 27 (March 2006): 71–92.

Flink, James J. "The Olympian Age of the Automobile." *American Heritage of Invention & Technology* 7 (Winter 1992): 54–63.

_____. "The Path of Least Resistance." *American Heritage of Invention & Technology* 5 (Fall 1989): 34–44.

_____. "Three Stages of American Automobile Consciousness." *American Quarterly* 24 (October 1972): 451–73.

French, Michael J. "Structure, Personality, and Business Strategy in the U.S. Tire Industry: The Seiberling Rubber Company, 1922–1964." *Business History Review* 67 (Summer 1993): 246–78.

Fuller, Wayne E. "Farmers, Postmen, and the Good Roads Movement." In *Indiana History: A Book of Readings*, edited by Ralph D. Gray, 221–7. Bloomington, IN: Indiana University Press, 1994.

Garamvári, Pál. "100 Years of the Carburetor." *Technikat Ort Enetio Szemle* 20 (1993): 11-15.

Gartman, David. "Three Ages of the Automobile: The Cultural Logistics of the Car." *Theory, Culture & Society* 21 (2004): 169–195.

Gerber, Timothy. "Built for Speed: The Checkered

Career of Race Car Designer Harry A. Miller." *Wisconsin Magazine of History* 85 (2002): 32–41.

Gianturco, Michael. "The Infinite Straightaway." *American Heritage of Invention & Technology* 8 (1992): 34–41.

Graebner, William. "Ethyl in Manhattan: A Note on the Science and Politics of Leaded Gasoline." *New York History* 57 (1986): 436–43.

Grammage, Grady, Jr., and Stephen L. Jones. "Orgasm in Chrome: The Rise and Fall of the Automobile Tailfin." *Journal of Popular Culture* 8 (1974): 132–47.

Grayson, Stan. "Crosley of Cincinnati." *Automobile Quarterly* 16:1 (First Quarter 1978): 6–20.

Greenberg, Harvey R., Carol J. Clover, et al. "The Many Faces of 'Thelma and Louise.'" *Film Quarterly* 45 (Winter 1991–1992): 20–31.

Griggers, Cathy. "Thelma and Louise and the Cultural Generation of the New Butch-Femme." In Jim Collins, Hillary Rader, and Ava Preacher Collins, eds., *Film Theory Goes to the Movies*. New York: Routledge, 1993: 129–141.

Hendry, Maurice D. "Henry M. Leland." In Ronald Barker and Anthony Harding, eds., *Automobile Design: Twelve Great Designers and Their Work*, 2nd ed. Warrendale, PA: Society of Automotive Engineers, 1992: 81–112.

_____. "Pierce-Arrow: An American Aristocrat." *Automobile Quarterly* 6:3 (Winter 1968): 240–265.

_____. "Thomas!" *Automobile Quarterly* 8:4 (Summer 1970): 418–30.

Herlihy, David V. "The Bicycle Story." *American Heritage Invention & Technology* 7 (Spring 1992): 48–59.

Howard, John Robert. "The Flowering of the Hippie Movement." *Annals of the American Academy of Political and Social Science* 382 (March 1969): 43–55.

Hugill, Peter J. "Good Roads and the Automobile in the United States, 1880–1929." *Geographical Review* 72 (July 1982): 327–349.

Hyde, Charles K. "The Dodge Brothers, the Automobile Industry, and Detroit Society in the Early Twentieth Century." *Michigan Historical Review* 22 (1996): 48–82.

Irwin, Howard. "The History of the Airflow Car." *Scientific American* 237 (August 1977): 98–104.

Jackson, Richard H., and Mark W. Jackson. "The Lincoln Highway: The First Transcontinental Highway and the American West." *Journal of the West* 42 (2003): 56–64.

Katz, John F. "The Challenge from Steam." *Automobile Quarterly* 25:1 (First Quarter 1987): 15–29.

Kimes, Beverly Rae. "The Dawn of Speed." *American Heritage* 38 (1987): 92–101.

_____. "His Cord and His Empire." *Automobile Quarterly* 18:2 (Second Quarter 1980): 193–201.

_____. "Plymouth: Walter Chrysler's Trump Car." *Automobile Quarterly* 5:1 (Summer 1966): 74–85.

Konig, Wolfgang. "Adolf Hitler vs. Henry Ford: The Volkswagen, The Role of America as Model, and the Failure of a Nazi Consumer Society." *German Studies Review* 27 (2004): 249–68.

Kosher, Rudy. "Cars and Nations: Anglo-German Perspectives on Automobility Between the World Wars." *Theory, Culture, & Society* 21 (2004): 121–44.

Laird, Pamela Walker. "'The Car Without a Single Weakness': Early Automobile Advertising." *Technology and Culture* (1996): 796–812.

Lamm, Michael. "Are Car Keys Obsolete?" *American Heritage Invention & Technology* 23 (Summer 2008): 7.

Langworth, Richard M. "The Glorious Madness of Kaiser Frazer." *Automobile Quarterly* 9:3 (Spring 1971): 266–83.

_____. "The True Tale of Uncle Tom McCahill." *Automobile Quarterly* 14 (First Quarter 1976): 68–73.

Lankton, Larry. "Autos to Armaments: Detroit Becomes the Arsenal of Democracy." *Michigan History* 75 (1991): 42–9.

Lee, Matthew T. "The Ford Pinto Case and the Development of Auto Safety Regulations, 1893–1978." *Business and Economic History* 27 (1998): 390–401.

Lewchuck, Wayne A. "Men and Monotony: Fraternalism as a Managerial Strategy at the Ford Motor Company." *Journal of Economic History* 4 (December 1993): 824.

Lewis, David L. "'Sex and the Automobile: From Rumble Seats to Rockin' Vans." In David L. Lewis and Laurence Goldstein, eds., *The Automobile and American Culture*. Ann Arbor, MI: University of Michigan Press, 1983: 123–133.

Lichtenstein, Alex. "Good Roads and Chain Gangs in the Progressive South: 'The Negro Convict as a Slave.'" *Journal of Southern History* 59 (1993): 85–110.

Lichtenstein, Nelson. "Auto Worker Militancy and the Structure of Factory Life, 1937–1955." *Journal of American History* 67 (September 1980): 335–53.

Lipski, Patricia W. "The Introduction of Automobile into American English." *American Speech* 38 (October 1964): 176–87.

Loeb, Alan P. "Birth of the Kettering Doctrine: Fordism, Sloanism and the Discovery of Tetraethyl Lead." *Business and Economic History* 24 (1995): 72–87.

MacDonald, Thomas H. "The History and Development of Road Building in the United States." *Transactions, American Society of Civil Engineers* 92 (1928): 1181–1206.

Maxwell, James A., and Margaret N. Blacom. "Gasoline Rationing in the United States, I." *Quarterly Journal of Economics* 60 (August 1946): 561–587.

McCaffrey, Donald W. "The Evolution of the Chase in the Silent Screen Comedy." *Journal of the Society of Cinematologists* 4 (1964–5): 1–8.

McCarthy, Tom. "The Coming Wonder? Foresight and Early Concerns about the Automobile." *Environmental History* 6 (January 2001): 46–74.

McIntyre, Stephen L. "The Failure of Fordism: Reform of the Automobile Repair Industry, 1913–1940." *Technology and Culture* 41 (2000): 269–99.

Melder, F. Eugene. "The 'Tin Lizzie's' Golden Anniversary." *American Quarterly* 12 (Winter 1960): 477–8.

Messer-Kruse, Timothy. "You Know Me: Barney Oldfield." *Timeline* 19 (2002): 2–19.

Moraglio, Massimo. "Per Una Storia Della Autostrade Italiane." *Storia Urbana* 26 (2002): 11–25.

Mueller, Mike. "Tucker: A Man and His Car." *American History Illustrated* 23 (1989): 36–41.

Nelson, Bruce. "Autoworkers, Electoral Politics, and the Convergence of Class and Race, Detroit, 1937–1945." In Kevin Boyle, ed., *Organized Labor and American Politics, 1894–1994*. Albany, NY: State University of New York Press, 1998: 121–58.

Newcomb, James. "Depression Auto Styling." *Winterthur Portfolio* 35 (Spring 2000): 81–100.

Norbye, Jan P. "Panhard et Levassor: Limelight to Twilight." *Automobile Quarterly* 6:2 (Fall 1967): 127–43.

O'Brien, Anthony Patrick. The Importance of Adjusting Production to Sales in the Early Automobile Industry." *Explorations in Economic History* 34 (1997): 195–219.

Oestreicher, Richard. "The Rules of the Game: Class Politics in Twentieth-Century America." In Kevin Boyle, ed., *Organized Labor and American Politics, 1894–1994*. Albany: State University of New York Press, 1998: 19–50.

Offer, Avner. "The American Automobile Frenzy of the 1950s." In K. Bruland and P. K. O'Brien, eds., *From Family Firms to Corporate Capitalism: Essays in Business and Industrial History in Honour of Peter Mathias*. Oxford: Oxford University Press, 1998: 315–53.

Ostrander, Stephen G. "A Car Worthy of Its Name." *Michigan History Magazine* 76 (January/February 1992): 24–7.

Peterson, Joyce Shaw. "Autoworkers and Their Work, 1900–1933." *Labor History* 22 (1981): 213–36.

_____. "Black Automobile Workers in Detroit, 1900–1933." *Journal of Negro History* 64 (Summer 1979): 177–90.

Peterson, Richard A. "Why 1955? Explaining the Advent of Rock Music." *Popular Music* 9 (January 1990): 97–116.

Pfau, Hugo. "Dr. Rumpler's 'Volkswagen.'" *Cars & Parts* 20 (August 1977): 28–32.

Rieger, Bernard. "'Fast Couples': Technology, Gender, and Modernity in Britain and Germany During the Nineteen-Thirties." *Historical Research* 76 (August 2003): 364–88.

Rollins, William H. "Whose Landscape? Technology, Fascism, and Environmentalism on the National Socialist Autobahn." *Annals of the Association of American Geographers* 85 (September 1995): 494–520.

Rosner, David, and Gerald Markowitz. "A 'Gift of God'?: The Public Health Controversy Over Leaded Gasoline During the 1920s." *American Journal of Public Health* 75 (1985): 344–52.

Sandoval, Denise Michelle. "Cruising Through Low Rider Culture: Chicana/o Identity in the Marketing of *Low Rider* Magazine." In Alicia Gasper de Alba, ed., *Velvet Barrios: Popular Culture and Chicana/o Sexualities*. Basingstoke: Palgrave Macmillan, 2003: 179–98.

Schuler, Dustin. "Skinning Cars in the American West: Transforming Automobile Bodies into Relief Sculptures." *Leonardo* 17 (1984): 241–44.

Scott, Cord. "The Race of the Century." *Journal of the Illinois State Historical Society* 96 (2003): 37–48.

Shand, James D. "The Reichsautobahn: Symbol for the Third Reich." *Journal of Contemporary History* 19 (1984): 189–200.

Smith, Julian. "Transports of Delight: The Image of the Automobile in Early Films." *Film & History* 11 (1981): 59–67.

Sonkin, Robert. "Bleeding Betty's Brakes: Or, the Army Names a Jeep." *American Speech* 29 (December 1954): 257–62.

Stewart, Doug. "Hail to the Jeep! Could We Have Won Without It?" *Smithsonian* 23 (1992): 60–73.

Todd, Jan. "Cars, Paint, and Chemicals: Industry Linkages and the Capture of Overseas Technology Between the Wars." *Australian Economic History Review* 38 (July 1998): 176–93.

Tuttle, William M., Jr. "The Birth of an Industry: The Synthetic Rubber 'Mess' in World War II." *Technology and Culture* 22 (January 1981): 35–67.

Wells, Christopher W. "The Changing Nature of Country Roads: Farmers, Reformers, and the Shifting Use of Rural Space, 1880–1905." *Agricultural History* 80 (2006): 143–66.

Wilkinson, Stephan. "Tanks, Hot Rods, and Salt." *Air & Space Smithsonian* 12 (1997): 60–3.

Wright, John L. "Croonin' About Cruisin'." In Jack Nachbar, Deborah Weiser, and John L. Wright, eds., *The Popular Culture Reader*. Bowling Green, OH: Bowling Green University Press, 1978: 109–17.

Yanik, Anthony J. "Harley Earl and the Birth of Modern Automotive Styling." *Chronicle: Quarterly Magazine of the Historical Society of Michigan* 21 (1985): 18–22.

Yates, Brock. "Duesenberg." *American Heritage* 45 (1994): 88–99.

Books

Adler, Dennis. *Chrysler*. Osceola, WI: MBI, 2000.

_____. *Duesenberg*. Iola, WI: Krause Publications, 2004.

Allen, Frederick Lewis. *Only Yesterday*. New York: Harper and Row, 1931.

Antonick, Michael. *California Screamin': The Glory*

Days of Corvette Road Racing. Osceola, WI: MBI, 1990.

Arnold, Horace Lucien, and Fay Leone Faurote. *Ford Methods and Ford Shops.* New York: Engineering Magazine, 1915.

Assael, Shaun. *Wide Open: Days and Nights on the NASCAR Tour.* New York: Ballantine, 1998.

Bailey, Beth L. *From Front Porch to Back Seat: Courtship in Twentieth-Century America.* Baltimore: Johns Hopkins University Press, 1988.

Baldwin, Neil. *Henry Ford and the Jews: The Mass Production of Hate.* New York: Public Affairs, 2001.

Barnard, John. *American Vanguard: The United Autoworkers During the Reuther Years, 1935–1970.* Detroit: Wayne State University Press, 2004.

Barnes, H.E. *Society in Transition.* New York: Prentice Hall, 1939.

Batchelor, Dean. *Dry Lakes and Drag Strips: The American Hot Rod.* St. Paul, MN: MBI, 2002.

Batchelor, Ray. *Henry Ford: Mass Production, Modernism and Design.* Manchester: Manchester University Press, 1994.

Bayley, Stephen. *Harley Earl and the Dream Machine.* New York: Knopf, 1983.

_____. *Sex, Drink and Fast Cars.* New York: Pantheon, 1986.

Beasley, David. *The Suppression of the Automobile: Skullduggery at the Crossroads.* Westport, CT: Greenwood, 1988.

Beatley, Timothy. *Green Urbanism: Learning from European Cities.* Washington, D.C.: Island Press, 2000.

Belasco, Warren James. *Americans on the Road: From Autocamp to Motel, 1910–1945.* Baltimore: Johns Hopkins University Press, 1979.

Bel Geddes, Norman. *Magic Motorways.* New York: Random House, 1940.

Belloc, Hilaire. *The Road.* New York: Harper & Brothers, 1925.

Berger, Michael L. *The Devil Wagon in God's Country: The Automobile and Social Change in Rural America, 1893–1929.* Hamden, CT: Archon Books, 1979.

Bernstein, Irving. *Turbulent Years: A History of the American Worker, 1933–1941.* Los Angeles: University of California Press, 1969.

Billington, David P., and David P. Billington, Jr. *Power, Speed, and Form: Engineers and the Making of the Twentieth Century.* Princeton, NJ: Princeton University Press, 2006.

Binder, Alan K., and Deebe Ferris, eds. *General Motors in the 20th Century.* Southfield, MI: Wards Communications, 2000.

Blackford, Mansel G., and K. Austin Kerr. *B. F. Goodrich: Tradition and Transformation, 1870–1995.* Columbus: Ohio State University Press, 1996.

Blank, Harrod. *Wild Wheels.* San Francisco: Pomegranate Artbooks, 1993.

Bliss, Carey S. *Autos Across America: A Bibliography of Transcontinental Automobile Travel: 1903–1940.* Austin and New Haven: Jenkins & Reese, 1982.

Blum, John Morton. *V Was for Victory: Politics and American Culture During World War II.* New York: First Harvest, 1976.

Bonsall, Thomas E. *The Cadillac Story: The Postwar Years.* Stanford, CA: Stanford University Press, 2004.

Borg, Kevin L. *Automechanics: Technology and Expertise in Twentieth-Century America.* Baltimore: Johns Hopkins University Press, 2007.

Borgeson, Griffith. *Miller.* Osceola, WI: Motorbooks, 1993.

Bottles, Scott. *Los Angeles and the Automobile: The Making of a Modern City.* Berkeley: University of California Press, 1987.

Boyer, Paul S. *By Bomb's Early Light: American Thought and Culture at the Dawn of the Atomic Age.* New York: Pantheon, 1985.

Bradsher, Keith. *High and Mighty: SUVs — the World's Most Dangerous Vehicles and How They Got That Way.* New York: Public Affairs, 2002.

Braverman, Harry. *Labor and Monopoly Capital: The Degradation of Work in the Twentieth Century.* New York: Monthly Review Press, 1974.

Breer, Carl. *The Birth of Chrysler Corporation and its Engineering Legacy.* Warrendale, PA: Society of Automotive Engineers, 1995.

Brinkley, Douglas. *Wheels for the World: Henry Ford, His Company, and a Century of Progress, 1903–2003.* New York: Viking, 2003.

Brown, Kurt, ed. *Drive, They Said: Poems About Americans and Their Cars.* Minneapolis: Milkweed, 1994.

Brown, Lester R., Christopher Flavin, and Colin Norman. *Running on Empty: The Future of the Automobile in an Oil-Short World.* New York: Norton, 1979.

Buehrig, Gordon M. *Auburn: The Year 1936 Is Viewed 50 Years Later.* Privately printed, 1986.

Buel, Ronald. *Dead End: The Automobile in Mass Transportation.* Englewood Cliffs, NJ: Prentice-Hall, 1972.

Burlingame, Roger. *Henry Ford.* New York: Knopf, 1955.

Burnside, Tom, and Denise McCluggage. *American Racing: Road Racing in the 50s and 60s.* Cologne: Könemann, 1996.

Burton, Walter. *The Story of Tire Beads and Tires.* New York: McGraw-Hill, 1954.

Butler, Don. *Auburn Cord Duesenberg.* Osceola, WI: Motorbooks, 1992.

Carson, Iain, and Vijay V. Vaitheeswaran. *Zoom: The Global Race to Fuel the Car of the Future.* New York: Twelve, 2007.

Casey, Robert. *The Model T: A Centennial History.* Baltimore: Johns Hopkins University Press, 2008.

Chandler, Alfred D. *Strategy and Structure: Chapters in the History of Industrial Enterprise.* Cambridge, MA: MIT Press, 1962.

Chrysler Corporation. *The Story of an American Company.* Detroit: Chrysler, 1955.

Clymer, Floyd. *Floyd Clymer's Steam Car Scrapbook.* New York: Bonanza Books, 1945.

_____. *Henry's Wonderful Model T 1908–1927.* New York: McGraw-Hill, 1955.

_____. *Those Wonderful Old Automobiles.* New York: Bonanza, 1953.

Cowan, Ruth Schwartz. *More Work for Mother.* New York: Basic Books, 1983.

Cray, Ed. *Chrome Colossus: General Motors and Its Times.* New York: McGraw-Hill, 1980.

Crews, Harry. *Car.* New York: William Morrow, 1972.

Critchlow, Donald T. *Studebaker: The Life and Death of an American Corporation.* Bloomington: Indiana University Press, 1996.

Crosse, Jesse. *The Greatest Movie Car Chases of all Time.* St. Paul, MN: Motorbooks, 2006.

Csikszentmihalyi, Mihaly, and Rochberg-Halton, Eugene. *The Meaning of Things: Domestic Symbols and Self.* Cambridge: Cambridge University Press, 1981.

Curcio, Vincent. *Chrysler: The Life and Times of an Automotive Genius.* New York: Oxford University Press, 2000.

Cusumano, Michael A. *The Japanese Automobile Industry: Technology and Management at Nissan and Toyota.* Cambridge, MA: Harvard University Press, 1985.

Dammann, George H. *Seventy Years of Chrysler.* Glen Ellyn, IL: Crestline, 1974.

Davis, Michael W. R. *Detroit's Wartime Industry, Arsenal of Democracy.* Charleston, SC: Arcadia Publishing, 2007.

Davis, Mike. *Buda's Wagon: A Brief History of the Car Bomb.* London: Verso, 2007.

Davis, Susan S. *The Stanleys: Renaissance Yankees: Innovation in Industry and the Arts.* New York: Newcomen Society of the United States, 1997.

Deming, W. Edwards. *Out of the Crisis.* Cambridge, MA: MIT Press, 1982.

Dettelbach, Cynthia Golob. *In the Driver's Seat: The Automobile in American Literature and Popular Culture.* Westport, CT: Greenwood Press, 1976.

Donaldson, Gary. *Abundance and Anxiety: America, 1945–1960.* Westport, CT: Praeger, 1997.

Donnelly, Nora, ed. *Customized: Art Inspired by Hot Rods, Low Riders and American Car Culture.* New York: Harry N. Abrams, 2000.

Downey, Fairfax. *Jezebel the Jeep.* New York: Dodd, Mead, 1944.

Duncan, Dayton. *Horatio's Drive: America's First Road Trip.* New York: Knopf, 2003.

Duryea, J. Frank. *America's First Automobile.* Springfield, MA: Macaulay, 1942.

Eastman, Joel W. *Styling vs. Safety: The American Automobile Industry and the Development of Automotive Safety, 1900–1966.* Lanham, MD: University Press of America, 1984.

Elbert, J. L. *Duesenberg: The Mightiest American Motor Car.* Arcadia, CA: Post-Era Books, 1975.

Farber, David R. *Sloan Rules: Alfred P. Sloan and the Triumph of General Motors.* Chicago: University of Chicago Press, 2002.

Faris, John T. *Roaming American Highways.* New York: Farrar & Rinehart, 1931.

Felsen, Henry Gregor. *Hot Rod.* New York: E. P. Dutton, 1950.

Finkelstein, Norman H. *The Way Things Never Were: The Truth About the "Good Old Days"* New York: Atheneum, 1999.

Flink, James J. *America Adopts the Automobile, 1895–1910.* Cambridge, MA: MIT Press, 1970.

_____. *The Automobile Age.* Cambridge, MA: MIT Press, 1988.

Ford, Henry. *My Life and Work.* Garden City, NY: Doubleday, Page, 1922.

_____. *Today and Tomorrow.* Cambridge, MA: Productivity Press, 1988.

Foster, Kit. *The Stanley Steamer: America's Legendary Steam Car.* Kingfield, ME: Stanley Museum, 2004.

French, Michael J. *The United States Tire Industry.* Boston: Twayne, 1991.

Frey, John W., ed. *A History of the Petroleum Administration for War, 1941–1945.* Washington, D.C.: G.P.O., 1946.

Gartman, David. *Auto Opium: A Social History of American Automobile Design.* London: Routledge, 1994.

_____. *Auto Slavery: The Labor Process in the American Automobile Industry, 1897–1950.* New Brunswick, NJ: Rutgers University Press, 1986.

Georgano, Nick. *Art of the American Automobile: The Greatest Stylists and Their Work.* New York: Smithmark, 1995.

Gladding, Effie Price. *Across the Continent by the Lincoln Highway.* New York: Brentano's, 1915.

Goddard, Stephen B. *Colonel Albert Pope and His American Dream Machines: The Life and Times of a Bicycle Tycoon Turned Automotive Pioneer.* Jefferson, NC: McFarland, 2000.

Granatelli, Anthony (Andy). *They Call Me Mister 500.* Chicago: Henry Regency, 1969.

Greenleaf, William. *Monopoly on Wheels: Henry Ford and the Selden Patent Suit.* Detroit: Wayne State University Press, 1961.

Gruskin, Paul. *Rock'n Down the Highway: The Cars that Made Rock Roll.* St. Paul, MN: Voyageur Press, 2006.

Gustin, Lawrence R. *Billy Durant: Creator of General Motors.* Grand Rapids, MI: Eerdmans, 1973.

Gutfreund, Owen D. *Twentieth-Century Sprawl: Highways and the Reshaping of the American Landscape.* New York: Oxford University Press, 2004.

Hagstrom, Robert G. *The NASCAR Way: The Business That Drives the Sport.* New York: John Wiley, 1998.

Hair, William Ivy. *The Kingfish and His Realm.* Baton Rouge: Louisiana State University Press, 1991.

Halberstam, David. *The Reckoning.* New York: William Morrow, 1986.

Hamper, Ben. *Rivethead: Tales from the Assembly Line.* New York: Warner Books, 1992.

Heat Moon, William Least. *Blue Highways: A Journey into America.* Boston: Little, Brown, 1982.

Hendry, Maurice D. *Cadillac, Standard of the World: The Complete History.* Princeton, NJ: Automobile Quarterly Publications, 1977.

Herlihy, David V. *Bicycle: The History.* New Haven, CT: Yale University Press, 2004.

Hokanson, Drake. *The Lincoln Highway: Main Street Across America.* Iowa City: University of Iowa Press, 1988.

Hounshell, David A. *From the American System to Mass Production 1800–1932: The Development of Manufacturing Technology in the United States.* Baltimore: Johns Hopkins University Press, 1984.

Hyde, Charles K. *The Dodge Brothers: The Men, the Motor Cars, and the Legacy.* Detroit: Wayne State University Press, 2005.

_____. *Riding the Roller Coaster: A History of the Chrysler Corporation.* Detroit: Wayne State University Press, 2003.

Iacocca, Lee, with Novak, William. *Iacocca: An Autobiography.* New York: Bantam Books, 1984.

Ikuta, Yasutoshi. *American Automobile: Advertising from the Antique and Classic Eras.* San Francisco: Chronicle Books, 1988.

_____. *Cruise O Matic: Automobile Advertising of the 1950s.* San Francisco: Chronicle Books, 1988.

Ingrassia, Paul. *Comeback: The Fall and Rise of the American Automobile Industry.* New York: Simon and Schuster, 1995.

Innes, C. D. *Designing Modern America: Broadway to Main Street.* New Haven: Yale University Press, 2005.

Jackson, Robert B. *Road Race Round the World: New York to Paris, 1908.* New York: Scholastic, 1965.

Jacobs, Timothy. *A History of General Motors.* New York: Smithmark, 1992.

_____. *Lemons: The World's Worst Cars.* Greenwich, CT: Dorsey, 1991.

James, Wanda. *Driving from Japan: Japanese Cars in America.* Jefferson, NC: McFarland, 2005.

Jardim, Anne. *The First Henry Ford: A Study in Personality and Leadership.* Cambridge, MA: MIT Press, 1970.

Jeffreys, Steven. *Management and the Managed.* London: Cambridge Press, 1986.

Jerome, John. *The Death of the Automobile: The Fatal Effect of the Golden Era, 1955–1970.* New York: Norton, 1972.

Kanigel, Robert. *The One Best Way: Frederick Winslow Taylor and the Enigma of Efficiency.* New York: Viking, 1997.

Kaszynski, William. *Route 66: Images of America's Main Street.* Jefferson, NC: McFarland, 2003.

Keats, John. *The Insolent Chariots.* Greenwich, CT: Fawcett, 1959.

Keene, Carolyn. *The Secret of the Old Clock.* New York: Grosset & Dunlap, 1930.

Kerouac, Jack. *On the Road.* New York: Viking, 2007.

Keyser, Michael. *A French Kiss with Death: Steve McQueen and the Making of Le Mans: The Man — the Race — the Cars — the Movie.* Cambridge, MA: Robert Bentley, 1999.

Kinsey, Alfred, et al. *Sexual Behavior in the Human Female.* Philadelphia: W.B. Saunders, 1953.

Kirby, Richard Shelton. *Engineering in History.* New York: McGraw-Hill, 1956.

Kirsch, David. *The Electric Vehicle and the Burden of History.* New Brunswick, NJ: Rutgers University Press, 2000.

Koistinen, Paul A. C. *Arsenal of World War II: The Political Economy of American Warfare, 1940–1945.* Lawrence: University Press of Kansas, 1994.

Kraus, Henry. *Heroes of Unwritten Story: The UAW 1934–1939.* Urbana: University of Illinois Press, 1993.

Laban, Brian. *Cars: The Early Years.* Köln: Könemann, 2000.

Lacey, Robert. *Ford: The Men and the Machine.* New York: Little, Brown, 1986.

Lackey, James H. *The Jordan Automobile: A History.* Jefferson, NC: McFarland, 2005.

Landis, Carole. *Four Jills in a Jeep.* New York: Random House, 1944.

Lane, Rose Wilder. *Travels with Zenobia: Paris to Albania by Model T Ford.* Columbia: University of Missouri Press, 1983.

Langworth, Richard M., and Jan P. Norbye. *The Complete History of Chrysler Corporation, 1924–1985.* New York: Beekman House, 1985.

_____. The *Complete History of General Motors, 1908–1986.* Skokie, IL: Publications International, 1986.

Laux, James. *In First Gear: The French Automobile Industry.* Montreal: McGill–Queen's University Press, 1976.

Lavine, Sigmund A. *Kettering: Master Inventor.* New York: Dodd, Mead, 1960.

Lears, T. J. Jackson. *Fables of Abundance: A Cultural History of Advertising in America.* New York: Basic Books, 1994.

Leavitt, Helen. *Superhighway — Superhoax.* New York: Ballantine, 1970.

Le Grand, Henderson. *Augustus Drives a Jeep.* Indianapolis: Bobbs-Merrill, 1946.

Leland, Ottilie M., with Minnie Dubbs Millbrook. *Master of Precision: Henry M. Leland.* Detroit: Wayne State University Press, 1996.

Leslie, Stewart W. *Boss Kettering.* New York: Columbia University Press, 1983.

Lesseig, Corey T. *Automobility: Social Changes in the American South 1909–1939.* New York: Routledge, 2001.

Levine, Leo. *Ford: The Dust and the Glory: A Racing History.* 2 vols. Warrendale, PA: SAE, 2001.

Levy, Lester S. *Give Me Yesterday: American History in Song, 1890–1920.* Norman: University of Oklahoma Press, 1975.

Lewis, David Lanier. *The Public Image of Henry Ford: An American Folk Hero and His Company.* Detroit: Wayne State University Press, 1987.

Lewis, Tom. *Divided Highways: Building the Interstate Highways, Transforming American Life.* New York: Viking, 1997.

Lewis, W. David. *Eddie Rickenbacker: An American Hero in the Twentieth Century.* Baltimore: Johns Hopkins University Press, 2005.

Lincoln, Natalie Sumner. *The Blue Car Mystery.* New York: D. Appleton, 1926.

Lincoln Highway Association. *A Picture of Progress on the Lincoln Way.* Detroit, 1920.

Livesay, Harold. *American Made.* Boston: Little, Brown, 1977.

Ludvigsen, Karl. *Battle for the Beetle.* Cambridge, MA: Bentley, 2000.

Lutz, Robert A. *Guts: The Seven Laws of Business That Made Chrysler the World's Hottest Car Company.* New York: John Wiley, 1998.

Lynd, Robert S., and Helen Merrell Lynd. *Middletown in Transition: A Study in Cultural Conflicts.* New York: Harcourt, Brace, 1937.

Lyons, Dan. *Cars of the Fantastic '50s.* Iola, WI: KP Books, 2005.

Madden, W. C. *Haynes-Apperson and America's First Practical Automobile: A History.* Jefferson, NC: McFarland, 2003.

Madsen, Axel. *The Deal Maker: How William C. Durant Made General Motors.* New York: Wiley, 1999.

Mantle, Jonathan. *Car Wars: Fifty Years of Greed, Treachery, and Skulduggery in the Global Marketplace.* New York: Arcade, 1995.

Marcantonio, Alfred, David Abbot, and John O'Driscoll. *Is the Bug Dead? The Great Beetle Ad Campaign.* New York: Stewart, 1983.

March, Peter, and Peter Collett. *Driving Passion: The Psychology of the Car.* Boston and London: Faber and Faber, 1987.

Marling, Karal Ann. *As Seen on TV: The Visual Culture of Everyday Life in the 1950s.* Cambridge, MA: Harvard University Press, 1994.

Marquis, Samuel S. *Henry Ford: An Interpretation.* Boston: Little, Brown, 1923.

Massey, Beatrice Larned. *It Might Have Been Worse: A Motor Trip from Coast to Coast.* San Francisco: Harr Wagner, 1920.

Maugeri, Leonardo. *The Age of Oil: The Mythology, History, and the Future of the World's Most Controversial Resource.* Westport, CT: Praeger, 2006.

Maxim, Hiram Percy. *Horseless Carriage Days.* New York: Dover, 1962.

May, George W. *Charles E. Duryea Automaker.* Chillicothe, IL: River Beach Publishing, 1996.

McCahill, Tom. *The Modern Sports Car.* New York: Prentice-Hall, 1954.

McCalley, Bruce W. *Model T Ford: The Car That Changed the World.* Iola, WI: Krause Publications, 1994.

McCallum, Iain. *Blood Brothers: Hiram and Hudson Maxim; Pioneers of Modern Warfare.* London: Chatham, 1999.

McKeon, Elizabeth, and Linda Everett. *Cinema Under the Stars: America's Love Affair with the Drive-In Movie Theater.* Nashville, TN: Cumberland House, 1998.

McNichol, Dan. *The Roads That Built America: The Incredible Story of the U.S. Interstate System.* New York: Sterling, 2006.

McShane, Clay. *Down the Asphalt Path: The Automobile and the American City.* New York: Columbia University Press, 1994.

Medley, Tom. *Tex Smith's Hot Rod History.* Osceola, WI: Motorbooks International, 1990.

Meier, August. *Black Detroit.* New York: Oxford University Press, 1979.

Miller, Ray. *Chevrolet: The Coming of Age, 1911–1942.* Oceanside, CA: Evergreen Press, 1976.

Mills, Katie. *The Road Story and the Rebel: Moving through Film, Fiction and Television.* Carbondale: Southern Illinois University Press, 2006.

Mom, Gijs. *The Electric Vehicle: Technology and Expectations in the Automobile Age.* Baltimore: Johns Hopkins University Press, 2004.

Monkkonen, Eric H. *America Becomes Urban: The Development of U.S. Cities and Towns 1780–1980.* Berkeley: University of California Press, 1988.

Moorehouse, H. F. *Driving Ambitions: An Analysis of the American Hot Rod Enthusiasm.* Manchester, England: Manchester University Press, 1991.

Morales, Rebecca. *Flexible Production: Restructuring the International Automobile Industry.* Cambridge, MA: Polity Press, 1994.

Moses, Sam. *Fast Guys, Rich Guys and Idiots: A Racing Odyssey on the Border of Obsession.* Lincoln: University of Nebraska Press, 2007.

Mueller, Mike. *The American Pickup Truck.* Osceola, WI: MBI, 1999.

Muir, John, and Tosh Gregg. *How to Keep Your Volkswagen Alive: A Manual of Step by Step Procedures for the Compleat Idiot,* 16th ed. Santa Fe, NM: John Muir, 1995.

Nader, Ralph. *Unsafe at Any Speed: The Designed-In Dangers of the American Automobile.* New York: Grossman, 1965.

Nauen, Elinor. *Ladies, Start Your Engines: Women Writers on Cars and the Road.* Boston: Faber and Faber, 1996.

Nelson, Walter Henry. *Small Wonder: The Amazing Story of the Volkswagen.* Boston: Little, Brown, 1967.

Nevins, Allan, and Frank Ernest Hill. *Ford: Decline and Rebirth, 1933–1962.* New York: Scribner's, 1963.

_____ and _____. *Ford: Expansion and Challenge, 1915–1933.* New York: Scribner's, 1957.

_____ and _____. *Ford: The Times, the Man, the Company.* New York: Scribner's, 1954.

Nye, David E. *Consuming Power: A Social History of*

American Energies. Cambridge, MA: MIT Press, 1998.

O'Barr, William M. *Culture and the Ad: Exploring Otherness in the World of Advertising.* Boulder, CO: Westview Press, 1994.

O'Connell, Sean. *The Car and British Society: Class, Gender and Motoring 1896–1939.* Manchester, England: Manchester University Press, 1998.

Olsen, W. Scott. *At Speed: Traveling the Long Road Between Two Points.* Lincoln: University of Nebraska Press, 2006.

Olson, Sidney. *Young Henry Ford: A Picture History of the First Forty Years.* Detroit: Wayne State University Press, 1963.

O'Neill, William L. *American High: The Years of Confidence, 1945–1960.* New York: Free Press, 1986.

O'Toole, Jack. *Forming the Future: Lessons from the Saturn Corporation.* Cambridge, MA: Blackwell, 1996.

Page, Victor W. *Prevention of Automobile Accidents.* New York: Henley, 1932.

Partridge, Bellamy. *Fill 'er Up! The Story of Fifty Years of Motoring.* New York: McGraw-Hill, 1952.

Patton, Phil. *Bug: The Strange Mutations of the World's Most Famous Automobile.* New York: Simon and Schuster, 2002.

_____. *Open Road: A Celebration of the American Highway.* New York: Simon and Schuster, 1986.

Pelfrey, William. *Billy, Alfred, and General Motors: The Story of Two Unique Men, a Legendary Company, and a Remarkable Time.* New York: AMACOM American Management Association, 2006.

Peterson, Joyce Shaw. *American Automobile Workers, 1900–1933.* Albany: State University of New York Press, 1987.

Post, Dan. *Cord: Without Tribute to Tradition.* Arcadia, CA: Post-Era Books, 1974.

Post, Robert C. *High Performance: The Culture and Technology of Drag Racing.* Baltimore: Johns Hopkins University Press, 2001.

Preston, Howard Lawrence. *Dirt Roads to Dixie: Accessibility and Modernization in the South, 1885–1935.* Knoxville: University of Tennessee Press, 1979.

Rae, John B. *The American Automobile.* Chicago: University of Chicago Press, 1965.

_____. *The American Automobile Industry.* Boston: G. K. Hall, 1984.

_____, ed. *Henry Ford.* Englewood Cliffs, NJ: Prentice-Hall, 1969.

_____. *The Road and the Car in American Life.* Cambridge, MA: MIT Press, 1971.

Ralston, Marc. *Pierce-Arrow.* San Diego: A. S. Barnes, 1980.

Rifkin, Herbert R. *The Jeep: Its Development, and Procurement Under the Quartermaster Corps, 1940–1942.* Washington D.C.: Quartermaster Corps, 1943.

Roberts, Peter. *Any Color So Long as It's Black ... the*

First Fifty Years of Automobile Advertising. Newton Abbott: David & Charles, 1976.

Rothschild, Emma. *Paradise Lost: The Decline of the Auto-industrial Age.* New York: Random House, 1973.

Rubenstein, James M. *The Changing U.S. Auto Industry: A Geographical Analysis.* New York: Routledge, 2002.

Saal, Thomas F. *Famous but Forgotten: The Story of Alexander Winton, Automotive Pioneer and Industrialist.* Twinsburg, OH: Golias Publishing, 1997.

Sachs, Wolfgang. *For Love of the Automobile: Looking Back into the History of Our Desires.* Berkeley: University of California Press, 1992.

Scharff, Virginia. *Taking the Wheel: Women and the Coming of the Motor Age.* Albuquerque: University of New Mexico Press, 1992.

Schneider, Kenneth. *Autokind vs. Mankind: An Analysis of Tyranny, a Proposal for Rebellion, a Plan for Reconstruction.* New York: Schocken Books, 1972.

Sedgwick, Michael. *Early Cars.* London: Octopus Books, 1962.

Seely, Bruce E. *Building the American Highway System: Engineers as Policy Makers.* Philadelphia: Temple University Press, 1987.

Setright, L. J. K. *Drive On! A Social History of the Motor Car.* London: Granta Books, 2003.

Sherman, Joe. *In the Rings of Saturn.* New York: Oxford University Press, 1994.

Sinclair, Upton. *The Flivver King.* Emmaus, PA: Rodale Press, 1937.

Sloan, Alfred P. *Adventures of a White Collar-Man.* New York: Doubleday, Doran, 1941.

_____. *My Years with General Motors.* Garden City, NJ: Doubleday, 1964.

Smith, George David. *Wisdom from the Robber Barons: Enduring Business Lessons from Rockefeller, Morgan, and the First Industrialists.* Cambridge, MA: Perseus, 2000.

Sorenson, Charles E. *My Forty Years with Ford.* New York: Norton, 1956.

Stanford, Don. *The Red Car.* Cutchogue, NY: Buccaneer Books, 1954.

Steacy, Ken. *Brightwork: Classic American Car Ornamentation.* San Francisco: Chronicle Books, 1999.

Steinbeck, John. *The Grapes of Wrath.* New York: Viking, 1939.

Steinwedel, Louis William, and J. Herbert Newport. *The Duesenberg.* New York: Norton, 1982.

Swope, Mary, and Walter H. Kerr, eds. *American Classic: Car Poems for Collectors.* College Park, MD: SCOP Eight, 1986.

Tarkington, Booth. *The Magnificent Ambersons.* Garden City, NY: Doubleday, Page, 1918.

Tedlow, Richard. *New and Improved: The Story of Mass Marketing in America.* New York: Basic Books, 1990.

Thompson, Mickey, with Borgeson, Griffith. *Challenger.* Englewood Cliffs, NJ: Prentice-Hall 1965.

Vargas, Zaragosa. *Proletarians of the North: A History of Mexican Industrial Workers in Detroit and the Midwest, 1917–1933.* Berkeley: University of California Press, 1993.

Vatter, Harold G. *The U.S. Economy in the 1950s.* Chicago: University of Chicago Press, 1963.

Vlasic, Bill, and Bradley A. Stertz. *Taken for a Ride: How Daimler-Benz Drove Off with Chrysler.* New York: HarperCollins, 2000.

Volti, Rudi. *Cars & Culture: The Life Story of a Technology.* Baltimore: Johns Hopkins University Press, 2004.

Wallace, Max. *The American Axis: Henry Ford, Charles Lindbergh, and the Rise of the Third Reich.* New York: St. Martin's, 2003.

Wallis, Michael. *Route 66: The Mother Road.* New York: St. Martin's 2001.

_____, and Williamson, Michael S. *The Lincoln Highway: The Great American Road Trip.* New York: Norton, 2007.

Walton, Mary. *Car: A Drama of the American Workplace.* New York: Norton, 1997.

Ward, James A. *The Fall of the Packard Motor Car Company.* Stanford, CA: Stanford University Press, 1995.

Watkins, Julian L. *The 100 Greatest Advertisements: Who Wrote Them and What They Did.* New York: Dover Publications, 1959.

Watts, Steven. *The People's Tycoon: Henry Ford and the American Century.* New York: Knopf, 2005.

Weibe, Robert. *The Search for Order, 1877–1920.* New York: Hall and Wang, 1967.

Wells, A. Wade. *Hail to the Jeep.* New York: Harper and Brothers, 1946.

White, Lawrence J. *The Automobile Industry Since 1945.* Cambridge, MA: Harvard University Press, 1971.

_____. *The Regulation of Air Pollutant Emissions from Motor Vehicles.* Washington, D.C.: American Enterprise Institute, 1982.

Whitney, Albert. *Man and the Motor Car.* New York, 1936.

Whyte, Adam Gowns. *Electricity in Locomotion: An Account of its Mechanism, Its Achievements, and Its Prospects.* Cambridge, England: Cambridge University Press, 1911.

Wik, Reynold M. *Henry Ford and Grass-Roots America.* Ann Arbor: University of Michigan Press, 1972.

Wilkinson, Stephan. *The Gold-Plated Porsche: How I Sank a Small Fortune into a Used Car, and Other Misadventures.* Guilford, CT: Lyons, 2004.

Williams, T. Harry. *Huey Long.* New York: Knopf, 1970.

Williamson, Harold F., et al. *The American Petroleum Industry, 1899–1959: The Age of Energy.* Evanston, IL: Northwestern University Press, 1963.

Williamson, Judith. *Decoding Advertisements: Ideology and Meaning in Advertising.* London: Boyars, 1978.

Witzel, Michael Karl. *Route 66 Remembered.* Osceola, WI: Motorbooks, 1996.

Wixom, Charles W. *A Pictorial History of Road Building.* Washington, D.C.: American Road Builders' Association, 1975.

Wolfe, Tom. *The Kandy-Kolored Tangerine-Flake Streamline Baby.* New York, Vintage, 2005.

_____. *The Electric Kool-Aid Acid Test.* New York: Farrar, Straus & Giroux, 1968.

Wollen, Peter, and Kerr, Joe, eds. *Autopia: Cars and Culture.* London: Reaktion, 2002.

Womack, James P., Daniel T. Jones, and Daniel Roos. *The Machine That Changed the World.* New York: Rawson Associates, 1990.

Wright, J. Patrick. *On a Clear Day You Can See General Motors.* Grosse Pointe, MI: Wright Enterprises, 1979.

Wrynn, V. Dennis. *Detroit Goes to War: The American Automobile Industry in World War II.* Osceola, WI: Motorbooks International, 1993.

Yates, Brock. *The Critical Path: Inventing an Automobile and Reinventing a Corporation.* Boston: Little, Brown, 1996.

Yergin, Daniel. *The Prize.* New York: Simon and Schuster, 1991.

Young, Rosamond McPherson. *Boss Ket: A Life of Charles F. Kettering.* New York: Longmans, Green, 1961.

Zeder, Fred Morrell. *Leadership: A Message to America.* New York: Newcomen Society, 1947.

INDEX

241